Jamie McGuinness left university mid-way through studying engineering to travel the world. After prospecting for gold in the western deserts of Australia, training huskies in Sweden and selling Trans-Siberian train tickets in Hong Kong, he finally found his place in it – as a Himalayan trekker.

To satisfy a yesteryear sense of exploration, for much of the year Jamie can be found in Nepal and Ladakh leading treks and climbs or exploring remote corners of the Himalaya. He has also begun managing 8000m expeditions. His latest project is the creation of a Great Himalayan Trail.

Trekking in the Everest Region
First edition: 1993; this fourth edition: October 2002

Publisher
Trailblazer Publications
The Old Manse, Tower Rd, Hindhead, Surrey, GU26 6SU, UK
Fax (+44) 01428-607571, info@trailblazer-guides.com
www.trailblazer-guides.com

British Library Cataloguing in Publication Data
A catalogue record for this book is available from the British Library

ISBN 1-873756-60-7

© **Jamie McGuinness**
Text, maps and photographs

The right of Jamie McGuinness to be identified as the author of this work has been
asserted by him in accordance with the Copyright, Designs and Patents Act 1988

Editor: Henry Stedman
Series editor: Patricia Major
Layout: Anna Jacomb-Hood
Cartography: Nick Hill
Index: Jane Thomas

Warning: mountain walking can be dangerous
Please read the notes on when to go (pp38-41), health and AMS (pp57-60 and pp276-94).
Every effort has been made by the author and publisher to ensure that the information
contained herein is as accurate and up to date as possible. However, they are unable
to accept responsibility for any inconvenience, loss or injury sustained by anyone
as a result of the advice and information given in this guide.

A note from the author: When I wrote the first edition of this guide in 1992 I began with
a few fundamental philosophies. First, I didn't want to recommend any lodges; everybody
has their own ideas of what makes a good lodge, very few of them are bad, and I have seen
first hand the change in fortunes a recommendation in a guide book can have. Instead, I
have simply listed them all by name. My second aim was to cover virtually every route and
track in the region so that you have the choice of where to go, rather than being forced to
go only to those areas where information is available. Perhaps 90% of trekkers still stick to
the main routes but at least the choice is theirs. It was also my hope that this info would
spread trekkers to equally deserving areas. Third, I wanted to write for everyone, from the
first time visitor to the Nepalophile; I have constantly been surprised at the number of reg-
ulars I meet year after year in the hills. My fourth aim was to have enough trail detail so
that at any confusing junction, you would be able to find your way by using this book.
Lastly I hoped that the book could act as a vehicle for the organizations and local peoples
involved with conservation and development.

For this fourth edition there are many changes. I have also taken advantage of the
power of the internet and corrections, additional info, useful links and updated info, particularly on the Maoist situation, is available at **www.trailblazer-guides.com**.

Printed on chlorine-free paper from farmed forests by
Star Standard (☎ +65-6861 3866), Singapore

★ TRAILBLAZER

TREKKING
IN THE
EVEREST
REGION

includes Kathmandu city guide

JAMIE McGUINNESS

TRAILBLAZER PUBLICATIONS

Acknowledgements

I am particularly grateful to the people of Nepal, who did much more than simply help with the research for this guidebook; living in their country has provided me with a diverse insight into life itself. The Sherpas and the mountains, especially of the Khumbu, hold a special place in my heart.

Many people have accompanied me to the region: thanks to all the group members who were so tolerant while I ran off to check something for this book, and for the good company. It is partly with the help of these groups that I have been able to visit this region no less than 20 times.

Each year the volunteer doctors and staff at the Himalayan Rescue Association posts and the Khunde Clinic share their accumulated knowledge on altitude sickness and the region with infectious enthusiasm and deserve a thousand thank-you's not just from me but from all the trekkers who have visited the posts.

At Trailblazer, thanks to Nick Hill for drawing and updating the maps, Henry Stedman for updating part of the Kathmandu chapter and for editing the text, Anna Jacomb-Hood for laying down the book, Tara Winterton for the Nepali words and phrases section and Jane Thomas for the index. The publisher updated the list of overseas trekking companies, had the difficult job of selecting the photos and provided material for the Kathmandu and Nepal chapters, and part of the minimum impact trekking section.

Along the trails in the Khumbu there are so many Nepalis that I'd like to thank by name but the vast majority are more easily recalled by their smiles and helpfulness, as are the many foreign trekkers I met.

While I am constantly surprised by the courtesy and warmth of the Nepali people in general, and the majority of government officials I have met, one can only hope that the more faceless side of the government and bureaucracy doesn't destroy the country before they act on the long-known realization that corruption is the root of many of Nepal's current problems.

A request

The author and publisher have tried to ensure that this guide is as accurate and up to date as possible. However things change quickly in this part of the world. Prices rise, new lodges are built and trails are rerouted.

If you notice any changes or omissions that should be included in the next edition of this book, please email Jamie McGuinness at jamie.mcguinness@trailblazer-guides.com or write to him c/o Trailblazer Publications (address on p2). A free copy of the next edition will be sent to persons making a significant contribution.

Updated information is available on the Internet at
www.project-himalaya.com/updates-everest.htm
www.trailblazer-guides.com

Front cover photograph: Pumori from the top of Kala Pattar © Jamie McGuinness

CONTENTS

To Lobuche and Kala Pattar

To Gokyo

Khumbu side trips and pass-hopping

Salpa-Arun to the Khumbu

From Bhojpur

Rolwaling

Trekking peaks

APPENDICES

INDEX

INTRODUCTION

The Solu-Khumbu region of Nepal has been a magnet for mountaineers, adventurers and travellers ever since its opening to foreigners in the 1950s, and with good reason. They may primarily be drawn by a desire to see the world's highest mountain but Everest is only one of a myriad of beautiful peaks in the area. Indeed, even if Everest wasn't here, the Khumbu (Everest region) should still be an extremely popular area, for it is a superb region for trekking, climbing and exploring.

Passing through populated areas, a trek in Nepal is very different from a wilderness hike in the USA or New Zealand, or a randonnaire route in the European Alps. The hills in Nepal are the life and soul of diverse ethnic groups, the most famous of which are the hospitable Sherpa people. What further sets trekking in Nepal apart is the low cost and the ease with which a trek can be arranged. There can be few countries where you can set off for a month-long walk carrying no food or shelter yet be 100% sure that every day you will be able to find these essentials, and on a budget of much less than twenty dollars a day. Alternatively, if you want an organized trek with an entourage of guides, cooks and porters to transport you back to the luxurious time of pukka sahibs and memsahibs, this can be quickly arranged with competent staff for a very reasonable cost.

Three areas in Nepal have become popular with trekkers for their scenic attractions and their established network of local lodges for accommodation and food. As well as the Everest region, there's the Annapurna region, north of Pokhara, which may have a greater range of terrain and cultures but receives nearly twice as many trekkers as the Everest region. The third area is Langtang, north of Kathmandu, which is quieter and less developed. What sets the Everest region apart from these two other areas is the fact that once above Namche and Lukla you are right among the mountains, continuously above 3000m/10,000ft with many chances to ascend above 5000m/16,400ft. The greater Khumbu (Everest) region also has immense scope for wild exploration.

One of the world's classic long trekking routes, the first part of the traditional 'expedition' route from Jiri to Everest crosses ridge after ridge of painstakingly-terraced hills populated by subsistence farmers. Semi-mediaeval villages cling to the hillsides with mysterious *gompas* (Buddhist monasteries) above them. Rural life, little-changed for centuries, surrounds the trekker, thought-provoking and very different from the Western way of life. You soon settle into the trekking lifestyle leaving the instant world of mobile phones far behind and rediscovering simple pleasures like the enduring glow of a sunset, the magic of flickering flames and the bliss of sleep to soothe naturally exercised muscles.

Namche, the capital of the Khumbu and a focal point for trekkers, is juxtaposed between the old and the new with traders well versed not only in the various types of Tibetan *tsampa* but also in the different brands of titanium ice screw. From the alpine valleys above Namche, the scenery is awesome: Ama Dablam, Kangtaiga, Cholatse and numerous other peaks, while the 8000-metre giants, Makalu, Cho Oyu, Lhotse and Everest command respect for their sheer height.

The highest mountain on earth has several different names. To the Western world it became Mt Everest in 1865 (and was pronounced 'Eve-rest') but to the Tibetans and the Khumbu Sherpas it has always been Chomolungma. The Chinese have wisely used the local name (transliterated as Qomolangma). Much more recently the government of Nepal has given it the name Sagarmatha. In this guide, it's referred to as Everest only because this is the name most readily recognized by readers. I personally prefer the original name, Chomolungma.

PART 1: PLANNING YOUR TREK

What is trekking?

The prospect of trekking for the first time in the Himalaya can be daunting as well as thrilling. Compared to a week's backpacking in the Rockies or bush-walking in Tasmania, trekking in Nepal is an altogether different experience. Rather than jumping into the wilderness to get away from it all, you walk into a countryside free from roads and discover villages caught in a time warp and terraced fields stacked up huge hillsides. The paths are timeless pilgrimage routes, trails between villages or tracks to high grazing pastures. It is by no means untouched, but it is an incredibly beautiful natural world. Higher up in the alpine valleys the villages are replaced by herders' huts and, higher still, the ice castles of the Himalaya.

Trekking is simply adventurous walking; it is not climbing or mountaineering and the practical aspects are surprisingly straightforward. In the villages and along the way are lodges and teahouses where meals are ordered from menus in English. Alternatively, on an expedition-style trekking tour three course meals are served by your crew. Without the need to carry food and camping equipment, backpacks are light, and if you have a porter you need carry only your daypack. So trekking is really little more than a pleasurable ramble through quaint villages, gazing in wonder at the terraced hillsides and wandering amid incredible mountain scenery.

The satisfaction of trekking is in the process; most trekking days are not particularly long so there is time to spot wildlife, take photographs, chat along the way and relax over lunch or a reviving cup of tea.

But there are challenges, predominantly the physical effort required: as well as the inspiring mountains there are huge hills some of which must be climbed. Although hopefully lightly laden, hill-climbing still means plenty of heavy breathing and sweat. Pleasure can be had from frequent rests to admire the scenery which, even after a mere ten minutes, alters satisfyingly and often dramatically. Take comfort, too, in the frequent teahouses which are often strategically placed.

The second is the discomfort of sickness. This is Asia and no matter how careful you are, you should count on some bowel problems and possibly a day or two that you would rather forget. Luckily, these seem trivial when compared to the whole wonderful experience.

To enjoy the Himalaya you don't have to be a tough outdoor type. Like backpacks and cameras, trekkers come in all shapes and sizes and with widely differing aspirations. Trekking is physically demanding but certainly not beyond the majority of people. Most important is knowing that you enjoy the concept. Bring along a traveller's curiosity and a sense of humour, and before you know it you will relish the thought of another trek.

TREKKING IN THE KHUMBU

Trekking is usually a wonderful experience; however, a reality check is in order. You are heading into an extreme mountain environment. It can snow unexpectedly. Emergency facilities are limited: most villages don't even have a phone. You will also be at extreme altitude and experience its discomfort and problems. Ignorance and foolhardiness on acclimatization can and does still kill, although it is entirely preventable: see p281.

With a group or on your own?

Nepal, long suspicious of foreign influence and colonial powers, began opening its borders only in 1948. The first tourists (as opposed to mountaineers and researchers) arrived in 1955 but it was not until 1965, when Colonel Jimmy Roberts set up Mountain Travel, that the first commercial treks began. The concept was similar to the expedition approach used by mountaineers, with guides, porters and tents. These holidays proved to be a great success and essentially the same expedition-style format is still used today by many trekking companies.

Alongside this self-sufficient approach to trekking is a second locally-based tourism industry catering to the needs of a different type of visitor. Along the main trade routes the hill peoples of Nepal traditionally had a code of hospitality towards travellers. It was only a matter of time before small groups of adventurers started taking advantage of this, staying in basic teahouses and lodges. In 1964 just 14 foreigners visited the Khumbu but by the 1970s the numbers were rapidly increasing. Now more than 15,000 people trek this way each year, staying in the much improved lodges and teahouses along the routes.

It used to be that most people knew instinctively whether they were an independent or a group trekker. A middle way has now developed, however, with trekking groups also using local teahouses; recently trekking companies have even started building chains of their own lodges. So now the trekking infrastructure in the Solu-Khumbu has developed to a stage where many options are possible, from a full-scale expedition with tents and porters through guided teahouse treks to an independent trek using the local lodges and carrying only a sleeping bag and jacket. It is simply a case of choosing the option most appropriate for you.

The convenience that each option offers will probably be the deciding factor. For a time-limited holiday it is nice to have everything pre-arranged, whereas on a budget part of the fun is organizing things yourself. Certainly with a company you have more back-up in case something goes wrong, but since it is often the rigidity of the planned itinerary that causes a problem, this is a dubious advantage. If the standard of guiding in Nepal were higher then there would be definite advantages to signing up with a guided trek. But most 'guides' are really just sirdars, competent organizers rather than knowledgeable wildlife and cultural interpreters; the guiding concept as we understand it in the West is little understood here. The majority of 'guides' have little or no training and are rarely fluent in English.

On an expedition-style trek and a teahouse trek, although the styles of interaction with locals are different they are equivalent. Staying in a lodge provides the rewarding opportunity to mix with your Nepali hosts, many of whom speak reasonable English. How much you interact depends on you; some trekkers seem happy to spend all their time just in the company of other trekkers. On an expedition-style trek or teahouse trek, although being self-sufficient removes the enjoyable need to interact with the villagers, this is redeemed by the crew who look after, entertain and add local colour to the trek. So making a choice probably comes down to your aspirations and the convenience factor.

INDEPENDENT TEAHOUSE TREKKING

Dotted along the main trails are privately owned teahouses and lodges. They can provide anything from a cup of tea to a full meal and a bed so, for the entire trek, there's no need to carry food or shelter. Teahouse trekking, as it's usually called, is easy to organize: just pack and go. It's also cheap: luxuries aside, US$20/£13 a day easily covers food and accommodation.

The level of comfort and facilities in the lodges has improved greatly. Once infamously smoky and rather too authentically mediaeval, many are now modest hotels which generally offer better facilities than the expedition approach. Because of the way that the lodges are managed in the Khumbu, they are universally regarded as the best in the country, on average significantly better than the lodges in Langtang and better than most lodges in the Annapurna region.

As well as being economical, teahouse trekking gives you the freedom to alter your schedule and stop where you wish. This is particularly handy if you are sick for a day or two or you feel like a rest; commercial group treks have to push on. The freedom to explore is slightly limited by the location of lodges and the restricting geography of the region, though in practice most trekkers follow a few standard routes and similar itineraries anyway, as do the trekking companies. This means that during the peak season the lodges in popular stopping places are crowded, although a meal and bed can always be found.

Trekking alone

Many people trek by themselves. Unless trekking during the monsoon or off the standard routes you constantly meet other trekkers in the lodges or on the trail so while you can remain by yourself if you wish, most people end up walking in small groups and staying at the same lodges. This process often begins on the bus out to Jiri or on the flight to Lukla, and more friendships evolve during the rest of the walk, one of the special joys of Nepal trekking.

Standard wilderness recommendations are to hike in a group of three or more, in case of accidents. However, there is less need to apply this reasoning in the Khumbu because there are several medical posts along the way, and lodge owners and other trekkers can render assistance. While many people would consider it foolish to rely on strangers, in fact very few trekkers have accidents or ever end up relying on – and inconveniencing – other trekkers so I feel there are few risks in hiking alone in the Khumbu (ie above Lukla). As a woman the risks of physical sexual harassment are also negligible above Lukla, for which you can thank the broad sexual equality accorded by the Sherpa culture. That said, dressing conservatively and behaving modestly is sensible, and when stopping for the night it's a good idea to check that there is another woman staying in the same lodge, or head for one of the busier lodges; if heading off the main routes you should team up with someone else, as much for general safety as anything else.

Trekking below Lukla alone (as a male or female) used to be safe but more caution is required now. Villagers often ask how many people you are trekking with and the best reply is always to say that your friend is just behind. Violent crimes against foreigners are still virtually unknown but the law and order situation in the country has deteriorated significantly.

If you would prefer to begin your trek with a partner, advertise on, or scan, the noticeboards around Thamel, especially at the Himalayan Rescue Association (HRA), Kathmandu Environmental Education Project (KEEP) office, Pumpernickel Bakery and the Kathmandu Guest House boards. There are many internet message boards, and there's a short list on : www.trailblaz er-guides.com (*Trekking in the Everest Region*, update pages).

Other options are to hire a porter-guide through a trekking company or in Lukla, or try to join an existing group.

Trekking the wild way
For climbers and experienced trekkers the region has an incredible amount to offer. At any major village on the main trekking routes you can pick up enough food (provided you're not a fussy eater) to disappear into the wilderness for a week or more, so the scope for exploring off the beaten track is immense. The main decisions boil down to selecting exactly what gear to take and deciding if you have enough experience for some of the wilder route options.

COMMERCIAL GUIDED TREKS

The decisions facing today's trekker are manifold. Even if you decide, for example, that you'd prefer to trek independently, you still have to decide whether you need a porter/guide, and if so, whether to hire him through a Nepali trekking company via the internet before you leave home, once you arrive in Kathmandu, or even at the trailhead. Alternatively, if you'd rather join a group, would you rather book through an unknown Nepali trekking company, which will be cheaper, or through a more expensive but usually more reliable foreign operator, who at least will take your complaints – should you have any – seriously? The internet has served only to increase the possibilities and options available – but the potential for pitfalls has also risen.

Is a guide or porter necessary?

Assuming you will be taking this book with you, there's no need for a guide of the human kind on the established trekking routes. The lodges are impossible to miss, route finding presents few problems and basic English is widely understood. However, trekking with some local people can be an enlightening, entertaining and a rewarding cultural exchange.

Hiring a **porter-guide** is an option that gives you the advantages of both the independent approach and the group trek. You retain control, but with the opportunity for the greater insight and interaction that a guide can provide, and you have your load pleasantly lightened. A porter-guide should speak reasonable English, know the region and carry 10-15kg plus their equipment. They are happy to work for one person or a small group, or if you have several loads to carry you could hire an additional porter to accompany the group. See p104.

A cheaper option is to hire a normal **porter**, who will probably speak little English but know the trail route well. You shouldn't feel the least bit guilty if you do hire a porter-guide or a porter. The money you give them directly benefits the local economy and the walk itself can be an enjoyable cultural exchange. See p105.

What you're paying for

A commercial trek, whether teahouse-style or expedition-style, is a pleasant routine suited to those who enjoy being looked after and, with everything planned in advance, is perfect for people with limited time. Pre-trek preparation should be easier and can all be arranged by telephone or email. Normally the package includes airport pick-up, a guided tour plus a day or two in Kathmandu, hotel accommodation, and everything while trekking. Advice is just a question away and there is security in knowing that back-up is readily available in case of real trouble.

Many trekking companies, however, still have significant flaws. A few fail to plan itineraries that allow for sensible acclimatization and many, if you do struggle, simply turn you back without the possibility of a slower ascent or an alternative lower altitude trek. Foreign trekking companies have comprehensive packing lists, jabs lists and offer tailored insurance yet the majority of Nepali companies don't. The local guides, or sirdars, leave a lot to be desired too: one would expect them to be trained in history and culture, first aid and group management, yet the majority are not. Even if they are adequately trained, many still struggle to act as a cultural interface between trekkers and Nepalis. Even among the professional agencies, while the leaders are *usually* good they are not always so, and many have surprisingly little real understanding of altitude sickness and other common medical complaints. To be fair though, this is more of a failing of Nepal's education and belief system because most good companies have training programmes. As a result, Western-led trips are generally more reliable, although usually pricier too. While the standards of a Nepali trekking company may not always be particularly high, one definite advantage is they will run a trek for just a couple of people.

Commercial teahouse trekking

Recognizing the improvements in lodges, many foreign and local trekking companies now also offer teahouse-style trek packages. The usually warm diningroom is much better than an often frigid dining tent, the lodge food is certainly equal to the average group cook's offerings and the bedrooms are more spacious than a tent. It is also much more convenient to be met at the airport with your hotel already arranged.

However, you pay well for the privilege of going on a tour compared to doing the same thing independently and there are some specific limitations that you should be aware of. Normally it is the trekking company or guide that chooses the lodges and unless you're willing to pay an additional sum the very best lodges and restaurants (eg pizza at the Namche bakery) will be off-limits. Some companies use a restrictive 'set meal' arrangement while others allow you to choose from the menu. In many cases you will be sharing a lodge with other trekkers and a late night party might keep you (or them) awake: most lodges are not particularly soundproof. On balance, however, teahouse trekking is more comfortable than camping.

Expedition-style trekking

The traditional idea of trekking evokes images of armies of heavily-laden porters catering to the every needs of a few pampered sahibs and memsahibs, while sherpas pitch the tents and kitchen staff serve magnificent dinners on tables complete with table linen. In fact this is still essentially the standard format today, and it's a glorious way to trek, especially off the beaten track where teahouses are rare, or during peak season when the lodges are overflowing.

The main advantage of this style of trekking is that you are independent of teahouses, though the porters are still reliant on finding food in villages. Some companies run expedition-style treks simply because they have large groups – for example KE Adventures' maximum group size is 16 clients – and lodges in a few places would struggle to cope with a party this big.

Adventure treks and recreational mountaineering

If you are considering a true wilderness trek across some of the wilder passes or fancy climbing a 6000m peak, you are probably better organizing such an expedition through a professional company unless you are supremely confident in your abilities and experience. However, even if you do arrange things through a company, caution is still required. Nepali companies, despite their claims, are notorious for getting out of their depth. Indeed, few local climbing guides can even belay – a standard climbing technique. This is a major failing of the whole trekking industry in Nepal and you should choose which company you sign up with carefully.

That said, the majority of Nepali-guided expeditions, such as those across the Tashi Labtsa or up to the summits of Island Peak and Mera Peak, do run successfully. With these treks, Western guides generally have higher success rates and if there is a problem, a much better understanding of what the safest course of action would be. Foreign trekking companies using Western guides are much more professional and have a lot more at stake too. You definitely pay for what you get.

NEPALI TREKKING AGENCIES

The internet has radically changed how many people book a trek in advance. A quick search throws up hundreds of Nepali trek operators and choosing between them can be difficult. Most compete on price and little else and will pull every trick in the book, fair or otherwise, to get you to sign up. One would assume that you could sort the good companies from the bad by the quality of the answers they give to your questions, but even this is not an entirely reliable method as it is rarely the trekking staff who answer the emails, but rather a computer-literate Nepali with relatively little trekking experience.

While it is pleasant to arrive in Kathmandu with everything already arranged, it is sometimes possible to wait until you meet the company face to face in Kathmandu before agreeing to sign up and finalizing your arrangements. If doing this, allow a day or two in Kathmandu to compare companies; then, having found a suitable trekking company, a couple more to allow them to get a crew and supplies together. One trick is to go rafting or on a jungle safari prior to the trek, which gives the trekking company time to prepare properly.

Either way, this approach is cheaper than a package tour booked in your own country. You are not paying for office services and pre-trek preparation, which may amount to more than the actual trek. You also have greater flexibility on the

---

Cheap trek: but who pays?

Walking the narrow streets of Thamel, Kathmandu's crowded, smog-filled tourist quarter, is to run the gauntlet of hustlers out to convince the gullible Western trekker that the firm they work for is the only one worth bothering with. With every step comes a fresh business card, every second of eye contact a potential booking. And they'll promise the earth to clinch a sale. But just how cheap will they go? I instantly invent a dozen keen trekkers who will join me in a fortnight. Now it's time to do business – and what a deal I can get. For just £12 a day, my imaginary companions and I will be able to walk the mountains of the Annapurna or Everest ranges – sleeping in teahouses by night, three hot meals a day, a rescue service on stand-by. We'll have two nights of three-star accommodation before we start, one porter to every two people. The deal's incredible. But it's not we who are really paying: it's the porters. In the Everest region, a hot shower costs £2, a pot of instant noodles, 65p; it doesn't take a genius to work out that at £12 a day there won't be much flowing through to them.

Stephanie Clark (excerpt from *The Times*)

choice of itinerary and changes you may wish to make to the route. Try to talk with other trekkers who have used a company's services too – they will know better than anybody what the company is like.

Another possibility is to join a group trek after you have arrived in Nepal, though for this option you must be prepared to wait, and you'll need a bit of luck too. The majority of pre-arranged treks are organized by foreign tour operators and are considered exclusive, with bookings via the overseas agent only. There are a few companies that advertise set trekking dates but these usually depart even if only two people book. Sometimes, although not always, this is just a different way of advertising trek-organizing expertise.

TREKKING AGENCIES OUTSIDE NEPAL

Some companies offer a general range of treks while others specialize in climbing and adventure treks. Brochures and websites usually stress the level of experience required for treks and climbs advertised. Don't, however, lose sight of the fact that although trekking is made easier by the need to carry only a daypack, it is still your legs that do all the walking. Don't be afraid to quiz the company on who is leading the trek, their group numbers policy, and on the detailed itinerary. All profess to following comfortable acclimatization rates but the hard reality is that many don't. They may have a good safety record of saving people before it's too late, but many itineraries cause undue and unnecessary discomfort. While the majority of operators have a slick website, curiously very few feature detailed itineraries or advertise the price of their trips.

Compared to Nepali companies the prices quoted by foreign agencies are higher, often much higher, but you'll also get a much higher standard of trek too. Furthermore, you have the consumer rights of your country on your side, so you should be well protected. In contrast, if booking through a Nepali company you'll have to deal with the slow-moving Ministry of Tourism should anything go wrong.

Costs

US companies quote land-only costs. For the shortest treks that fly to Lukla and explore as far as Tengboche, they charge US$1500-2500. The longer standard treks start at US$2000 but most are around US$3000 and climbing treks cost US$3000-5000. US companies that offer Australian-operated treks are usually a little cheaper.

In the UK, trek costs are generally quoted including return airfares. Treks start from £1200 with most around £1650 and the longer climbing treks range between £1850 and £2500. US companies (bar one) don't operate in Europe because they are not competitively priced; the Australian and UK markets, however, seem to mix well.

Australian companies quote air and land costs separately. A return flight to Nepal is around A$1700. Short treks are A$1300 and upwards, and the standard treks are from around A$2000 to A$3000. Trekking peak expeditions cost A$3400-4500.

Tours and trekking agencies in the UK and Ireland

● **Bufo Ventures** (☎ 01539-445445, ✉ bufoventures@btconnect.com, www.bufoventures.co.uk), 3 Elim Grove, Windermere, Cumbria LA23 2JN, organizes tailor-made treks for groups or individuals.

● **Classic Journeys** (☎ 01773-873497, ✉ info@classicjourneys.co.uk, www .classicjourneys.co.uk), 33 High St, Tibshelf, Alfreton, Derbyshire, DE55 5NX.

● **Exodus Travel** (☎ 020-8675 5550, ✉ sales@exodus.co.uk, www.exodus .co.uk), 9 Weir Rd, London SW12 OLT, has a wide range of guided treks with accommodation in tents or tea houses.

● **Explore Worldwide** (☎ 01252-760000, ✉ info@exploreworldwide.com, www.exploreworldwide.com), 1 Frederick St, Aldershot, Hants GU11 1LQ, offers a number of treks.

● **Footprint Adventures** (☎ 01522-804929, ✉ sales@footprint-adventures. co.uk, www.footprint-adventures.co.uk), 5 Malham Drive, Lincoln LN6 0XD, offers several guided treks in the area.

● **Guerba Expeditions** (☎ 01373-858956, ✉ res@guerba.co.uk, www.guer ba.com), Wessex House, 40 Station Rd, Westbury, Wilts BA13 3JN.

● **High Places** (☎ 0114-275 7500, ✉ treks@highplaces.co.uk, www.high places.co.uk), Globe Centre, Penistone Road, Sheffield S6 3AE.

● **Himalayan Kingdoms** (☎ 01453-844400, ✉ info@himalayankingdoms .com, www.himalayankingdoms.com), Old Crown House, 18 Market Street, Wootton under Edge, Glos GL12 7AE, has several treks in the region.

● **Jagged Globe** (☎ 0845-345 8848, ☎ 0114-276 3322, ✉ climb@jagged-globe.co.uk, www.jagged-globe.co.uk), The Foundry Studios, 45 Mowbray St, Sheffield S3 8EN, offers more ambitious trekking and mountaineering holidays.

● **KE Adventure Travel** (☎ 017687-73966, ✉ info@keadventure.co.uk, www.keadventure.com), 32 Lake Rd, Keswick, Cumbria CA12 5DQ, offers treks and trekking peaks including Mera.

● **Maxwells Travel** (☎ 01-677 9479), D'Olier Chambers, 1 Hawkins St, Dublin 2, Ireland.

● **Mountain Travel & Sobek Expeditions** (☎ 01494-448901, ✉ sales@ mtsobekeu.com, www.mtsobek.com), 67 Verney Ave, High Wycombe, Bucks, HP12 3ND. See also Trekking agencies in the USA.

● **Naturetrek** (☎ 01962-733051, ✉ info@naturetrek.co.uk, www.nature trek.co.uk), Cheriton Mill, Cheriton, Nr Alresford, Hampshire SO24 ONG, offers bird-watching tours in several regions of Nepal.

● **Palanquin Travels** (☎ 01937-587152, ✉ info@palanquintravels.com, www .palanquintravels.com), 15 Bank Street, Wetherby, West Yorkshire LS22 6NQ.

● **Roama Travel** (☎ 01258-860298, ✉ roama@city2000.net, www.roama .com), Shroton, Blandford Forum, Dorset DT11 8QW, specializes in individual treks.

● **Sherpa Expeditions** (☎ 020-8577 2717, ✉ sales@sherpaexpeditions.com, www.sherpaexpeditions.com), 131a Heston Rd, Hounslow, Middx TW5 ORF, has a wide range of guided treks.

- **Specialist Trekking Co-operative** (☎ 01228-562358, 🖳 trekstc@aol.com), Chapel House, Low Coethill, Carlisle, Cumbria CA4 0EL.
- **Terra Firma** (☎ 01691-870321, 🖳 info@terrafirmatravel.com, www.terra firmatravel.com), Eunant, Lake Vyrnwy, Powys SY10 0NF, offers several treks in the region.
- **Tribes Travel** (☎ 01728-685971, 📧 info@tribes.co.uk, www.tribes.co.uk), 12 The Business Centre, Earl Soham, Woodbridge, Suffolk IP13 7SA, offers tailor-made treks.
- **Walks Worldwide** (☎ 01524-262255, 🖳 info@walksworldwide.com, www.walksworldwide.com), 15 Main St, High Bentham, Lancaster LA2 7LG.
- **World Expeditions** (☎ 0800-0744135, 020-8870 2600, 🖳 enquiries@world expeditions.co.uk, www.worldexpeditions.co.uk), 3 Northfields Prospect, Putney Bridge Rd, London SW18 1PE.

Trekking agencies in Continental Europe

- **Austria** **Oekista** (☎ 1-401 487001, 🖳 info@oekista.at, www.oekista.at), Turkenstrasse 6, 1090 Wien; **Supertramp Reisen** (☎ 01-533 51 37, 🖳 travel@ supertramp.co.at, www.supertramp.co.at), Helferstorferstrafle 4, A-1010 Wien.
- **Belgium** **Joker Tourisme** (☎ 02-648 78 78) Boondaalsesteenweg 6, Chaussée de Boondaal 6, 1050 Bruxelles. **Roadrunner** (☎ 052-211511) Grote Markt 22, 9200 Dendermonde. **Divantoura** (☎ 09-223 00 69, 🖳 info@divan toura.com, www.divantoura.com), Bagattenstraat 176, 9000, Gent; also (☎ 03-233 19 16) St Jacobsmarkt 5, 2000 Antwerpen.
- **Denmark** **Inter-Travel** (☎ 33-15 00 77, 🖳 inter-travel@inter-travel.dk, www.inter-travel.dk), Frederiksholms Kanal 2, DK-1220 Kobenhavn K. **Marco Polo Tours** (☎ 33-2818 7540, 🖳 marcopolo@marcopolo-tours.dk, www.marco polo-tours.dk), Borgergade 16, 1300 Kobenhavn K.
- **France** **Club Aventure** (☎ 08 25 30 60 32, 🖳 info @clubaventure.fr, www .clubaventure.fr), 18 rue Séguier, 75006 Paris. **CTS Voyages** (☎ 01 43 25 00 76, 🖳 info@ctsvoyages.fr, www.ctsworld.com), 20 rue de Carmes, Paris 75005.
- **Germany** **DAV Summit Club** (☎ 089-64 24 00, 🖳 info@DAV-Summit-Club.de, www.dav-summit-club.de), Am Perlacher Forst 186, 81545 München. **Kilroy Travels** (☎ 30 31 00 040, 🖳 es@kilroytravels.com, www.kilroytrav els.com), Hardenbergstrasse 9, 10623 Berlin.
- **Netherlands** **Adventure World** (☎ 023-5382 954, 🖳 atc@euronet.nl), Muiderslotweg 112, Haarlem 2026 AS. **Snow Leopard Adventure Reizen** (☎ 070-388 28 67, 🖳 info@snowleopard.nl, www.snowleopard.nl), Treubstraat 15 F, 2288 EG Rijswijk. **Himalaya Trekking** (☎ 0521-551 301, 🖳 info@htwan delreizen.nl, www.htwandelreizen.nl), Ten Have 13, 7983 KD Wapse. **Nederlandse Klim en Bergsport Vereniging** (☎ 030-233 40 80) Oudkerkhof 13, 3512 GH Utrecht.
- **Norway** **Worldwide Adventures** (☎ 22-404890, 🖳 post@worldwide.no), AS Nedre Slottsgate 12, Oslo 0157.
- **Spain** **Banoa** (Bilbao) (☎ 944-232039), Ledesma (Musico), 10-bis, 2°, 48011 Bilbao. **Banoa** (Barcelona) (☎ 93-318 96 00), Ronda de Sant Pere, 11, 8906

Barcelona. **CTS Viages** (☎ 91 559 31 81, 💻 www.cts.world.com), Edificio Espana, Plaza de Espana, 28013 Madrid and (☎ 933 1825 93), El Palau Nou de la Rambla, Las Ramblas 88-94, Ir C 08002 Barcelona.
● **Sweden   Himalayaresor** (☎ 08-605 5760, 💻 explore@himalaya.se, www.himalaya.se), Bjorkallen 45, 14266 Trangsund, Stockholm.

Agencies in the USA

● **Adventure Center** (tollfree ☎ 800-227-8747, 💻 tripinfo@adventurecenter. com, www.adventurecenter.com), 1311 63rd St, Suite 200, Emeryville, CA 94608.
● **GAP (USA)** (☎ 914-666-4417, ▤ 914-666-4839, toll free ☎ 1-800-692-5495, 💻 adventure@gap.ca, www.gap.ca), 760 North Bedford Rd, Suite #246, Bedford Hills, New York 10507. See GAP (Canada) for a description.
● **Geographic Expeditions** (☎ 415-922 0448, toll free ☎ 800-777 8183, 💻 www.geoex.com), 2627 Lombard St, San Francisco, CA 94123, run a number of tours around Nepal including an 18-day tour around Everest villages and a 27-day 'Great Route to Everest' trek.
● **Himalayan Travel** (☎ 800-225 2380), 2nd Floor, 112 Prospect St, Stamford, CT 06901 – agents for Sherpa Expeditions (UK).
● **Journeys International** (☎ 734-665 4407, ☎ 800-255 8735, 💻 info@jour neys-intl.com, www.journeys-intl.com), 107 April Drive Suite 3, Ann Arbor, MI 48103. Also includes some treks specially for families.
● **Mountain Travel & Sobek Expeditions** (☎ 510-527 8100, ☎ 888-687 6235, 💻 info@mtsobek.com, www.mtsobek.com), 6420 Fairmount Ave, El Cerrito, CA 94530. Wide range of upmarket treks.
● **Overseas Adventure Travel** (☎ 800-221 0814), 349 Broadway, Cambridge, MA 02139, offers a number of treks in this area.
● **Safaricentre** (☎ 310-546 4411, ☎ 800-223 6046, 💻 info@safaricentre.com) 3201 N Sepulveda Blvd, Manhattan Beach, CA 90266 – agents for Exodus (UK).
● **Wilderness Travel** (☎ 510-558-2488, toll-free ☎ 800-368 2794, 💻 info@wildernesstravel.com, www.wildernesstravel.com), 1102 9th St, Berkeley, California 94710-1211, offers a 14-day trek to Khunjung, Phortse and Tengboche and a 25-day trek to Everest Base Camp.
● **World Expeditions** (☎ 415-989-2212, toll-free ☎ 1-888-464-8735, 💻 con tactus@weadventures.com), 6th Floor, 580 Market Street, San Francisco, CA 94104. A volume operator with a wide variety of trips.

Agencies in Canada

● **The Adventure Center** (☎ 416-922 7584, 💻 toronto@theadventurecenter. com, www.theadventurecenter.com), 25 Bellair St, Toronto, Ontario M5R 3L3.
● **Canadian Himalayan Expeditions** (☎ 416-360-4300, toll free ☎ 800-563-8735, 💻 info@HimalayanExpeditions.com, www.HimalayanExpeditions. com), 2 Toronto St, Suite 302, Toronto, Ontario M5C 2B6. This is one of the few Canadian companies that runs their own treks, rather than acting as agents for other companies.

● **GAP** (Canada) (☎ 416-260-0999, toll-free ☎ 1-800-465-5600, 🖳 adven ture@gap.ca, www.gap.ca), 19 Duncan St, Suite 401, Toronto, Ontario M5H 3H1. This is a very large, well-run organization.

● **Trek Holidays** (☎ 780-439-9118, toll-free ☎ 1-888-4566-3522, 🖳 adven ture@trekholidays.com, www.trekholidays.com), 8412-109th St, Edmonton, Alberta T6G 1E2.

● **Westcan Treks** has offices in Calgary (☎ 403-283 6115, 🖳 calgary@west cantreks.com, www.westcantreks.com), 336 14th St NW, Calgary, Alberta T2N 1Z7), and Vancouver (☎ 604-734-1066, 🖳 vancouver@westcantreks.com), 2911West 4th Ave, Vancouver BC V6K 1R3.

● **Worldwide Adventures Inc** (☎ 416-633-5666, from USA ☎ 1-800-387-1483), 1170 Sheppard Avenue West, Suite 45, Toronto, Ontario, Canada MK3 2A3 – agents for World Expeditions (Australia).

Agencies in Australia

● **Adventure World** has branches in Perth (☎ 08-9226 4524, 🖳 info@adven tureworld.com.au, www.adventureworld.com.au), 4th Floor, 197 St George's Terrace, Perth, WA 6000) and Sydney (☎ 02-8913 0755), 3rd Floor, 73 Walker St, Sydney, NSW 2000.

● **Exodus Expeditions** (☎ 02-9251 5430), 1 York St, Sydney, NSW 2000 – agents for Exodus (UK).

● **Outdoor Travel** (☎ 03-9670 7252), 60 Hardware St, Melbourne, Vic 3000 – agents for Sherpa Expeditions (UK).

● **Peregrine Travel Centre** (☎ 03-9663 8611, 🖳 sales@peregrine.net.au, www.peregrine.net.au), 258 Lonsdale St, Melbourne, Victoria 3000: also in Sydney (☎ 1300-854 444, ☎ 02-9290 2770, 🖳 enq@peregrine.net.au), 5th floor, 38 York Street, Sydney NSW 2000; Brisbane (☎ 07-3854 1022, 🖳 pere grine@backtrack.com.au), 1st Floor, Scout Outdoor Centre, 132 Wickham St, Fortitude Valley, Queensland 4006 and Perth (☎ 08-9321 1259, 🖳 pere grinewa@tpg.com.au), 1st Floor, 862 Hay St, Perth, WA 6000.

● **Summit Travel** (☎ 09-321 1259) 1st floor, 862 Hay St, Perth, WA 6000.

● **World Expeditions** (☎ 02-9279 0188, 🖳 enquiries@worldexpeditions. com.au, www.worldexpeditions.com.au), Level 5, 71 York Street, Sydney NSW 2000. Also in Melbourne (☎ 03-9670 8400, 🖳 travel@worldexped itions.com.au), 1st Floor, 393 Little Bourke St, Melbourne, Victoria 3000; Brisbane (☎ 07-3216 0823, 🖳 adventure@worldexpeditions.com.au), Shop 2, 36 Agnes St, Fortitude Valley, Queensland 4006; and Perth (☎ 08-9221 8240, 🖳 holiday@worldexpeditions.com.au), Suite 2, 544 Hay St, Perth, WA 6000. The main competition for Peregrine. As well as a range of standard treks, some climbing expeditions are offered.

Agencies in New Zealand

● **Venture Treks** (☎ 09-379 9855), PO Box 37610, 164 Parnell Rd, Auckland – agents for Sherpa Expeditions (UK).

● **Project Himalaya** (☎ 06-868 8595, 🖳 info@project-himalaya.com,

www.project-himalaya.com), 54a Darwin Rd, Gisborne. Run by the author of this guidebook.
● **World Expeditions** (☎ 09-368 41611, toll-free ☎ 0800-350354, 💻 enquiries@worldexpeditions.co.nz, www.worldexpeditions.co.nz), Level 1, 11 Cheshire St, Auckland.

How long to go for

If time is the ultimate luxury a trekking holiday should be a decadent one. The more time you have in the mountains the better, especially if the concept of trekking appeals. It takes a day or two to adjust to the trekking lifestyle and exercise, and it's usually only in the last couple of days that you'll start to feel that it is time to clean up and fatten up. If you want to sample trekking rather than eat the whole pie, a week to ten days is a good length; anything less is just a stroll.

Time planning

Arriving in Nepal from Australia or Europe it's best to allow a whole day in Kathmandu (ie two nights), while from New Zealand and the USA allow two whole days to recover and adjust to the different time zone and climate. If arranging a trek on arrival, two or three full days are better. Try to have at least one day in Kathmandu at the end of a trek in order to clean up and shop. More time can easily be filled by exploring the Kathmandu Valley, relaxing in cafés and bargaining with tea-serving Kashmiri carpet salesmen and Thangka-hawking Tibetans. Slowly Nepal is becoming an adventure destination, so plan extra time if rafting, bungee jumping, canyoning, mountain-biking, paragliding or visiting Tibet appeals.

❖ Acute mountain sickness (AMS) primer

The key to planning a trekking itinerary is awareness of altitude sickness: going up too fast causes a medical condition serious enough to kill you. The higher the altitude, the less oxygen there is in the air. On the lower summit of Kala Pattar (5554m/18,222ft), for example, there is 50% less oxygen than at sea level. Your body needs many days to adapt to this phenomenon so for a safe trek it is absolutely essential that you **allow sufficient time for acclimatization**. The doctors at Khunde Hospital and the HRA Pheriche clinic both stress that in virtually all of the cases they treat, the patient has ascended faster than the guidelines. In a surprising number of cases trekkers were forced to ascend too quickly by their group's itinerary. Sometimes this has been because a delayed flight has meant they have had to cut a vital acclimatization day. The Japanese are perhaps the most notorious for rushing and by all accounts also seem to be the most susceptible to AMS. See p281 for more information.

Avoid the trap of planning a whole itinerary down to the last minute and allow plenty of time for the inevitable delays and interruptions to your schedule. Domestic flights can be delayed, so allow an extra day or two to accommodate for this. Once on the trail, especially on a longer trek, allow a couple of days for inclement weather, sickness or a gloriously lazy day for eating and reading. Although many people have never been hiking for more than four or five days at home (or indeed never been hiking at all), two or three weeks in the mountains of Nepal usually flies by all too quickly.

Route options

Since ancient times caravans have followed trade routes across many parts of Asia. The advent of motorized transport brought great changes but these developments passed Nepal by until the 1950s. The first road link, the Rajpath between Kathmandu and India was opened only in 1956 but road construction is now a government priority (rail is impractical). With much of the countryside being not far off vertical, only the low-lying Terai and the Himalayan foothills have been penetrated and even then the roads are rough. The rest of the country still relies on the footpaths and mountain trails that form an age-old network across the country. Looking at a map it's easy to plan some weird and wonderful routes in wild and isolated areas. However, only a few major routes are suited to trekkers wanting to stay in lodges – but what routes some of them are!

Planning
Most people start planning with the intention of seeing Everest. Basically this entails going to the Khumbu region and up a hill to view the mountain. So the majority of trekkers fly to Lukla, trek to the top of Kala Pattar, then fly out of Lukla. This standard route is popular, and with good reason, but options are much broader. All routes to Everest pass through Namche (except a few tough options mentioned later on in this guide) so the first decision to make is how you're going to get there. If you plan to fly one way only then flying out is best since the walk in aids acclimatization (the process of getting used to altitude, see p273) and fitness. If flying in and out, although the vast majority of people begin and end in Lukla, flying in to Phaplu is a sensible alternative (see p24). For sample itineraries see pp273-5.

WALKING IN OR OUT

From Jiri – the expedition route
Jiri, a day's journey by bus or taxi from Kathmandu, is the usual starting point for trekkers who prefer to walk in. This route features numerous pleasant lodges and teahouses catering for trekkers. While during peak season the regions above

Lukla are congested, the Jiri walk-in never suffers this feeling. The majority of trekkers are individuals rather than groups, giving the lodges a carefree air. It is a surprisingly strenuous walk with the route crossing three large ridges, but it's also a rewarding one that prepares you for the higher altitudes ahead. See p145 for more details.

This route is often called the expedition route because it follows the trail that the majority of climbing expeditions took (although when Everest was first climbed the trail began on the edge of the Kathmandu Valley).

The Salpa-Arun route from Hille/Basantpur or Tumlingtar
On this route, compared with the Jiri to Namche walk, the number and height of the hills are similar but the overall distance is slightly greater. Route-finding is more challenging and many lodges are a half- or full-day's walk apart, so it's better attempted by trekkers with some experience. It is still a surprisingly rustic experience.

Walking from Hille to Leguwa Ghat or Basantpur first involves a rough 24-hour bus ride from Kathmandu, then a short but hot two-day walk to Tumlingtar airport. Flying directly to Tumlingtar is good value, relatively reliable and generally the better option.

A variation on this route is to begin from Bhojpur. The facilities are less than basic – see p248.

Beginning your adventure with a wet and wild rafting trip on the Sun Kosi is a great way to combine a rafting expedition with a Salpa Arun trek. See p227.

The Salpa-Arun route was used by the first few expeditions into the Khumbu but it didn't really catch on, perhaps because they trekked it during the monsoon. See p226 for more details on the route.

Avoiding altitude sickness
Most scheduled flights arrive in Lukla before lunch so it's usual to hit the trail and stay at Phakding or Monjo for the first night. Nevertheless, some sensible planning is required to lessen the risk of altitude sickness occurring later. Already at Lukla there is only 70% of the oxygen compared to sea level. Altitude-specialist doctors recommend taking a minimum of 2-3 nights to reach 3000m/9843ft. Since Lukla is at 2850m/9350ft you are already close to that altitude limit and Namche, at 3450m/11,319ft, is well above it; yet most trekkers who fly in, trek to Namche in just over 24 hours. These people are twice as likely to experience troublesome AMS (Acute Mountain Sickness) and form the majority of serious cases. Caution at this point will undoubtedly lessen the impact of problems experienced later. Diamox may also help: see p286.

There are many people in the trekking industry who would consider the above advice over-cautious. However, two American studies found that 9-12% of people who ascend directly to 2800m (Lukla: 2850m) suffered noticeable AMS, admittedly usually non-life-threatening, but definitely uncomfortable. The AMS tended to resolve itself within 2-3 days of staying at the same altitude. Arriving directly at 3860m (ie Syangboche) caused AMS in 84% of people.

❖ **Salpa-Arun or Jiri?**
Previously the decision was easy to make: the Jiri route had superior facilities and the route is straightforward, while the Salpa-Arun route had far more basic facilities and there was a high probability of getting lost. But now, though the Jiri facilities are still better, those on the Salpa-Arun have improved and getting lost is no longer so easy. However, there still remains much less choice on this route and the distances between some lodges are still relatively big. It is also slightly longer, and slightly more strenuous too.

In all other ways, each advantage is matched by a disadvantage. Culturally the Arun has a greater variety but fewer people speak English so it is perhaps less accessible; scenically, the Salpa-Arun has more variety, for it begins in the low country, but this also makes the first stretch hot and sweaty. If the decision is still difficult, flip a coin, or take one route for the walk in, and the other when walking out.

FLYING IN

Flying to Lukla (2850m/9350ft)
This is the most popular way to begin the trek because it's the quickest: Lukla is only one-and-a-half day's walk from Namche. However, the risk of altitude sickness is double that of alternative routes unless at least one extra acclimatization day is scheduled. Trekkers in organized groups should particularly note this; see the discussion on p274.

In the past there were nightmarish flight-booking queues but with the introduction of private airlines and the upgrading of Lukla airport this problem has been alleviated. Indeed, the flights are surprisingly reliable given that they are fair-weather only.

Flying to Phaplu (2350m/7710ft)
If you wish to fly, flying to Phaplu is an under-used route and yet the most sensible choice. It saves what some consider an arduous day on a bus (ie to Jiri) and a few days' walking. Compared with flying to Lukla, it allows a safer and more gentle introduction to altitude and reveals a richer cultural variety with the added bonus of being able to visit Junbesi and Chiwang Gompa. The government has recognized the potential and introduced tourist-priority flights, but trekking companies have yet to adapt their itineraries to include this alternative trail: flying to Lukla saves that extra day or two, all-important in today's package trek market. See p223.

Flying to Syangboche (3700m/12,139ft)
There are no scheduled flights to Syangboche, the airstrip just above Namche. The runway here is used by charter and cargo helicopters only although there are plans to extend the runway to allow passenger flights. Without previous acclimatization, flying to Syangboche and descending to Namche, at 3450m/11,319ft, is uncomfortable and potentially dangerous; Lukla is a much better option. However, for flying out of the region a new service would be convenient.

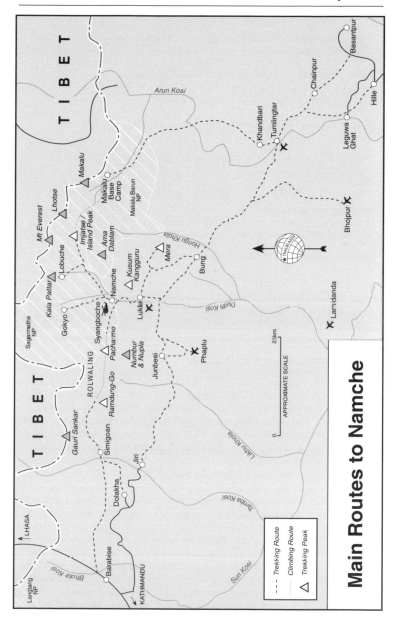

Main Routes to Namche

- - - Trekking Route
.... Climbing Route
△ Trekking Peak

TIMEFRAMES – KATHMANDU TO KATHMANDU
The following are overall times needed for a trek, assuming normal pace with acclimatization days and including travel days, ie buses and/or flights. Remember to allow an extra day or two for flight delays, sickness etc.

Flying in and out of Lukla
Quickest Everest view (to Namche with a day trip there) 5-6 days
To Tengboche Gompa 7-9 days
Khumbu culture (with time around Thame, Namche, Tengboche) 10-12 days
Everest Base Camp (actually Kala Pattar) 13-16 days
Gokyo Lakes 12-14 days
Explore the Khumbu (Gokyo, Kala Pattar, Chukhung) 18-21 or more days
Attempt Island Peak (or similar) 18-21 days
Mera Peak 19-23 days
For flying in to Phaplu instead of Lukla add 4-6 days

Walking into the region
Expedition route Jiri start, trek to Kala Pattar then fly from Lukla 20-22 days
Exploring the Khumbu Jiri start, look up the main valleys then fly from Lukla 23-28 days
Expedition route in (Jiri start) plus walking out via Salpa-Arun to Tumlingtar 27-30 days
Sun Kosi rafting beginning add 8-9 days
Arun-Salpa route fly to Tumlingtar, trek to Kala Pattar then fly from Lukla 22-25 days
Tilman-Shipton route Hille start, Salpa-Arun to Kala Pattar, fly from Lukla 24-27 days

ROUTE OPTIONS ABOVE NAMCHE

Above Namche there are four main valleys (see map opposite), each spectacular and worthwhile exploring. The westernmost valley in the Khumbu is the lower Bhote featuring Thame with its old gompa – a good day or overnight trip from Namche. The upper Bhote valley leads to the 5700m Nangpa La trading pass which was opened to trekkers in 2002, although you can only go to the top of the pass and cannot actually cross into Tibet. Above Thame there are no lodges so any walk here is serious wilderness trekking and incredibly spectacular – perfect for some wild exploration. See p222.

Moving eastwards, the valley featuring Gokyo has a stunning set of turquoise lakes, multiple Everest viewpoints and offers incredible potential for exploration. Its lower reaches are good places for wildlife spotting.

The next valley east features Kala Pattar, the most popular point for viewing Everest, and Everest Base Camp. These are accessible from Lobuche and Gorak Shep, the highest places you are likely to stay. One detail that should be clearly understood is that although most people are initially drawn to Everest and usually harbour ideas of visiting Everest Base Camp, there are actually no views of the upper part of the mountain from there. For this reason almost everyone climbs Kala Pattar, which features a spectacular panorama, including Everest.

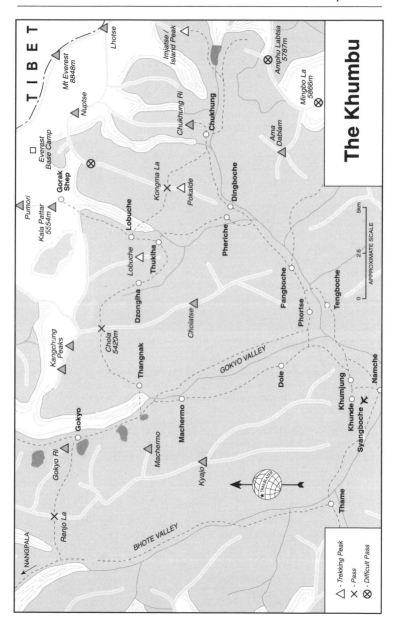

The Khumbu

T I B E T

Mt Everest 8848m

Lhotse

Nuptse

Everest Base Camp

Pumori

Kala Pattar 5554m

Gorak Shep

Kongma La

Pokalde

Lobuche

Lobuche

Thukla

Dzonglha

Cholatse

Chola 5429m

Kangchung Peaks

Thangnak

Machermo

Gokyo

Gokyo Ri

Machermo

Kyajo

Renjo La

NANGPALA

BHOTE VALLEY

Imjatse / Island Peak

Amphu Labtsa 5787m

Chukhung Ri

Chukhung

Mingbo La 5866m

Ama Dablam

Dingboche

Pheriche

Pangboche

Tengboche

Phortse

Namche

GOKYO VALLEY

Dole

Khumjung

Khunde

Syangboche

Thame

APPROXIMATE SCALE

0   2.5   5km

△ - Trekking Peak
✕ - Pass
⊗ - Difficult Pass

You should check your itinerary or allow an extra day if you wish to climb Kala Pattar and visit Everest Base Camp, which can be quite a tough walk.

The final valley above Namche is home to Chukhung and offers good exploring and climbing, although no Everest views. Chukhung is the stepping point for Island Peak/Imjatse, an over-popular 6173m mountaineering climb.

In addition to trekking through each valley, there are also several high passes that run between them and provide a greater challenge.

Other considerations are the gompas – Buddhist temples – that dot the region. Tengboche, en route to Lobuche and Chukhung, is popular and well set up to accept visitors. It is also modern, having been rebuilt in grand scale after the 1989 fire; as such, a comparison with older gompas such as Pangboche, Thame or Khumjung can be enlightening. Although many visitors are keen to experience the Sherpa culture, to do so in depth is more difficult than you would expect, see box p30.

The amount of time spent above Namche varies with your ambitions. To spot Everest from the top of Kala Pattar, or Gokyo Ri in the Gokyo Valley, a minimum of thirteen days must be allowed (including a day for flying out). This includes several consecutive nights spent at the same point while ascending, essential for adequate acclimatization. Lovers of grand mountain scenery and explorers, however, could spend weeks wandering up the high valleys above Namche, only returning to hunt down a hot shower and good pizza. In addition to incredible scenery, staying in quieter lodges and spending time with Sherpas and other local people is all part of a rewarding experience. It is this that separates trekking in Nepal from trekking in wilderness areas in Western countries.

Lobuche or Gokyo??

Years ago, heavy marketing for treks to Everest Base Camp excluded other less goal-orientated options. This is still reflected in the brochures of many trekking companies which barely mention a trek up Gokyo Valley. It is, however, well worth considering, though if you're limited by time choosing an itinerary may be difficult.

The pros and cons The views from **Kala Pattar** (near Lobuche and Everest Base Camp) are fantastic. Although only the upper part of Everest can be seen, spectacular sheer mountains and glaciers entirely surround you. Most people don't end up visiting Everest Base Camp, partly because many don't have enough time and also because the trail there is rough and the only view is of the fearsome icefall. However, during the main expedition season, April-May, visiting the tent city is fascinating.

From **Gokyo Ri** the mountains are just as spectacular but not so close, affording views that extend into the distance. The sunset from Gokyo Ri far surpasses that from Kala Pattar. Perhaps the major advantage is Gokyo's exploration potential: there are five day trips possible, each even offering a view of Everest.

Trekking to Gokyo also has the advantage of taking one day less, and the highest sleeping altitude is lower too, at 4750m as opposed to Lobuche's

4930m. On the other hand, if you plan to spend only a single day at one or the other, Lobuche is possibly the better option because the views are great from nearby Kala Pattar and the walk is perhaps more spectacular, although tougher.

If you have more time options broaden. Having been to one of either Gokyo, Lobuche or Chukhung, you should now be acclimatized sufficiently so that you no longer have to plan with altitude in mind. The distances in the Khumbu are not, in fact, very great, with each valley being only a day or two apart. Deciding between visiting Chukhung en route to Lobuche or going to Lobuche first and then Gokyo is such a difficult choice that it's tempting to add a couple more days and visit all of them!

Some examples of itineraries are given on p273 and they can be joined together to create more interesting combinations.

Gokyo and Lobuche
Keen to visit both? If you plan to visit both, but not Chukhung, it may be slightly more sensible to visit Gokyo first since the maximum sleeping altitude there is slightly lower. Crossing the Tsho La (Cho La) between the valleys takes most people two days while walking around the bottom route via Phortse takes two to three days.

If you plan to visit Chukhung as well then beginning with Gokyo or Chukhung makes equal sense. Gokyo and Chukhung offer many days' worth of side trips while Lobuche/Gorak Shep is more limiting.

The Chugyima La / Tsho La / Chola (p215) is a tempting option when contemplating visiting both Gokyo and Lobuche valleys but the conditions must be good. This trip normally takes two days. The alternative walk via Phortse offers a less alpine landscape but is just as rewarding, though it involves two or, more normally, three days of tough trekking.

LEAVING THE REGION

Flying out
The majority of trekkers fly out of Lukla. Although the walk from Namche to Lobuche or Gokyo takes a week going up, the return trip takes most trekkers just two days, then one more to Lukla. It isn't possible to fly out of Syangboche, except by helicopter charter.

Walking in and out
The most obvious route is to walk from Jiri to the Khumbu, then exit via Tumlingtar or Hille/Basantpur. It is slightly better attempted in this direction because the Jiri route is a more gentle introduction to trekking.

However, retracing your steps to Jiri is not a boring alternative; returning, the views are different and the seasons change the colours of the countryside. You'll get a warm welcome from lodges you return to, and being wiser to the ways of the land you'll probably find this part of the walk more rewarding than before.

OTHER OPTIONS

Recreational mountaineering

Fancy climbing a 6000m Himalayan peak? In the jagged world of the Everest region there are a few peaks that can be relatively straightforward to climb and some of these so-called 'trekking peaks' have become increasingly popular objectives. Despite the term 'trekking peaks', all involve real mountaineering, and climbing at 6000m is more challenging than most people expect.

For many climbers and would-be climbers, the combination of a trek to Everest Base Camp and the climb of a 6000m/20,000ft peak has unbeatable appeal – it's one of the reasons Island Peak/Imjatse is the most popular of the 'trekking peaks'. That means it is very busy during the main October-November season, sometimes chaotically so. With ropes fixed along all the tricky sections it is simply a case of clipping on a jumar (a one-way device) and heading off, hopefully to the summit. As such, it is very much big Himalayan climbing style rather than the more admired alpine style.

❖ Cultural treks

The Salpa-Arun and Solu-Khumbu regions are perfect areas for a culture-ori-entated trek. In many ways time is the most important factor. Taking a Sherpa guide and staying in lodges gives you an immediate introduction to a local house (ie their lodge). If the lodge isn't busy you can sit at the kitchen fire and chat with the owner. This is more easily accomplished off-season from Namche and above. Thame and the small settlements en route, Upper Pangboche and Phortse are less frequently visited villages.

Below Lukla the main trails aren't heavily trekked and there are not many trekkers in the shoulder season, eg late September, December through March and mid-May to mid-June. You can get off the tourist-frequented routes by either tak-ing an expedition crew, or, if you have the right guide, simply by staying in peo-ple's houses. But be warned the food will be simple, hygiene will be marginal at best, and there may be little privacy. Perhaps the best way to experience the culture is to briefly live it, eg help with the harvest.

There are some loops that take you off the main trekking routes. For a sample of **Rai culture** consider staying in Bung or Gudel for at least several days and visit a few of the villages nearby, eg Cheskam. There is a route south of the main trekking route, via Somtang, to or from Phaplu.

Phaplu and the surrounding region is barely visited by trekkers. There are sev-eral interesting old and new gompas and Salleri is the district headquarters, the real Nepal, although half modern. Chialsa is a **Tibetan enclave**, as is Thubten Choeling, north of Junbesi. Trekking up from Okaldunga to Phaplu would be an experience. Around Bhojpur, Dingla, Tumlingtar, Khadbari and Chainpur is a mainly Hindu region. Trekking to the Rolwaling Valley is rewarding and it is possible to exit via a different route. You will have to camp a few nights but the hardy could mostly stay in local lodges and people's houses.

For all the ideals involved in taking a cultural trek, it is difficult to really expe-rience or get deeply into the culture especially without speaking the language. It helps to read as much background information as possible, particularly anthropo-logical papers. Few guides, however, are adept at explaining their culture.

OTHER ACTIVITIES
Nepal offers a lot more than just trekking. Unless your schedule is tight, these activities don't need to be planned in advance, just remember to allow some extra time to make arrangements.

Activity	Costs (in US$)
Chitwan – staying inside the park	140 up (plus 80 by car)
Chitwan – outside the park (Sauraha)	65 up
Bardia National Park	220 up (plus 200 if flying both ways)
Rafting:	15-65 a day
Karnali	350-450
Sun Kosi	250-400
Kali Gandaki	75-150
Marsyangdi	180-250
Bhote Kosi	60-80
Trisuli	25-80
Mountain biking	20-65 a day
Mountain flight	109
Balloon flight	195
Canyoning	80 (including transport)
Bungee jump	80 (including transport)
Tibet 8-day overland	700-1000 (including flight)
Tibet 11-day Tibet side Everest BC	1000-1200 (including flight)

Chitwan National Park wildlife safari (3-4 days)

Fancy shaking trunks with an elephant or sipping exotic cocktails under a crimson sunset? How about wildlife spotting by dugout canoe and elephant-back or watching rhinos forage in the savannah from the breakfast table? Royal Chitwan National Park is one of Asia's premier game parks, a mix of jungle, grasslands and river plains teeming with wildlife, including the endangered **royal bengal tiger**, the rare **gangetic dolphin** and the usually seen **one-horned rhino**. It is well managed with buffer zones and the local people are beginning to see the long-term benefit, essential for the long-term future of the park.

Safari, Asian style, is quite different from the African approach. The game, although abundant, is often more elusive and shy. It is also better hidden in the long elephant grass or jungle undergrowth, hence the advantage of spotting by elephant-back, from canoes and from *machans* (hides or blinds). However you will see lots of game and there's a special thrill finding it in its natural environment.

There are two distinct ways of enjoying Chitwan: staying inside the park, or staying outside. Sauraha, the travellers haunt outside the park, is the cheaper but less satisfactory alternative; the Government elephant ride is short so most of the game spotting is done on foot (and by climbing trees if a rhino charges) or by jeep. And in the cosmopolitan village, you miss the absolute serenity of the morning and evening jungle. So, while the experience is good, there is a better way.

Scattered through the park jungle, the wildlife resorts are secluded and more than comfortable. The well-planned activities flow and the service is superb. Each has its own fleet of elephants, dugout canoes and jeeps, handled by guides who know the animals' habits, usually spotting game long before you do. The resorts are peaceful and deliciously relaxing, making the Chitwan Experience a brilliant way to begin or end a holiday in Nepal. *(cont'd over)*

OTHER ACTIVITIES

(cont'd from p31) Other pachyderm-related entertainments include **elephant polo**. If polo is a gentleman's sport, elephant polo must be the sport of kings. Tiger Tops hosts an annual tournament at its Chitwan Jungle Lodge. It is a fun social occasion well attended with teams sponsored by liquor and adventure companies.

Bardia National Park (4-8 days)

Lost in Nepal's Wild West, Bardia is almost undiscovered compared to Chitwan, probably because it is either inconvenient or more expensive to access. Here four- or five-day safaris penetrating well into the park are better. Access is from Nepalganj, a US$109 flight (one way) or a gruelling 14-18 hour night bus journey. From Pokhara the flights costs US$67 and the bus journey is a similar length.

Further hidden in the West are **Kaptada National Park**, a middle-altitude forest plateau which can only be reached by walking (7-14 days total) and the Royal Suklaphanta Wildlife Reserve, close to Mahendranagar. The reserve is a grassland area rich in rare swamp deer and with the occasional tiger and wild elephant. It is a staggering 30 hours by bus or a US$160 flight from Kathmandu.

Rafting (2-12 days)

While Nepal is famous for mountains it should also be renowned for rafting. Huge mountains mean big, steep rivers, perfect for rafting and kayaking. For thrill-seekers no trip to Nepal would be complete without a wild water expedition. The nervousness, no, the plain fear of being committed to a rapid, then the sheer exhilaration of running and surviving the huge white-water make rafting one of the most thrilling life experiences. Between the roller-coasters are peaceful stretches, chances to splash around and relax, letting the adrenaline highs give way to that priceless inner glow. Also special is the warmth and fun of being an integral part of the team.

For a mild, cheap intro try the **Trisuli**. Almost every rafting company runs this 2-4 day river and it can be run year-round. If you know you will enjoy the thrills and spills then don't muck around, hit a river with a higher scare factor. The **Bhote Kosi** (two days) and the **Marsyangdi** (five days) are steep, technical and fun. For the ultimate try the massive waters of the **Karnali** (8-9 days plus 3 travelling) and the **Sun Kosi** (8-9 days plus 2 travelling), which have rapids that will make even the coolest cucumber gulp in disbelief. Another world-class river is the exhilarating **Tamur** (Kanchenjunga region), with its magic trek in and approximately 130 rapids in 120km. For a shade off full throttle consider the cultural **Kali Gandaki** (5 days, out of Pokhara) or the **Sun Kosi** in low water. Want to learn how to kayak? Kayak Clinics come highly recommended, though first ensure the instructors are qualified.

The high water season, for those with no fear, is late September-early October and May. Trips run into November then begin again in March and taper off by late May.

Wherever you go, safety should be paramount. The more difficult the river is, the more you should check the company's ability, and make sure you ask if the rafting guides and safety kayakers are swift-water-rescue trained. Take a look at Peter Knowles' *Rafting: a consumers' guide*, available in Kathmandu; for more info on all the rivers of Nepal read his delightfully-written *White Water Nepal*.

Mountain biking (1-4 days)

The Kathmandu Valley and the surrounding hills offer some of the best mountain biking there is: endless interesting trails, many technical, and, much more than that, a cultural experience and insight into the real Nepal. Although you can go alone the guides know the best loops and the companies have good bikes.   *(cont'd opposite)*

OTHER ACTIVITIES
Mountain biking
(cont'd from p32) Trips can be organized through **Himalayan Mountain Bikes**, **Dawn till Dusk** and others in Thamel. Costs begin at around $20 a day with a minimum of two, sometimes four people required. For more information see Trailblazer's new *Tibet Overland* guide which has a chapter on mountain biking in Nepal.

Cycling/motor-biking around the city
Once cycling was the most pleasant way to see Kathmandu. Now with the dust, pollution and lack of road rules few people cycle in Kathmandu for pleasure, but once outside the city limits it's a different story. Clunky Indian mountain bikes (better kept on the tar seal) cost US$2-4 a day while motorbikes go for around US$10 a day plus petrol.

Mountain flight
Almost every morning during the high seasons, Buddha Air, Mountain Air and others operate a 'mountain flight' for close-up views of the Himalaya including Everest. It costs US$109 and departs only if the sky is clear. During the autumn peak season highly rated mountain flights around the Annapurna Circuit also operate out of Pokhara. Tickets are refundable and bookings may be moved to the following day if the flight is cancelled. Taking any other domestic flight is, if the weather's perfect, also spectacular.

Balloon flight
Based in Kathmandu and piloted by a colourful Australian, the hour or so flight is uplifting, peaceful and somewhat random; you land where the gods have taken you.

Canyoning
More wet fun. Up near the Tibetan border both **The Last Resort** and **Borderlands** are developing canyoning in the stunningly steep hillsides around there.

Bungee jump
This is the ultimate for adrenaline junkies, a leap off a bridge 160m/520ft (!) above the Bhote Kosi. **The Last Resort** operates the only jump in the country and this can be combined with canyoning and rafting.

Paragliding
This sport is in the process of floating into Nepal with at least one operation in Pokhara, and plans for another near Kathmandu.

Rock climbing
It has taken a while, but finally you can get vertical on warm rock. A couple of camps by good rock and a couple of climbing gyms in Kathmandu are now open.

Visiting Pokhara
Beside a lake gazing up at the huge Annapurna range, the delight of Pokhara is that there's nothing to do besides enjoying the cafés. It is also a good base to begin or end Annapurna treks and ties in well with trips to Chitwan National Park and rafting the Trisuli, Seti and Kali Gandaki.

A second trek
Trekking can be addictive! Around 20% of trekkers do it again in the same holiday. Trekkers also have one of the highest tourism return rates in the world; an amazing number of people just keep coming back year after year. After a first trek you'll know how the teahouse system works and be comfortable with the way Nepal is in general.

(cont'd overleaf)

OTHER ACTIVITIES
A second trek
(cont'd from p33) Teahouse trekking is still only easy in the three main areas of Annapurna, Everest and Langtang, but based out of teahouses some wild routes with plenty of exploring are possible. Trailblazer publishes two other Nepal trekking guides – *Trekking in the Annapurna Region* and *Trekking in Langtang, Helambu and Gosainkund.*

On a more generous budget (US$30-60 a day, plus flights), heading away from the main areas and camping makes sense. This could be a full-service trek or you could adopt a mixed approach, using local teahouses where possible and camping where not, taking lightweight camping gear and a minimum of porters. During the October-December season or late spring, the more ambitious may want to throw in a 6000m/20,000ft trekking peak too. Looking through picture books in Kathmandu can give you a better idea of the differences in the areas. A map of Nepal is useful for planning.

Visiting Tibet
If you already have a Chinese visa, you can sometimes cross the border as an individual, though often it is prohibited unless you're in a group of five. On the other side, since there are (officially) no buses, you often have to hire a Landcruiser (minimum US$60 per person) to Shigatse. This also gets around random permit problems. See the website : www.project-himalaya.com for up-to-date details.

An easier and quicker way is to book one of the 8- to 11-day fixed departure tours in Kathmandu, although you should book well in advance as the operators need time to process the paperwork. These drive to (or from) Lhasa, stopping at most points of interest along the way. The budget versions cost US$600-1000, including the US$253 flight between Kathmandu and Lhasa. Tours generally run from March through to mid-November. There are four or five operators in Thamel with little to distinguish between them, and most trekking and travel companies organize through them too.

Visiting Bhutan
The Land of the Thunder Dragon is an exclusive, particularly rewarding destination. The friendliness of the people and the smooth organization come at a price of around US$200 a day whether trekking or travelling. It also takes time to arrange – a minimum of two weeks, and allowing more time is better.

The second busiest peak is **Mera**, offering a sensational summit panorama including a bunch of 8000m mountains. It is little more than an intimidating snow plod up, so it suits people with little skill. It is in a remote area with few villages, which contrasts with Island Peak.

On both mountains there is a mixture of clients, from those whose mountaineering experience is close to zero and are on guided ascents to more skilled climbers using basically the same techniques. For people who consider themselves confident or experienced mountaineers and want an uncluttered peak-season climb there are a few other mountains worthy of your attention. See p261 for detailed individual descriptions, cautions and an explanation of the trekking peak and expedition peak system.

Note that on even a basic expedition the costs quickly mount up so especially for less-focused, novice or budget mountaineers it is generally better to simply go exploring around the Khumbu. There is a glorious freedom in the host of 5800m scrambles and 5400m pass crossings, unencumbered by harness, rope or even guide.

Other non-technical trekking routes into the Khumbu

The standard routes (Jiri and the Salpa-Arun) are the most logical and direct ways into the Khumbu, reinforced by chains of lodges. However, walking from Barabise to Jiri is feasible, as is flying into Lamidanda, Okhaldhunga, Bhojpur (p248) or Taplejung, or trekking up from the Okhaldhunga road to the south. These alternatives are not on difficult or dangerous trails but they traverse hot low country and lack lodges, so they are better attempted with a guide and after acquiring some Nepalese trekking experience. Check the political situation carefully, too (see p266).

Technical passes into the Khumbu

There are four challenging 5700m-plus (18,700ft) passes that drop into the Khumbu and require mountaineering competence. Generally it's better to visit the Khumbu first and acclimatize properly, then exit via one of the high passes. The tough and dangerous **Tashi Labtsa** is at the head of the Rolwaling Valley and can be reached from Barabise or Dolakha. If you're trekking with a group, a climb of the trekking peak Ramdung-Go is usually included as acclimatization and to ensure that you are capable of the crossing.

The **Mingbo La** and the **Amphu Labtsa** are technically difficult and isolated, and are generally only crossed in conjunction with climbing the trekking peak Mera (6476m/21,246ft) or crossing a couple of 6100m/20,013ft passes from Makalu Base Camp. Read the detailed route descriptions on p252, p220 and p221 for scare factors. The **Nangpa La** (5716m/18,753ft) is the highest and one of the more arduous trading passes in the world. It was recently opened to visit but not to cross. See p222.

The high passes of the Khumbu and the trekking peaks are better attempted during the October to Christmas season. Later the numbing cold and increasing snowfall can make these already tough propositions more challenging, highly dangerous or even impossible.

Alternative treks

The psychological omnipotence of Everest is so great that few people contemplate trekking in this region without the aim of seeing it from close quarters. Star attraction aside, however, there are other areas that offer fantastic trekking amid stunning mountains. These all require a degree of self-sufficiency and camping out. Many would be particularly suited to the classic style of Nepal trekking – a crew to carry the excess, and a few Sherpa companions to round the experience. Going without local support is for the tough and experienced and even then a porter for some sections would be invaluable. The best suggestions are:
● **Exploring above Junbesi**, to Dudh Kund (Milk Lake) below the holy moun-

tain of Numbur and in the Lumding Kharka area, south of Kongde (a 'trekking peak') and Nupla. This could be combined with the trek to Namche.

● **South of the Rolwaling Valley** is a region that hides untold exciting possibilities – high kharkas and ridges littered with mountains a touch under 6000m/19,685ft. Several circuits are possible over unused passes.

● **The Hinku and Hongu valleys** offer challenging and remote treks amongst mind-blowing mountains. A circuit including Mera would be attractive.

The Barun and Makalu region

This is an isolated area with only a fraction of it used for grazing and expedition access to Makalu. Otherwise it's impenetrable forest topped by savage mountains. A trek to Makalu Base Camp is the only feasible option. See : **www.project-himalaya.com** for enough details to whet your appetite for visiting a little explored area.

Mountain-biking

A picture of a Japanese man astride a mountain bike atop Kala Pattar set off a raft of would-be imitators. Each found the hard way that bikes have to be carried at least 95% of the time, effectively the whole way. Now, sensibly, Sagarmatha National Park has put a ban on mountain-biking in the park.

Budgeting

The price of material progress is too often to replace a smile with a worried frown, the god being money instead of inner peace **Tom Weir**

Nepal is undoubtedly one of the cheapest countries to travel around. It's possible to survive on US$5/£3.50 a day and for under US$25/£20 a day you can live quite comfortably. There's also a tempting array of services and souvenirs to mop up any excess funds.

COSTS IN KATHMANDU

Your choice of hotel will largely determine the amount spent on basics. A spartan double room with communal bathroom facilities goes for US$2-5/£1.50-3 a night, and with attached bathroom US$5-12/£4-9; a pleasant 2- or 3-star room is about US$20/£13. The 4-star hotels are around $100/£65 and the 5-stars begin from $140/£100 a night.

Food is of a more uniform price. If you avoid the ten most expensive restaurants, meals are US$2-5/£1.50-3, so US$6-10/£4-7 a day is plenty. What you spend on drinks depends on your poison: large bottles of beer and double nips of cheap spirits are around US$1.75-2/£1.20-1.60, while soft drinks cost less than US$0.50/£0.30.

For a budget traveller, around US$120/£80 a week is adequate for cheap hotels, good food, sightseeing, visa extensions and other necessities such as chocolate, newspapers and a quick call home. It is the avoidable one-off expenses, such as flights, rafting trips and quality souvenirs that will have a large impact on your budget plans. With much less than US$100/£60 per week careful budgeting is required.

THE TREKKING BUDGET

Independent trekkers

Once it was difficult to spend even US$5 a day but there are now double rooms and some extensive menus in lodges, tempting trekkers to spend more. Around US$15/£10 a day per person gives you good food and accommodation, plus a few treats. Lodges charge under US$1/£0.60 for dormitory accommodation while doubles go for US$1.50-4/£1-2.60, and main courses are around US$1-2.50/£0.60-1.60. Chocolate, beer and Coke are not so cheap but even with an excess of these luxuries spending more than US$20/£13 daily would be a challenge. Trekking in the middle hills, i.e. below Lukla is far cheaper than the Khumbu and US$10/£6 should suffice.

There are, however, other things than just those necessary for day-to-day survival and you should allow money for: extra films, souvenirs and, most importantly, emergency situations. Many trekkers end up taking a doctor's consultation at Khunde or the HRA post, and a few end up being rescued or hiring a porter. The doctors report that many budget trekkers don't have enough cash on them. It's best to take at least US$100-200/£66-132 in rupees more than your budget. You will most likely spend this in Kathmandu upon your return, or if heading to India, this can easily be converted to Indian rupees. If you intend to take advantage of leftover mountaineering gear sold in Namche (see pp51-2) you'll need lots of rupees, and sometimes dollars (cash). It is increasingly difficult to change money in the hills so begin your trek with all the rupees you are likely to need.

If you're planning to organize a guided trek on arrival in Nepal or to hire a porter see p103 for the costs.

Commercial treks

With all the money paid upfront it's simply a case of following company guidelines and allowing for the few extras. While trekking there are no expenses bar the odd bottle of beer so just allow for souvenirs, extra film, bars of chocolate and the tips for your crew (covered on p105).

CURRENCY

The Euro, British pounds, US, Canadian, Australian, Hong Kong and Singapore dollars are accepted in Nepal, both in cash form and as travellers' cheques (all major brands are welcome, although only American Express has an office in Kathmandu). Major credit cards are accepted by star-class hotels, in some shops and trekking companies, and for cash advances at a few banks. At last, Kathmandu and Pokhara have cash machines (ATMs). Be aware that normally there is a daily limit on your transactions (set by your bank), but you can get around this by withdrawing over the counter at a bank.

Eurocheques and Post Giros are not accepted. As in the rest of Asia some US$ cash is handy. Nepal still has a small black market and in Thamel carpet shop touts offer to exchange dollars for rupees at marginally more favourable rates. You should, however, be aware that exchanging money on the black market does nothing to help the country's balance of payments.

For rates of exchange see p74.

When to go

Trekking the standard routes in the Khumbu is possible and can be pleasant at almost any time of the year; just tailor your route and your expectations to the prevailing seasonal conditions. However, for climbing and crossing high passes the classic trekking time (October–December) is best, with April to early June a distant second.

Most years winter falls of snow are surprisingly light and, providing you can cope with the numbing cold, exploring and climbing is possible. Other years a week or two's unstable weather kicks in usually during January or February and snow drifts bank up, limiting trekking to the main trails.

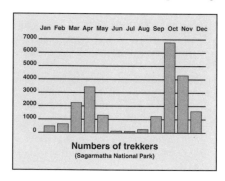

Numbers of trekkers
(Sagarmatha National Park)

The post-monsoon season (October and November edging into December) offers the clearest weather and stunning views but since it's also the busiest time many lodges are full. Winter in the Himalaya is more manageable than you would first think since the weather is mainly fine, so for the well-prepared trekking is still rewarding at this time. Winter thaws to the spring reawakening: the flowers bloom, leaves sprout and the rhododendrons blossom for the March to May trekking season. During this increasingly warm period the afternoons are hazy unless there's been a shower of rain to clear it away.

By the end of May and into June it's hot and the approaching monsoon occasionally shakes its clouds. When this does arrive, at the end of June or the beginning of July, everything flourishes under the life-giving rain. Except at high altitudes, leeches abound and coupled with the humidity are enough to put off all but the most determined trekkers.

Global warming
Though how it is being caused is still being debated, global warming is now a fact. Most recent research has pointed to the fact that the recent changing of weather patterns is not temporary, so the weather of the last five years or so is the weather we are likely to be stuck with, only with greater fluctuations likely. For the trekker expect a large dump of snow (rain in the low country) in October or November as a cyclone degenerates on the Himalaya, but otherwise it should be mostly fine. Monsoon-like conditions seem to prevail earlier, starting sometime in May, although the official monsoon (a distinct weather pattern in the Bay of Bengal) still seems to begin mid-June.

SEASONAL CONDITIONS

Early autumn (mid-September to mid-October)

The monsoon has dwindled but a few tail-end clouds and showers (or short-lived snow at altitude) must be expected. Locals and trekkers simply take cover in the nearest teahouse and wait the afternoon shower out. There's also a chance that the monsoon may not quite have ended, staging a dramatic return for a few weeks. The Jiri to Namche section is either hot and sweaty under the fierce sun or perpetually grey and cloudy, while higher up it's pleasant with cool but mostly frost-free nights. If you skip the lower country, this is a particularly pleasant and under-trekked season. At this time the whole country changes from a lush, verdant green into the harvest colours.

The approach of winter (mid-October to Christmas)

This is classic trekking time, famed for clear skies and fantastic fine weather. Early October through to late November is also the busiest period with most lodges and camp sites brimming with trekkers.

The long fine periods are occasionally broken for a day or two by a front sweeping overhead causing high cloud or cloud banks that roll up the valleys, then usually clear at altitude with the sunset. The odd stronger front brings a spot of wet weather as well but it is impossible to tell (even the locals can't) whether a front contains rain. Barring unusual conditions during this trekking season, perhaps two or three periods of showers and drizzle, or short-lived snow at altitude, can be expected. In an odd year there is perpetual high cloud and less than crystal clear skies.

Tengboche begins receiving frosts in October and by November at altitude evenings are chilly. During a cold clear snap in the up-valley lodges (Lobuche, Gokyo and Chukhung) a water bottle beside your bed will partially freeze overnight and the lakes above 5000m/16,404ft begin to ice over. Shorts can still be worn above Namche on windless days by the determined; but light pants feel more comfortable. December is one of the most pleasant months for trekking because statistically it is the driest month of the year and the vast majority of trekkers have already headed down. The shorter winter days are cooler but on the walk in you'll still sweat on the hills. Above Namche it is cold but a thick down jacket, good sleeping bag and lots of hot drinks can ward the cold off effectively.

Winter (January through March)
New Year or sometime into January-February usually brings a week or so of disturbed weather. Frequently this is the snowfall that puts a stop to the easy pass-hopping and climbing, or at least brings more challenging conditions. This semi-regular fall is sometimes followed by more winter storms breaking the fine periods. Two closely spaced storms can lead to snow drifts above Namche. A bad year will see the high lodges snowed in for a few days and a sudden rush on plastic boot rentals in Namche. The shaded snow has no chance of melting while the rest of the snow patchily clears over a week or two. In other years, and this is increasingly the trend, there'll be only light falls that burn off quickly in the sunny spots. Air temperatures stay around 0°C/32°F during the warmer days, and nights are all below 0°C/32°F and can even hit -30°C/-22°F at 5000m/16,404ft. All the high altitude lakes sport ice thick enough to skate on and many (for example Gokyo lake) will not thaw until May.

March has a reputation among the Sherpas as being colder than December, and with snow lying around, trekking is more challenging. This is no time to take an expedition-style trek; stick to teahouse trekking. Below Namche, down to an altitude of about 2600m/ 8530ft, periodic snow falls and ice can occasionally be expected. Flights to Lukla are sometimes disrupted by snow during January and February but only for a day or so.

Spring (April to early June)
The second trekking season commences at the end of March and continues into May with the atmosphere becoming increasingly hazy. The fine periods will be broken by lots of cloud rolling up the valleys during the afternoon, often bringing drizzle that clears during the evening. On the trekking peaks and above there is a pattern of daily light powder snow that shortens the usable part of the day. A torrential pre-monsoon downpour is also possible, though rare.

The temperatures warm up considerably and by the end of April are hot at low altitudes and sometimes on the warm side higher up too. The rain, sun and warmth spark a flourish of growth with rhododendrons painting the hillsides, beginning in late February at lower altitudes and blooming ever higher during March and April.

In May the middle hills are sweltering; beginning early, having a long lunch and sometimes walking in the late afternoon minimizes the discomfort. The low altitude haze and occasional cloud reduce the strength of the sun. In the high country, early May is an under-utilized time. While the weather may be less stable than November-December, the warmth, lushness and the comparative lack of trekkers mean it is still great trekking.

The monsoon (late June to early October)
The Indian monsoon rains usually hit the eastern Himalaya around mid-June, although it can, rarely, be as much as a month early or late. Below 3000m/

9843ft it's oppressive, muddy and leeches abound but planes still operate flights (on an irregular schedule: planes may not be able to get to Lukla for as many as 15 days in a row) so it's possible to avoid the worst areas. There are frequent showers, mainly in the afternoon and at night, and occasional heavy deluges, especially in July. Everybody dives under the nearest shelter to drink tea and wait it out. Infrequently these cloudbursts create dangerous flash-floods and mudslides which can put paid to the day's walking.

Above Namche the days are warm and the nights are frost-free although short-lived snow can fall on Kala Pattar and even down as far as Chukhung. Rainfall is uneven with the southernmost mountains bearing the brunt; this is the reason the glaciers on Numbur and in the Hongu/Hinku are so big. Above Namche is a partial rain-shadow area and consequently in the higher reaches of the main valleys the rain is reduced to occasional showers and drizzle. The rain pattern is not regular; it might be misty and rain every afternoon for a week, then clear for a couple of days. Slippery trails can be a problem, particularly for porters. The monsoon always eventually manages to find its way into tents and dining tents are restrictive for an afternoon's rain; better to stick to teahouse trekking. Overall, the almost perpetual cloud cover is more of an annoyance than the drizzle. The views are stunning when they clear but you often wait days for this to happen, although Kala Pattar does clear more frequently. The rewards of this season are lush green valleys carpeted by petite flowers, though this is also true of late May and early June. For a person who likes wandering, rather than trekking to a schedule, it's a wonderful time to observe the other way of life of the Sherpas, the monsoon cycle of agriculture and festivals.

By September the monsoon is in retreat. Officially the monsoon rains usually stop around mid-September but sometimes they cease as early as the beginning of the month or as late as early October.

Although the monsoon conditions in the Bay of Bengal may have finished, the unsettled pattern of cloud and periodic drizzle usually continues into early October. Increasingly frequently during October or November the remains of a

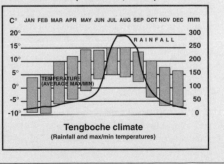

CLIMATE STATISTICS FOR TENGBOCHE (3867M/12,687FT)

In October an average night minimum of -4°C/24°F and an average day maximum of 10°C/50°F can be expected. For January the average night minimum is -9°C/16°F and the average day maximum is 4°C/39°F. In this chart for Tengboche average monthly rainfall is shown as a line and maximum/minimum temperatures are indicated by grey blocks.

Tengboche climate
(Rainfall and max/min temperatures)

Bay of Bengal cyclone unload in a torrential downpour lasting a day or two. This falls as troublesome deep snow at altitude that generally clears rapidly in the sunny regions.

THE KATHMANDU CLIMATE

At the moderate altitude of 1400m/4600ft, the capital's climate is quite mild. The monsoon showers keep the temperature down mostly to the high 20s°C/80s°F during summer, although it's humid and uncomfortable if it does not rain. By the end of September the tropical temperatures cool and by late October the evenings are a little cold for just a shirt. The early winter days are sunny and agreeable, the evenings require a thick jacket and there's the occasional frost. From Christmas onwards a morning fog pattern sometimes settles on the valley making rising early a challenge. This also disrupts some flights but by 10 or 11am schedules are back to normal. Visiting Kathmandu is pleasant during any of the seasons although spring and autumn are the most popular, and crowded, times.

What to take

FACTORS AFFECTING EQUIPMENT SELECTION

For the trek in (if you are not flying), regardless of the season, you'll want mainly cool, loose clothes for the warm days. Above Namche the days are cooler and a set of interchangeable warm/windproof layers is best. These layers will also do for sitting around in the high lodges from late April to October but at other times a thick down jacket for cold mountain tops and evenings in the lodges is essential. An important key to staying healthy is sleeping well and warmly so that your body doesn't waste energy trying to keep you warm. Don't skimp on your sleeping bag.

During the main trekking season, October to December, it is nearly always dry so you need one set of clothes, ie only what you can wear at once (plus an extra shirt and a change of underwear). During late winter into May clothing may get wet so an extra thermal or light fleece might be appreciated.

All this can add up to a lot of equipment and since you (or a porter) must carry it all consider carefully how to keep it to a minimum. On domestic flights the usual luggage limit is 15kg (34lb) before surcharges apply. Except at the beginning of the Everest climbing season, early April, the airlines are happy to take considerably extra.

The layering principle

If you wear a number of thinner layers of clothing you can simply shed a layer if you get hot or add a layer if the temperature drops. In spite of the fact that this

The bare necessities

What to take is simply a question of what is essential. I met some Tibetans travelling without yaks over the 5716m/18,735ft Nangpa La. We looked at each others' lunches (my biscuits and their *tsampa*) and then compared rucksacks: my fancy expedition-sized pack versus their grubby day-packs. One Tibetan unpacked the rest of his bag to show me what the essentials were: gloves, an extra pair of socks and shoes (Chinese shoes are not known for durability), a jersey and grass (for starting yak dung fires). After lunch into the bag went a 2kg sack of tsampa, a stomach of butter, a brick of tea, spoon, cup and the ancient teapot, and on top went the all-too-thin bedding roll. A hat was already on his head and his jacket pockets held a knife and lighter. They laughed as I shouldered my 20kg backpack and followed them.

Assuming you will be staying entirely in lodges, confident trekkers can get away with very little equipment. **For Sept-Oct and May-June**: 50 litre backpack, T-shirt, thermal top for evening wear, light down jacket (or a thick thermal plus fleece top), rain jacket, mid-weight longjohns, light trekking pants.

For Nov to May: 60 litre backpack, 2 thermal tops (one for walking, one for the evening), down jacket (thicker is better), good breathable rain jacket (Goretex or similar), thick longjohns, light trekking pants, optional snow gaiters.

keeps your clothing dry (more comfortable and much warmer than if wet) you still see many people wearing a fleece jacket and dripping with sweat during the day. Of course the layer next to your skin will probably get wet with sweat so you should carry an extra T-shirt or thermal top. When you stop, change the wet top for a dry one and then put an extra layer or two on to keep warm. This is a good principle for walking during the day but cold Himalayan nights require another. Forget the layers and simply put on dry thermals and the thickest down jacket you can find. Down is comfortable over a large range of temperatures, so even during a mild evening, thick jackets are still functional.

Don't under-estimate the high country cold

Above 4000m it is cool year-round. Even after a warm sunny day the evening temperature is dramatically lower. From November through to April the nights are *very cold*. While many Canadians, Americans and Scandinavians understand the cold, Brits, Kiwis and Aussies don't have exposure to these low temperatures. High altitude winter night temperatures are similar to your freezer at home (which is normally set at -18°C) and even in the trekking areas can drop to as low as -30°C. In admittedly extreme trekking situations I have several times measured temperatures of close to -40°C/-40°F.

In real winter a windless sunny day doesn't feel cold, even though the air temperature might be around 0°C, but a blustery, cloudy day requires being well protected.

There is another factor that conspires to cool you: the lack of oxygen. It is largely oxygen in the blood that keeps fingers and toes warm. When bottled oxygen was first tested on Everest in the 1920s the first effect noticed was that everyone felt warmer. The trick at altitude is to carefully manage and regulate your body temperature. If possible avoid getting sweaty and damp and the moment you start cooling down add some layers. The most critical time is at the end of the day, when you might be low on energy. Having a snack at this time or at minimum a hot drink helps. It is far easier to stay warm than try to warm up after getting cold.

What to sleep in when it's cold

Surprisingly, if you put on all your clothes to go to bed you feel constricted and not a lot warmer. Using a sleeping sheet and one layer of thermal underwear is better and if that's not enough put your down jacket over your sleeping bag. Alternatively, wear the down jacket but with only a T-shirt or thermal top on underneath. What keeps you warm is trapped air, not the materials themselves. Pull the draw-cords tight and ensure your head and shoulders are well insulated.

Foot care

Your feet will be doing far more work than they're probably used to so take great care of them. The rest of your body has the luxury of changes of clothes but your feet are confined to a single pair of boots that must cope with the extremes of heat and cold so air them, and your socks and boots, frequently – lunch in the sun is an ideal time. Consider changing your socks more than once during the day and wash your feet and socks, if nothing else, at least every few days. If you feel a hot spot or a blister developing, you should stop immediately and cover it with a tape before it's too late to prevent damage.

EQUIPMENT LIST

● **Sleeping bag** Essential. A down bag is lighter and more compact than a synthetic one of the same warmth. From late April to the end of October a three-season bag is adequate, ie 700 grams of good down. For the cold months, November to March, take particular care to choose a warm four-season bag, ie 900+ grams of high quality down. When buying a down bag look for good and even thickness; the down should be fluffy and light. A muff around the top of the bag makes a big difference to overall warmth.

In Kathmandu you can easily rent ordinary sleeping bags and there are also a few good down bags. Trekking companies often provide bags but if you already have a good one it's worth taking it instead. There are also fleece liners for approximately US$15 that can boost a tired bag's warmth.

● **Sleeping-bag liner** (cotton or silk). Saves washing your sleeping bag and adds warmth. In Kathmandu, these can be easily and cheaply made up from light cotton. Lightweight silk is harder to find and the more easily available imitation silk is not as good. Hygiene fanatics may also want to bring their own pillowcase.

● **Rucksack/backpack** It's important to have a comfortable one. The feature that will help most in this respect is a good waistband – it should fit snugly without riding up your stomach (which interferes with breathing). At the same time

> **The top half**
> Working out a good combination of tops can be tricky, especially if you want to travel light or can't afford the works. For me I go without a fleece jacket, instead taking a mid-weight and expedition-weight zip T-shirt (or shirt and expedition-weight for warm weather), a light but good down jacket and a Goretex jacket, lined for winter, unlined for warm weather.
>
> A friend uses a completely different combination, T-shirts and the occasional thin thermal top with a Windstopper jacket and a down or fleece vest. If it is likely to be wet he includes a Goretex jacket; if it is winter, a thick down jacket.

it must not sit too low and touch your walking muscles. Small backpacks are neat and look trendy but often are not big enough. For winter a larger pack is preferable since gear does not have to be tightly compressed and this makes packing easier. Group trekkers will need only a daypack but once you put in a down jacket, wind pants, camera and water bottle, plus more odds and ends, you will doubtless find that you need a bigger one, 30 litres or more; again, a proper waistband will make it far more comfortable. It's possible to rent daypacks of varying sizes in Kathmandu. Renting full-size rucksacks is not so easy, although there are plenty of shoddy ones for sale.

● **Boots** One of the most important things for ensuring a happy trek is having comfortable feet. Carrying a backpack places a greater load on your feet than normal so rigid supportive boots will feel more comfortable in the long run. It's possible to trek in running shoes but the new generation lightweight trekking boots are far superior. Trekkers seem to get away with these boots even in winter but this can be dangerous during a snowfall. Sturdy but fairly light all-leather boots are better for cold weather (although should be treated with waterproofing agents after a snowfall or if the trails are muddy).

When choosing boots look for good ankle support, plenty of toe room essential for the long descents (but don't overdo this), a stiff sole (helps prevent tired feet by lessening twisting) and, furthermore, remember that the boots should not be too heavy. Check the inner lining – leather is OK and Cambrelle (which can destroy the bacteria that causes foot odour) is even better. The trend is towards Goretex or similar waterproof but breathable inner linings. These

> **The bottom half**
> Again there are a multitude of combinations. Thin leggings/longjohns, fleece pants and travel pants are a good combination, likewise thick expedition-weight leggings plus travel pants that can fit over the top (and gaiters in winter) are often enough. A third combination is thin or mid-weight leggings, travel pants and waterproof breathable pants.
>
> Many people pack expensive waterproof breathable pants. Most of the time they remain unused though they come into their own, especially bibs, when climbing in winter.

Dress standards
These vary considerably around the country. Kathmandu is the most liberal and culturally diverse place though Western women will find dressing modestly attracts far less attention. The well-off (locals and foreigners) are expected to dress conservatively, casual but clean. Along the regular trekking routes the Nepalese are used to (though have never understood) the comparatively odd and occasionally indecent ways in which Westerners dress, but in less frequented areas locals may still be quite shocked. Even with the Khumbu Sherpas' familiarity with foreigners, you will rarely see more than their head and forearms. Being dressed in a culturally acceptable way gains you much greater respect among the local people, a fact that many trekkers have commented upon.

For men, shorts are more or less acceptable although often you will be looked upon in a strange way because the only Nepalese who wear shorts are the porters (for the caste conscious, low status). T-shirts are OK, but singlets, running shorts or cycle pants, despite the fact that some porter-guides wear them, are going too far; bare chests are rude.

For women double standards exist. Long baggy shorts are worn although a skirt that falls at least to the knee, or light baggy trousers, are definitely more appropriate. A T-shirt is the minimum for modesty but Lycra pants invite unwarranted attention.

render boots even warmer, very often too warm for normal trekking. For the drier seasons less technical boots are more comfortable.

Lightweight trekking boots generally have good shock-absorbing qualities but some foams can actually be crushed if too heavily loaded. Boots must be worn in before trekking and this should include some steep hills.

For independent trekkers weight and space are of prime importance so a single pair of comfortable boots is generally enough. If trekking with a group, another pair of shoes for relaxing around camp can be useful. In cold weather down booties are an option worth considering.

● **Socks** Most of the time your feet will be warm or even hot while walking so quality cotton-mix sports socks are better than wool-based trekking socks, at least until it gets really cold. Few people seem to believe this so I suggest you test this out at home. Three to four pairs are enough. It's during some evenings and a few cold days that you will need good warm socks. Lightweight trekking boots generally fit snugly so wearing two pairs of socks at the same time (originally used in stiff boots to prevent blisters) is not practical. Instead a single pair of quality socks is quite adequate, with an extra pair in reserve.

● **Down jacket** This is essential during the cold months. Find one of bum-warming and hand-warming length, big and thick with a hood. If trekking during the warmer months you will not need it until above Namche and even then a hat and a jersey or fleece combined with a rain jacket may well be adequate.

● **Down pants/trousers** These are a good idea if you are on a high-altitude camping trip from December to March. Teahouses are much warmer and down pants are completely unnecessary.

● **Wind/rain jacket** Essential. High up, if the sun is shining, it can be wonderfully warm. When a breeze picks up the true air temperature becomes apparent and wind protection is a necessity. Since it rarely rains all day – or even at all in peak season – having an expensive, totally waterproof jacket (if there is such a thing) is not necessary. When it starts raining everybody simply takes cover in the nearest shelter. During the finer months the daring have got away with Windstopper or similar fleece and no waterproof jacket.

Plastic ponchos are only of use during the monsoon.

● **Jersey/fleece top** Opinions vary: when it's cold people with down jackets consider down essential, but those with only fleece say it's adequate. Fleece is no substitute, however, for a down jacket in real winter. From May to October, the wet times, fleece may be a better choice.

● **Shirt/blouse** T-shirts are popular but thin long-sleeved cotton shirts/blouses are more versatile: the collar protects the back of your neck and the sleeves can be rolled up or down. Take two so that you have a dry one to change into after trekking. For winter trekking ditch the shirt and take high-neck thermals instead.

● **Underwear** Along the trails into Namche washing every day or two is never a problem. Higher up, when it is cold, the inclination to change your underwear and wash may occur less frequently. Four to five pairs is plenty. (When Ranulph Fiennes and Mike Stroud crossed Antarctica they took only one pair each for over 100 days, though this just about ended the expedition.) If you frequently wear a sports bra bring two; otherwise, what you normally wear is fine.

● **Thermal underwear** Longjohns/legging and some sort of a top are essential unless substituted by fleece for the warmer times. In winter a mid-weight zip T is good lower down, while for higher up an expedition-weight for wearing every day plus a spare for sleeping in is advisable.

● **Pants/trousers** Light material, loose and dark-coloured is best. Cotton/polyester travel pants/pack pants or rock-climbing baggies in nylon or cotton/nylon

---

❖ **Old clothes needed by Kathmandu charities**
If you have a little space in your luggage there are a couple of worthy local charities that would be very grateful for some old clothes.

Kumbeshwar Technical School (☎ 536483) in Patan was set up to cater specifically for the very low caste groups. It incorporates a small orphanage, a primary school and a technical school where carpet weaving and carpentry are taught. High quality sweaters are on sale in the showroom here.

Child Workers in Nepal (CWIN, ☎ 271658) is a charity working for the rights of children and the abolition of child bonded labour (16% of children in the country are bonded labourers). They also run a 'Common Room' to support the 1000 children who live on the streets of Kathmandu. Clothes are always needed; children's clothes are best but they can alter adults' clothes. They can also make use of any medicines you may have left after your trek. CWIN is near the Soaltee Holiday Inn in Kalamati.

mixes are perfect. Throwaway cotton pants are easily bought in Kathmandu. Jeans are not practical; they are restricting and cold when damp.

● **Fleece pants** Good to have though during the warmer seasons they are not strictly necessary; thermals and walking pants will do. In winter they are almost essential.

● **Windproof/waterproof pants/trousers/bibs** If your trekking pants are partly windproof an additional waterproof pair isn't needed.

● **Warm hat** Essential.

● **Sun-hat** You need something to protect your head in hot sunny weather, particularly from April to the end of October. A light hat with a wide brim is good, as is a cotton scarf with a visor.

● **Mittens/gloves** Essential except during the monsoon. The cheap fleece gloves available in Kathmandu are fine for anything except winter climbing. Ski gloves tend to be too warm and heavy, although they are good for climbing. In particularly cold conditions a pair of thin liner gloves when walking is invaluable.

● **Snow gaiters** Leggings that protect from the ankle to the knee are useful in Nepal only when it has snowed heavily. On the main trails, after a large fall of snow a path is cleared quickly so if you can wait you can survive without gaiters. Off the main trails or when climbing they are essential and often, in combination with a longer waterproof jacket, are a good substitute for waterproof pants.

● **Towel** Doesn't need to be big. Quick-drying sarongs seem to be better than most high-tech travel towels.

● **Bathing suit** – only useful while walking along the Arun, where the water is less than glacial in temperature.

● **Insulating pad** – not needed for teahouse trekking unless you plan to spend a night or two outside. For expedition-style treks you will be provided with a pad of sorts but a self-inflating (Thermarest) pad is an improvement.

● **Water bottle** A one-litre water bottle is essential and should be leakproof, tough and able to withstand boiling water. Two are useful, but unless you will be in the hot country, not essential. Some people swear by the convenience of drinking systems but they often fail. In winter they are not worth the trouble, even insulated tubes often freeze in a trekking setting.

● **'Green tea' (pee) bottle/jar** The effects of altitude test even the largest of bladders. Especially in winter when staying in double rooms this luxury will be appreciated. One litre is the minimum, though more capacity can cater to multiple night-time pees.

● **Sunscreen** – essential. The ultra-violet (UV) concentration increases around 4% for every 300m gain in altitude and snow reflects 75% of UV. Having said that, the sun is not nearly as strong as in the ozone hole Oceania regions. Except in snow the thick high-factor creams are unnecessary and 8-15 factor creams are more comfortable. In snow apply frequently and extensively even on cloudy days and offer some to your crew too.

● **Sunglasses** These are essential and must protect against UV – virtually all sunglasses, even the cheapest, now do. For prolonged high altitude sojourns side pieces are useful but ski goggles are not. If you wear prescription glasses it's best to get a pair of prescription sunglasses made. Alternatively, detachable dark lens have proved adequate.

● **Contact lenses** Wearers report problems with grit and pollution in Kathmandu but few problems in the hills except cleaning them in cold conditions. To prevent the cleaning solution from freezing it's best kept in your sleeping bag on cold nights. Also bring your glasses. Many people become blasé about cleaning/changing their lenses but complacency often leads to problems later.

● **Torch/flashlight** – essential. The new LED-based torches are perfect for trekking, and a set of new batteries will last several treks. Head torches are particularly handy for group trekkers in tents. Budget trekkers may get by with a cheap Kathmandu torch.

● **Trekking poles** Particularly useful for stiff descents on rough terrain. If you are already in the habit of using them, bring them. If you are exploring with a heavier pack they are invaluable. If you have never used them, consider buying one if you are older or feel twinges in your knees. They really can make a difference.

● **Umbrella** Most useful during late spring and the monsoon through to the end of September, an umbrella also offers great protection against the sun and, coupled with a good rain jacket, is essential for surviving the monsoon. Available in Kathmandu.

● **Pack cover** Potentially useful from March to the end of September. A large, carefully cut plastic bag can be a reasonable substitute. Both are available in Kathmandu; you can also buy plastic bags in main villages on the trail.

● **Toiletries** This is where you can really save some weight. There is no need for a half-litre bottle of shampoo; chances are you will only wash your hair a few times and one-use packets are available in Kathmandu. Finding hot water for a shave is not always easy and there are no plugs for electric razors except possibly in Namche. The smallest size of toothpaste sold is perfect for a month. Most critically don't forget your deodorant ('the trekker's shower'). Natural anti-bacterial mineral crystals are available, but hard to find, in the Assan Tol market.

● **Toilet paper** Available on main routes so start with only one roll.

● **Lighter** Essential for burning used toilet paper and handy for lighting candles in lodges.

● **Moisturiser** A small tube for sensitive or well cared for skins is useful as the air is dry and the sun harsh.

● **Lip balm with sunscreen** Essential to prevent chapped and blistered lips. From Namche and above use all the time, even on cloudy days. Banana Boat seems to be the best brand.

● **Tampons/sanitary napkins** The supermarkets in Kathmandu always have limited stock, Namche generally has some but they're unavailable elsewhere.

● **Pre-moistened towelettes ('Wet ones')** Handy for group trekkers but bulky for individuals.

● **Camera** If you bring one always keep it with you. Thieves are well aware of the value of cameras so check your insurance policy to ensure your camera is

---

❖ Digital cameras

At last there are some solutions that are workable for a trekking setting. For a shorter trek rechargeable batteries will probably do since you can definitely charge them in Namche/Khumjung. Models that can substitute normal batteries instead are better. The common 2CR5 lithium alternative is relatively cheap to buy in Kathmandu and they last much longer than the normal rechargeables. A big capacity storage card is the way to go, but unless you have several, you are likely to be shooting at resolutions better suited to viewing on screens rather than printing. Note that IBM microdrives are specifically rated to only 3000m.

---

fully covered. A modern compact, especially with a zoom lens, is light and convenient but lacks the versatility of the SLR (interchangeable lens camera). Most come with a zoom that begins from 35/38mm but for trekking a wider-angle zoom, eg from 28mm, is far more useful.

SLRs with zoom lenses provide brilliant flexibility. For portraits and stunning landscape details take a telephoto zoom (70-210mm) as well as a wider lens. Experienced photographers will appreciate a very wide-angle lens.

A polarizing filter is useful and learning its tricks can be fun. It can significantly cut down reflection, giving skin, landscapes (tree leaves in particular) and the sky a deeper, richer colour. It does this best when used in bright sunlight at approximately 90 degrees to the sun. It should not be used for every shot and it's possible to overdo the effect, especially with films that saturate colours (ie virtually all of them).

Auto-everything cameras place high demands on batteries which sometimes give out in the cold so take several spare sets. One trick is to keep a set warm in a pocket ready to substitute. Don't dispose of batteries in the hills. Bring some cleaning equipment as lenses can get dusty.

Having a single, cheap, disposable camera is good insurance against breakdowns. Standard rather than panorama models offer better quality.

● **Film** Kathmandu stocks a wide variety of the standard films (Kodak, Fuji, Konica, Agfa) at competitive prices. Slide film is available everywhere but supplies of Kodachrome are erratic. Black and white film is scarce.

● **First-aid kit** See the medical section, p293.

● **Water purification kit** It is possible to get away with using lodge-boiled water or environmentally unsound bottled water but you have more flexibility with another solution, see p280.

● **Reading matter** Owing to the social nature of trekking, there's often not much time for reading. One or two paperbacks are usually enough for a deliciously lazy day and can be exchanged in Namche or with another trekker.

● **Diary** Many people like to write a diary while they trek.

● **Money pouch/belt** Most people find wearing one while trekking a hassle and keep it buried in their pack until they stop for the evening. More money belts are left behind under pillows than stolen; think of a better way of hiding it at night and develop a habit.

If you plan to stay only in lodges then camping equipment (tent, foam pad, stove, food, cutlery, plate and mug) is not needed. On an expedition-style trek everything is provided, but you may want to bring your own self-inflating mattress (eg Thermarest) as an improvement over what will be supplied.

Modern equipment aside, in Kathmandu it's possible to buy a thick jersey, cotton thermal underwear and socks, and then hit the trail having spent little money. Whatever else you don't already have can be rented.

RENTING OR BUYING EQUIPMENT IN NEPAL

In Kathmandu

There's a great variety of rental equipment here which saves buying expensive specialized gear. Easy-to-rent items include down jackets, sleeping bags, insulating pads, plastic boots, ice axes and crampons.

Many items can also be bought here, mostly for less than in the West. A lot of equipment is locally made, some well designed and strong, most of it adequate or barely so, but you pay for what you get so gear doesn't cost much. In contrast to the uniformly high standard of gear in the West, you will have to look carefully at every aspect of design and manufacture in Kathmandu; in particular carefully feel the quality of down. Some store owners are happy to point out the differences in quality along with the commensurate differences in price, though the less honest will still sometimes insist that a fake label is genuine. You can rely on finding an odd variety of lightweight trekking boots, daypacks and smaller backpacks, large 'porter'/duffel/kit bags, down jackets, down sleeping bags, fleece jackets, pants and accessories, and also a variety of semi-waterproof breathable jackets and pants. Now that Goretex is out of patent similar material is available, usually from Korea. It is basically waterproof but generally the seams are not sealed.

What is still missing is quality thermal gear for next to the skin, Windstopper fleece, large volume backpacks and stretch-fabric clothing.

The vast majority of accessories are genuine: branded knives and pliers sets, trekking poles, torches, sunglasses, harnesses, karabiners, gas stoves, crampons, ice axes and altimeter watches. There are a few things conspicuous in their absence like drinking systems, GPS's, walkie talkies, brand new self-inflating mattresses and quality socks. There is a strange variety of brands.

Snow bars are untested and locally made, but generally do. Most ice screws are Russian titanium. Serviceable down suits are made for 8000m expeditions and the warm One Sport/Millet boots are available new and used.

In Namche

If you are flying in and out of the Khumbu it's better to rent most of the equipment you require in Kathmandu. You can rent passable sleeping bags, down jackets, down pants and down boots. Comparing daily rates, renting gear in Namche tends to be marginally more expensive than in Kathmandu though you don't have to carry it up or pay for the time it's not in use.

Original, brand new clothing and left-over expedition equipment is also available, sometimes almost enough to equip a serious expedition with high quality gear: ice axes, crampons, plastic boots, climbing hardware, tents, down suits, the latest Goretex clothing, fleece, socks and more. The only problem is you never know exactly what will be there, and in what sizes. Increasingly this equipment has been imported but some has been left behind from previous expeditions. Prices are similar to USA prices, but often there are real bargains around too.

ADVENTURE TREKKING EQUIPMENT

Group trekkers are provided with extensive lists. Climbers and experienced adventure trekkers planning to camp out frequently really need to plan carefully: too much is horribly heavy unless you recruit a porter, and too little is limiting.

If trekking alone, or in a small group without a full trekking crew, it's really worth employing a porter who has trekked the route before. Not only will all your packs be lighter (often making the difference between an endurance test and an enjoyable trek) but experienced porters know the bivvy caves, the local herders, the track details and the latest on where you can find supplies in unusual places.

In Namche it's possible to rent everything necessary to climb a trekking peak: harnesses, snow stakes, ropes, crampons, tent etc, but the quality leaves a lot to be desired. If you have your own favourite gear, bring it.

High altitude – October

Day temperatures rarely drop below zero, except above 6000m, so good fleece and thick thermals are enough although down jackets are still handy and a better choice. Although the weather is mostly fine you should be prepared for a fall of snow. Good leather boots are adequate for 6000m peaks and the high passes in perfect conditions; however, most people attempting trekking peaks do wear plastics.

High altitude – November and December

Be prepared for real cold. Day temperatures range from 10°C/50°F to -10°C/14°F and at night expect -10°C/14°F to -25°C/-13°F .

● **Day wear for climbing** should include thin/mid-weight longjohns plus semi-windproof trousers, T-shirt or mid-weight top with expedition weight top (or fleece) and a Goretex shell for more demanding conditions. Liner gloves (thin and not windproof) are essential, backed up by something more substantial. The higher you go the better your mittens must be. Conditions vary considerably, often you can get away without waterproof pants/bibs, but they are invaluable if windy while climbing.

● **Boots** This is the most difficult choice. You have to be planning a lot of pass-hopping and peak-bagging in rough country to wear plastics the whole time above Namche. Walking from Jiri in plastics is absolutely out of the question. Tough well-insulated leather boots backed by full insulating gaiters are more manageable, even for a single trekking peak or high pass in reasonable conditions. Foot care is incredibly important and should never be neglected; if there is only one part of you that you wash in weeks at high altitude, it should be your feet.

● **In the evening** you'll need a substantial down jacket, thin balaclava, and perhaps thick longjohns or fleece pants. Down pants are a luxury.

● **At night**, for several people a tent might be comfortable but a bivvy bag will do. However, if your sleeping bag is exceptionally warm even a bivvy bag is superfluous (provided you have an emergency space/survival blanket for an unexpected snowfall).

If using a Thermarest self-inflating mattress, an ultra-lite with a very thin back-up pad is a comfortable and safe combination, otherwise a thick foam pad will suffice.

High altitude – January to mid-April

Be prepared for extreme cold. Light down jackets or, better, thermals with fleece, and expedition-weight longjohns are comfortable to walk in. Plastic boots above 4000m/13,123ft are good for trekking if it has snowed, with some trekking crews and most lodge owners wearing them; and they are essential for climbing. If trekking in leather boots use gaiter protection and take care to keep them dry. A tough tent is essential. You must be prepared for savage cold and infrequent snowstorms. Above 5000m/16,404ft a cold clear night can put thermometers off the scale.

Frostbite is something to be aware of. For hands, tough liner gloves are invaluable. Take great care of your feet too: lacing boots tightly compresses both the lining and the socks that are meant to keep your feet warm and restricts vital circulation. Inner boots may need lacing only around the ankle. The soles suck heat out and insulating inner soles are invaluable. A single extra layer of material around the whole boot (like a stuff sack) can make a big difference on the coldest mornings when climbing in crampons.

High altitude – Mid-April and May

The warmer conditions are tough with soft, wet and often deep snow. Bring an alarm clock for early starts and a few novels for long snowy afternoons. Tents and clothing should be waterproof and plastic boots are still best for climbing. Goretex pants/bibs and fleece are in their element; carry spare dry clothing and perhaps some camp shoes.

General gear

● **Stoves** Kathmandu and Namche have Epigas-Primus and most other canisters, usually with matching stoves for rent or for sale. Ask the supplier if they have been refilled with Kathmandu gas, which smells more, or are original. Dirty, low quality kerosene is available in small quantities at virtually every lodge, and there is a reasonable chance of finding petrol at two or three lodges above Namche. Petrol is easier to light and significantly cleaner than kerosene. All fuel should be filtered.

● **Water bottles/bags** A total capacity of three litres per person is useful for camping.

Climbing gear

See the trekking peak descriptions for recommendations. For a first trip in the Himalaya, I strongly advise beginning with a trek and a light climb or exploration rather than focusing on the vertical. With this approach you can get away without taking any climbing gear or just bringing enough for walking on glaciers. There's lots of new and second-hand climbing gear for sale in Namche and Kathmandu. Always available are cheap titanium ice screws, snow stakes, jumars, karabiners, slings, ice axes, crampons (step-in and strap-on) and used ropes (fixed and climbing, but exercise caution).

Don't neglect your crew's equipment

While you may have the latest and best equipment your crew certainly will not. Sirdars usually have reasonable gear although it is worth checking their climbing gear and sleeping bag. The sherpas and kitchen hands are less well-equipped and generally appreciate cast-offs, perhaps a Kathmandu fleece or a good piece of clothing as part of the tips. Porters have nothing and appreciate clean serviceable clothes of any sort and especially old running shoes or boots. See pp102-6 for notes on employing and looking after crew.

RECOMMENDED READING

Kathmandu has the world's best selection of books on Nepal and the surrounding mountain areas and prices are often below normal cover prices so it's also an attractive place to buy them. The Thamel area boasts many second-hand bookshops with hundreds of cheap paperback novels.

Guidebooks

For exploring the Kathmandu Valley and the rest of the road-accessible country there's a wide range, all available in Kathmandu. Apa's *Nepal Insight Guide* has beautiful coffee-table photos and an informative text but is, however, of limited and dated use as a practical guide. Apa also has a *Pocket Insight Guide* featuring self-guided tours which is perfect for a flying visit.

Lonely Planet's *Nepal* is comprehensive and good on practical information while Moon Publications' *Nepal Handbook* is a literate, sensitive and in-depth guide. The *Rough Guide to Nepal* offers stiff competition to both, with its comprehensiveness and enthusiastic chatty style. Footprint's *Nepal Handbook* is particularly strong on culture and history; all could be called bibles.

When it comes to trekking the choice thins. Both the Nepal handbooks and Rough Guide are good for deciding how to and where to go and Lonely Planet's *Trekking in the Nepal Himalaya* is thorough in many ways but lacks detailed trail info such as the times between places. Stephen Bezruchka's dated *Trekking in Nepal* (7th edition) has the trail times, interesting cultural and environmental discussions but no lodge information. *Trekking Peaks of Nepal* by Bill O'Connor is the standard but dated reference for climbing these limited-bureaucracy mountains.

Trailblazer publishes detailed regional guides to trekking in other parts of the Himalaya – *Trekking in the Annapurna Region, Trekking in Langtang, Helambu and Gosainkund* and *Trekking in Ladakh* (see pp303-4). A new Nepal climbing guide is in preparation and will be published in late 2003.

Mountaineering books

Hundreds of expedition accounts have been published but many are of interest only to avid climbers. The books that I particularly enjoyed are listed below.

Bill Tilman and Eric Shipton are names closely linked with much of the early exploration of the Himalaya and Karakoram. Even judged by modern standards the ground they covered and the peaks that they conquered is incredible. Their legacy is a series of books written in elegant prose with vivid and interesting descriptions that twinkle with penetrating insights, often curiously and hilariously funny. Their individual books have been reprinted in several volumes.

Eric Shipton's *The Six Mountain-Travel Books* (The Mountaineers, Seattle, 1985) includes two books about Everest: *Upon That Mountain* and *The Mount Everest Reconnaissance Expedition 1951*. HW Tilman's *The Seven Mountain-Travel Books* (The Mountaineers, Seattle, 1983) includes *Everest 1938* and *Nepal Himalaya*, which has been reprinted and is widely available in Kathmandu.

Everest by Walt Unsworth (Oxford Illustrated Press, 1989) is a climbing history capturing the hopes and fears of the attempts on Everest.

Everest: The Best Writing and Pictures from 70 years of Human Endeavour, edited by Peter Gillman (Little, Brown & Co, London 1993) features interesting historical snapshots of the climbing of Everest.

Cho Oyu by Favour of the Gods by Herbert Tichy covers the first ascent of Cho Oyu. With only three members this was not the usual grand expedition, and neither is the book written in the traditional heroic style.

Nothing Venture Nothing Win by Sir Edmund Hillary is an interesting autobiographical account of his adventures including the scaling of Everest. His *Schoolhouse in the Clouds* offers an insight into the development of the Khumbu and other Sherpa areas.

Sherpas: Reflections on Change in Himalayan Nepal by James F Fisher is an interesting and readable investigation into the changes in the Khumbu that tourism and schooling have brought, with perceptive feedback from local people.

Into Thin Air by Jon Krakauer is the compelling story of how so many climbers died (and some miraculously lived against the odds) on two commercial expeditions in 1996, but to get a sense of the other side of the story, read *The Climb* by Bourkreev.

MAP RECOMMENDATIONS

This guide specifically includes many maps, enough to cover a normal trek to the Khumbu from Jiri or Lukla. However, for identifying the many surrounding peaks and features, detailed topographic maps are invaluable and essential for exploration off the beaten track.

Once there was only one set of reliable detailed maps but now shopping in Kathmandu shows there is an almost bewildering range. Out of Nepal, however, finding maps can still be a mission. The three main series are:

The **Schneider 1:50,000 series** published by Freytag-Berndt und Artaria of Vienna covers the entire area in beautiful four-colour topographic maps. The Khumbu Himal is the most useful for all trekking, exploring and climbing from Namche to the north. Tamba Kosi covers Jiri to Junbesi (and the approaches to the mountains south of the Rolwaling but not the range itself), including from Dolakha. Shorong/Hinku includes the trekking routes from Junbesi and Lukla to Namche as well as north of Junbesi, the Hongu (the area surrounding Mera peak) and the eastern Arun trekking route from Lukla/Kharikhola to the Surkie La. Dudh Kosi covers Phaplu to Junbesi, and also from the Rumjatar and Lamidanda airports up the Dudh Kosi. Rolwaling Himal includes the area from the Tashi Labtsa to Simigoan and the Tamba Kosi, and is useful for exploring the Rolwaling range. Lapchi Kang covers from the Tamba Kosi to Barabise. These maps are available in Kathmandu for around $10-12.

The **National Geographic** series has maps of the Everest, Annapurna and Langtang regions. Despite their heritage they still have minor mistakes but nevertheless are great both for planning and once on the trail.

The yellow bordered magazine published a beautiful map of the area surrounding Everest but, unfortunately, it does not cover the Gokyo Valley, or even below Pangboche. Inserted in the 1988 centennial issue, it was the most accurate and detailed 1:50,000 map ever made. Use it for the Amphu Labtsa, Mingbo La, Sherpani Col and climbing around Chukhung. It's stocked by most bookshops in Kathmandu.

The **Himalayan Map House series** is produced in Nepal and readily available in Kathmandu and increasingly overseas. Confusingly they come under several names – Nepa Maps, Himalaya Kartographisches Institut to name but two – and in a bewildering variety of titles, but are basically all the same. Look carefully for the most detailed scale for the region you need.

Also readily available in Kathmandu are several cheap general maps covering either Jiri to Kala Pattar or Lukla to Kala Pattar. There is little to choose between them, and even 'Latest updated editions' are loaded with minor inconsistencies but they are adequate for trekking. The names and spelling used in this guidebook are more accurate than any map.

If trekking and travelling the country extensively, a map of Nepal that marks all the district headquarters and roads and rivers is invaluable, although none is particularly accurate.

❏ **Further information and useful websites**

For more information and links to websites see the updates section for this book at 🖳 www.trailblazer-guides.com.

Health precautions and inoculations

For this fourth edition Dr Jim Litch reviewed and partially revised this health section.

Nepal is a developing country with a marginal infrastructure and in rural areas like the Solu-Khumbu it is even more limited. One impact of this is on health, both of the local people and visiting trekkers. It is therefore important to attend to your health and fitness before you even arrive in Nepal. Pre-trip preparations are described in this chapter. Health information while trekking is presented separately in the Appendix (pp276-94).

The physical aspects of trekking

Trekking means walking almost every day for four to seven hours, often for three weeks or more. Many people begin only moderately fit but generally cope well and end the trek feeling amazingly healthy. A few find the reality of continuous walking difficult. If you lead a sedentary life plan an exercise programme well before you go. Brisk walks are a good start, building up to include walking up and down hills with the boots you plan to wear trekking, to introduce your body to the rigours of hill walking. Jogging and aerobics are reasonable substitutes. Muscles strengthen fairly quickly, although painfully if you overdo exercise.

It is important to realize that while trekking you can be a long way from help, and sometimes you will have to be your own doctor. However, the Khumbu region is better endowed with medical facilities than anywhere else in rural Nepal. There is an excellent hospital at Khunde (an hour above Namche) staffed by a doctor throughout the year. The Himalayan Rescue Association post at Pheriche is staffed by two Western short-term volunteer doctors and open for 7-8 weeks during the peak of the two main trekking seasons.

SPECIFIC AGE GROUPS

● **Older people** Many recently retired people have made it to the top of Kala Pattar (5600m/18,373ft) so age alone need not be a barrier. The older you are, the more important prior fitness preparation is. Older trekkers are also more likely to have chronic medical conditions that should be assessed by a doctor before committing to a trek.

● **Younger children** Caution should be exercised when taking children trekking. Although younger people seem to acclimatize as well as adults, they generally trek much slower. Very young children have difficulty in communicating exactly how they feel, which can lead to confusion regarding illness. Remember with small children, if in doubt: descend. Cautious doctors recommend a safe maximum altitude for pre-teenage children of 3000m/9843ft, though there is little evidence to support this recommendation. After all, a number of young children have made it to the top of Kala Pattar, and even 18-month-old babies have visited Everest Base Camp and stayed several days there. Trekking with children can be very rewarding and bring you closer to the locals. You share a common bond for there are few people without children in Nepal. Little legs are easily carried by a porter when tired, and Sherpanis are good babysitters. Remember, however, that's it's not only the altitude that's a potential problem, but also the fact that you'll be visiting a remote area.

● **Teenagers** There is no evidence to suggest that teenagers adapt more slowly to altitude than adults. However, they do appear to be more at risk. This is likely to be because of competitiveness and a will not to give in. School groups should allow an extra day or two over and above even the most conservative itineraries and be particularly watchful. An extended conservative itinerary allows for greater flexibility necessary to cope effectively with illness and other problems that typically arise.

MEDICAL CONDITIONS

Anyone with heart, lung and blood abnormalities or a continuing medical condition should have a check-up and get a medical opinion before setting off. A summary letter from your doctor describing your medical condition, treatment including any medications and contact information should be carried with your personal documents. It is important that you remember to pack a second set of any required medications, and that they are stored separately while flying and trekking so a back-up is available should a bag be delayed, misplaced or stolen.

● **Asthma** is no reason to avoid trekking. Except in polluted Kathmandu there are fewer irritants in the air at high altitude so most asthmatics actually feel better while trekking. Look after your medication by keeping it with you at all times – wear your inhaler on a chain around your neck or keep it in a pocket. There is still the normal risk of a serious attack so brief your companions on what to do.

● **Diabetes** If it is well-controlled, diabetes is no reason to avoid trekking. You cannot afford to lose the medication so keep it with you at all times. Advise your friends on the procedures in case there's an emergency. Your increased energy expenditure will change carbohydrate and insulin levels so it's very important to **monitor your glucose levels** frequently and carefully and to keep blood sugar levels well controlled. Insulin that has been frozen loses potency, so care must be taken to adjust your dosage in relation to blood sugar levels measured by your monitor.

● **High blood pressure (hypertension)** Blood pressure will fluctuate more and be higher than usual while on a trek, particularly as you ascend to high altitude. Therefore it is important that your blood pressure be well-controlled prior to your departure. You should seek the advice of a doctor who is aware of the history of your condition.

● **Previous heart attacks** The level of exertion required on a trek is more significant than the altitude factor for normal trekking elevations. If your condition at home is well-controlled during brisk exercise levels comparable to trekking, going on a trek may be a reasonable decision for you. However, do consider that you are just as likely to suffer a recurrence abroad as at home, and you will be entering a remote region of the world with very limited health facilities. Seek the advice of your doctor.

● **Epilepsy** There may be a small increased risk of a seizure at altitude, but this is not necessarily a reason to stop trekking if your condition is under good control at home. Your companions must be briefed on all the relevant procedures.

● **Pregnancy** To embark on a trek to moderate altitude while pregnant is a personal decision. Prior to the 35th week of the pregnancy, and assuming there have been no complications, there is no convincing evidence against trekking. After 35 weeks, however, airlines do not allow air travel on normal passenger flights. Furthermore, one must consider that you are entering a remote area, so should any problems or concerns develop, medical care may be a long way away.

INOCULATIONS

'For residents and travellers, one proper jab now can save dozens later....'
Dr Jim Litch, Khunde Hospital

The majority of Nepal's population has limited access to basic infrastructure, so the health situation is extremely poor. Disease and malnourishment are rife and even sickness easily cured by simple measures often leads to death without basic health education. Visitors arriving with immunizations, healthy bodies and access to clean water are much less at risk. A bout of diarrhoea, however, is almost inevitable, no matter how careful you are. There are no official immunization requirements to enter Nepal but the following should be considered. Access to up-to-date information is readily available on the internet, and general clinics now have the capability to advise you on travel vaccinations.

● **Hepatitis A** Usually passed on in contaminated water; immunization is considered a must by most doctors unless you have had hepatitis A before. The new vaccine is Havrix and a full course will give up to ten years protection. A cheaper but less effective alternative is a gamma globulin injection, given just before departure and repeated every 4-6 months while travelling. Although this is a blood-based product there is no chance of contracting HIV from this immunization.

● **Hepatitis B** This disease is avoidable since, like HIV, it's passed by unsafe sex or contaminated blood products. A vaccine is available.

● **Meningitis** Occasional cases of meningococcal meningitis occur in Nepal. The disease is often fatal but the vaccine is safe and should be considered.

● **Cholera** The World Health Organization no longer recommends this vaccination. It is only partially effective and early treatment with antibiotics is extremely effective. The risk of travellers acquiring cholera in Nepal is extremely low.

● **Typhoid** is common in Nepal. There are various vaccines and one should be obtained; the injectable vaccine has been found to be more effective than the oral one.

● **Tetanus-Diptheria** This vaccine is recommended if you have not had a booster in the last 10 years.

● **Polio** If you did not receive this immunization as a child a series of vaccinations is recommended. If you have not had a booster as an adult, one may be required. Check with your doctor.

● **Measles, mumps and rubella** If you did not have these diseases (or the vaccinations) as a child you may need a vaccination.

● **Japanese Encephalitis B** This disease is transmitted by mosquitoes and there have been sporadic outbreaks in the Terai (lowland Nepal) and India. Western doctors based in Kathmandu suggest the vaccination is recommended only for people visiting the Terai or middle hills for extended periods during the monsoon season.

● **Rabies** This deadly virus is transmitted by the bite of an infected animal, usually a monkey or dog. The risk of being bitten is small, but should the animal be infected with rabies you are likely to die unless you get treatment. Travellers have died of rabies in Nepal. A vaccination is available but even if you've had it you'll still need a follow-up course of two further injections for full protection after a bite. If you've not been vaccinated and are unlucky enough to be bitten, a single injection of a very expensive rabies immune globulin **and** a series of five injections of vaccine over a four-week period is required. These should be started as soon as possible, preferably within a week of the bite. The rabies immune globulin and vaccine are available only from the CIWEC clinic in Kathmandu. In any case, thoroughly washing the site immediately following the bite, with disinfectant or even soap and water, has been found in one study to be effective in preventing rabies.

● **Malaria** Carried only by the Anopheles mosquito, malaria exists in the Terai and middle hills in Nepal (ie below 2000m/6562ft), and across much of the rest of rural Asia. There's no risk in Kathmandu or while trekking (except possibly at lower altitudes during the monsoon). If visiting Chitwan or going rafting consider taking tablets to protect against malaria. The drug of choice varies for different areas of the world, and for each individual depending on health issues and other factors. If you have just visited a malarial area, for example India or Thailand, it's vital to continue taking your medication for the recommended length of time. The first line of protection, however, is to avoid being bitten. The Anopheles mosquito is active only between early evening and dawn so you should cover up well between these times and use mosquito repellent on any exposed skin.

MEDICAL INSURANCE

A combined travel/medical insurance policy is a sensible choice for any traveller and a requirement for most tours booked in your home country. Since trekking may require helicopter rescue which is not always covered by general travel schemes, some alpine clubs and trekking companies have specially-tailored policies, as do a variety of traveller evacuation insurance companies worldwide. Independent trekkers should register with their embassy which will be contacted if helicopter rescue is required. Forms are available at each embassy and the Himalayan Rescue Association in Kathmandu. Note that a rescue mission does not take place unless there is a guarantee of payment by a third party such as a trekking company or your insurance provider (see p294).

If you are behind on any of the immunizations listed above, they can be safely obtained at clinics in Kathmandu. For health precautions in Kathmandu see p97, and for a detailed discussion of staying healthy on the trek see p276.

PART 2: NEPAL

Facts about the country

GEOGRAPHICAL BACKGROUND

Perilously placed between the Asian superpowers of India and China, Nepal is a land-locked rectangle roughly 800km by 200km (500 by 120 miles). It straddles the hills and mountains between the enormous Ganges plain and the high Tibetan Plateau. In the south is a narrow strip of flat land known as the Terai. Rising abruptly from this are the small Siwalik hills and the Mahabharat range. Between are broad valleys, the Inner Terai, which were once infested with malaria. Thanks to DDT spraying in the 1950s that threat has been virtually eradicated and this rapidly developing area is now the fertile bread basket of Nepal. The wide band of steep middle hills shelter the older centres of population – Kathmandu, Pokhara and smaller towns like Jiri. To the north are the majestic Himalaya, including Kanchenjunga, Makalu, Lhotse, Everest, Cho Oyu, Manaslu, Annapurna and Dhaulagiri – eight of the ten highest peaks on the planet.

The Himalaya

As well as being the world's highest mountains, the Himalaya are also the youngest. What fascinated early explorers was the fact that they did not form the continental divide. This is, in fact, to be found further north on the Tibetan Plateau.

The Himalaya were formed by the collision of two continental plates, with the Indian plate being forced under the edge of the Asian plate, pushing up part of the Tibetan Plateau into jagged mountains. However, as fast as the Himalaya rose, the rivers to the north cut their southern paths faster, which accounts for the great depth of many of the valleys in the region.

The patterns of formation can be seen on many of the rock faces, especially the Lhotse-Nuptse wall (where distorted sedimentation lines are quite obvious) and from Kala Pattar (where continuation of the yellow band near the top of Everest can be seen in Changtse/Bei Peak, the mountain to the north in Tibet).

 Earth Mother
When geologists first came to Nepal Sherpas were horrified to see them breaking rocks and digging holes without first apologizing to the land. Sherpas perceive the earth as mother earth: the soil is her flesh, the rocks her bones, the water her blood. They depend on her for their lives and when they die their flesh becomes one with the earth.

CLIMATE

Nepal is at the same latitude as Florida and Cairo so the climate in the lowland areas is hot with temperate winters. The trekking areas are, however, well above sea level and consequently temperatures vary considerably.

The climate comprises distinct seasons but with an important additional feature: the monsoon. This moisture-laden wind amasses in the Bay of Bengal and sweeps up across India to spend its forces on the Himalayan mountain chain between late June and mid-September. It does not rain continuously or even every day. Rather there may be a couple of heavy downpours during the day that usually last less than an hour, keeping the summer heat down to bearable levels. Sometimes it rains only at night. After the monsoon retreats, the climate is mainly dry and sunny for the remainder of the year.

Autumn is renowned for clear skies and pleasant temperatures. By winter the high hills take on dry brown shades and the mountains are occasionally dusted with fresh snow. The colourful spring, March to May, is punctuated by the odd shower of life-giving rain but the heat builds until the monsoon relief arrives. The trekking seasons are detailed on pp39-42.

HISTORICAL OUTLINE

Facts and fables

Nepal's early history is clouded in folklore and legend. One story relates how the Kathmandu Valley, then a huge sacred lake, was emptied through a channel cut by the stroke of a god's sword. The Chobar Gorge, which drains the Valley, indeed fits the description and geologists maintain that the soil in the Valley gained its renowned fertility as a lake bed.

At the time of the Buddha, in the second half of the 6th century BC, the Kirati ruled the Kathmandu Valley. They were a Mongol race whose descendants include the Rai and Limbu now settled in the east of Nepal. Buddhism spread slowly and the arts and architecture developed under the 28 successive kings. Around AD300 the Indian Licchavi dynasty invaded Nepal, introducing the caste system and Hinduism, which intermingled with Buddhism, a process continuing to this day. Around AD900 power struggles enveloped the Valley and it was not until AD1200 that the Malla dynasty became established. The caste system was rigidly defined and (although there was occasional in-fighting that laid the towns of the Valley to waste) trade, cottage industries and the enduring Newar culture blossomed. The 1400s left the wealth of architecture, carving and sculpture that surrounds the Durbar Squares in Kathmandu, Patan and Bhaktapur. Known then as Kantipur, Lalitpur and Bhadgoan respectively, these three cities divided into separate flourishing but quarrelsome kingdoms in 1482 on the death of Yaksha Malla.

Unity, treachery and extravagance

In 1768 Prithvi Narayan Shah of Gorkha (a princely kingdom between Kathmandu and Pokhara) conquered the Kathmandu Valley and began the Shah dynasty that continues by direct blood line to this day. He started by consolidating the many individual kingdoms that now form the basis of Nepal. His successors, although 'honourably defeated' in the 1814 war with British India were able to resist colonial domination, a fact that the Nepalese are proud of to this day.

Overall control by the Shah dynasty was undermined by the rich nobles whose constant struggle for power often led to violence. However, in 1846 unequivocal control was seized by Jung Bahadur Rana who killed all the ministers and high officials in what became known as the Kot Massacre. He declared himself Maharajah, and the founder of a second line of Nepalese kings. To ensure continuity of the line his family married into the Shah dynasty and other high caste families. Jung Bahadur Rana alone fathered over 100 children. He and his heirs effectively ruled the country, although the king, kept in seclusion, was the highest authority. The Rana family amassed incredible wealth, visible in the numerous European-style palaces (inspired by Jung Bahadur's visit to Europe) which now house various government departments in Kathmandu. This feudal dynasty held Nepal in its grip for over a century until 1950, when the puppet king Tribhuvan outwitted them and escaped to India.

The post-war period
Following the end of the Second World War much of Asia was in turmoil. Newly independent India, and China, both seemed to have their hungry eyes on the tiny neighbour that divided them. Political discontent and fear were growing in Nepal.

Now known as the father of democracy in Nepal, BP Koirala managed to undermine the Ranas' control and India assisted in engineering the return to power of King Tribhuvan in 1951. In a checkmate move, ostensibly on a tiger hunting trip, the king drove into the Indian Embassy giving the Ranas the choice of giving up power or giving up the country to India. Nepal quickly invited foreign countries to open consulates in Kathmandu, keen to maintain its independence. Thus ended more than a century of isolation.

The panchayat system
In 1955 King Tribhuvan died and was succeeded by his son, Mahendra. The constitution was reformed and in 1957 the people of Nepal voted in the Nepal Congress Party with a decisive majority. However, bribery and corruption played a large part in the country's first elections and continued in the new government. This gave King Mahendra the excuse to step into power and at the end of 1959 he arrested the entire cabinet. He took direct control himself, later instituting the *panchayat* system. Under this system the locally-elected leaders of village councils nominated the candidates for higher posts, all ultimately under the king. In theory, this was quite a reasonable system and was endorsed by the new Eton-educated King Birendra when his father died in 1972.

Democracy established
Corruption and self-interest prevailed and popular discontent spread again, erupting in 1979 with rare violence in Kathmandu. The panchayat system was

put to the test by public referendum and survived, but only just. Its days were numbered and the government's inability to solve a serious trade dispute with India in 1990 and its continued persecution of the opposition caused public protest. Meetings dispersed with bullets became riots and the palace was surrounded by machine-gun toting soldiers.

Under mounting public and private pressure King Birendra lifted the ban on political parties in April 1990. He readily agreed to become a constitutional monarch and a temporary government was formed.

In 1991 the promised elections were held in first-past-the-post system. The Nepal Congress Party (symbol: the tree) won, putting the Communist Party (the sun) in the role of opposition party.

The Nepali Congress have a supposedly pro-business stance, and in this respect can be compared with the Conservative party in the UK and the US Republican parties; like those parties, many perceive the Nepali Congress to be arrogant and out-of touch with the man on the street, particularly as the party is made up largely of high-caste people. The communists are the opposite, mainly from the low castes, and despite a red name, are more socialists – the equivalent of the (Old) Labour party in the UK, or the US Democrats. The third main party, the RPP, are the remaining members of the reformed Pancha (Panchayat) leaders, who despite being well connected and articulate, have never become a force to be reckoned with.

Congress versus communists

Nepal has had democracy for more than a decade now – but has little to show for it. The Communist Party United Marxist-Leninist (CP-UML, or simply UML) in their brief mid-1990s' reign introduced a far reaching decentralization policy, now stalled, that allotted a yearly allowance to the smallest administrative unit, the Village Development Committee (VDC), so that they can help themselves. Then a faction split off, confusingly calling itself the Communist Party Marxist-Leninist (CPML or ML), and since then there has been a lack of any serious, united opposition to the Congress party. This should have been an ideal opportunity for development, since Congress had already been in power for more than five years, but factionalism between two geriatric leaders, KP Bhattarai and GP Koirala (brother of the late BP Koirala) has destroyed the general population's faith in Congress and possibly even in democracy itself.

While Bhattarai has bowed out gracefully a number of times when criticized, and suggested handing over to the younger generation, the 79-year-old Girija Prasad Koirala has almost destroyed the country – literally. He is a skilled power broker and has installed a loyal coterie of family members and friends, ruling by cunning and sheer force. His critics, however, maintain that

Opposite: Porters are the real heroes of the Himalaya, often carrying loads a Westerner would have difficulty just picking up – and yet still managing a smile.

The peoples of eastern Nepal

A cultural bridge between Tibet and India, Nepal is a colourful patchwork of ethnic groups, castes and clans. Although officially the only Hindu kingdom in the world, tides of history have also deposited Buddhists and even a few Muslims and Christians. Unlike in India the caste system is not institutionalized and is generally only observed by the beneficiaries, the higher castes.

Newars, with their rich urban-based culture and separate language, are the traditional inhabitants of the Kathmandu Valley, responsible for much of the famous architecture and art. Outside Kathmandu they are mainly merchants, particularly shop owners. **Brahmins** are the high Hindu priestly caste rather than an ethnic group. Traditionally they earn money from performing religious rituals and must avoid being polluted by people of a lower caste. Many now work in the government and in business. In the hills they are often little better off than the lower castes and intermarriage has taken place.

Sherpas (see p122), Kirat (Rai and Limbu, see p127) and Tamangs are the ethnic groups most commonly encountered on the Everest trek. **Rais** are found south of Solu and Pharak, particularly in the area between the Khumbu and the Arun. The villages of Bung and Gudel are exclusively Rai and you'll also meet them at Namche's Saturday market. Usually stocky and short, the Rai have Mongoloid features, a round face and a tanned but fairly light skin and they wear light-coloured clothing. The diet staples are rice, maize, wheat and millet, mixed with a variety of vegetables. The Rais are well represented in Gurkha battalions of the Indian and British armies.

Tamangs are people of the middle hills who very often act as porters. The women are distinctive with nose jewellery that hangs over their lips while the men wear a rough sleeveless woollen tunic when it is cold. They are Buddhists and, like the Sherpas, have their roots in Tibet.

his time in power has been spent trying to further consolidate power and politicize every aspect of bureaucracy sometimes at the expense of promoting development and progress.

By some counts there have been 15 governments in 11 years and it cannot be understated how pig-headed and greedy each has been. The Communists, who have grouped the six leftist parties, are not blameless either, often resorting to less than constitutional means to overthrow Koirala, preferring to try a 'people's power' approach instead.

The monarchy

King Birendra, after giving the people democracy, sat back and watched the outcome. It is often said that he, and his brother the current king Gyanendra, are the only people of power that have stayed within the letter, and more importantly, the spirit of the constitution. Paradoxically as the general population

Opposite: Statue at Tengboche Gompa (see p188). This famous monastery is spectacularly-situated below the Kangtaiga and Thamserku mountains.

THE MAOISTS

 I have been filled with deep sadness. At the time of going to print rural Nepal was in the midst of a Maoist insurgency, a period of great tragedy and uncertainty. It was still safe to trek in October 2002 but for a regular update and assessment visit Trailblazer's website: ⌨ www.trailblazer-guides.com and go to the updates page for this guidebook.

Background

On 13 February 1996 the underground Maoist party called a 'People's War' with the aim of overturning the semi-feudal, semi-colonial nature of the state. The plan was perhaps doomed to failure and was almost certain to be a disaster for the masses they were trying to assist; nevertheless by 2000 the Maoists had managed to amass a reasonable level of support in poor regions of the country, mainly because corruption and mis-management had reached monumental proportions, the blame for which can be laid largely at the doors of the opulent houses and shiny four-wheel drives of the ruling Nepali Congress party. For all the prime minister's talk of high principles, it is they who are emptying the honey pot and seem unable to extract their fingers. Many people have thus become so disenchanted that they now consider any alternative better – with unfortunate consequences for the country as a whole.

The Maoists began their campaign in the middle hills of West Nepal but by 2001 they controlled large swathes of countryside and had taken over at least seven out of 75 districts. Their tactics were to brutally attack isolated police posts in overwhelming numbers and kill or maim any corrupt officials, particularly those belonging to the Nepali Congress party. There were few major incidents before 1999 but in 2000 the situation rapidly worsened and in early 2001 the Maoists were winning every battle with the ill-equipped police. After using the pretext of talks to build forces the Maoists took on the army at the end of 2001. Although the Maoists won a few battles, in hindsight it seems like a mistake since the army is developing counter-insurgency tactics and has better equipment. As of late 2002 the Maoists continue to suffer serious defeats, but a wounded animal is at its most dangerous...

Today

It takes years to win a guerrilla war only with weapons, if it is even possible. Instead Nepal's politicians must rid themselves of the pervasive corruption and administrative stagnation, something they are talking about with a fervour that shows they are worried about their necks, but they have yet to act upon. The years 2001 and 2002 were wasted with damaging political in-fighting, and now the general feeling is that the politicians and officials are truly incapable of the changes needed. Increasingly it looks as if the king may have to take over the country.

This has been a horrible human tragedy for Nepal, sadder for the fact that it could so easily have been prevented, if only government corruption and indifference had not wasted so much development aid and public money. Some argue that foreign aid is in one sense to blame for helping to maintain a system that would otherwise have collapsed long ago. But the truth is that Nepal has been failing in its own complex way for a long time now, with intrigue, corruption, high caste pontificating rather than direct action and a deliberate attempt by the authorities to stymie the education of the masses all conspiring to bring about the current crisis. In theory the solution to the troubles would thus seem fairly simple – sound management, selfless energy and an immediate end to the rampant corruption are all that's required – but these things are a lot less easy to put into practice; until it does, the country is doomed to be far less prosperous than its people deserve.

have got more frustrated with politics and politicians, many ordinary people would welcome the return of the king to real power. Brokering behind the scenes with people like Koirala has not worked.

The royal massacre

In June 2001 the country was in political crisis but the massacre of King Birendra and much of the family overshadowed everything. On the night of June 1, Crown Prince Dipendra, slightly intoxicated on alcohol and dope, returned to a family dinner, heavily armed and in combat fatigues. He cold-bloodedly shot his father with an M16 rifle and then injured or killed eleven other family members. The queen and Nirajan, Dipendra's brother, initially escaped but he shot them outside. The rules of accession were clear: he knew he was now king. But then, distraught, he turned a pistol on himself through the head. Though he lived in a coma long enough to be declared king, he died a couple of days later.

Like a Shakespearean tale, Dipendra had everything he could want except the woman of his dreams. He was thirty-ish and frustrated: his choice of a wife was the bright and beautiful Devyani Rana, a woman of most royal blood but from a family that the queen's side of the family had been feuding with. The queen insisted that he marry one of two other women. In a drunken rage one night he threatened to kill anyone who got in his way. Later, in a tragedy of epic proportions for Nepal, he did just that.

In the period of disbelief and disillusionment, the king's brother Gyanendra was crowned king. In this country that thrives on intrigue there was a feeling of distrust but a year into his reign this has settled and as many people expected, he has become an able ruler. The major blot was his son, the unruly prince Paras who had an unsavoury reputation. He, however, has since cleaned up and recently been named the crown prince.

ECONOMY

Nepal's rural backwardness may be attractive to tourists but the mediaeval way of life is not easy for most Nepalese. In the past tenant farmers, the majority of the population, paid crippling taxes to landlords in a vicious semi-feudal system. The 1964 reforms sought to redress this by land redistribution and reducing rental to a (still unbearable) 50% of the crop but they were only partly successful.

In 2000 the bonded labour system was abolished but despite assistance being readily available the freed *Kamaiya* have struggled against Government indifference to get their government-promised land. Even now 90% of Nepal's population lives off the land with the majority existing at subsistence level. It's a simple, hard life with virtually no money, with the average annual per capita income a mere US$150.

This legacy means the prospects for the farmers' children are indescribably bleak. Nepal's astronomical birth rate and a lack of new arable land are the main problems. The ever-expanding population has been partly absorbed by the Inner

Terai but the amount of arable land available per person continues to drop. Crop yields have increased but cannot keep pace with demand so Nepal has become a net food importer. There are dire predictions about the decline of land fertility and the destruction of the forests; already there are food and firewood shortages. Without development miracles this situation can only get worse.

Nepal is barely industrialized. Demand for jobs far outstrips supply resulting in exploitative wages and appalling working conditions. With no manufacturing base all machinery and construction materials must be imported which means paying hard currency or Indian rupees, and earning these is difficult. Of the few exports, the majority go to India since reliable and cheap shipping is problematic for greater distances. Main sources of hard currency include Nepalese working overseas – particularly the Gurkha soldiers – carpets and pashmina (in a boom-bust cycle) and tourism (450,000 people a year). Foreign aid programmes are, however, big business in Nepal and a third of government funding comes from this source.

Critics of the government point to powerful vested interests as a reason for why Nepal is not growing at a faster rate. Everybody knows that far-reaching change is the only way forward, but nobody in the power elite can or is willing to introduce it – the fuel for the Maoist insurgency.

DEVELOPMENT

There is no doubt that considerable development is needed in Nepal, if only to avert tragedy. The root of the problem is the spiralling population growth. Nature's harsh natural balance was upset by the introduction of a few simple life-saving measures such as oral rehydration salts and basic hygiene principles. The five million people that lived in Nepal in 1950 have multiplied to 22.6 million, and this population is expected to double in the next 30 years, with possibly catastrophic results.

It's difficult to get the message of birth control across to Nepal's peasant farmers when to them more hands are an asset and extra children an insurance against others that may die. Obviously education and health care are a good start. If you are secure in the knowledge that your children will live (their health protected by vaccines and clean water) and believe that their quality of life may be better (with education) you will be more interested in trying to limit the size of your family. Electricity and roads provide opportunities for diversification from agriculture and a move to a more cash-orientated society, where the benefits of birth control become more obvious.

Such massive changes don't happen overnight, certainly not in Nepal, despite vast quantities of (mostly squandered and plundered) foreign aid.

RELIGION

Nepal describes itself as a Hindu Constitutional Monarchy. Official statistics state that 89.5% of the population is Hindu, 5.3% Buddhist, 2.7% Muslim, 2.4% shamanist and animist, 0.1% Jain and 0.04% Christian. Since being Hindu and

---

❏ **Buddhism – the Four Noble Truths**
1. Life is suffering.
2. The cause of suffering is thirst or desire.
3. Ending desire ends suffering.
4. And this means taking the Noble Eightfold Path: right view, right thought,
   right speech, right action, right livelihood, right effort, right mindfulness
   and right concentration.

Nepali-speaking can confer greater employment opportunities and higher social standing, it's likely that there are more Buddhists and fewer Hindus than these figures suggest.

The long tradition of religious toleration has led to a blurring of distinctions, especially between Hinduism and Buddhism. You'll see Buddhist prayer-flags fluttering over a Hindu temple and statues of Hindu gods in Buddhist *gompas* (monasteries). In fact, many Hindu deities have their Buddhist counterparts.

Practical information for the visitor

VISA AND TREKKING REGULATIONS

Visas
All visitors except Indians require a visa for Nepal, easily obtained at the airport or border on arrival (one passport-sized photo required, although if you don't have one you may be able to persuade them to let you through, perhaps with a small financial 'token' by way of reward) or at Nepalese embassies abroad, sometimes the more expensive option.

At the airport a single entry visa valid for 60 days costs US$30. At the airport this is payable in cash in any major convertible currency but for the land borders it is safer to stick to US dollars cash. A 60-day double-entry visa costs US$55 and a multiple-entry visa US$90; these are valid for 60 days from the date of entry into Nepal, whether you actually stay in Nepal or not. Check your visa and change carefully before leaving the counter: if there is a mistake you can bet it is in the official's favour. Visas are free for children under ten years old. All visas can be extended and converted from single entry to double entry (US$25 equivalent) or multiple entry (US$60 equivalent) in Kathmandu and Pokhara.

If you have previously been in Nepal during the calendar year and don't have a double- or multiple-entry visa then you will have to pay the same as if you were buying an extension, ie US$50 for 30 days ($75 if you want double entry and $110 for multiple entry within the same 30 days) but if you have already been in the country for more than 90 days in the calendar year (ie the new visa takes you past 120 days) your passport might be taken from you and you will have to go to the Department of Immigration the next working day to pick it up. Normally they want to see a confirmed air ticket out of the country.

Throughout 2001-02 various newspaper articles announced that new classes of visa would become available but there has been silent inactivity within the department and nothing had happened at the time of printing.

Transit visa The 48-hour transit visa won't get you far in the hills. It is available only for transit in and out of Kathmandu's airport with a confirmed ticket and currently costs US$5. This charge was temporarily dropped in 2002 and may be restored in 2003.

Other visa categories For information on diplomatic, official, study, pilgrims, non-tourist and business visas talk with Immigration or see their website and take a look at the updates section of our website.

Restricted area trekking permits

Nepal used to have an odd trekking permit system but this was scrapped for the main trekking regions, including the Everest region, in July 1999. Additionally, the restrictions on Rolwaling have been lifted: no trekking permit is now required, so in theory the only area that *is* restricted is north of Thame to the Nangpa La. The permit fees and procedures were not decided at the time of writing.

Trekking peak permits are covered on p262.

Visa extensions

Applications are accepted at the Department of Immigration, located around the side of Bhrikuti Mandap, the tourist service centre building that houses the Nepal Tourism Board (at the back is the Ministry of Tourism and the less than helpful tourist police). It is a taxi ride (approximately $1) from Thamel. Bhrikuti Mandap has a modern traditional look and is a block south of the old bus station near the clock tower. Touts promise special service; unless you want your passport dropped off at your hotel, ignore them and instead deal directly with the officials inside. The office is open for applications Monday to Friday 9am to 3pm in summer, and 9am to 2pm in winter, and is closed Saturdays, Sundays and the main public holidays. If you apply in the morning you can collect your extension in the afternoon of the same day – before 5pm in summer and 4pm in winter – although there is no rule that says you have to pick up your passport the same day.

Visa extensions cost US$50 per 30 days (paid in equivalent Nepalese rupees; they don't take dollars), for up to a maximum of 150 days in one calendar year. If your visa expires you must pay the extension fee plus a fine: the equivalent of US$2 per day up to 30 days expiration and after that $3 for days 31-90. If you are late because the Department of Immigration is closed, eg weekends and public holidays, there is no fine.

Leaving the country

You are given one day's grace, ie allowed to leave the day after your visa expires.

If your visa has expired by less than a week the fine (US$2 per day) and visa extension (US$50) can be handled at the airport, otherwise sort it out at Immigration beforehand. For those heading to India excess Nepalese rupees are easily converted into Indian rupees, but do this in Kathmandu or at the land border. In Delhi and other major centres it is almost impossible to change Nepali rupees.

GETTING TO NEPAL

By air

The best airlines for Kathmandu are Thai, Qatar and Gulf. Other carriers include Bangladesh's Biman, Indian Airlines, Pakistan International Airlines, China South-West, Aeroflot and Royal Nepal. Apart from Thai and Indian Airlines, which operate daily flights, most airlines have two or three flights a week.

● **From the West** For the cheapest flights check the travel advertising section of the major papers and on the internet. From the UK the cheapest return ticket is on Bangladesh Biman at around £400.

● **From India** On Indian Airlines there are daily flights between Kathmandu and Delhi (US$142 with 25% discount if you are under 30) and Varanasi (US$71 with a similar discount). There are also less frequent flights between Kathmandu and Calcutta (Kolkotta, US$96) and between Biratnagar and Calcutta and Patna on private airlines.

● **From Thailand** Since the land border with Burma is closed the only way is to fly. There are direct flights or the cheapest combination is to fly from Bangkok to Calcutta, then take surface transport.

● **From Tibet** The surface route is the more interesting but you can fly between Kathmandu and Lhasa for a monopolistically priced US$253. See p34.

See p83 for information on arrival at Kathmandu airport.

Overland from India

From Delhi there are direct buses to Kathmandu, but it is a tough journey taking 36-60 hours. An alternative is to take a train to Gorakhpur and then catch a local bus (don't believe touts who say there is a tourist bus) to the border crossing of Sunauli/Belahiya. From Varanasi you can take a train or bus to Gorakhpur, from where it is approximately three hours to Sunauli.

Immigration is staffed from dawn to dusk although the border does not physically close at night. If you arrive late simply walk across and stay at the better hotels on the Nepalese side, then visit immigration the next morning. Without a visa and entry stamps you'll encounter a big problem in Kathmandu or when leaving. Buses to Kathmandu (US$2, 11 to 14 hours) leave from 5am to 9am for the day service and from 4pm to about 8pm for the night buses. For much of the way the route follows the Trisuli River and the scenery is an impressive introduction to the middle hills of Nepal.

From Calcutta the usual route is via Patna to the border at Birganj/Raxaul and then the 15-hour bus journey to Kathmandu. The border crossing from Darjeeling is called Kakarbhitta (spelt various ways) and it is at least 18 hours to Kathmandu.

LOCAL TRANSPORT

● **Air** Nepal has an extensive network of domestic flights to make up for the lack of roads. With many competing airlines, services, although basic, are surprisingly convenient. Since there are no radars at hill strips bad weather can occasionally postpone flights, sometimes for several days. Tickets can be bought direct from the airlines but travel agents and trekking companies get them for the same price too. Avoid the grossly mismanaged national airline, Royal Nepal, if possible – though for the more unusual sectors they are often the only choice. Fares must be paid in hard currency, cash or travellers' cheques, not rupees. For more details see p106. Domestic tickets are not readily available over the internet.

Once the domestic fleet was almost exclusively sturdy Twin Otters but with the proliferation of airlines, demand and improved airstrips a variety of turbo-prop planes are now flown. There are still no regional runways long enough to take 737 jets, but with the upgrades and new international airports planned, they will become a reality too.

Increasingly smaller 4-9 passenger helicopters are used for sightseeing, charter and rescue. For a while the large Russian MI-17 helicopter workhorses were used for passenger service, but now they are only permitted to carry cargo and up to seven cargo handlers; this is a shame since they provided a better and more extensive service than the Twin Otters could, especially during the winter snows.

● **Long-distance bus services** are run using sturdy Indian buses that cope well with the rough roads but night coaches are for masochists and perhaps better avoided because of the now numerous security checks. The day buses are often filled to bursting point and feature a variety of seating, mostly unsuitable for long legs. The spectacular scenery can, however, make up for the lack of comfort. It's important to realize that, when you buy a ticket, you are paying to get from A to B, regardless of whether you actually have a seat or not.

For journeys to Pokhara and Chitwan tourist coaches, with seated passengers only and safe luggage storage on the roof, are the best especially as they depart from near Thamel, saving a taxi journey. See a travel agent or hotel reception for tickets.

● **Taxis** are plentiful and cheap, though ensure they use the meter; for ordinary taxis, just hop in, tell them where you want to go (Bhrikuti Mandap *jannhos*, for example) then, as they begin, check that they have turned on the meter. There is a special night rate, also on the meter.

● **Hiring a vehicle** is best organized directly with a driver for a tourist car, or through a travel agent for mini-buses and four-wheel drives.

● **Local buses** In Kathmandu a small revolution is happening: the smoke-belching Vikram tempos have been banned, replaced by cooking-gas powered Suzuki micro-buses, tough Toyota Hiaces and electric 'SAFA' tempos (which means 'clean' in Nepali). There are, however, still some of the large Mercedes vans, occasionally impossibly crowded.

● **Tempos** are small three-wheeled vehicles. The majority are 'SAFA' that run on batteries, however the cost of electricity means that the newer petrol-powered ones will become more common.

● **Auto rickshaws** These are the black-and-yellow three-wheelers that spit noxious fumes because although they can pass emission tests, the owners dilute the petrol with oil so that they are more economical. They never use the meters.

● **Cycle-rickshaws** are environmentally sound and are found in all major towns and bargaining is required before you depart.

● **Bicycles** used to be a good way to get around Kathmandu but the pollution and lack of road rules is so bad that they are hard to recommend. Once out of the city they are a great way to explore the Valley. Standard bikes and mountain bikes are easily hired in the Thamel and Freak Street areas.

In theory you should have an international licence to **hire a motorbike** but mostly you can get away without one – all you need to do is leave some security with the owners. Costs start from US$10 a day; look around Thamel, where there are several places.

LANGUAGE

Nepali, a Sanskrit-based language similar to India's Hindi, is the country's official language. For approximately half the population Nepali is not the mother-tongue; ethnic languages such as Sherpa and Newari being widely used in local areas.

Nepali is the medium for schools but English is also taught and you'll meet a surprising number of children who know at least a few English words. In the tourism industry English is the main language, although it is by no means fluently spoken. In the main trekking areas it's quite possible to get by speaking only English.

It is handy to learn a few phrases if trekking without a guide (see Appendix p296). Learning more is rewarding and will provide many amusing reactions. Simple spoken Nepali is not difficult and most Kathmandu bookshops sell small phrasebooks.

ELECTRICITY

The electricity grid covers only the major towns and cities and power cuts are frequent, especially in springtime and during rain. The supply is 220V and 50Hz using round two-pin and three-pin sockets in two sizes. Rural Nepal has little electricity, apart from a few very small-scale private or foreign aid hydro schemes.

While trekking it is impossible to recharge batteries for camcorders or digital cameras other than with a solar panel because even if a village has electricity, the power is rationed to a few bulbs per house and turned on only for the evening. The exception is Namche-Khumjung-Khunde where there is plenty of power and, just as importantly, power points.

TIME

Nepal is 5 hours and 45 minutes ahead of Greenwich Mean Time (GMT), and 15 minutes ahead of India (as a show of independence). There is no daylight saving scheme.

MONEY

The Nepalese rupee (Rs or NC) comes in banknote denominations of 1, 2, 5, 10, 20, 25, 50, 100, 250 (rare), 500 and 1000 rupees, each featuring an animal. There's a surprising variety of coins worth from 1 to 10 rupees, and plans for bigger denomination coins; so far, all of these coins are confusing to foreigners because the value is written only in Nepali.

❏ **Rates of exchange**
The Nepali Rupee is tied to the Indian rupee and tracks it at exactly 1.6 times the value; it therefore also slowly but constantly loses value.

These were the rates as of Oct 2002; current rates are available on 🖳 www.nepalnews.com:

US$1	Rs78
Euro 1	Rs76
UK£1	Rs122
A$1	Rs42.42
Indian Rs1	Rs1.60

Rates of exchange vary depending on whether the exchange is an official government transaction or a transaction being made by a tourist in a commercial bank or moneychanger; there's also a third, black market, rate. However, the spread of rates is not great.

Note that Indian Rs500 notes are illegal in Nepal and will be confiscated if found. This is because Pakistan was forging them and distributing through Nepal.

Changing money
This is supposed be to done at your hotel or at a bank or moneychanger, not on the (now small) black market. The star-class hotels have banking facilities at their reception counters. Ensure you are given a receipt. Some small change is useful, in particular Rs100 bills. For larger transactions it is worth shopping around.

Tipping
Once virtually unknown in Nepal, this custom is spreading through the tourism services. Tipping hotel and restaurant staff is not necessary but if the service was good, a 5% tip or the small change will be appreciated. Tipping trekking crews is now normal, for guidelines see p105.

POST AND TELECOMMUNICATIONS

The Nepalese postal system is slow and unreliable. Letters to or from Europe, USA and Australasia usually take around two weeks but can take up to six weeks while surface mail takes three to six months and occasionally simply never arrives.

The **poste restante** service in the GPO consists of large boxes for each letter of the alphabet, each one containing hundreds of letters that anybody can look through, although it's rare for ordinary letters to go missing. Sending to star-class hotels and communication centres are an alternative.

Kathmandu is blessed with a reasonable telephone system but so far international calls are unrealistically priced, although cheaper internet calling systems and fax systems are changing this. The international dialling code for Nepal is +977 followed by 1 for Kathmandu.

Internet and email

Nepal is up with technology and there are hundreds of internet cafés in Kathmandu and some in other centres; it is hard to imagine that in 1997 the internet was just arriving. Costs are roughly US$0.33 an hour. Places in Thamel often have scanners and colour printers too. Unlike Pakistan, for example, there is virtually no pornography visible, at least in the Thamel cafés popular with tourists.

TV, RADIO, NEWSPAPERS AND MAGAZINES

Television

Nepal Television (NTV) has news in English at 9.15pm followed by the BBC TV World Service. International satellite/cable TV with a range of the popular channels is available in most hotels and bars.

Radio

Radio Nepal's short-wave transmissions reach the whole country. News in English is broadcast at 2pm and 8pm, followed by the general weather forecast. Note that they have a hopeless record in predicting huge snow storms. Try Voice of America's hard to find Lhasa forecast or the BBC. Only in 1997 were commercial radio stations allowed on the airwaves. The music is more modern but they are only just beginning to reach out of the Kathmandu Valley.

Newspapers, magazines and books

There is a growing crop of **local** English-language dailies, the *Kathmandu Post*, the *Rising Nepal* and the rather better *Himalayan Times*, all cost less than Rs5 and mostly are available at your favourite breakfast spot. The government-controlled *Rising Nepal* is still obsessed with the comings and goings at the royal palace and naming politicians, so international news is usually confined to a few columns. The paper gives a rosy and vague outline of what the government is currently up to and also includes odd titbits such as the state of the New Zealand economy. The *Nepali Times*, a colour weekly that comes out Friday is absolutely the best paper overall. The *Nepali Times*, *Rising Nepal* and the *Kathmandu Post* are available online too.

International papers and magazines, such as the *International Herald Tribune*, *USA Today*, and the *Asian Wall Street Journal* are sold everywhere as are magazines including *Time*, *Newsweek*, *Fortune*, *The Economist*, *Stern* and *Der Spiegel*. Once it was all news, but now you don't have to miss much at all, fashion magazines such *Cosmopolitan* and *GQ*, car and computer magazines are also on the stands. There's a plethora of Nepali magazines, many advertising tourist orientated services and interests. One that is worth looking out for, although its views are rather negative, is *Himal*, a quarterly Himalayan development and environmental discussion magazine. The British Council has a reading room with a variety of magazines and papers.

Kathmandu has some of the best **bookshops** on the subcontinent, including some second-hand shops where you can trade in your novel for another.

HOLIDAYS AND FESTIVALS

Government office hours are 10am to 5pm (4pm in winter). On Saturday and Sunday, in Kathmandu only, government offices (including Immigration) and embassies are closed. Banks are mostly open on Sundays, a few on Saturday morning, and of course the cash machines don't close, although they have a habit of running out of money during festivals. Souvenir shopping and sight-seeing are possible every day although all museums are closed on Tuesday.

Nepal is a land of colourful festivals and these are celebrated with fervour, especially by the less well-off masses. Dates are generally determined by the lunar calendar so fall on a different day each year. The following will be of particular interest to visitors:

● **Dasain** (Durga Puja) is a ten-day October festival, the most important of the Hindu year, and commemorates the victory of good Lord Rama over Ravana, the demon king of Lanka. Rama, an incarnation of Vishnu, is venerated by Hindus as the paragon of all virtues, so the victory symbolizes the ultimate triumph of good over evil. This is a time of family reunion and consequently results in total chaos as everybody heads home. On days eight and nine there's a mass slaughter of buffaloes, goats and chickens. Vehicles are blessed by having their wheels doused in blood. Government offices are closed for at least three days, and rural offices generally don't function until after Tihar.

● **Tihar** (Deepavali/Diwali) is the five-day Festival of Light that takes place in late October or early November. Amongst the symbolism is an acknowledgement of the value of brothers and sisters, dogs and cows. Children go from house to house singing and dancing and are given a little food or money. At the height of the festival on the third day people light their homes with candles to welcome Laxmi, the goddess of wealth.

Sherpa festivals

● **Mani Rimdu** is the popular three-day Sherpa festival held at Tengboche in November and at Thame in May. Monks perform ceremonies and dances, both serious and fun. It is a major social occasion.

● **Losar** Tibetan New Year is celebrated during mid-February. It is a time to receive new clothes (making them is a winter job) and put up new prayer flags.

● **Orsho** is a rite to protect the crops and takes place at the beginning of April.

● **Ch-rim**, to rid the land of evil spirits, occurs twice a year. The rite is enacted first after potato planting, then again after the harvest when the livestock returns from the summer pastures.

● **Dumji** is an important five-day festival that takes place during the monsoon, over the anniversary of the Khumbu's patron saint, Lama Sange Dorje. The gods are requested to subdue the evil spirits of the village. A group of eight families (different each year) lays on the feast. There are separate festivals in Namche, Thame and Khumjung.

● **Buddha's birthday** falls in May and the **Dalai Lama's birthday**, particularly celebrated by Tibetan refugees, is on 6 July.

FOOD

Despite the ethnic mosaic the local cuisine is not particularly inspiring (unless you stay with well-off Nepalese friends). Standard Nepalese fare, *dal bhaat*, consists of rice, lentils and a few vegetables. It can become monotonous but is certainly nutritious, cheap and filling – your plate is topped up until you've had enough. In the Khumbu, potatoes form a major part of the diet of the Sherpas.

In response to travellers' requests the restaurants of Kathmandu (and along some trekking routes) experimented with foreign dishes with surprising success. There's now an incredible variety of non-Nepalese cuisines at these places. Authenticity is not always a strong point but you can eat passably Mexican, Italian or Thai food. There are excellent restaurants in Kathmandu specializing in tandoori and other styles of Indian food. 'Buff' (buffalo) steaks are a feature on many menus, the killing of cows for beef being outlawed in this Hindu kingdom, although some restaurants import it from, of all places, India. The range of Tibetan food includes *momos* (meat or vegetables encased in dough and steamed or fried), and meat soup known as *thupka*.

The cakes and pies can be a real delight. These vary from restaurant to restaurant but many are wholesome and just as Mum would make them. The vast choice includes apple pie, apple strudel, cheesecakes, chocolate cakes, lemon meringue pies, cinnamon rolls and banana cream pie.

DRINK

All water should be treated (see p280) before it is safe to drink. Plastic bottles of mineral water are available but from an environmental point of view drinks such as Coke are better since the glass bottles they come in are returnable.

Several beers are brewed here, some under licence from foreign companies: Tuborg, San Miguel, Carlsberg and Guinness. Chang is locally brewed 'beer' produced by villagers.

THINGS TO BUY

In Kathmandu and at a few of the larger centres along trekking routes, shops selling souvenirs and handicrafts abound. They offer Newari art, Tibetan *thangkas* (intricate paintings of religious symbols and figures, done on cloth), jewellery, bronze Buddhas and Hindu deities. Boys wander around the streets of Thamel pestering you to buy khukri knives, chess sets and Tiger Balm. Carpets come in a great variety, many with modern designs in vegetable-dyed pastel shades. Luxuriously thick, they are made mainly in Kathmandu from a blend of New Zealand and Tibetan wool. When buying jewellery finding quality silver is not easy and you should beware of glass 'rubies' and dyed concrete-dust or glass 'turquoise'.

Hand-knitted jerseys/sweaters and clothing are made in distinctive styles of the regional cultures and are popular with travellers. In Kathmandu, embroidered T-shirts are a speciality. There's a wide range of motifs to choose from and they look good on fleece jackets too.

Bargaining

Throughout Asia, bargaining is a part of life, although trekking exposes you to few situations that require bargaining. Most lodges have a menu with fixed prices that really are fixed – where you eat or stay is your choice. Buying at markets or from a farmer or hiring a porter may require some negotiation. As a foreigner (incredibly wealthy in comparison to most rural Nepalese) you start at a disadvantage and this will be utilized. Bargaining need not be aggressive – it's better to treat it as a game with smiles and jokes. Basically you are trying to agree a price that leaves you both happy. After a price has been agreed it must be honoured. Once the transaction is complete that is the end of the matter, all is forgiven and forgotten. Harbouring resentment comes across as a small-minded Western attitude.

SECURITY

Kathmandu is safer than most Western cities. Violent crime is virtually unknown, and it is safe to take taxis, cycle and walk the streets and alleys at night, although women may be safer in a group. Despite the relaxed atmosphere in hotels, staff are honest, rooms have barred windows and managers are security-conscious, keeping an eye on who goes in or out. In the cheaper hotels other travellers are a greater risk, if anything. The better hotels have security boxes for valuables and all will store luggage safely while you trek.

Around town, adept pickpockets work crowded local buses. The usual ploy is to distract you with conversation or by pretending to be interested in your watch, or simply to rush and jostle as you board a long distance bus.

> **Tourist police?**
> Set up to help tourists, this one-roomed office is where you report incidents of theft so that you can get a police report for insurance purposes. The trouble is often they doubt you and will not provide complete reports. That may sound ridiculous, but there is little you can do other than insist on seeing a superior or insist they do their job properly. They have zero interest in actually solving crime. They are located in Bhrikuti Mandap, the same building as Immigration, but right around the back.

Pickpockets have a field day at busy festivals, as the queues of foreigners outside the American Express office the following day testify. Keep your travellers' cheques and money in a pouch or moneybelt and never let your camera and other valuables out of your sight.

In **Thamel** the nightlife has blossomed and so has the late night trouble. After 11pm or so single women walking home have (rarely) been hassled, usually by Nepali guys that have followed them out of a club. Inside occasional fights erupt, often over young foreign girls who are acting naïvely, and pickpockets sometimes work the clubs so either leave valuables at the hotel or be extremely careful. The Thamel bars which close around 11pm or so are generally trouble-free; it is the nightclubs – Liquid, Underground, Jump and Scores – where things can happen.

There is a gang of Tibetan women and a separate group of black leather jacketed Tibetan men who are the smoothest thieves you can imagine. They only occasionally enter Thamel restaurants and bars, but with serious consequences to wallets, bags and moneybelts.

The **trekking regions** were once crime-free but as the population is exposed to the wider ways of the world, occasional cases of theft now occur. Violent attacks are almost unheard of in the Solu-Khumbu although the tents of trekking groups are very occasionally slit during the night and valuables disappear. Trekking crews are trustworthy, although if you lend gear you might have to ask to get it back. In the crowded lodges during high season occasionally the odd thing goes missing, generally a camera or valuable trekking equipment, but in a quiet lodge things are absolutely safe.

You are incredibly wealthy by most rural standards so don't flaunt your gear or openly display large quantities of money and camera equipment. You should show that you value and care for all your belongings.

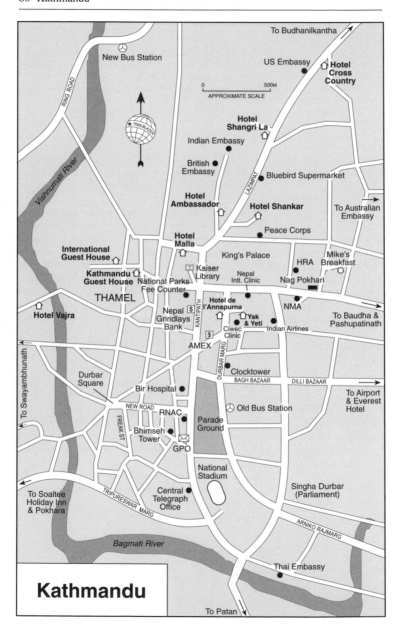

To Budhanilkantha

New Bus Station

US Embassy

Hotel Cross Country

RING ROAD

0   500M
APPROXIMATE SCALE

★ TRAILBLAZER

Hotel Shangri La

Indian Embassy

Vishnumati River

British Embassy

LAZIMPAT

Bluebird Supermarket

Hotel Ambassador

Hotel Shankar

To Australian Embassy

Peace Corps

Hotel Malla

International Guest House

King's Palace

HRA

Mike's Breakfast

Kaiser Library

Nepal Intl. Clinic

Nag Pokhari

Kathmandu Guest House

National Parks Fee Counter

THAMEL

Hotel de l'Annapurna

NMA

Hotel Vajra

Nepal Grindlays Bank

KANTIPATH

$

Yak & Yeti

Ciwec Clinic

Indian Airlines

To Baudha & Pashupatinath

$

AMEX

DURBAR MARG

Clocktower

To Swayambhunath

Durbar Square

Bir Hospital

BAGH BAZAAR

DILLI BAZAAR

NEW ROAD

RNAC

Old Bus Station

To Airport & Everest Hotel

FREAK ST

Bhimseh Tower

Parade Ground

GPO

National Stadium

TRIPURESWAR MARG

Central Telegraph Office

Singha Durbar (Parliament)

To Soaltee Holiday Inn & Pokhara

ARNIKO RAJMARG

Bagmati River

Thai Embassy

Kathmandu

To Patan

PART 3: KATHMANDU

The city

Nepal's capital city (population 600,000) is a fascinating mélange of mediaeval and modern that combines astounding beauty with appalling squalor and poverty.

Time has stood still in parts of Kathmandu. In the narrow alleys, around the numerous temples and shrines and along the banks of the Bagmati River people go about their daily lives in much the same way as their ancestors did hundreds of years ago. Yet the contrasts between old and new become ever more bizarre. A porter struggles under the weight of two colour-television sets, carrying them in the traditional fashion supported only by a *namlo*, the strap around his fore-head. A young Tibetan monk in ochre robes passes on his way to the great stupa at Baudha, his shaven head in the grip of the head-phones of his walkman.

For first-time Asian visitors, Kathmandu is a visual feast but for long term travellers who've journeyed up from India it's also a feast of a more basic nature. The city has some of the best travellers restaurants on the subcontinent dishing up everything from pepper steaks to enchiladas, chocolate cake to apfel-strudel. Accommodation, too, is excellent and can be better value than in India.

It's well worth setting aside at least a few days to see something of the city.

HISTORY

Origins
The name Kathmandu is believed to be a corruption of Kasthamandap ('square house of wood'), the 1000-year-old dharamsala (rest-house) that still stands in Durbar Square.

The first identifiable civilization in the Kathmandu Valley was that of the Kirats, who occupied a number of sites in the region in the second half of the first millennium BC. They were succeeded by the Lichhavi in the ninth century AD and the Malla in the 13th century. The settlements were centred around religious sites known as piths or power places, usually on the tops of hills.

Early urban planning
Kathmandu was a town of almost 2000 houses by the beginning of the Malla period (13th century), centred on Pashupatinath. Like the other two large towns in the Valley, Patan and Bhaktapur, it was an independent kingdom. Religion controlled not only the lives of the people but also the layout of these towns. Wandering through the chaotic maze of streets and temples in modern Kathmandu, it's difficult to believe that there has ever been any town planning here; but, in fact, centuries ago Hindu philosophy determined the design of whole towns based on the Vastupurusa Mandala, a complex layout in the shape

of a square. This was composed of many smaller squares assigned to different deities and their temples. The main temple and palace, the centres of spiritual and temporal power, were symbolically placed at the very centre. Agricultural land surrounded each town.

Newar architectural heritage

The dominant culture in the Kathmandu Valley, until the unification of Nepal by the king of Gorkha in 1768, was that of the Newars. They are best known for their spectacular architectural legacy – the temples and palaces that surround the Durbar Squares in Kathmandu, Patan and Bhaktapur. They built with brick, wood and tiles and are said to have invented the pagoda. Until the introduction of reinforced concrete in Nepal just 50 years ago, Kathmandu was truly the Florence of the East. Visiting in 1959, Michel Peissel described the city as 'simply one vast work of art, from the humblest of the peasant's rectangular brick homes to the most impressive of the two-thousand-odd pagodas whose gilt roofs rise above the neat rows of houses. Each house, each temple, each shrine is decorated with delicately carved beams representing gods and goddesses, or animals drawn from reality and from fantasy, carved in dark wood that stands out against the background of pale pink bricks' (*Tiger for Breakfast*).

Rigid town planning did not allow for the enormous growth that has taken place in the area. Satellite towns were developed to house the growing population and these often became associated with a particular industry. (Thimi, for example, is still a pottery centre). Most of the towns in the Kathmandu Valley did, however, manage to conform to their original plans at least until the time of the Ranas. Jung Bahadur, the first of this line of prime ministers, visited Europe in 1850 and introduced the bizarre neo-classical style of architecture exemplified in the vast whitewashed edifices that can be seen in various stages of dilapidation in the city. Large areas of agricultural land were taken over for their construction.

Modern Kathmandu

The real attack on the strongly inter-related cultural, social and religious framework of the Valley's urban centres did not, however, really begin until the 1950s after the restoration of the monarchy and the opening up of the country. The effects have been dramatic, though, and many parts of Kathmandu have degenerated into an urban sprawl of unsightly concrete and brick buildings. The district of Thamel, that today looks no different from tourist ghettos in the other Asian capitals on the backpackers' route, was largely fields 30 years ago. The Kathmandu Guest House, opened in 1968 to house Peace Corps volunteers, was the first hotel here.

Kathmandu today is plagued with the problems that beset all rapidly expanding developing world cities: overcrowding, severe pollution and traffic congestion to name but a few. The population of the Kathmandu Valley now stands at 1.4 million, with a high growth rate of almost five per cent. None of these problems seems to tarnish the allure of the city as far as the tourist is concerned.

ARRIVAL AND DEPARTURE

By air

● **Arrival** Tribhuvan International Airport is a 20-minute drive from the centre of Kathmandu. Once off the plane you are led to the Immigration hall. If you already have a visa look for the appropriate queue. If you need to get one, however, fill out a visa form (available in the hall or in advance on the net) and line up at the queue for paying visa fees (see p69). You can pay in most hard currencies, cash only, but US dollars are by far and away the most convenient. This done, take the receipt to the Immigration counter.

In the arrival hall there's a basic but cheap duty-free shop and two foreign exchange counters. Downstairs is the luggage carousel staffed by predatory porters for whom the money you give is never enough (although a dollar or equivalent should be plenty) and luggage carts designed to travel in every direction but straight ahead.

Customs don't generally offer problems for tourists, although you may be required to put all your luggage through an X-ray machine (they are looking for gold being smuggled). Remember to ask to have your camera and films checked by hand: the X-ray machines are not film-safe.

Through customs is the quiet main hall where the tourist information booth gives out free copies of *Travellers' Nepal* (in which the star-class hotels advertise heavily) and a free map of Kathmandu, both worth picking up. There's a bank open during the day. The hotel reservation counter deals with star-class hotels, making reservations and organizing a free taxi service. The pre-paid taxi counter organizes transport into town for around the equivalent of US$3.50. Sometimes bargaining with the taxi drivers outside is slightly cheaper but often more hassle. There is no bus service.

Outside the building is a chaotic scene similar to any developing world airport forecourt. Taxi drivers pull you every which way offering discount hotel rooms while boys eagerly try whisking away your luggage to another taxi. It is extremely rare for anything to be stolen but expect to have to tip: a dollar is more than plenty, or possibly coins from your home country. There are also plenty of hotel representatives, with many offering a free taxi if you check out their hotel first. Most work directly for the hotel so there are rarely commissions involved. Travellers usually head for Thamel or Freak Street for budget accommodation. Taxi-drivers recommend the marginally more expensive Thamel hotels (where they can sometimes get commission) but it's easy enough to find your own hotel when you get to either of these places, once you have got rid of the taxi driver.

The several routes to Thamel pass through narrow streets lined with crumbling red brick houses and shop after tiny shop. You know you've arrived in Thamel when, after driving by a few roundabouts, you see Westerners everywhere and the road ahead narrows to a jumbled mass of vehicles. This is as good a place as any to get out. Alternatively, ask for the Kathmandu Guest House, to land yourself in the centre of it all.

● **Departure** If you leave Nepal by air there is a departure tax of Rs1100 (Rs770 for India and SAARC countries) which is payable in local currency only at the labelled bank counter before you pass your luggage through the X-ray machine.

In the bank here you can reconvert rupees into hard currency. Alternatively you can dispose of surplus rupees at the shop in the corner of the departure hall that sells gift packs of tea and Coronation Khukri rum in exotic khukri knife shaped bottles.

By land

Most **buses** (except buses for the Everest region) terminate at the new main bus station which is in the north of the city. If you're coming into Kathmandu by bus it's worth asking the driver to drop you off as near Thamel as possible. From the new bus station, however, there are frequent shuttle buses (Rs5) which pass by the northern end of Thamel on their way to the old bus station near the clock-tower. A **taxi** to Thamel will cost just under the equivalent of US$2.

ORIENTATION

Greater Kathmandu, which includes Patan as well as Kathmandu itself, lies at about 1350m/4428ft above sea level. The Bagmati River runs between these two cities. The airport is 6km to the east, near the Hindu temple complex of Pashupatinath, with the Buddhist stupa at Baudha 2km north of Pashupatinath. The other major Buddhist shrine, Swayambhunath, is visible on a hill in west Kathmandu. The third city in the Valley, Bhaktapur, is 14km to the east.

Within Kathmandu, most tourist hotels and guest houses and restaurants are to be found in Thamel, north of the historic centre of the city, Durbar Square. Freak Street, the hippie centre in the '60s and '70s which still offers some cheap accommodation, is just off Durbar Square. Some of the top hotels and the international airline offices are along Durbar Marg which runs south from the modern royal palace, scene of the grisly massacre in June 2001.

WHERE TO STAY

Hotel areas

● **Thamel** Most travellers find Thamel the most convenient area to stay in, although it's now largely a tourist ghetto. Everything you could want is available here, with over 100 guest houses and hotels (from US$1/£0.65 to US$90/£60 per night), good restaurants, souvenir shops, book shops, communication centres and travel agencies.

● **Freak St** In the halcyon days of the '60s and '70s when Kathmandu was a major stopover on the hippie trail, Freak St, just off Durbar Square, was the place to hang out. Although the hash dens are now all closed it still retains a quaint, almost timeless charm, and it's recently hung up a banner proclaiming *Welcome to Freak Street – free entry to all tourists*, presumably in a sly dig at the recently introduced Durbar Square entrance fees. Its 15 or so hotels and restaurants are all in the rock bottom to cheap bracket.

> **Hotel receptions are not trekking companies**
> An increasingly bad practice at many of the budget hotels is to pressure new
> arrivals into booking a trek with reception. Naturally this involves a hefty
> commission, usually to the detriment of the services, and some hoteliers will tell
> outright lies (eg 'it is impossible to find the way, there are so many trails') in their
> attempts to get you to sign up with them. Move hotels if they don't desist.

● **Other areas** Away from the intense tourist scene are other small hotels scattered throughout Kathmandu. In Patan, there are two budget hotels off Durbar Square and also a few good upmarket hotels. Baudha and Swayambhunath have some simple hotels favoured by Buddhists and travellers.

Prices
Prices given in this section are for the high season (Oct-Nov/Mar-Apr) for single/double rooms, with **common (c)** or **attached (a)** bathrooms as indicated. You may be able to get a discount of anything up to 50% on prices below outside the high season, depending on the length of your stay. Many hotel owners quote their prices in US dollars; you pay in rupees, though. Given the changing rate of inflation in the country, this is a sensible idea so US dollars are also used here. The dollar/pound exchange rate hovers around US$1.50=£1.

While the following prices were accurate at the time of research, note that this section is particularly liable to change. The low tourist numbers in Nepal over the past few years have meant that hotel prices are at an all-time low.

Budget guest houses (US$5/£3 or less)
In Thamel there are around 50 places to choose from in this price bracket, and in some you'll even get an attached bathroom for this price. A few hotels have triple or quad bed rooms. Check that the hot water works and try to get a room that faces away from the roads – Kathmandu is plagued by noisy dogs and honking taxis. The cheapest hotels tend to be in Narsingh Camp (behind Pumpernickel Bakery), in Chetrapati, a suburb adjoining Thamel to the south, or on the outskirts of Thamel.

A few Thamel hotels offer dormitory accommodation for around US$1 a bed. These include the basic *Hotel California* [122] and *Hotel Jjang* [21] as well as some of the smarter hotels such as *Shanti Nepal* [114] ($3 per bed) and *Villa Everest* [35] ($5 per bed or, oddly, $1 if used between 9pm and 9am only!). These may be the cheapest options, but they're not the best value: for just a few rupees more you can have your own room. Recommended budget hotels include the wonderful *Hotel Potala* [89], run by a Tibetan family, with satellite TV lounge and a roof terrace, which is swamped by gap-year students who take over the place for much of the year. Nearby, there's a knot of very cheap hotels behind the Maya Pub, including *Cosy Corner* [87] and *Pheasant Lodge* [88]; these two currently have the cheapest rooms in the area and are in an extremely central location. (*continued on p88*).

ACCOMMODATION IN THAMEL

01 Kathmandu Garden GH
02 Tibet Peace GH
03 Royal Peace GH
04 Ktm Peace Guest House
05 Green Peace Ktm GH
06 Pumori Guest House
07 Hotel Manang
08 Hotel Impala
09 Hotel Tenki
10 Hotel Marshyangdi
11 Microne Hotel
12 Hotel Blue Ocean
13 Sweet Dreams GH
14 Hotel Nature
15 Hotel Mt Fuji
16 Hotel Florid
17 Holyland Guest House
18 Hotel Lily
19 Hotel Iceland View
20 Hotel Buddha
21 Jjang Hotel
22 Hotel Namche Nepal
23 Hotel Gauri Shankar
24 Hotel Greeting Palace
25 Pilgrims GH
26 Laughing Buddha Home
27 Encounter Nepal
28 Dolphin GH
29 Tata GH
30 Hotel Crown
31 Hotel Heritage
32 Hotel Norbu Linka
33 Hotel Shakti
34 Villa Everest
35 Hotel Malla
36 Souvenir Guest House
37 Hotel Yeti
38 Hotel Thamel
39 Hotel Moon Drops
40 Hotel Panda
41 Namaskar Guest House
42 Maryland GH
43 Hotel Karma
44 Hotel Tashi Dhargey
45 Hotel Peninsula
46 Hotel Vaishali
47 Hotel Shree Tibet
48 Eco 2000
49 Hotel Mandap
50 Hotel Bikram

51 Peak Dhaulgiri GH
52 Yeti Guest Home
53 Mustang Guest House
54 Shim Ter
55 Hotel Mona
56 Hotel Garuda
57 Holy Lodge
58 Hotel Down Town
59 Hotel Tradition
60 International GH
61 Dolpo GH
62 Hotel 7 Corner
63 Prince Guest House
64 Classic Down Town GH
65 Travellers' Home
66 Acme Guest House
67 Hotel Red Planet
68 Hotel Nana
69 Deutsch Home
70 Kathmandu GH
71 King's Land GH
72 Samjhya GH
73 Surya GH
74 Hotel Centre Point
75 Tourist Home
76 Hotel Earth House
77 Hotel MM International
78 Potala Tourist Home
79 Hotel Tilicho
80 Tibet Holiday Inn
81 Student Guest House
82 Marco Polo
83 Newa Guest House
84 Sagarmatha GH
85 Hotel Star
86 Star Rest House
87 Cosy Corner
88 Pheasant Lodge
89 Hotel Potala
90 Highlander
91 Mini Om Guest House
92 New Look
93 Hotel Excelsior
94 Memorable GH
95 Hotel Pacifist
96 World Wide
97 Hotel The Earth
98 My Mom's House
99 Sherpa Guest House
100 Hotel Gaia
101 Hotel Swoniga
102 Hotel Puska

103 Shiva's Damaru GH
104 Om Buddhist GH
105 Hotel Tashi Dhele
106 Thorong Peak GH
107 Universal Guest House
108 My Home
109 Hotel Pisang
110 Gorkha Guest House
111 Mont Blanc GH
112 Fujiyama Guest House
113 Hotel Millennium
114 Hotel Shanti Nepal
115 Hotel Discovery
116 Imperial Guest House
117 Shangri-La GH
118 Hotel White Lotus
119 Mustang Holiday Inn
120 Dynasty
121 Fuji
122 Hotel California
123 Hotel Cheng Chang
124 Hotel Horizon
125 Nirvana Garden Hotel
126 Hotel Hama
127 Sun Rise Cottage
128 Tibet Guest House
129 Mount Holiday GH
130 Kathmandu City GH
131 Hotel Poon Hill
132 Khangsar Guest House
133 Hotel Tayoma
134 Potala Guest House
135 Hotel Ktm Holiday
136 Om Tara Guest House
137 White Lotus GH
138 Yak Lodge
139 Hotel Heera
140 Tibet Home
141 Tibet Cottage
142 Hotel Blue Diamond
143 Hotel Radiance
144 New Tibet Rest House
145 Lhasa Guest House
146 Sidharta Garden Hotel
147 Mt Annapurna GH
148 Hotel New Gajur
149 Hotel Elite
150 Hotel Norling
151 Hotel Utse
152 Diplomat
153 Hotel Jagat
154 Lucky Guest House

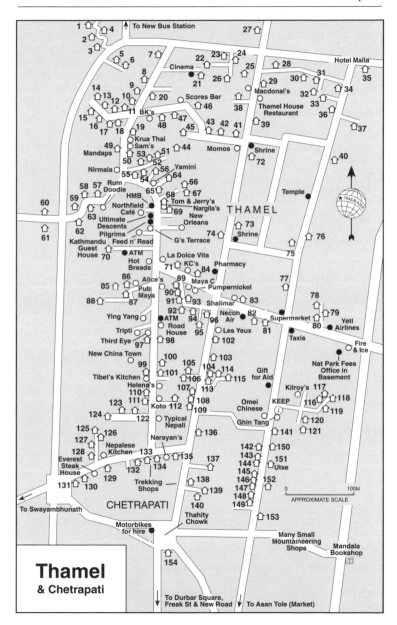

To New Bus Station
1
4
2
3
27
Hotel Malla
5
6
7
Cinema
22 23 24
28
31
35
8
25
9
29 30
32 34
14
20
Macdonal's
33
13
Scores Bar
Thamel House
36
12 10
38
Restaurant
15 11 BK's
46
39
37
16 17 18 19
43 42 41
47 48 45
Krua Thai
Momos
Shrine
49 Sam's
44
72
40
Mandaps
50 53 51
Nirmala
55 52 56 Yamini
64
58 57 Rum 54
66
Temple
59 Doodle
65
67
60 HMB 68
Tom & Jerry's
Northfield 69
Nargila's
THAMEL
Café
New
Ultimate
Orleans
63 Descents
74 73
61 62 Pilgrims
Shrine
76
Kathmandu Feed n' Read
G's Terrace
75
Guest
House 70 ATM
La Dolce Vita
Hot
71 KC's 84
Pharmacy
Breads
89 Maya C
77
86 Alice's
Pumpernickel
85
90
78
Pub
83
79
88 Maya
91 93 Shalimar
87
92 Necon 82
Yeti
Ying Yang
94 Air
Supermarket
Airlines
ATM
96
81
80
Tripti
Road
Les Yeux
Taxis
Fire
House
102
& Ice
Third Eye 95
98
New China Town
100 103
Nat Park Fees
99
105
104 114
Office in
Tibet's Kitchen
101 106
115 Gift
Basement
107
113 for Aid
Helena's
108
Kilroy's 117
110
112 109
Omei
KEEP
116 118
123 111 Koto
Chinese
119
124 122
Typical
Ghin Tang
120
Nepali
141 121
125
136
127 126
142 150
128 Nepalese
143
Kitchen 133
Narayan's
144 151
Everest
135
Utse
Steak 132 134 137
145
House
146 152
131 130 129
138
147
Trekking
139
148
Shops
CHETRAPATI
140
149
Thahity
153
Chowk
To Swayambhunath
Motorbikes
for hire
Many Small
Mountaineering
Thamel
Shops
Mandala
& Chetrapati
154
Bookshop
To Durbar Square,   To Asan Tole (Market)
Freak St & New Road

Temple

0   100M
APPROXIMATE SCALE

(*cont'd from p85*) For a bit of peace and quiet away from the dogs, discos and drunks of Thamel, check out the collection of four guest houses just to the north which each have their own garden area. Though the quality of all four suggest that they should belong in a higher price bracket, at least two – **Tibet Peace Guest House** [2] and **Royal Peace Guest House** [3] – are prepared, after a little bargaining on your part, to offer huge discounts, presumably because they have difficulty attracting custom being a ten-minute walk away from the centre of Thamel.

The following are **keyed to the map on p87**:

02 Tibet Peace GH (415026) dbl $4 (c), $4/5-8 (a)
03 Royal Peace GH (414623) $2/3 (c)
05 Green Peace Ktm GH (426817) $3 (c), $5 (a)
06 Pumori GH (417830) sgl $3/4 (c) $4/5 (a)
17 Holyland GH (429384) $3-6/5-9 (c), $6/6-12 (a)
18 Hotel Lily (426264) $4/5-6 (a)
21 Jjang (412715) dorm $1.30, sgl/dbl $3.50 (c)
22 Hotel Namche Nepal (417067) $3/4 (c) $4/5 (a)
26 Laughing Buddha Home (425056) $4/7 (a)
29 Tata GH (416951) $2/3 (a)
36 Souvenir GH (410277) $1.50/3 (c), $4/4-5 (a)
37 Hotel Yeti (414858) $3/4 (c) $8 (a)
39 Hotel Moon Drops (424704) $2/3 (c), $3/4 (a)
41 Namaskar GH (421060) $4/5 (a)
42 Maryland GH (416953) sgl $3 (c), $4-5/4-9 (a)
45 Hotel Peninsula (414209) $3/4-6 (a)
50 Hotel Bikram (425827) $3/4 (a)
51 Peak Dhaulagiri GH (432887) $4/5 (c), $6/8 (a)
52 Yeti Guest Home (419789) $4/5 (c), $6/8 (a)
53 Mustang GH (426053) $2/3 (c), $3-4/4 (a)
54 Hotel Shim Ter (434738) $3/3 (c), $5/6 (a)
57 Holy Lodge (416265) $3/4 (c), $7-12/15 (a)
64 Classic Down Town GH (426156) $3/4 (a)
65 Traveller's Home (416917) $5/6 (c)
67 Red Planet (432879) $5-8/7-11 (a)
69 Deutsch Home (415010) $4/6 (c), $5/7 (a)
71 King's Land GH (417129) $2/3 (c), 3/3.50 (a)
72 Samjhya GH (418399) $2 (c), $3-4/5-10 (a)
73 Hotel Surya (429386) $3/5-8 (a)
75 Tourist Home (418305) $4/6 (c)
76 Hotel Earth House (418197) $4/6 (c), $10/16 (a)
77 Hotel MM International (416797) $3.50/5 (a)
81 Student GH (251448) $4/6.50 (a)
82 Marco Polo (251914) $3/3 (c), $6-8/5-10 (a)

85 Hotel Star (411000) $2/4 (c), $6/8 (a)
86 Star Rest House (424044) $4/5 (a)
87 Cosy Corner Lodge (438409) $1.50/2 (c) $5 (a)
88 Pheasant Lodge (417415) $1.50/2 (c)
89 Hotel Potala (419159) $2/3-3.50 (c)
91 Mini Om GH (259036) $1.50/2 (c)
92 New Look GH (437988) $1.75/2 (c), $2/3 (a)
94 Memorable GH (419288) $2/2 (c), $3/3 (a)
95 Hotel Pacifist (258320) $1.50/2 (c), $2/3-3.50 (a)
96 Hotel World Wide (437033) $3/3 (c), $4/4 (a)
98 My Mom's House (266897) $2/3 (c), $3/4 (a)
100 Hotel Gaia (260555) $2/4 (c), $3/5 (a)
102 Hotel Puskar (262956) $3 (c),$4/5-7 (a)
103 Shiva's Damaru GH (264489) $2 (c), $3 (a)
104 Om Buddhist GH (255755) $1-2/2 (c), $2/3 (a)
105 Hotel Tashi Dhele (251720) $4/4 (c), $6/10 (a)
107 Universal GH (259382) $3/4 (c), $5-8/6-10 (a)
110 Gorkha (267660) $1.50/3-4 (c), dbl $4-6 (a)
111 Mt Blanc GH (223318) $2/2-3 (c), $3/3-4 (a)
112 Fujiyama GH (244074) $2 (c) $3/3-4 (a)
117 Shangri-La GH (250188) sgl $3 (c), dbl $5 (a)
118 Hotel White Lotus (249842) $3/6-8 (a)
122 Hotel California (242076) $1.50/3 (c), $3/4 (a)
129 Hotel Mount Holiday (240193) dbl $4-15 (a)
130 Kathmandu City GH (260624) $3/4 (c), $4/5 (a)
132 Khangsar GH (260788) $6/8-10 (a)
135 Hotel Ktm Holiday (230293) $4-9/5-10 (a)
136 Om Tara GH (259634) $3/4 (c), dbl $6-9 (a)
137 White Lotus GH (258996) $3/5-9
138 Yak Lodge (259318) dbl $3 (c), $4 (a)
139 Hotel Heera (259542) dbl $4 (c), $3/5 (a)
140 New Tibet Home (269092) sgl $2 (c) dbl $3 (a)
154 Lucky GH (259415) $2/3 (a)

Freak Street, near Durbar Square, is one of the few places in the world where it is still possible to find a room, admittedly small, for around one US dollar a night. A slightly larger budget widens the choice considerably. The majority of hotels are on the main street but looking down alleys nearby yields more.

Cheap hotels in Thamel (US$6-15/£3.50-9)
Most Thamel hotels offer a range of rooms, the majority falling in this price bracket. The hotel should provide clean sheets and blankets while the better ones will also supply towels and toilet paper and perhaps be carpeted. Little fea-

❏ The Kathmandu **area code** is 01. If phoning from outside Nepal dial ☎ +977-1

tures to check are: is there a vent or window in the bathroom, a clothes line and a rooftop garden? Features aside, when choosing a hotel, go by the reception staff – are they friendly and helpful or lackadaisical? Most people new to Kathmandu begin looking at hotels in the heart of Thamel. However, there are plenty of hotels in every direction, none of which are more than a few minutes' walk from the centre. The best known of the hotels in Kathmandu is the long-running *Kathmandu Guest House* [70] (☎ 413632, 🗎 417133, 🖳 www.kath manduguesthouse.com), a Thamel landmark. Popular with groups, it's bursting in the high season. They have a few rooms from US$4-10/$6-12 (c) but most accommodation here is US$17/20 or more in the new wing.

Another hotel that is winning a fine reputation is the wonderful *Pilgrim's Guest House* [25] (☎ 413260, 🗎 422914, 🖳 pilgrimshouse@yahoo.com), set in its own peaceful and sunny grounds at the northern end of Thamel. The *Hotel Karma* [43] (☎ 417897) also enjoys a burgeoning reputation and the patronage of many expats. The following are **keyed to the map on p87**:

01 Ktm Garden GH (415239) $4/13-20 (a)
04 Ktm Peace GH (439369) $8-12/12-16 (a)
08 Hotel Impala (415549) $5/8-16 (a)
11 Microne Hotel (437569) $15/20-35 (a)
13 Sweet Dream GH (440080) dbl $5-15 (a)
15 Hotel Mt Fuji (422684) $8-16/10-26 (a)
16 Hotel Florid (416155) $3/4 (c), $5/10-25 (a)
19 Hotel Iceland View (416686) $12-25/18-44 (a)
20 Hotel Buddha (413366) sgl $6 (c), $15/18-30 (a)
23 Hotel Gauri Shankar (417181) $15/20 (a)
24 Hotel Greeting Palace (417212) $12/18-30 (a)
25 Pilgrims GH (413260) $10/15 (c), $20/25-68 (a)
27 Hotel Encounter Nepal (414848) $6/15
28 Dolphin GH (429280) $6/8 (c), $10/12 (a)
31 Hotel Heritage (422686) $6/8-12 (a)
33 Hotel Shakti (410121) $7/9 (c), $12-18/18-25 (a)
34 Villa Everest (413471) $7 (c), $16/30 (a)
40 Hotel Panda (424683) $6/8 (c), $10/12 (a)
43 Hotel Karma (417897) $12-22/18-32 (a)
44 Hotel Tashi Dhargey (415378) $20-35/25-40 (a)
47 Hotel Shree Tibet (419902) $10/15-60 (a)
48 Hotel Eco 2000 (436913) $15-25/20-30 (a)
55 Hotel Mona (422151) $15/20 (a)
56 Hotel Garuda (416340) $10-35/15-40 (a)
58 Hotel Down Town (430471) $5/7 (c), $8/8-20 (a)
61 Dolpo GH (251193) $6/6-10 (c), $6-15/8-20 (a)
62 Hotel 7 Corner (415588) $6/8 10 (a)
63 Prince GH (414456) $6-8/10-12 (a)
66 Acme GH (414811) $5-20/8-25 (a)
68 Hotel Nana (413960) $10/15-25 (a)
70 Kathmandu GH (413632) $4/6 (c), $17/20 (a)
78 Potala Tourist Home (410303) $3/4 (c) $7/10 (a)
83 Newa GH (415781) $6-12/8-14 (a)
84 Sagarmatha GH (410214) $5/7 (c), $8/10-20 (a)

90 Highlander (424066) $8/12 (a)
97 Hotel The Earth (260312) $12/15-25 (a)
99 Sherpa GH (221546) sgl $9 (c) $12-18/17-20 (a)
106 Thorong Pk GH (253458) $8/12 (c), $14/18 (a)
108 My Home (256238) $10/14 (c) $14/18 (a)
109 Hotel Pisang (252540) $25-50/30-60 (a)
113 Hotel Millennium (249579) $6/8-12 (a)
114 Hotel Shanti Nepal (262986) $15-25/25-40 (a)
115 Hotel Discovery (229889) $6/8-20 (a)
116 Imperial GH (249339) $12/15 (a)
119 Mustang Holiday Inn (249041) $8-40/10-45 (a)
121 Fuji GH (250435) $6/10 (c), $10-20/15-30 (a)
123 Hotel Cheng Chang (246949) $6 (c), $20/25 (a)
124 Hotel Horizon (220904) $4 (c) $25 (a)
126 Hotel Hama (251009) $3/5 (c), $8-10/10-12 (a)
127 Sun Rise Cottge (256850) $8/10 (c), $13/17 (a)
128 Tibet GH (254888) $16-55/19-59 (a)
131 Hotel Poon Hill (257666) $12-20/18-25
134 Potala GH (220467) $10-15/20-60 (a)
141 Tibet Cottage (226577) dbl $8 (c), $10/15 (a)
142 Htl Blue Diamond (226320) $12-23/15-27 (a)
143 Hotel Radiance (220264) $8-15/12-20 (a)
144 New Tibet Rest House (225319) $8/12 (c), $15/20-25 (a)
145 Lhasa GH (226147) sgl $5 (c), $12/18 (a)
146 Siddharta Garden Htl (222253) $10/12-25 (a)
147 Mt Annapurna GH (255462) $10/15 (a)
148 Hotel New Gajur (226623) $15/18 (a)
149 Hotel Elite (227916) $5/8-25 (a)
150 Hotel Norling (240734) $12-16/19-28 (a)
151 Hotel Utse (226946) $15-24/21-30(a)
152 Hotel Diplomat (267996) $14-25/20-35 (a)
153 Hotel Jagat (250732) $7/15 (a)

Moderately-priced hotels

There are numerous reasonable hotels in the US$15-30/£9-18 price range, most of them with a restaurant attached. All rooms have attached bathrooms with hot water, and in the more expensive rooms a TV and perhaps an air-conditioner and heater. Some hotels have a few de luxe rooms in this price range too. Once again, a little bargaining with these hotels can go a long way if they're not full, and many of them were offering rooms with attached bathroom for as little as $4-5 during the recent tourist slump.

The following are **keyed to the map on p87**:

09 Hotel Tenki (425694) $25-40/35-50 (a)
12 Hotel Blue Ocean (412577) $15-25/20-30 (a)
14 Hotel Nature (425823) $35-45/50-60 (a)
30 Hotel Crown (416285) $20/25 (a)
38 Hotel Thamel (417643) $30-40/45-55 (a)
49 Hotel Mandap (413321) $21/27--45 (a)
59 Hotel Tradition (428217) $30-55/40-65 (a)
60 International GH (410533) $16-20/20-25

74 Hotel Centre Point (424522) $55/65-85 (a)
79 Hotel Tilicho (410132) $15-35/20-45 (a)
80 Tibet Holiday Inn (423530) $25/30 (a)
93 Hotel Excelsior (411566) $20-32/25-40 (a)
101 Hotel Swoniga (253253) $35-45/45-55 (a)
120 Hotel Dynasty (263172) $40-60/50-95 (a)
125 Nirvana Garden (256200) $30-55/40-65 (a)
133 Hotel Tayoma (260617) $15-52/30-62 (a)

Three-star standard hotels

Around the three-star standard are two well-managed traditionally built hotels. *Hotel Vajra* [see map on p80] (☎ 272719, 🖻 271695, 🖳 www.hotelvajra.com) was conceived and paid for by a Texas billionaire, and built by Newar craftsmen, with wall-paintings by Tibetan and Tamang artists. Rooms are US$33/38 with attached bathroom and there are cheaper rooms for under US$20 with wash-basins and shared bathrooms. It is located near Swayambhunath.

The traditionally decorated *Summit Hotel* (☎ 521810, 🖻 523737, 🖳 www.summit-nepal.com) in Patan is popular with expeditions wanting a peacefully-located hotel. Prices range from US$25/35 to US$125. Both have a pleasant atmosphere, attractive gardens, restaurants and appropriate amenities.

Close to each other in north Thamel are *Hotel Marshyangdi* [10] (☎ 414105, 🖳 www.catmando.com/marshyangdi/) and *Hotel Manang* [07] (☎ 410993, 🖳 www.hotelmanang.com), both popular with trekking groups. There are rooms here from US$55-80/65-90. *Hotel Norbu Linka* [32] (☎ 414799, 🖳 www.web-nepal.com/norbulinka/index.htm) is slightly cheaper at US$35-55/45-65.

Four- and five-star hotels

Until its unfortunate demise in 1970, the top place to stay was the Royal Hotel. Its success was largely due to its proprietor, the legendary White Russian émigré, Boris Lissanevitch. It was the country's first Western hotel, opened in 1954 in a wing of the palace that is now the Bahadur Bhavan. Virtually everything for it had to be imported from Europe, shipped to India and then carried in by porters. Staying here you'd be guaranteed to meet interesting people and many of the mountaineering expeditions made it their Kathmandu base.

Most of the city's top hotels are now much like expensive hotels anywhere in the world. *Hotel Yak & Yeti* (☎ 248999, 🖻 227781, 🖳 www.yakandyeti.com, see map on p80), has rooms from US$185 to US$625 for a suite. Centrally located, it has everything you'd expect from a five-star hotel, although the modern wings don't exactly blend with the old Rana palace which forms part of it. The Yak & Yeti Bar with its excellent Chimney Restaurant was moved here from the Royal Hotel when it closed. Rich Indians, however, consider *Soaltee Holiday Inn Crowne Plaza* (☎ 272555, 🖺 272205, 💻 crowneplaza@shicp.com.np) as the best of the big hotels, although it's not so well located, being in the west of the city, in Kalimati. Rooms range from US$170/180 to US$675. It's said to have the best casino on the subcontinent.

Back on Durbar Marg is *Hotel de l'Annapurna* (☎ 221711, 🖺 225236, 💻 www.taj-annapurna.com.np) with rather ordinary rooms from US$135-360/130-360, a large pool and seedy casino. Similarly priced but inconvenient-ly located is *Everest Hotel* (☎ 488100, 🖺 490288) on the road to the airport.

Hotel Malla [35] (☎ 418385, 🖺 418382, 💻 malla@htlgrp.mos.com.np), just north of Thamel, is pleasant with rooms from US$130/156. It has a fitness centre and swimming pool. The best value in this group is *Hotel Shangri-La* (☎ 412999, 🖺 414184, 💻 www.nepalshangrila.com), in Lazimpat, with rooms from US$130 and a peaceful garden. Both *Hotel Radisson* (☎ 411818, 🖺 411720, 💻 www.radisson.com/kathmandune) and a 400-room branch of the *Hyatt Regency* chain (☎ 491234, 🖺 490033, 💻 www.sales .kathmanduhr .hyatt.intl.com), near Baudha, have opened in the last few years. Both are very clean and modern and have rooms from around $175 per night.

The Indian-owned *Hotel Vaishali* [46] (☎ 413968, 🖺 414510, 💻 www.vais hali.com.np) is Thamel's first four-star hotel. Rooms are from US$90/110 although travel agents can offer substantial discounts.

Probably the best hotel in Kathmandu is *Hotel Dwarika's* (☎ 470770, 🖺 471 379, 💻 www.dwarikas.com), which has opted out of a star classification. If Kathmandu is a living museum, this is the ultimate place to experience it. The red-brick buildings are decorated, inside and out, with ornate panels lovingly restored from old Kathmandu houses. Every room (US$135/155) is an individ-ual work of art, and the restaurant's offerings are similarly exotic.

Golfers may be interested in the new branch of *Le Meridien* (☎ 244154) which is now open beside the Gokarna Forest Golf Club – an eco-friendly course designed by Gleneagles.

Note that all star-class hotels add a 10-14% government tax to the bill.

WHERE TO EAT

Kathmandu's restaurants are renowned amongst travellers throughout South Asia for their ability to serve passable approximations of Western dishes. Authenticity isn't the strong point of the real budget restaurants but the better restaurants really do serve some good food. Cheap main courses start at around US$1.50 or around US$2.50 at better-quality places. There is a 10% tax and a further 2% tourist service charge (which goes to the Nepal Tourism Board for promotion) at the better restaurants; sometimes this is included but in some of the upmarket restaurants this is added to the bill.

Be especially careful about what you eat before you set out on your trek: you're much more likely to pick up a stomach bug in a Kathmandu restaurant than in the hills. A test on the quality of the tap water in Thamel showed it to contain more than ten times the WHO recommended safe maximum level of faecal matter. The better restaurants are serious about hygiene but don't believe all restaurants that tell you their salads are washed in iodine. Similarly, filtered water is only reliable at the better places; otherwise stick to bottled or hot drinks.

Unless otherwise indicated the restaurants described are in Thamel (see map p87).

Breakfast

Even the smallest guest houses offer breakfast and snacks either as room service or in their own snack bars. Most of the Thamel restaurants have set breakfasts that can be good value but for a leisurely breakfast/brunch in the sun there are a few places worthy of special mention:

The *Pumpernickel Bakery* does a roaring trade in cinnamon rolls, bagels and other pastries and cakes. There's a pleasant garden behind it and the noticeboard here is a good place to track down trekking partners. *Brezel Bakery*'s rooftop offers competition especially with its quick service. Close by and offering similar fare is the *Hot Breads Bakery*, also with its own roof terrace; they also have a branch on Durbar Marg.

Most places offer yoghurt with fruit and/or muesli but the two best (with little between them) are *New Orleans* with great curd and *Northfield Café* with better fruit. Both places have decent coffee, a great variety of food, tasteful music and the morning papers.

Decent bacon can be found at *New Orleans* and at *Helena's*, perfect with fried eggs sunny-side up. It may be flights of stairs to Helena's rooftop, but the view is extensive. Other places with sunny terraces are *Mandaps*, which is good all round, *Le Bistro* and *G's Terrace*.

If you don't mind being indoors, *K-too* has hearty breakfasts while *Himalatte* and *Himalayan Java* specialize in good coffee; Himalatte even offers café latte in a bowl (Rs120) while Himalayan Java's cold blended banana mocha (Rs90) is hard to beat. There is still no Starbucks chain in Nepal, indeed none of any of the major food-beverage chains has made it here.

Out of Thamel the place to go for a relaxing start to the day is *Mike's Breakfast*. You breakfast on authentic American (hash browns, pancakes and syrup, fresh coffee with free refills etc) and Mexican fare in a garden, serenaded by the sounds of the ex-Peace-Corps owner's classical record collection. Lunch and dinner are also good.

Lunch and dinner

● **Budget** The cheapest restaurants in Kathmandu serving 'Western' fare are in and around Freak St. There are a handful of restaurants all offering main courses that start for less than US$1 and top out at around US$2. Back in Thamel, restaurant prices can be much higher, but there are still places where you'll get a cheap meal that's reasonably filling.

At the long-running *Tashi Deleg* everything is under Rs100, except steaks which are Rs115. *Nargila's* is good value too with steaks topping out at Rs150;

it is popular with Israelis for its Middle Eastern food – a plate of falafel with pita, tahina and salad costs Rs105. There are many momo and dal bhaat restaurants, ask local friends which they like and think are reasonably hygienic.

● **Western** The recently-relocated *Helena's* is a popular place: main dishes are Rs135-260, everything is good but nothing really stands out, similar to *Alice's* and *Jalapeno*.

K-too! is a beer and steak house; a great no-brainer is the toasted minute steak 'Bookmaker' Rs155; they also have full-flavoured onion, anchovy and spinach quiche for Rs190 and to go with the large cable TV behind the bar is the best range of bar snacks in Thamel.

For a refreshingly different menu and great atmosphere *New Orleans* is recommended. Try their jambalaya (Rs220 with chicken, veg for Rs165) or for a lighter meal spinach rice and steamed vegetables. It's the only place that is a successful blend of a restaurant and bar; a White Russian made with blended ice cream (Rs175) will even do as a dessert.

Many places have steak on the menu, usually (but not always) buffalo steak. It's often served as a 'sizzler' and arrives in front of you on a heated cast-iron plate doing just that. The enduring *Everest Steak House*'s speciality is a wide range of real beef fillet steaks, beginning from Rs175, although most, eg the brandy sauce steak, are around Rs250. If you have the appetite of a yeti try the Rs1000 chateaubriand (better split between two or three people). In this Chetrapati restaurant there are virtually no vegetarian dishes.

G's Terrace is a Western-Nepali joint venture with a diverse range of cuisine, including authentic Bavarian. The Schwabischer zwiebelrostbraten (special roast beef) costs Rs210 at this pleasant roof-top restaurant. *Old Vienna Inn*, now in the centre of Thamel, serves Austrian cuisine for similar prices. On the ground floor is a pseudo-deli/fast-food counter for meals in quick time and opposite are a couple of bakeries: the *Hot Shoppe's* spinach and mushroom quiche (Rs45) can be eaten on the run or upstairs. Their strawberry tart (when in season) will bring you back again.

KC's Restaurant & Bambooze Bar is as much a Thamel institution as the Kathmandu Guest House. A sizzling steak from the people who introduced the 'sizzler' to Kathmandu now costs Rs250; and if that doesn't fill you up you can round off your meal with their cheeseboard (yak, mozzarella and cottage cheese

---

Baber Mahal revisited

This place has to be seen to be believed! The crumbling stables of a Rana palace between Kathmandu and Patan have been converted into a chic shopping centre that wouldn't look out of place in California.

There are some distinctly exclusive boutiques and one of Kathmandu's best restaurants, *Chez Caroline*. Not to be missed for a celebratory dinner is *Baithak* (☎ 248747). In the grand long gallery, past Ranas stare down from their portraits as you feast on 'delicacies from the Rana court'. Main dishes are Rs500 and the set dinner, the Maharaja's Feast (Rs945) is recommended.

with wholewheat bread and pickles. Another Kathmandu institution recommended for its food is the **Rum Doodle**. It is one of the very few places that offers mashed potato. Try lemon grilled chicken (Rs220) or the Rum Doodle BBQ, your choice of meat for Rs240. During winter enjoy a real fire without guilt: the logs are made from crushed rice husks.

Showing that they care about hygiene, **Himalatte** has an open kitchen. Vegetarian stir fry with rice is Rs140, and beef stir fry Rs170. If you are suffering try their hangover helper – carrot, ginger and parsley juice for Rs90.

Kilroy's has an original menu and competes to be the best restaurant in the tourist area. For a starter, chargrilled market vegetables (Rs115) is interesting, their royal dal bhaat (Rs330, veg Rs280) is royal indeed – the King and Queen have eaten here. Irish stew and even a beef and Guinness hotpot (Rs355) gives away the chef's origins. Lunchtime sandwiches are cheaper and good value.

Nepal isn't the place to suffer a Mac Attack: McDonald's hasn't arrived. The alternatives are **Neerula's** and **Wimpy**, both on Durbar Marg. Beefburgers are out of the question, mutton burgers being the less tasty alternative.

Video restaurants around Thamel show Hollywood's latest but feature unmemorable food and low-quality recordings. A better alternative is the Kathmandu Guesthouse's large-screen video disc cinema which seats about 25 people. The quality comes at the modest price of Rs100 including drink and snack.

In the five-star hotels there are some excellent Western-style restaurants, probably the best is upstairs at the **Hyatt**; a huge slab of salmon cooked to perfection is Rs1200. The **Yak & Yeti** and the **Radisson** often have specialty functions that are heavily advertised.

Lazimpat has a wide range of good if more upmarket restaurants catering to the large expat community around there.

● **Nepali & Newari** There are many cheap local Nepali places out of Thamel that serve dal bhaat or momos, usually for less than Rs50. In Thamel the **Nepalese Kitchen** has a range of superior dal bhaat specials (Rs80+) and live traditional music several times a week. The **Typical Nepali Restaurant** does the same in a typical building – you won't miss the typically dressed tout outside either.

Lowland has perhaps the largest traditional Nepali menu in central Thamel. *Nepali khasi* (boneless mutton) is Rs165; order separately or go for a fixed menu. A great accompaniment is tomato achaar, a traditional boiled tomato sauce, which is rarely found on menus. They also have a popular range of fish dishes: the grilled trout is superb at good value too at Rs195. **Northfield's** fancy dal bhaat is also recommended.

The upmarket **Bhanchha Ghar** (meaning 'Kitchen House') in Bagh Bazaar offers wild pork or dried deer meat to accompany drinks and the dinner menu is similarly exotic. Imitating this is **Thamel House Restaurant** (☎ 410388) set in a renovated 100-year-old Newar house. Main dishes start from Rs180 and the nine-course set meal costs Rs695.

● **Tibetan** The best-known Tibetan place is **Utse**, in the hotel of the same name. The pingtsey soup (meat soup with wontons) is excellent, as are their momos (vegetable, mutton, buffalo or pork) which cost Rs55 for ten. Given a couple of hours' notice, they will prepare a complete Tibetan banquet. *Tibet's Kitchen* in the Sherpa Guest House has an open-plan kitchen and food is similarly clean and fresh.

● **Indian** Serving reasonable Indian food has made *The Third Eye* popular (paneer tika is Rs160, chicken tika masala Rs215) but *Mandaps'* quality is more consistent, even if the menu is limited. Delicious yogurt chicken costs Rs195. Palak paneer (spinach cheese) is Rs115 and each dish includes hot nan or rice.

Surprisingly *Feed n' Read* is the only place in Thamel that serves southern Indian Masala dosas which, for Rs100, make a great lunch. Their momos are original too.

The top Indian restaurant is Hotel de l'Annapurna's *Ghar-e-kabab* (☎ 221711). It specializes in the rich cuisine of north India, main dishes are around Rs300 and there's live music in the evenings. You may need to book in advance.

● **Mexican** The latest place is *Walter's Bodega*, chimichangas (meat-filled tortilla with green rice) is Rs220 and they offer no fewer than 10 different tequila cocktails (Rs180 each).

Northfield Café and *Mike's Breakfast* are the only places for a tostada. They are also among the most hygienic of Thamel restaurants. The Jesse James Bar, attached to Northfield Café, serves free corn chips and salsa with drinks.

● **Italian** Many restaurants serve pizza and pasta but one place stands way above the rest, however, *Fire & Ice Pizzeria & Ice Cream Parlour* has to be experienced to be believed. Run by an Italian woman who's imported her own computer-controlled Moretti Forni pizza oven, some of the best pizzas on the subcontinent are now turned out here. Prices range from Rs170 to Rs 290 and there's wine by the glass for Rs130. *Northfield Café* turns out the best pizzas in central Thamel and at two-thirds of the price.

For authentic pasta, try *La Dolce Vita*, great food though the service is lacklustre, or the more consistent *Casa Della Pasta* where cannelloni Fiorentina (pasta stuffed with spinach, ricotta and mushroom) costs Rs145. Their continental barbequed wild boar for Rs210 is good, too.

● **Chinese** Most cheaper 'do everything' restaurants have spring rolls and chow mein on their menus although what appears on your plate is usually unmemorable. The *New China Town Restaurant* is good, sometimes excellent, but inconsistent. Probably the best Chinese restaurant is the *Mountain City* at Malla Hotel, just north of Thamel.

● **Thai** *Ying Yang*, opposite the Third Eye, is one of Thamel's best restaurants. Their Phad Thai for Rs210 is the most consistent and best, and with the curries you have a choice of heat. They also have a range of Western cuisine and their pastas in particular are good value at Rs150-160.

● **Japanese** All serve authentic portions at almost authentic prices. *Koto*, towards Chetrapati, is the most conveniently located. Warm towels greet you and the dishes are works of art.

● **Vegetarian** *New Nirmala* is simply the best-value restaurant in Thamel: soups are Rs48, lasagne al forno Rs98, quiche mushroom spinach is Rs105 and a small pot of herbal tea is Rs30 yet the meals are consistent, delicious and wholesome. On Freak St, *Paradise Vegetarian Restaurant* is an excellent place to eat.

● **Juices** *Just Juice and Shakes* down the alley heading to Hotel Red Planet is a favourite with anyone who really knows Thamel. Their secret is using frozen fruit instead of ice for incredibly thick shakes: a coffee banana shake is Rs60, and their cappuccino (Rs50) is one of the best in Thamel if you prefer a strong and rich flavour.

● **Desserts** After a long trek there's hunger enough in the stomach for a substantial dinner *and* dessert. In Freak Street *the* place is the long-running *Snowman*. It has been renovated, leaving it a little sterile compared to its hippie past, but the desserts are still astounding value at Rs30-40. The crème caramel is still the best in Kathmandu.

Back in the Thamel area *Narayan's*, in Chetrapati, has a window filled with cakes and pies, as does *Helena's*, that taste as good as they look. *Roadhouse* has a good ice-cream bar and at *Pumpernickel* there's excellent ice cream by the scoop, though they are only open during the day.

La Dolce Vita's tiramisu, served in a cocktail glass, is addictive as is *Rum Doodle's* excellent cheesecake for Rs70. At *Kilroy's*, the skill Thomas Kilroy gained making over 20,000 lemon tarts in Bermuda has certainly paid off – they're so good you may even convince yourself that perhaps one is not enough. At *Northfield Café* try the chocolate sundae or the brownie sundae (Rs95) at your peril; hungry trekkers will be back for one for breakfast, too!

NIGHTLIFE

Rum Doodle Restaurant & 40,000½ft Bar is a Kathmandu institution, with yeti prints on its walls inscribed by the members of many mountaineering expeditions and is a good place to catch the stories at the end of the expedition season. Hot rum punch costs Rs70. *Tom & Jerry's* is noisy and popular, an old favourite. There's a couple of pool tables and satellite TV. *Pub Maya*, *Maya Cocktail Bar* and *Tongues 'n Tales* are all similar with their three-hour-plus happy hours. *Sam's* is a friendly old-style local, while *Full Moon* is a hip hangout place.

The **clubs** – *Jump*, *Scores*, *Underground* and *Liquid* – pump until late (when there isn't a noise crackdown) and the crowd is increasingly Nepali. Further afield, and usually with entrance fees, are *Club X-zone*, *Woodlands*, *Dynasty* and others.

There's **live music** every Wednesday at *Bamboo Club*, with a band or jam session; on Friday *Himalatte* has funk and acoustic jam, Saturday is New Orleans band night and Sunday is unplugged, and no, it isn't all the same band.

Opposite Top: The stupa at Bodhnath (Baudha, see p99) is one of the largest in the world and the centre of a large community of Tibetan Buddhists. **Bottom**: Musicians at a festival in Kathmandu. **Following page**: Surveying the bustling street scene below.

During the trekking season there are sometimes other places, including *Les Yeux*. The *Hyatt* on a Friday night also pumps with the wealthy Nepali crowd; beers are Rs275.

Hotel Sherpa and Hotel de l'Annapurna (both in Durbar Marg) and the Shankar Hotel (off Kantipath) put on **cultural shows**. Both the French and Russian cultural centres occasionally sponsor a play, jazz night or films; details are advertised. The top hotels all operate **casinos**. If you flew into Nepal recently you're entitled to Rs100-worth of free coupons if you show your air ticket.

Look out for posters in Thamel advertising **Chris Beall's slide shows** covering the main trekking regions of the country. He's a professional photographer and lecturer and the slide shows, held in the early evenings at Kathmandu Guest House, offer good unbiased advice for trekkers about to head into the hills and are well worth the ticket price.

SERVICES

Banks
Larger hotels can change money at reception. Around every corner in Thamel are authorized moneychangers but their rates, like the hotels, are not quite as good as the banks.

Automatic cash dispensers (**ATMs**) have finally arrived in Nepal. In Thamel the most convenient machines are in the courtyard of the Kathmandu Guest House and opposite Ying Yang restaurant. There are a few more machines around Kathmandu including one at the Kantipath branch of Standard & Chartered. There is a daily withdrawal limit of Rs20,000 but the limit set by your bank may be lower.

You can withdraw unlimited amounts in person from banks, either in rupees or travellers' cheques, but not in foreign cash. The most convenient foreign-exchange counter is at Nabil Bank, 50m down (south) from Ying Yang. Upstairs in the shopping centre in the same building as Fire & Ice is the Himalayan Bank, though its cash dispenser is for account holders only. The most efficient bank is Standard & Chartered (ex Nepal Grindlays) in Kantipath; Nabil Bank is also in Kantipath and offers some of the most competitive rates in the city. Tucked way near the Vaishali Hotel in Thamel is a branch of Kathmandu Bank.

The **American Express** office (☎ 226172, open Sunday to Friday 10am-1pm and 2-5pm) is in front of the Hotel Mayalu, Bagh Bazaar.

Bookshops and libraries
Kathmandu has some of the best bookshops on the subcontinent, including many small second-hand shops where you can trade in your novel for another. Most international news, computer and fashion magazines are regularly available.

The **Kaiser Library**, Kaiser Shamsher Rana's private collection, is worth visiting as much for the building as for the 30,000-plus musty volumes. This Rana palace is now the Ministry of Education and Culture, just west of the modern royal palace. The **British Council Reading Room** by the British Embassy is open to all and has the main UK newspapers and plenty of magazines.

Post and telecommunications

There are **internet cafés** everywhere but many have grimy keyboards. The rates are semi-standardized at around Rs25-30 an hour. Many of them also offer **internet phone services**, but the quality is often low, including the calls made through internet call-back systems, ie they dial many numbers before yours. The standard but monopolistically expensive **Nepal Telecom** service still offers the clearest line

although it is far from perfect; getting people to call you back seems to result in a clearer line. However, for **fax** anything works well.

Snail **mail** (and it is that in Nepal) and **poste restante** are found only at the GPO, which is a 25-minute walk south of Thamel, on the corner of Kantipath and Prithvi Path. When sending a letter don't put it in a post-box but ask them to frank it or the stamps may be removed and resold. Sending mail is far more easily but less reliably attended to by the numerous **communication centres** and book shops in Thamel. For parcels you have the choice of international couriers with reliability at a price, the numerous cargo agents who specialize in bigger cargo consignments, and the less than reliable GPO.

Medical clinics

CIWEC (☎ 228531, open Monday to Friday 9am-noon, 1-4pm) is an exceptionally competent clinic located just off Durbar Marg, near the Hotel Yak & Yeti. Consultations cost US$40 or equivalent in any currency.

The long-running **Nepal International Clinic** (☎ 434642, 435357, open Sunday to Friday, 9am-5pm, Saturdays after 3pm for $50) is also good. A first consultation costs US$35 or equivalent, a follow up's $20. It's 200m east (ie continuing away from Thamel) from the main Durbar Marg Palace gate.

There are a couple more convenient and slightly cheaper clinics in Thamel. Try the **Himalayan Traveller's Clinic** on the edge of Chetrapati (☎ 263170, after hours ☎ 372857) or the **Himalaya International Clinic** (☎ 225455, 223197, open 9am-5pm everyday) virtually next to the Hotel Norling in Jyatha.

With all clinics there are additional charges for medicine (if they provide it) and for lab services.

Voluntary work

The **Gift for Aid Nepal** office (☎ 259567) on Jyatha in Thamel (opposite KEEP and Kilroy's) opened in 2001 with the aim of providing tourists in Nepal with the opportunity to make a contribution to the structural improvement of Nepal's development. This can be done either with a donation or by carrying out voluntary work. There's also information on Nepalese non-profit organizations and their ongoing development projects. Visits to projects can be arranged.

TRANSPORT

By **bicycle** is a good way to get around although traffic and pollution problems get worse each year. There are lots of rental stands around Thamel. No deposit is required; you sign the book and pay the first day's rental. Be sure you check the tyres, brakes, lock and bell before you cycle off. Lock the bike whenever you leave it as you'll be held responsible for its replacement if it gets stolen. A mountain bike for a day costs Rs100-200. If you're renting for more than one day (a good idea as you can keep the bike overnight at your guest house) you can usually negotiate a lower rate. For serious mountain biking the best place is **Himalayan Mountain Bikes** (☎ 442345 🖳 www.bikeasia.info), by Northfield Café. They introduced mountain-bike tours to Nepal and pioneered most of the trails. They offer a range of tours (1-21 days) and there's a workshop in Lazimpat-Radisson Lane for servicing, bike clothing, parts, plus tour and rental bikes (US$10-15 per day for a modern bike). Bikes are also bought and sold.

A number of places in Thamel, particularly around Thahity Chowk, now rent out **motorbikes**, mostly 100-250cc Japanese bikes made under licence in India. They cost around Rs350 (for 100cc) to Rs550 (for larger bikes) per day, plus Rs30 for a helmet; a cash deposit is sometimes required, usually they simply want to know where you're staying. You're supposed to have either an international driving licence or a Nepali one.

There are lots of **taxis** around Kathmandu but it's difficult to get drivers to use their meters, especially if you pick one up in a tourist district like Thamel or Durbar Marg. You won't get away paying less than Rs150 for the ride in from the airport to the city centre although the metered fare would be about Rs120.

There are also **auto-rickshaws**, metered and costing about a third less than taxis. Kathmandu's **cycle-rickshaw** wallahs understand just how your delicate Western conscience ticks, so hard bargaining is required if you're going to pay anything like local prices. There are extensive **bus** routes around the city and out to the airport but this is a very slow and crowded transportation option.

WHAT TO SEE

A virtual living museum, the Kathmandu Valley is crammed with sights and scenes and it's well worth setting aside several days to take some of them in. The most popular attractions are mentioned below. Aimless wandering through the narrow streets also has its rewards though. Amongst the colourful confusion you'll come upon numerous temples, stupas and other holy places.

Durbar Square

First stop on the Kathmandu sightseeing trail is Durbar Square, also known as Hanuman Dhoka. This complex of ornately carved temples and monuments includes the old royal palace (closed Tuesday; entry Rs250), the Kumari Bahal (the home of the Kumari, the 'living goddess', a young girl chosen as the incarnation of the Hindu goddess, Durga), the Kasthamandap (the wooden pavilion from which the city's name is said to have been derived) and the tall Taleju temple, built in the 16th century. The best time to be here is early in the morning when people are going about their daily pujas. The authorities have recently started charging foreigners an entrance fee of Rs200 to get into the square. Whilst this has raised complaints from travellers, nobody should begrudge paying – the entire square has, after all, been declared a World Heritage Site by UNESCO and vast funds are required to restore and maintain the many buildings. Having paid the fee, visit the offices at the southern end of Durbar Square (to the west of the entrance to Freak Street, behind the souvenir market) to pick up a free **Visitor Pass**. Bring one passport photo and your passport. You can then visit Durbar Square as often as you like for free for the rest of your stay.

Swayambhunath

From this huge stupa on a hill in the west of the city, the all-seeing eyes of the Buddha overlook the entire Kathmandu Valley. It's also known as the Monkey Temple and dotted around it are several other shrines and temples. There's a pilgrims' rest house, a Buddhist library and gompa (Buddhist temple) as well as a Hindu temple dedicated to the goddess of smallpox. Behind on a smaller hill is a favourite temple for children, dedicated to Saraswati, the goddess of learning. Walking (half an hour from Thamel) or cycling through the colourful streets is the most pleasant method of reaching the hill.

Pashupatinath

Beside the sacred Bagmati River, this is one of the most revered Hindu temples on the Indian subcontinent. Entry to the main temple is barred to non-Hindus but there are numerous other shrines in this large religious complex. Dedicated to Shiva – the destroyer and creator – stone linga fertility symbols are everywhere. Cremations take place on the banks of the river, providing a morbid tourist attraction. You'll see lots of sadhus, saffron-robed holy men, who perform various feats here (including rock-lifting – with their penises no less!). Pashupatinath is on the eastern outskirts of Kathmandu, easily reached by bike or taxi.

Bodhnath (Baudha)

One of the largest stupas in the world, Bodhnath is surrounded by a thriving Tibetan community. Prayer wheels line the mandala-shaped base. These must be turned clockwise, the direction in which you should walk around the stupa. There are lots of souvenir shops as well as Tibetan restaurants and a few guest houses. Close by are a variety of Tibetan gompas. Leave a small donation when visiting.

Patan

Once a separate city-state, this ancient historical centre is now a southern suburb of Kathmandu. It's an architectural feast, at the centre of which is Durbar Square. Temples abound and it is best to explore on foot or by bicycle. The outskirts of the town are beautiful and semi-rural, the most desirable residential area for wealthy Nepalese and expatriate staff.

Bhaktapur

Compared with Kathmandu and Patan, the other cities in this mediaeval trio, time has stood still in Bhaktapur. Wandering round the narrow streets and temple-filled squares is fascinating and schoolboys act as surprisingly knowledgeable guides, though they'll want some baksheesh (Rs30 or so, though they'll try for more). Staying here overnight, especially during a festival, is well worthwhile.

It's 14km from Kathmandu and you can get here by taxi, minibus or trolley-bus. You can also cycle here although the pollution on the outskirts of the city is horrific. Hiring a mountain bike to combine with a steep ride to Nagarkot makes for an adventurous expedition.

Nagarkot
Perched on the eastern rim of the encircling hills, the Himalaya from the Annapurnas to Everest are visible from Nagarkot on a clear morning. It's a popular overnight excursion though the exploring possibilities on foot or by mountain bike warrant more time. There are plenty of cheap lodges, and buses from Bhaktapur leave every hour or so. A tourist mini-bus leaves outside the Kathmandu Immigration office at 1.30pm and early morning sunrise tours are easily arranged by travel agents or with a taxi driver. Close by is Dhulikhel, another favourite viewing spot. Just off the Arniko Highway this is also easily reached.

Dakshinkali
Sacrificial blood flows freely on Tuesdays and Saturdays for the goddess Kali at this temple. Like hungry hyenas tourists jostle to take red-splashed photos and a few turn vegetarian. It is 20km from Kathmandu, an uphill cycle ride. Alternatively, buses leave from Martyrs' Gate, just east of the GPO in Kathmandu.

SIGHTSEEING TOURS

Most hotels and travel agents can arrange custom tours. To get the most from these ensure you will be accompanied by a qualified guide. For a small group half-day guided tours cost around US$5 plus entrance fees.

Trek preparation in Kathmandu

TREKKING EQUIPMENT

Things have changed. In the late 1980s buying a pair of boots in Kathmandu meant trying on second-hand boots but now there are perhaps a hundred models of brand new lightweight boots, sandals and running shoes. The majority are made in Korea or China and the quality varies considerably: none are guaranteed. Finding tough all-leather boots or plastics still means resorting to hunting every shop for a good second-hand pair. The exception is Millet One Sports, the boots for climbing 8000m peaks, which are usually available new in most sizes.

Now quite a bit of gear is imported, especially aluminium water bottles, Swiss army knives (the full range from both manufacturers), Leathermans and Chinese copies, Petzl head torches, Maglite torches, Camp climbing gear (especially their ice axes and crampons), some of the Leki range of trekking poles and more. The vast majority of rain, fleece and down jackets and pants are locally manufactured. The quality of workmanship and materials varies enormously so look carefully and try everything on for size and fit. The majority of it is serviceable but none is up to Western standards. Much of the 'Goretex' is Korean, perhaps breathable, but not seal-sealed. A cheap down jacket will have mainly feathers instead of down so ask and feel carefully if you want a quality down sleeping bag or jacket and be prepared to pay more.

Although many shops/manufacturers have their own logo there are still numerous copies of 'The North Face' or 'Lowe Alpine', both on clothing and backpacks. All are fakes unless in rare exceptions it is second-hand gear. Ask the shop owner, most will tell you they are fakes; if they don't, shop elsewhere.

The range of gear is such that if you are not fussy about quality, colour or style you can easily outfit yourself for a trek once in Kathmandu. Readily available are daypacks, sleeping bags, down jackets, fleece jackets, pants, gloves and hats, lightweight trekking boots and not so well designed kitbags. Still better brought from home are socks, – cotton and wool – thermal tops and bottoms, large packs and your favourite accessories.

There are shops scattered about but the main concentration is in Chetrapati. Some stock new goods only but others stock a wide variety of gear, each slightly different from the other. For hard to find items it pays to ask around.

For people who appreciate good gear bring everything from home. Label freaks should also take extra money to Namche where one shop stocks lots of real Mountain Hardwear and North Face goodies as well as woolly socks and accessories and the owner is honest and knowledgeable.

Renting gear
The alternative to buying is renting. It's easy to rent down jackets and sleeping bags, and plastic boots, ice axes and crampon sets. There is a huge variety so it pays to shop around. Large deposits are required: money of any sort or valid airline tickets should be fine but credit cards should not be trusted to anyone.

ORGANIZING A GUIDED TREK IN KATHMANDU

If you're planning to organize a trek with porters, tents and a cook along a standard route to the Khumbu it's worth pointing out that the better lodges here offer a competitive standard of service. As an alternative to the full organized trek you could hire a porter-guide or porter and use the lodges and their facilities. The expedition-trekking style is, however, best suited to lightly-trekked routes, remote areas and for climbing trekking peaks.

Trekking companies in Nepal
All trekking agencies in Nepal must be owned by Nepalese nationals so foreign companies have to operate through them. A few have a Western operations manager indirectly in charge. Despite the small offices, most trekking companies are well practised at organizing treks, though a few have yet to perfect the art. Go with your instincts (do the office staff really know what they are talking about?) and try to talk to another foreigner who's been on one of the treks organized by the company before signing up. For climbing trips be especially careful, ensure you meet the guide, carefully question him about the peak and check that he is NMA-registered.

Trek personnel

A **sirdar** (trekking guide) is an organizer rather than a trained specialist of history and culture; guides as such don't exist for the trekking regions. He (virtually never she) will speak English and carry only his personal equipment. The older Sherpa sirdars are generally more knowledgeable about the region but few guides are expansive; displaying their culture is not a widely understood tourism concept.

The sirdar, who is often the leader as well when there is no foreign representative, hires and/or supervises the porters and the sherpas (who are not necessarily from the Sherpa clan, and distinguished by the lack of a capital 'S'),and is usually in charge of the money. It is therefore a powerful position and a good sirdar will ensure the trek functions in a trouble-free manner. A bad sirdar can cause endless problems. The sherpas are the sirdar's assistants, general helpers who erect and pack the tents, serve the meals and help in any way they can. They ensure nobody gets lost and carry bags if the members tire. Most speak some English. The cook is another key figure, heading a small army of kitchen helpers.

A **porter** is a load-bearer, who generally speaks little or no English. The standard trekking company load is 30-35kg/66-77lb but if you are doing the hiring then a more gentle 20-25kg/44-55lb will leave a spring in your porter's step and flexibility about the stages.

Operating independently from the above personnel there is the **porter-guide**, usually someone who is not experienced enough to be a sirdar, but speaks some English and wants to try their luck at making more than the usual paltry wage. Since few people hire only a guide, they are willing to carry your backpack, leaving you with just a daypack. By asking around you may be able to find a porter-guide in Lukla; but they are scarce in Jiri.

Yaks and **zopkios** (a sterile cross between a yak and a lowland cow) are also load-bearers and are usually used in the Khumbu instead of porters, especially by large groups. Yaks are normally used only above Namche while zopkios are to be found from Lukla and above. They carry double the load of a porter, 60-70kg/132-154lbs, for double the cost. Normally the minimum number you can hire is three, with a **yak driver** to look after them.

Costs

At present the official minimum charge for a fully organized trek (all food, tents and crew) is US$20/£13.50 per person per day, for which you get a simple yet usually adequate level of service. US$30-40/£20-27 per person per day should provide a reasonable standard of service. The top companies charge around US$35-80/£23-50 a day for slightly better food and slicker service. The cost also depends on the number of people in the trekking group: a bigger group should be significantly cheaper.

Make sure it is clear exactly what you are paying for and, more importantly, what is not included. All the wages for the crew must obviously be included, and all food plus tents, but are bus tickets, taxes and the National Park entrance fees additional? Decide also on the rates for extra days, for example if you decide to trek for longer, or if the flight is delayed. Generally you pay for what you get. If you want a high standard trek, climbing trip or real remote-area trek it is often better to deal with companies out of Thamel, the ones who organize mainly for overseas agents.

Complaints

The Ministry of Tourism is the official body to talk with. Everything has to be done in writing. Although there may be some honest staff there, you can bet there will be talk of kickbacks and some possibly strange decisions. It pays to present yourself well, be humble most of the time and respect the officials; they have a tough job. All official trekking companies are registered there and have a monetary bond lodged with the Ministry so the officials really can do something about it. They are in Bhrikuti Mandap, the tourist service centre, the same building as the Department of Immigration.

The majority of trekking companies also belong to the Trekking Agents Association of Nepal (TAAN, ☎ 427473). While there is relatively little they can actually do in a dispute, talking with TAAN can shame a company.

HIRING GUIDES AND PORTERS

When looking for a porter/porter-guide, follow your instincts. A pleasant manner is more important than fancy clothes, and in fact for porters, the older and scruffier, the more reliable. Mutual respect is important so don't be afraid to show who's boss. They are being paid comparatively well and the working conditions are less demanding than a normal porter's job. By hiring somebody you take on the responsibility of an employer. One couple who had previously hiked a lot in the Rockies said, 'It was like having a child with you'. Others find the experience rewarding and at the very least it makes getting up the hills easier.

Trekking personnel look after themselves in most situations, finding food and lodgings (and often assisting you in this task), but when it comes to snow conditions with the risk of frostbite and snow-blindness, they are notoriously naïve. Usually it is you that will have to take preventative action and pay for hired boots and jackets and sunglasses (take a spare pair) for porters.

Sexual harassment

One of the advantages of arranging your trek through a company or hiring a porter-guide is the extra security this affords. Thanks to a broad equality, the vast majority of Sherpa guides won't hassle their female clients. Most guides over about 20 years old are married and not far from home territory. In some other regions (Annapurna, in particular) some guides do hassle women trekkers and turn sour when you won't hop into bed with them.

● Insist on meeting your guide or porter-guide before you set off

● Go with your instincts. Sound out the company and guide and, if there is any hint of sleaze, be direct: 'I have a boyfriend' often works, or even better simply say 'I am not going to sleep with you'.

● Guides from the Sherpa ethnic group tend to be more reliable.

Hiring in Kathmandu

Trekking companies are happy to arrange crew but be clear what the charges include. It must include their meals: if a company suggests that you pay for the guide's food, avoid that company. Since you will be spending a great deal of time together, talk to the guide beforehand, perhaps even go out for a meal with him and, if you have doubts, ask for someone else. With porters, if they are going to high altitudes, insist on knowing the arrangements for hiring their gear, because otherwise, no matter what's agreed, once you're up there the crew often lack the right clothing and equipment.

The daily rates for guides are US$6-12/£4-8, the higher rates being the norm. Rates for porters are slightly less, normally around US$5-8/£3.50-5.50 but prices vary considerably between the many agencies. Some trekking companies exploit their employees mercilessly. The crew may often receive no more than standard wages but must hire cold-weather gear themselves and pay for food which is progressively more expensive higher up.

Hiring on the trail

At Lukla, guides, porters and porter-guides are usually easy to find. At Jiri only porters are readily available, with lodge owners often knowing who is looking for work. Families with young children or a group of women trekking together may be able to hire female staff. Independent porter-guides can be hired for an all-inclusive rate of Rs400-800 per day, though bargaining is often required. Bear in mind that for menial jobs in Kathmandu the wage is Rs1500-2500 a

---

Tipping your crew

Many good crew members are super-heroes. Take the kitchen hands: they prepare all the meals, wash the dishes afterwards until late into the evening and then, early the next morning, you will hear the roar of the stoves well before it is light as they set to work making your breakfast – after which they spend the rest of the day running between the meal stops until it's evening again! And all for around US$2.50 a day.

Similarly, porters are the equivalent of Olympic athletes. Try lifting a load sometime and imagine carrying that every day for the distance that you walk.

I feel that the trekking companies should pay more realistic wages but it isn't going to happen. Instead it has become customary for trekkers to tip their crew, and the amounts trekkers dish out really matter. The majority of crew members will take their hard-earned cash back to their family and then try living on this for months – the reality of the developing world can be scary.

Simply put, tip money is vital, and providing the crew have done a good job a tip is definitely in order. Budget something like $50 per week of trekking, and if every member puts this amount in a kitty for you (rather than the sirdar) to divide up at the end, you should have enough to give a minimum of Rs1000 per crew member. (Though if you tip more, it certainly won't be wasted.) It is normal to tip in a graduated scale with porters getting the least and the sirdar the most but there is merit in tipping the porters, sherpas and kitchen hands a similar amount, and the cook and sirdar only slightly more. After all, the cook and the sirdar are in charge of the budgets for the trek and may have already done well out of this.

month. For a real guide – someone who speaks good English and doesn't carry a load – expect to pay well over the equivalent of $10 a day.

Note that if you hire through a trekking company all staff are fully insured (though ask the company to confirm this) while those hired independently on the trail are not. Also, many people have mentioned that with hiring locally the rates are often as high as those of a Kathmandu trekking company.

MONEY FOR THE TREK

Provided you're not planning to buy a ticket at a rural airport (payment in hard currency only), it's best to take your entire budget as cash in Nepalese rupees since the only exchange facilities are at Lukla and Namche, and they may disappear too. About a quarter of the total amount should be in medium- and small-denomination notes. The most frequently used notes are Rs100 but busy lodges can usually break down Rs1000 notes. For the Arun, Makalu and Rolwaling areas it's best to have all the money you'll need for that section in denominations of Rs100 and less.

LUGGAGE STORAGE

Most hotels will store whatever you want to leave behind. Normally there's no charge if you'll be staying on your return. Things are secure, and better hotels have safety deposit boxes.

GETTING TO THE KHUMBU

By air

The popular Lukla tourist sector is flown by several airlines, including the inefficient and corrupt (but safe) state-run Royal Nepal Airlines Corporation (RNAC) and the far more reliable Yeti Airlines. So it is a question of finding who has space, a job best left to a travel agent or trekking company. It is better to book well in advance but even if you book a day before it is usually possible to find seats.

Schedules and costs Airlines quote their prices in US$ but tickets can be paid for in most hard currencies, but not Nepalese rupees.

The flight timetables and routes change frequently. The fares for different airlines for the same sector are all similar although often RNAC is cheaper. There are no early booking discounts and return fares are double one-way fares. Only double-sector flights are cheaper than adding the two single sector fares together. There is a temporary $3 insurance surcharge on most tickets. There is also a departure tax of Rs165 payable at the airport for all domestic flights. The following are some sample prices; increases are, however, expected soon.

- **Lukla** US$91 (return $182) ● **Tumlingtar** US$72 ● **Biratnagar** US$85
- **Phaplu** US$85 ● **Bhojpur** US$85 ● **Syangboche** charter helicopters only.
- **Mountain flight** US$104-109 ● **Pokhara** US$67

Nepalis (such as your trekking crew) get significantly cheaper fares (eg Lukla Rs1460 and Phaplu Rs1380) and so getting tickets for them is sometimes more difficult when the flights are nearly full as airlines refuse to take them.

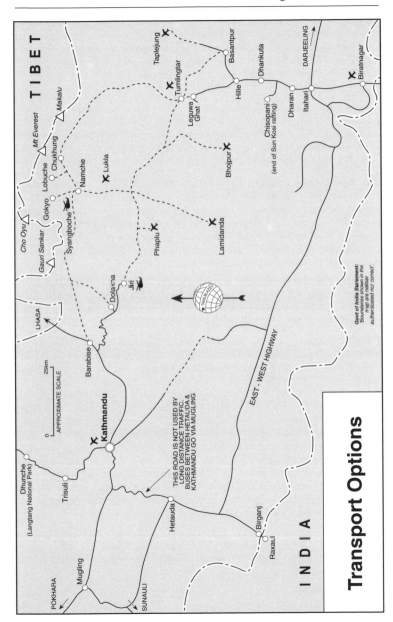

Transport Options

TIBET

Mt Everest

Makalu

Taplejung

Basantpur

Tumlingtar

Dhankuta

DARJEELING

Biratnagar

Leguwa Ghat

Hille

Chukhung

Lobuche

Namche

Lukla

Bhojpur

Chisopani
(end of Sun Kosi rating)

Dharan

Itahari

Cho Oyu

Gokyo

Syangboche

Lamidanda

Gauri Sankar

Phaplu

Dolakha

Jiri

LHASA

Barabise

Kathmandu

25km

0

APPROXIMATE SCALE

Dhunche
(Langtang National Park)

Trisuli

THIS ROAD IS NOT USED BY
LONG DISTANCE TRAFFIC.
BUSES BETWEEN HETAUDA &
KATHMANDU GO VIA MUGLING

EAST - WEST HIGHWAY

Govt of India Statement:
'Boundaries shown in the
map are neither
authenticated nor correct'.

Mugling

Hetauda

Birganj

Raxaul

POKHARA

SUNAULI

INDIA

Buying tickets at a rural airport On most flights tourists are given priority over locals. The fare must still be paid in hard currency. You are safest using US$ cash or travellers' cheques. Change and refunds are given in Nepalese rupees only. It is, of course, hard to book in advance but anyway you have at least a 90% chance of getting on a flight the next day.

By bus

Most bus rides are long and mostly uncomfortable but stops are made for meals. Roadside stalls sell biscuits, fruit, sweets and soft drinks. Restaurants serve little more than dal bhaat and are not too hygienic. It's wise to be cautious, especially at the start of your holiday. Buses for Jiri, Dolakha and Barabise still use the old central bus station near the clocktower, not the new bus station north of Thamel.

Jiri Between five and twelve buses a day leave Kathmandu's old bus station for Jiri (around US$4 with backpack, 9-12 hours) between 5.30am and 7.30am. Tickets for the first bus can be bought a day in advance; for subsequent buses you must buy your ticket on the day of departure. From Jiri the last bus leaves at around midday. You may be able to get a lift back on privately-hired transport returning to Kathmandu, which should be more comfortable than the buses. Ask around at the lodges in Jiri.

Dolakha There are three direct buses a day at 6am, 8am and 10am which leave from the old bus station in Kathmandu. Otherwise you can catch any bus heading to Jiri and get off at Charikot (US$1.50). It takes less than an hour to walk down to Dolakha from there. For the return journey buses leave at the same times.

Hille/Basantpur The road north from Dharan to Dhankuta and Hille is in the process of being extended and now goes as far as Basantpur. Kathmandu to Hille takes around 24 hours although it'll take less time when the new Eastern Highway is finished (in 2005/6). At present it's one of Nepal's more uncomfortable nightbus journeys. However, it certainly gives an interesting insight to life in the hot Terai and given the right frame of mind the ride can even be fun. There is no direct bus to Hille/Basantpur so book to Dharan (US$4, night buses only leaving Kathmandu's new bus station from 4pm), then change for Hille. It's better to book a seat a day or two ahead at the main bus station or perhaps through a travel agent, and ask for a seat near the front. Buses between Dharan and Hille leave in the mornings. An alternative route is to go to Itahari, then Dharan and Hille.

For the return journey the last bus for Dharan leaves Hille at around 2pm. The Dharan–Kathmandu bus leaves at 4pm but if you miss this catch a bus to Itahari and a connection to Kathmandu from there.

Barabise There are frequent buses leaving Kathmandu's old bus station between 5am and 4pm for Barabise (Rs30, six hours). The buses generally stop at the office on the west bank in Barabise, which is where you get tickets for the return trip to Kathmandu.

Tourist vehicles

The most pleasant way to travel is by car or van: Kathmandu–Jiri from US$80.

PART 4: THE EVEREST REGION

Mountaineering history

EVEREST

Meantime let us count our blessings – I mean those thousands of peaks, climbed and unclimbed, of every size, shape and order of difficulty, where each of us may find our own Mt Everest.

HW Tilman *Mount Everest 1938*

The search for the world's highest mountain

In 1808 the Survey of India began the daunting task of mapping the whole of the subcontinent. One of the goals was to discover if the Himalaya was indeed the highest mountain range in the world, as had previously been suspected. Already challenging, the project was made even more difficult by the fact that Nepal and Tibet, wary of foreign intervention, were closed to outsiders.

By 1830 the survey had reached the border between India and Nepal. Unable to cross into Nepal, surveyors resolved to continue the project from the plains. A baseline the length of the range was marked and in 1847 surveying of the northern peaks began, using trigonometrical calculations based on the heights and distances of known points. Conditions were terrible: malaria was rife and monsoon rain eroded the observation towers each year.

Until the mid-19th century it was thought that Kanchenjunga, in Sikkim, at about 28,000ft (8534m), was the highest peak in the range. In 1856 calculations published by the Survey of India revealed that a mountain on the border between Nepal and Tibet was higher. This mountain was designated 'Peak XV' and its height stated to be 29,002ft (8839m); Kanchenjunga was 28,156ft (8582m).

The accuracy of this first survey is astounding considering the fact that the mountains were measured from survey points from 108 to 150 miles away from the peaks. In their calculations surveyors had to take account of the earth's curvature and the changing air density, which bends light. It's a sad fact that a survey made from the same points would not be possible today. Dust and air pollution are now so bad that it's rare to be able to make out even the second foothills of the Himalaya from the plains.

The currently accepted height of Everest is just 26ft (less than 9m) higher: 8848m/ 29,028ft, from an Indian survey taken in Nepal in the 1950s. It's interesting to note that when National Geographic made their much lauded 1:50,000 map of Everest, instead of re-measuring the mountain they used its accepted height as a base for all the other altitudes on the map. Most recently an altitude of 8850m has been quoted, as measured by a sophisticated GPS system.

However, there is controversy over whether this height is that of the mountain including the hard ice on its very top or just the rock base.

The naming of Everest

It was not until 1865 that Peak XV was named. The accepted method of naming peaks at the time was to use the local name if one could be found. The first map of the area, made in the 1700s, marked this peak as **Tschoumoulancma** but the Surveyor General, Andrew Waugh, chose to name Peak XV **Mount Everest** after his predecessor, Sir George Everest, who oversaw the great survey of India.

This appropriately grand appellation stuck in the West, but Tibetans and Sherpas have always used some variation of the name used on the 18th-century map. The Dalai Lama, giving permission for the 1921 Reconnaissance Expedition, called it **Chha-mo-lung-ma**, the name adopted by the Chinese (but transliterated as Qomolangma or Chomolungma). This is also the name that the Sherpas use. Difficult to translate directly, it is usually said to mean: 'Mother Goddess of the World'. Sherpas sometimes translate it as 'Home of the Goddess of the Wind' or 'Home of the God or Goddess that Looks After Mothers'. (Makalu is said to be the home of the deity who protects daughters.)

The Nepali government's name is an even more recent creation than the English designation. They call it **Sagarmatha**, which has been variously translated as: 'Forehead Touching the Sky', 'Head in the Sky', 'Head above All Others' or 'Churning Stick of the Ocean of Existence'.

The Dalai Lama permits the first Everest expedition

Once Everest had been identified as the world's highest mountain nearly three-quarters of a century were to go by before an expedition could be set up to reach the area. The main interest was originally from the British but Nepal and Tibet were suspicious of this colonial power's intentions. Nepal already had a British Resident living in Kathmandu, installed as a permanent observer after they had lost the 1814 war to the British, and one resident foreigner was more than enough. Tibet's capital Lhasa had been a closed city for more than a century but in 1904 Francis Younghusband led a British expedition which fought its way through Tibet, killing many Tibetans, ostensibly to negotiate trade links between the two countries. For more than a decade the Dalai Lama withheld his permission for a British party to make an attempt on Everest. However, eventually he yielded to British demands and the first expedition was mounted in 1921. It was organized by the Royal Geographical Society with climbers from the Alpine Club and was followed by further attempts in 1922 and 1924.

1921 Reconnaissance expedition

The first expeditions were remarkable for a number of reasons. Many of the most promising young mountaineers had been lost in the battles of the First World War so the average age of members of the reconnaissance expedition was an almost geriatric 44. Although composed of experienced mountaineers, their experience was of European mountains half the height of Everest. Very little was known about the effects of altitude and their equipment and clothing, although the best available at the time, would seem totally inappropriate by modern standards. It was not a strong team and only six of the nine members reached the base of the mountain after the long walk from Sikkim.

A major figure in the first expeditions was George Mallory. With his mountaineering partner, Bullock, he first spent a tough month exploring the area to find the easiest access to the mountain, the hidden East Rongbuk Glacier. It was immediately obvious that summer, the monsoon period, was not the most favourable time for climbing. But despite this and their appalling equipment, three Sherpas and three climbers reached the North Col, 6990m/23,000ft. By the end of the expedition a thorough exploration of the Tibetan side of the Everest Massif had been made, and Mallory had even peered into the Western Cwm, as he named it, from the Lho La.

Frozen spaghetti on the 1922 expedition

The 1922 expedition, led by Brigadier-General Bruce, arrived before the monsoon and boasted a 13-member team (including a film crew) and rather superior food supplies. As well as champagne and caviar there were tins of Heinz spaghetti which, like most of the other foodstuffs, froze solid at the higher camps.

They may have been better fed but the team members were still woefully under-clothed. A famous picture of Mallory and Norton, high on the mountain, shows them dressed in wool trousers and jackets with little room for more than a jersey or two and longjohns under this. They sported medium brimmed hats and, aside from the goggles, ice axes and rope, would not have looked out of place strolling in an English park on a winter's morning.

A series of camps was established. Camp IV was set up on the North Col and the primitive Camp V at a height of over 7600m/25,000ft. Although experience showed that this was too low for a serious attempt on the summit, the first attempt was launched from here. Nevertheless, Mallory, Norton and Somervell reached a height of 8150m/26,800ft without oxygen, before descending, all slightly frostbitten.

The second attempt was by Finch, accompanied by Bruce's son. Spurred on by hot tea and the discovery that using oxygen at night aided warmth and sleep, they climbed to 8320m/27,300ft. For Bruce this must have been especially satisfying since this was his first climbing trip. It was also the first time that oxygen had been used on Everest and some members of the group were very much against it, maintaining that its use was most unsporting.

The third attempt ended prematurely, 200m below the North Col with a fatal avalanche. Nine Sherpas were caught and seven of them killed. The Everest toll had begun.

'Because it's there' – the 1924 expedition

It is immaterial whether or not George Mallory coined the immortal phrase: 'Because it's there', when asked in 1923 why anyone would want to climb Everest; it's for his pioneering contribution towards its conquest that he should be remembered; the fateful 1924 expedition was to be his last.

Team members were still inadequately clothed; they had no down clothing. Each climber was given an allowance of £50 to kit himself out. Norton boasted windproof overalls and a leather, fur-lined motorcycle helmet plus the usual all-too-thin layers, hardly sufficient against temperatures as low as -40°C (-40°F).

Early storms battered the group forcing them to retreat to Rongbuk Monastery. Here they received the Lama's blessing which they'd imprudently not bothered to seek out when they'd first arrived in the area. The freak weather patterns held up stocks of oxygen sets, leading to a shortage at Camp IV on the col; despite this, Camp V was established. Camp VI was set at an altitude of 8170m/26,800ft, with Norton and Somervell staying there overnight. They set off early the next morning but Somervell was overcome by a serious coughing attack. He had developed frostbite in his throat and almost choked on a lump of his own frostbitten flesh which he later coughed up, giving him much relief. Norton was forced to struggle on alone and, labouring up steep ground covered with powder snow, reached a record altitude of 8570m/28,126ft, a phenomenal achievement. One has to wonder how much further Norton would have been able to climb if he had had an oxygen set.

That evening, with Norton suffering from snow-blindness and Somervell also out of action, Mallory chose the young and relatively inexperienced Irvine to accompany him the next day. Odell, who was older and more acclimatized might, in fact, have been a better choice. Sherpas climbed with Mallory and Irvine up to Camp VI, returning to report that apart from a stove rolling off the mountain, all was well.

Next morning the weather was not perfect, and it is assumed that Mallory and Irvine left after sunrise since they left their torch and magnesium flares behind. Behind them, Odell climbed from Camp V to Camp VI studying the geology of the rocks along the way, and through a brief hole in the clouds saw the two climbers ascend a step. Initially he was inclined to think it was the second step before the summit but later suffered doubts.

This was around 1pm so the climbers were far behind their schedule: Mallory had intended to be at the second step by 8am. A snow storm blew up and then cleared two hours later leaving the ridge and the summit cone fully visible but there was no sign of Mallory or Irvine. The night was also clear and a watch was kept on the ridge to the summit. However, they were never to be seen alive again.

Their disappearance began endless conjecture as to whether or not they reached the summit before they died. Subsequent climbers have remarked that Odell's description of where he saw them fits the third and final step better than the second; climbers are still easily visible at that point. If this were the case Mallory and Irvine quite possibly made the summit. To the day he died Odell wasn't sure which step he saw them on but thought it likely that they attained the summit.

Telephones on Everest – the 1933 expedition

It was not until 1933 that another attempt was made. This boasted technical innovations: radio and, from Camp III to Camp IV, a telephone line. It was a strong team but bad weather interrupted the process of setting up intermediate camps, putting the expedition behind schedule. Nevertheless, they equalled Norton's altitude record, climbing without supplementary oxygen on bad snow.

British institutions like the Royal Geographical Society and the Alpine Club considered Everest their own preserve, jealously guarding it from attempts by outsiders. They were not amused, therefore, by the announcement, in 1933, by the wealthy adventurer, Maurice Wilson, that he would climb Everest alone. He bought a light aircraft and flew himself from Britain to India. Despite having no previous climbing experience he managed to get as far as the North Col before succumbing to the cold. His body was found by the next group of climbers.

The 1935 Reconnaissance expedition
Led by Eric Shipton, this was the first of several expeditions to be headed by this famous explorer-mountaineer. He preferred to travel light, living off the land, which was a major departure from the normal expedition approach. Since eggs were the most accessible source of protein they regularly appeared on the expedition menu, and Shipton notes that 'though many of them were rather stale we consumed enormous quantities. Our record was 140 in a single day between four of us, and many times our combined party of seven put away more than a hundred.' (*Upon that Mountain*).

One of the Sherpas Shipton took with him was an enthusiastic nineteen-year-old named Tenzing Bhotia (later Norgay), who proved to be ambitious and strong. Amongst the other team members was Dan Bryant, a cheerful Kiwi. The expedition had instructions not to climb Everest but the monsoon broke late so there would, in fact, have been time for a serious attempt that season. It was, however, a surprisingly successful climbing expedition in other respects, with an impressive total of 26 peaks over 6095m/20,000ft climbed by the seven-man group, and all for a total cost of a mere £1500.

The finding of Mallory's body
In May 1999, a season of exceptionally little snow, an expedition dedicated to researching the Mallory-Irvine mystery found Mallory's body, intact and in an amazingly preserved condition, high up on Chomolungma on the Tibetan side. Intriguingly, one of Mallory's or Irvine's oxygen bottles was found at a point higher than the fall, indicating that Mallory, at least, was returning from a higher point. It is also significant that the clip for his oxygen mask was found in his pocket, indicating that he had taken it off, either because of a malfunction or, more likely, because he had used up all his oxygen, a supply of 8-11 hours.

Also intriguingly, one of the climbers of the 1975 Chinese expedition reported finding a body with a hole in the cheek, which could only have been Mallory or Irvine. Mallory's body was discovered further away from this reported location than would have been expected and his cheeks were not damaged. No more is known because the Chinese climber who told this to one member of the Japanese Women's Everest Expedition died the next day.

The search for Irvine's body continues and there is still not enough information to confirm whether or not they did actually summit.

Monsoon stops play

The following year the 1936 Everest attempt, for which the 1935 expedition had been preparing the way, was unfortunately washed out by the early arrival of the monsoon. Then came a low-budget expedition in 1938 led by HW Tilman (recounted in his *Mount Everest 1938*). Having learnt lessons about the monsoon from previous expeditions, they arrived early but to no avail. The monsoon broke three weeks earlier than it ever had previously. Still, they continued, even trying a different route, until worsening snow conditions for the last 1000m forced them to retreat.

Nepal at last

In 1948 the Kingdom of Nepal for the first time opened its doors a crack, though only to parties interested in scientific research. Tilman was not a scientist (he claimed that he 'had hitherto refused to mingle art with science') but he compromised his principles and squeezed in a year later. He was allocated the Langtang area, which to his delight was marked 'unsurveyed' on his map. Later he was lucky enough to be invited to visit Namche, walking in from Dharan via the Arun River. As part of this trip he made the first ascent by a foreigner of the now famous Kala Pattar.

The 1951 Reconnaissance Expedition

After the Chinese invasion of Tibet the northern route to Everest was sealed off with the closure of the border. An expedition, led by Shipton, was dispatched to reconnoitre an alternative, southern route through newly-opened Nepal. Although Shipton had turned down many suitable applicants for the team in Britain, recalling instead New Zealander Dan Bryant from the 1935 Expedition, in a moment of weakness he accepted a request from the NZ Alpine Club for two unnamed climbers to join the team. They were George Lowe and Edmund Hillary. It was to be the first time that a party had climbed after the monsoon, the traditional season being in the 'lull before the storm'. They arrived in Namche at the end of September and climbed to the Western Cwm. In spite of the danger from the Khumbu Icefall it was clear that the south side route up Everest was indeed feasible.

1952 – the competition closes in

Time was running out for the British and what they arrogantly considered their exclusive 'right' to the area. In 1950 the first 'eight-thousander' (8000m peak), Annapurna, had been conquered by the French. After the British 1951 Reconnaissance Expedition to the Khumbu, there came an unwelcome piece of news: the Swiss had been given permission to make an attempt on Everest in 1952 and the British would have to wait until the following year. A French attempt was scheduled for 1954. Surprisingly, the Swiss almost agreed to a joint Anglo-Swiss expedition (obviously wanting to make use of Shipton's wide experience of the mountain) but the details could not be worked out to everyone's satisfaction. The Swiss chose Tenzing Norgay as their sirdar. He held them in high esteem because it was with two of the Swiss expedition members that he had successfully climbed a peak in 1947, his first despite 12 years climbing with expeditions.

The trek to Base Camp took 23 days from the newly-opened airfield in Kathmandu. They established five camps between Gorak Shep and the head of the Western Cwm and conclusively proved that it was a feasible route. Tenzing and Lambert climbed to just below the south summit but could go no further. It was realized that an additional camp and further logistical support were needed for an attempt to succeed. Their second attempt after the monsoon was dogged by bad luck, bad planning and the ferocious high-altitude winter winds.

Preparations for the 1953 British Everest Expedition

The Swiss attempts gave the British a chance to prepare properly. Training included an expedition to Cho Oyu in 1952, led by Shipton. Although they failed to reach the summit (see p120), the expedition was of great value: as a result important refinements were made to oxygen sets and clothing.

In planning the 1953 expedition internal politics played a large part. Though Shipton had led many previous expeditions and had immense popularity with the public, some members of the Alpine Club committee felt that he might not be the right man to lead an expedition of such size and under such pressure. This would surely be the final chance for them to reach the summit first. Diplomatic to the last, Shipton agreed that he was indeed happiest climbing with the minimum of encumbering resources and it was decided that John Hunt, an army officer, should lead the expedition which would be run on military lines. Strangely, most of the committee had never met Hunt, and he had been turned down for the 1935 Everest expedition for reasons of health.

'We knocked the bastard off!' – success in 1953

The 1953 expedition was an all-out assault. It was decided that oxygen was to be used to the limit of its advantages, for aiding sleep and climbing – anything to conquer. With all this equipment the walk-in was on a grand scale: the first of two groups of porters numbered some 350 people. Since the only currency accepted in the hills at the time was silver coins it took several porters just to carry the wages. There were 13 climbers, with Tenzing Norgay added to the climbing ranks, plus a reporter and cameraman.

The team spent two weeks climbing in the Khumbu area to aid acclimatization before tackling the Icefall. It was while forging a route through this mon-

Tenzing Norgay was Tibetan
Throughout his life Sherpa Tenzing was coy about where he was brought up. It turns out he was Tibetan, only briefly spending time in Thame, Nepal. The reason for the cover-up was that he had no passport and with the backing of Prime Minister Nehru, it was the Indians who gave him one, much to the annoyance of the Nepali authorities who would have loved to claim him as their own. Either way, neither country wanted to hand a propaganda coup to the Chinese, who had recently invaded Tibet.

strous obstacle that Hillary and Tenzing first got to know each other and Tenzing demonstrated that he could match the very competitive Hillary. Once the camps in the Western Cwm were established sickness took its toll, setting back the schedules. However, after a 13-day struggle, Camp VIII on the South Col was established. Evans and Bourdillon made the first summit attempt from this camp although it was clearly too far away to allow a safe return if they did succeed. In the event snow conditions deteriorated and one of the oxygen sets caused problems, so the climbers settled for the south summit. This was less than 100m/328ft below the real summit, but at that altitude, even with oxygen, the climbers estimated it to be three hours away.

The second assault was better planned. A higher camp, Camp IX, was established and Hillary and Tenzing rested here for the night, drinking quantities of hot lemon and even eating a little. At 6.30am on 29 May, they began the climb. They reached the south summit by 9am, and the snow conditions past this first critical point were good. What is now known as the 'Hillary Step', a 13m/43ft barrier, was overcome by chimneying up a gap between a cornice and the rock wall, a dangerous but necessary move. The summit, only a short distance away, was reached at 11.30am. In the words of Hillary:

I looked at Tenzing and in spite of the balaclava, goggles and oxygen mask all encrusted with long icicles that concealed his face, there was no disguising his infectious grin of pure delight as he looked all around him. We shook hands and then Tenzing threw his arm around my shoulders and we thumped each other on the back until we were almost breathless.   John Hunt *The Ascent of Everest*

By evening they had struggled down to the South Col where Hillary told his team mate: 'Well, George, we knocked the bastard off' – though this was not exactly what was printed in the press at the time!

Chinese attempts on Everest

The pressure bubble burst with the success of the British expedition. It was some time before further attempts were considered as now the other unclimbed 'eight-thousanders' commanded attention. The Swiss climbed Everest after their conquest of Lhotse in 1956. In 1960 the Indians came close to success and at the same time the Chinese attempted the pre-war route via Tibet. It was a mammoth affair, mounted on a grander scale than any previous attempt. Success was announced but no photos could be produced and the expedition account, after being suitably embellished by the propaganda department, made entertaining reading but was inconsistent with the mountaineering thinking of the time. We join them on the second step on a four-metre wall:

Each one made several attempts but fell back each time. They looked at each other for inspiration. Time was marching on mercilessly, and according to the weather-station forecast, it was the last day of the fine weather period ... Then Liu Lien-man had an idea that the 'courte echell' (short ladder) technique might help, so crouching down he offered his companion a leg-up. Ignoring the biting cold and the danger of freezing, Chu Ying-hua took off his high-altitude boots and his eider-down stockings to make the climb easier.... It had taken them five full hours to overcome this obstacle ... dusk came and an icy wind howled dolefully. The three members of the Communist Party of China, Wang Fu-chou, Chu Ying-hua and Liu Lien-man, discussed the situation and it was decided to leave Liu Lien-man behind and press on.   *Mountaineering in China* (People's Physical Culture Publishing House)

They claimed to have left a plaster bust of Chairman Mao Tse-tung near the summit. Although at the time the attempt was ridiculed by the Western media (this was during the Cold War) it's now considered that the expedition did succeed in reaching the summit.

Sydney Wignall, in his book *Spy on the Roof of the World*, suggests another reason for the attempt. In 1955 he gained permission to climb Nalkanbar, on Nepal's far western border with Tibet. In fact they planned to make a clandestine attempt on Gurla Mandhata, 7800m. They made the mistake of confiding in Tibetan traders, whom they later found out could only cross the border with a Chinese spy among them, who ensured they said only good, entirely fictitious things about the invaders. They were soon caught and taken to Taklakot, where they were interrogated for two months.

In desperation to please his captors, Sydney told them that Hillary and Tenzing had placed a sort of nuclear-powered radar capable of seeing all the way across Tibet to Lop Nor (where, unbeknown to him, the Chinese were developing their first nuclear weapon). Among his interrogators was the General in charge of Tibet. He appeared technologically naive. Later, after a diplomatic hiatus they were released but were only allowed to return over a route known to be impossible in winter. Much to the dismay of the Chinese the

---

✦ Conquering the world's top 20 peaks
The world's 20 highest mountains were almost all climbed in a relatively short span of frenetic mountaineering activity between 1950 and 1960.

1 Everest/Sagarmatha/Chomolungma	8848m	29,028ft	1953
2 K2 (Pakistan/China)	8611m	28,251ft	1954
3 Kanchenjunga (Nepal/India)	8586m	28,169ft	1955
4 Lhotse (Nepal/Tibet)	8501m	27,890ft	1956
5 Makalu (Nepal/Tibet)	8463m	27,765ft	1955
6 Cho Oyu (Nepal/Tibet)	8201m	26,906ft	1954
7 Dhaulagiri (Nepal)	8167m	26,794ft	1960
8 Manaslu (Nepal	8156m	26,758ft	1956
9 Nanga Parbat (Pakistan)	8126m	26,660ft	1953
10 Annapurna (Nepal)	8091m	26,545ft	1950
11 Gasherbrum I (Pakistan/China)	8068m	26,470ft	1958
12 Broad Peak (Pakistan/China)	8047m	26,401ft	1957
13 Gasherbrum II (Pakistan/China)	8035m	26,261ft	1956
14 Shishapangma (Tibet)	8027m	26,335ft	1964
15 Gasherbrum III (Pakistan/China)	7952m	26,089ft	1975
16 Gyachung Kang I (Nepal/Tibet)	7952m	26,089ft	1964
17 Annapurna II (Nepal)	7937m	26,040ft	1960
18 Gasherbrum IV (Pakistan/China)	7925m	26,001ft	1958
19 Himalchuli I (Nepal)	7893m	25,896ft	1960
20 Distaghil Sar I (Pakistan)	7885m	25,869ft	1960

mountaineers succeeded in returning; as a result it was proved the Chinese had been lying since they had announced that they had released them a month earlier in a different region. Sydney brought valuable information out, which unfortunately was ignored by India: the Chinese invasion of Indian Aksai Chin (Ladakh) should not have been a surprise at all.

There were rumours of another Chinese attempt in 1966 in which 24 climbers died but Chinese officials refused to discuss the incident. In 1969 it was claimed that three surveyors reached the summit without oxygen or additional support; and in 1975 another Chinese team was said to have reached the summit. Proof of their success was found by Doug Scott and Dougal Haston of the 1975 British South-West Face Expedition. On the summit they came upon a red Chinese tripod.

1996: The best guides or not, Everest is still the limit

In 1996 some high profile deaths and some surprising survival stories put Everest in the world headlines again. Rob Hall, a Kiwi guide who had summitted Everest three times previously, and Scott Fisher, who had summitted previously without oxygen, were the respective leaders of two commercial groups of climbers. Due to some bickering between the climbing sirdars ropes up the Hillary step were fixed late, creating a bottleneck. Then, unheralded, a light storm caught the late climbers unaware. A group made it down to the 8000m South Col, only to lose the way, forcing them to spend the night huddling together for their lives. In a brief early morning clearing a few struggled into camp. Rescuers dragged a couple more climbers back but left Beck Weathers and Yakuso Namba, who were badly frost-bitten and barely alive, to die.

Amazingly, in the morning Beck suddenly awoke and staggered into camp. After a heroic rescue effort including a 6000m helicopter landing, he survived losing a hand, fingers and his nose to frostbite. Yakuso died on the col.

Meanwhile, higher up the mountain a similar struggle was happening. Rob Hall and Andy Harris, New Zealand guides, valiantly struggled with Doug Hansen on his second attempt at the mountain with Rob Hall and Adventure Consultants. By morning only Hall was left, and he knew he was in deep trouble. By the wonders of modern communications he was able to talk with his wife in New Zealand, seven months pregnant. Jan had climbed Everest with Rob previously and immediately understood that death was clawing at her partner's back. Two sherpas attempted a rescue in bone-chilling conditions and climbed to 200 vertical metres below Hall before being driven back. Hall, by this stage was badly frost-bitten and even oxygen and dexamethasone weren't enough. He died by the south summit.

Scott Fisher and a reckless Taiwanese, 'Makalu' Gau, made it further down the ridge to approximately 400 vertical metres above the South Col before giving up. When sherpas found them the next morning, although both were alive, only Gau revived. The sherpas, who could only manage one person at this altitude, had to leave Fisher to die.

The deaths may have shocked the world but in fact that season climbers got off relatively lightly, as John Krakauer in *Into Thin Air*, his first hand account of the disaster, points out. Historically approximately one in four summiteers had died, whereas in 1996 only one in approximately seven summiteers died.

Recent attempts on Everest

More than a thousand mountaineers have now stood on the summit of Everest and it continues to attract attention. In 1970 an intrepid Japanese adventurer skied part of the way down using a parachute to slow himself and in 1988 Frenchman Jean-Marc Boivin jumped off the summit with a paraglider. New routes have been climbed, such as the south-west face in 1975 and the west ridge from Lho La. Different mountaineering methods have been applied and in 1978 Reinhold Messner and Peter Habeler reached the summit without the use of bottled oxygen, the first to do so. Messner went on to make a successful solo climb without oxygen in 1980 and has since soloed all 14 of the world's 'eight-thousanders'. Recently Hans Klammerlander repeated Messner's climb solo from 6400m to the top in a staggering 17 hours, and without oxygen. Partly using skis, he managed to return to his high base camp in less than 24 hours total. However, the first all ski descent was made by Davo Karnicar in autumn 2000 and six months later in 2001 Marco Siffredi snowboarded from the summit in impressive style, jumping rocks and carving slopes that climbers use ropes on.

As of 2002 the record for the most successes on Everest was Appa Sherpa, who has summitted an amazing 12 times, two more than Ang Rita Sherpa's and Babu Chiri's 10 times.

Sadly Babu Chiri died falling into a crevasse while photographing around Camp Two on the Nepal side in May 2001. He was the first Sherpa to break out of the high altitude guide/porter mould, being a Mountain Hardwear-sponsored climber and having set records for spending the night (21 hours) on top of Everest and climbing from Base Camp to the summit in under 16 hours (!). Self assured and on the point of what could be called 'tubby', he occasionally delighted in teasing Western notions of what one of the greatest Sherpa mountaineers should look like, asking people what they thought he did. Until his picture was splashed around the world, few people would believe on sight this heavy man was the fastest high-altitude climber in the world.

Walt Unsworth's book, *Everest,* and Peter Gillman's similarly-titled book are highly recommended for more information on the history of climbs on the mountain.

The Everest industry

During the main season, counting both sides of the mountain, there will be approximately 600 people camping, around 200 people attempting the climb and some 1000 plus tents on the mountain at any one time, not to mention fax machines, computers, satellite phones and cappuccino machines. Historically approximately 10% of climbers attempting the mountain actually succeed, although with the advent of commercial expeditions this ratio is increasing.

CHO OYU (8201m/26,906ft)

The name Cho Oyu is almost certainly Tibetan in origin and is transliterated in several ways. My favourite is Chomo Yu which means 'Goddess of Turquoise', the colour the mountain often assumes at sunset when viewed from the Tibetan side.

The 1952 British attempt

In 1952, while the Swiss were attempting Everest, Eric Shipton led a British expedition to Cho Oyu. They failed to reach the top probably because Shipton was unwilling to build a supply line up the mountain on the Tibetan side. Tibet was now in the hands of the Communist Chinese and Shipton was wary of doing anything that might jeopardize the planned 1953 Everest Expedition. In 1951 he'd been caught by the Tibetans on the wrong side of the border. Quite prepared to hand over everything he possessed (Rs1200) when they brandished their swords and demanded a ransom, he was soon amused to discover that his ever-faithful Sherpas had bargained the final sum down to a mere Rs7!

Herbert Tichy's style of mountaineering

An Austrian attempt on Cho Oyu was launched in 1954, led by Herbert Tichy. The decision to climb was made on the spur of the moment after a conversation with a Sherpa, before Tichy had even seen the peak. The team consisted of three Austrians and seven high-altitude Sherpas but their prospects did not look good. One of the Austrians had previously been shot through the lung, another suffered severely from sciatica and Tichy admitted to smoking a lot and drinking 'without reluctance'. In addition, the attempt was launched after the monsoon, without oxygen, with little equipment and less than Rs1000-worth of food. At that stage in the history of Himalayan mountaineering, success had occurred only on well-equipped pre-monsoon expeditions.

On the walk in, Tichy soon noticed that changes were afoot in the area: 'We followed in the tracks of other expeditions – notably Everest expeditions. They had rubbed off the bloom which I was still able to enjoy in the west of Nepal the year before: they had also spoilt the market (four eggs for a rupee instead of ten) and the villagers treated us with that mixture of interest and condescension people bestow on a travelling circus' (*Cho Oyu by Favour of the Gods*).

Tichy's relaxed approach to climbing left much time for merry-making with friends in the Khumbu. On one such occasion he notes that the Sherpa porters had done full justice to the parting from their friends and their families and when 'we overtook our proud array we saw that some of our Sherpanis were so drunk that their male companions had to carry them and their loads as well. This predicament was taken as a great joke' (*Cho Oyu by Favour of the Gods*).

1954 – Austrian success

The walk up to Base Camp, slightly north of the Nangpa La (just inside Tibet), was accomplished with only 27 porters. Camp IV was established at 6980m/22,900ft, ten days from Base Camp, but then disaster struck. In savage winds with the temperature below -35°C Tichy made a desperate dive to save one of their tents and suffered frostbite on his fingers. The climb had to be temporarily abandoned. Nevertheless nine days later he and his companions set off again, spurred on by meeting a Swiss expedition that had been rebuffed by Gauri Sankar and had just arrived with the similar intention of attempting Cho Oyu. A storm pinned the Austrians down for two days before they could return to Camp IV. However, on the following day, 19th October 1954, Tichy, Sepp Jochler and Pasang Lama made the summit.

For Pasang Lama the ascent was all the more remarkable, indeed the stuff of legends. Having returned to Namche to pick up more supplies, at Marulung (4150m/13,615ft), a day's walk from Namche, he heard of the Swiss plans and so raced, heavily loaded, in a day up to Base Camp. Then, even more remarkably, the next day he ascended with a load to Camp IV and on the following day climbed to the summit.

MAKALU (8475m/27,805ft)

British/American 1954 Expedition

In the line-up for attempts on Everest, the French had been allotted the year following the British. The same order was established for Makalu (8475m/27,805ft), with the British and Americans given permission for the spring of 1954 and the French scheduled to follow them. The French were naturally not keen to follow in the wake of a British success (as on Everest) and the results were anxiously awaited. With a strong team that included Hillary, it looked as if success on Makalu was likely. However, the summit was not reached. Interestingly the expedition took approximately 250 porters over the Mingbo La, West Col and East Col to Makalu Base Camp.

1955 – French success

The French were spurred into action with an autumn reconnaissance and gear-testing trip. Chomo Lonzo (7790m/25,557ft), just inside Tibet, and Makalu II (7640m/25,065ft) were both climbed from the Nepalese side.

The 1955 attempt was a classic assault of the mountain, superbly organized, kitted with the best of equipment and conducted as if the pride of the country was at stake. They were prepared for the worst and ready to make repeated attempts. However, perfect weather allowed all the expedition members, as well as some of the Sherpas, to reach the summit of Makalu between 15 and 17 May. Now around 100 foreign mountaineers pass through Tashigoan to attempt Makalu, Makalu II, Baruntse or Chamalang each year.

LHOTSE (8501m/27,890ft)

Lhotse was so named by one of the British expeditions in the 1920s; no local name for it could be found. It is Tibetan for 'South Peak' and Lhotse Shar is the south-east peak of Everest.

The 1956 Swiss Expedition

In the spring of 1952 the Swiss had climbed to 250m/820ft below the summit of Everest before being forced back. In 1956 an expedition was mounted with permission for Lhotse (at that stage the highest unclimbed mountain) as well as Everest. It was a very well planned and provisioned expedition and the team worked well together. A cautious acclimatization programme was followed, with many rest days at Tengboche and Pheriche. It's interesting to note that in an effort to make the route through the Icefall safer, explosives were used!

Success came on 18 May, when Ernst Reiss and Fritz Luchsinger, using oxygen, fought their way up the steep slopes in unsettled weather to the summit. The second goal was also attained and four climbers reached the summit of Everest on the same expedition.

The people

THE SHERPAS

Years of living in their villages left me well aware that Sherpas are no more strangers to greed, pride, love of power, jealousy or pettiness than other mortals. They seem still, for all the close familiarity, a singularly appealing people.
Stanley Stevens *Cultural Ecology and History in Highland Nepal* (Univ of California)

The mountaineering exploits of the Sherpas on foreign expeditions since the 1920s brought them clearly into the world spotlight. Sherpa Tenzing's conquest, with Hillary, of Everest in 1953 was a fitting tribute to the part played by Sherpas in the history of mountaineering, not just in the Khumbu but in many parts of the Himalaya. Although the lure of Everest has brought crowds of foreigners to their land, they seem to have weathered the cultural invasion surprisingly well. Theirs is an ancient culture which Westerners have learnt to respect, indeed admire, for its tolerance, comradeship and many other positive values.

Origins
Shar-pa is Tibetan for 'Eastern People' and the first Sherpas were almost certainly migrants from 1300km away in Kham (north-east Tibet) possibly fleeing from Mongol incursions. It's thought that they tried settling in a number of places en route but were consistently driven on, crossing the Himalaya about 500 years ago over Nangpa La. Migration occurred in several successive waves with large numbers of people arriving in the late 1800s and early 1900s and another major migration in the 1960s after the Chinese invasion of Tibet. Settlements first appeared in the mid-1500s on both sides of Lamjura La (Junbesi and north of Kenja), where Sherpas still live today. The Thame and Pangboche gompas were established later, possibly during the 1670s, though it's likely that the area had been populated previously. It's thought that the Khumbu was used for pastures by Rai shepherds before the Sherpas arrived; the Dudh Kosi is known as 'Khambu' by Rais today. The Sherpas have always considered the Khumbu a Beyul or hidden valley, free from the troubles of the outside world.

A year in the Khumbu

Many trekkers have mistakenly come away with the impression that Sherpas don't seem to do anything in the Khumbu apart from looking after trekkers. This is not the case. The Sherpa calendar of activities is governed entirely by the seasons with a short cultivation period. It's most fortunate that the main trekking season occurs at the end of the harvest.

● **April-May** After the fields have been prepared, the potatoes are planted, followed by barley and buckwheat. These are labour-intensive activities.

● **May-June** Traditionally, this is a time of trading. The high passes to Tibet are open for a short while after the winter snows have melted and before the snows of the monsoon arrive. It's also the season of yak-shearing and calving.

● **June-July** The fields are weeded: a laborious job that may have to be done several times.

● **June-September** After calving, the yaks and naks are herded up to the high summer pastures to protect the crops and save the grass lower down for the spring. Summer is the time of butter, cheese and curd production.

● **September-October** These are the busiest months. At the high pastures hay is cut, while in the villages the potatoes are dug up and the barley and buckwheat harvested and threshed. Once this is completed the cattle can return to the villages. It's also the breeding season for cattle and the beginning of the trekking season.

● **November-March** The long, cold winter months are filled with spinning and weaving, collecting firewood and feeding the animals by hand. It's also a time for trading, not only with Tibet, but also Kathmandu and trips to the capital are also made to beat the cold and visit friends. Losar, the Tibetan New Year which usually occurs in February, is the main festival.

Agriculture

The crop with the highest yield in the Khumbu is the humble potato and about 75% of the cultivated area is planted with them. Growing enough, however, is not easy and most families have always supplemented their income, originally by trading with Tibet and now mainly through tourism. Their agricultural methods are quite sophisticated even though their tools may be primitive. Land holdings are scattered and several crop varieties are used in order to minimize the risk of blight and other diseases. The soil is not naturally very fertile but large quantities of organic fertiliser (compost, human waste and animal manure) have worked well, according to soil scientists. Women and children do much of the work but the roles aren't rigidly defined. Up until the 1950s all ploughing was done by hand with four men to a plough but now animals are used. The men tend to the animals and are also occupied with trade, often leaving their wives to manage the entire affairs of the household.

The Sherpas of Pharak and Solu live at lower altitudes and the milder climate enables them to grow a wider range of crops. In Junbesi, many of the vegetables served to trekkers are grown locally. Apples thrive in this area and apple pies and jams are on every lodge menu. Yaks, naks (female yaks) and crossbreeds are kept high in the mountains away from the villages. Their milk that was once made into butter and traded with Tibet to keep the monastery lamps burning is now sold to local cheese factories. Sherpa trade in this area is now mainly with passing trekkers.

Diet

As one might expect, potatoes are eaten at almost every meal, although the well-off also eat rice. Potatoes are usually boiled and once they've been peeled (the skin is never eaten) they're dipped in salt and a chilli sauce. Savoury pancakes, made from a mixture of buckwheat (the non-sweet variety) and grated potatoes, are eaten with butter and chillies. However, the great Sherpa favourite is shakpa, a thick soup made with whatever comes to hand – usually potatoes (!), a few other vegetables and sometimes chewy balls of wheat flour.

With potatoes being a staple, it's not surprising that the Sherpas are connoisseurs of the varieties that are suited to the Khumbu. Trekkers also consume huge quantities of potatoes, not because there are no alternatives on the menu but because they're surprisingly tasty. If you show an interest, the lodge owner may show you the different types. The highest yielding variety (commonly served to trekkers) is not considered quite as tasty as some of the older types.

The Sherpa diet is fairly healthy. Naks and dzums (a yak/cow crossbreed) provide dairy products and meat is occasionally eaten, dried or fresh. In the past the diet lacked only iodine, a deficiency of which causes goitres and cretinism. The situation was quickly solved by the first doctor at Khunde hospital. Now the majority of salt in Nepal, instead of coming from Tibet, is naturally iodised sea-salt from India.

The Sherpa house

Unlike the Tibetan house, which is flat-roofed and built around a courtyard, the Sherpa house features a roof adapted for the monsoon rains and has no courtyard. Although it does bear a superficial resemblance to the Tibetan house, the Tibetan architectural style is reserved for gompas.

The size of a house is a sign of prosperity. In the Rolwaling there are still many single-storied houses, whereas in wealthy Namche there are now even some four-storey hotel 'sky-scrapers'. However, the majority of Sherpa houses consist of two levels. The ground floor is for stabling cattle and is a storage area for grain, animal fodder, firewood and tools. It's also where the *chang* (home-brew made from rice or barley) is fermented. The upper level of the house is usually an open living-room, sometimes with the kitchen partitioned off.

Roofs are made of slate or wood, though slates are now being replaced by corrugated iron sheets. Walls are usually stone with huge wooden beams running between them to support the floor. In some of the older houses, the beams can be up to 25 metres long which gives some idea of the size of the trees in the forests that once covered this area of the Himalaya.

The layout of the interior is dictated by tradition. The west wall is for a shrine with Buddha images, candles or butter lamps and pictures of the Dalai Lama and the King and Queen of Nepal. Beneath the sunny south-facing windows are long benches, often covered with thick Tibetan rugs. The south-east corner is for the master bed, usually the only bed, in which the whole family sleeps. If there are visitors for the night, they sleep on the carpeted bench seats. The sunless north wall is windowless and lined with shelves displaying the valuable kitchen-ware. The long tea-churn for making salt-butter tea should always be near the stairway. Many tea-churns are cherished family heirlooms, passed down from generation to generation.

The Sherpa view of life

Most Sherpas are followers of the Nyingmapa ('Red Hat') sect of Tibetan Buddhism, the most ancient and least reformed of the four major Tibetan sects. It developed out of the Tantric practices introduced by the Indian Padmasambhava (Guru Rinpoche or 'precious teacher') and is combined with older beliefs of the Sherpas: the Bon-po religion and animism. Spirits and demons (*lu*) inhabit the springs, trees and rocks, and there are detailed rites for protection and exorcism.

As Buddhists, Sherpas view life as an endless cycle of rebirth into a world of suffering. Escape (*nirvana*) is possible only by accumulating a series of 'good' lives. The measure of good and evil is *sonam*. By carrying out virtuous deeds you gain merit, but sinful acts reduce the total at a rather unequal rate. One sin is far more powerful than a few good deeds so constant work is required to keep ahead. If you fall far behind you may not even be born human again: monastery dogs are jokingly considered reincarnations of the not-so-studious monks. The meritorious who have finally escaped may return to assist their brethren as reincarnate head lamas, such as the Rinpoche at Tengboche.

All forms of life are treated with respect since to kill something is regarded as one of the greatest demerits. However, Sherpas relish meat and to eat it is no sin as long as the consumer was not responsible for the animal's death. The Sherpas' approach to life is remarkably unpuritanical and considerably more

---

❖ Prayers for the world

In addition to general good conduct, repeating *mantras* (prayer chants) is an important means by which to gain *sonam*. Most common is the mantra *Om Mani Padme Hum*, meaning 'hail to the jewel in the lotus', the jewel being the Buddha.

The more times a mantra can be repeated the better, so Tibetan Buddhism has evolved many ingenious labour-saving methods to mass-produce these prayers. **Prayer wheels** are filled with a long paper roll inscribed with mantras that are activated by turning the wheel. They come in many forms, from the portable hand-held device so admired by tourists to huge wheels that with a single turn repeat astronomical numbers of prayers. There are also water-powered prayer wheels and multicoloured fluttering **prayer flags**, printed with mantras which infuse the winds with prayers to travel the world. The mantra may be carved onto a **mani stone**, which benefits both the carver and the person who has paid for the work. Large numbers of these stones are piled up into the mani walls you see along the trails.

Note that you should always pass to the left of a mani wall and walk clockwise (the direction in which prayer wheels must always be turned) around Buddhist shrines and monuments.

liberated than that of the Hindu Nepali. There is no caste system and women (Sherpanis) are treated much more equally. In most cases it is the Sherpani rather than the Sherpa who controls the family finances.

Mountaineers, sirdars and porters

Sherpas are well known for their dedicated service to mountaineering expeditions, first as porters and sirdars and later also as participating climbers. The part they play in many expeditions has often been behind the scenes but it is nonetheless crucial for that. On the 1922 Everest attempt, six Sherpas climbed to Camp VI (8170m/26,800ft) from Camp V 800m below, merely to deliver thermos flasks of beef-tea to the sahibs after a storm.

Shipton, who always took Sherpas on his long and unbelievably wild treks in the Himalaya and Karakoram, thoroughly admired them:

One of the most delightful things about the Sherpas is their extraordinary sense of comradeship. During the six months we were together, I never detected any sign of dissension among our three. . . .This quality of theirs is due largely, I imagine, to their robust sense of humour. It hardly ever failed. Each enjoyed jokes against himself as delightedly as those who he perpetrated. Two of them would conceal a heavy rock in the load of the third, and when, after an exhausting climb, this was discovered, all three would be convulsed with mirth. . . .They were forever laughing and chatting together as though they had just met after a prolonged absence.   **Eric Shipton**, *The Six Mountain Travel Books*

Today, Sherpa high-altitude porters still play a vital role in many expeditions and the opportunity for mountaineering training has spawned local heroes. Sungdare Sherpa was one among many. He climbed many mountains, often at great speed (Cho Oyu, 8201m/26,905ft, in 18 hours), and had attained the summit of Everest five times before he died a premature death (not as a result of a mountaineering accident). The majority of Sherpas who work for expeditions do so for money, however, and consider the risks a trade-off for income. Ang Rita, ten times Everest summiteer, says simply that expeditions keep paying him more and more so he can't refuse. Most admired now, apart from the mountaineers, are the sirdars and trekking company directors who have broken through Hindu caste barriers to become some of the most successful businesspeople in Nepal.

Coping with development

The Sherpas' liberal and positive outlook on life combined with the head-start they were given through the Himalayan Trust (see p173) have enabled them to develop and adapt at a far quicker rate than most peoples in Nepal. Although community spirit is strong, individual endeavour and achievement through hard work are respected. There is little resistance to change that is obviously beneficial. If a new strain of potato, for example, proves to be an improvement on a previous type, it will be widely adopted.

Change in the Khumbu has been rapid but not overwhelming. Houses are bigger, smarter and less picturesque but their basic design and the style of construction are still close to time-honoured methods. The diet is generally healthier and more varied but an increase in sugar consumption has led to a greater incidence of tooth decay, especially among children. The worldliness of the Sherpas has undoubtedly increased with the steady stream of visitors and themselves travelling overseas but they are nonetheless still delightful people and can be entertaining hosts if you have time to spend with them.

THE RAI

At Namche's Saturday market the squat, almond-eyed people are Rais. A surprising number work in the fields and even in the lodges of the Khumbu. Trekking via Salpa-Arun you pass through many Rai villages.

Rai can be easily distinguished by their attire and accessories. The women wear a large round nose ring through the left nostril, while another ring hangs from the middle of the nose over the mouth. The musical clang of this ring with the tea cup is a constant melodic reminder of her wealth. They favour a wraparound patterned lungi (tight skirt). The men often wear a wool vest called *lukunis* and always carry a khukri, a large knife used for cutting firewood, splitting bamboo and cleaning fingernails.

Origins

Rai, along with the similar Limbu ethnic group, are collectively referred to as Kirat. They are considered the original inhabitants of Nepal. Having first lived in the Kathmandu Valley these people moved eastward – possibly from the second century on. Once in the east, the Rai were later confronted by the Sherpa, and were pushed still further east. However, mythology also relates how the mongoloid (Tibetan-style people) descended from seven brothers, Sherpa, Rai, Limbu, Tharu, Tamang and various Tibetan groups.

There are many Rai sub-tribes but the Kulung Rai consider themselves the original inhabitants of the Majh-Kirat area (what is now called the Makalu-Barun Conservation Area). The main concentration of this sub-tribe live in Bung and Gudel.

Religion

The religion of the Rai ethnic group is called Mudum; although somewhat influenced by Hinduism and Buddhism it retains much of its originality in its animistic heritage through oral myths, ceremonial dialogues and ritual recitation. Oral myth transmission is preserved by priests, shamans and elders. Natural spirits form the basis for the Mudum religion, including the 16 gods of the forest. Mudums worship in the home whereas Sherpas worship in gompas and Hindus in temples. For the Rai, the cooking area is considered one of the most sacred places in the home where three stones are placed to represent the stages of marriage. One stone looks in the direction of where the father sits (called *Pakalung*), one stone looks in the direction of where the mother sits (*Makalung*) and the third stone looks outside the house (*Sabelung*). A bowl (*dampay*) is kept on a shelf near the cooking area; it is filled with local beer (*chang*) four times a year and is used to bless the stones. If a new stove is built in a home, the original is not destroyed but kept as the place of worship.

Another important divinity resides in the main pillar of the house – a myth relates how a god or goddess became very angry with his child and tried to kill it by the fireplace in the courtyard and at the bottom of the door but could not. Finally he tried by the main pillar and the child died. Soon he was filled with deep remorse for killing the innocent child in a fit of rage so he blessed him to become the protector divinity of the house.

A Rai family has one major ceremony (*puja*) a year which takes place in the fall. A holy man (*dhami*) is hired for one full day to bless the home. The puja begins outside during daylight hours. The dhami sits and chants next to offerings of food, alcohol and tree branches while a feast of chicken and millet is prepared. In the evening, the ceremony is moved inside to the cooking area where the family is blessed and another chicken, also blessed with rakshi and rice, is sacrificed for the second feast of the day.

Agriculture and work

The life of the Rai is deeply rooted in their natural surroundings. Living at a lower elevation than the Sherpas, Rais have access to a greater variety of natural resources, such as bamboo – seven different species are found in the surrounding area. Being strong, versatile, and fast growing, it is highly valued and can be made into over 50 different domestic articles. A keen eye can spot some of these items including mats, vessels, hunting and fishing implements, toys and musical instruments.

Economically, the needs of locals are not met by subsistence farming forcing many young men to seasonally migrate to other regions for additional work. Some men work in the Khumbu or on farms in the Terai, while others go to fruit orchards in Bhutan or join the Indian army. Many also join the forces of the trekking business. Being less of a celebrity than the Sherpas, most Rai are left with the less glamorous job of porter where a day's work often earns only the day's food. Still, mixed groups of them often treat the work as a non-stop party.

Values

A study of the Rai reveals an appealing culture. They have a long tradition of reciting mandhums, poetic expressions of legends, mythology, history and stories. Some explicitly deal with various taboos: promiscuity after marriage, incest, and bad/unequal treatment of women – the problems that every society faces. Several stories altruistically tell of the dangers of polluting the environment, especially the water in the lakes. They share community values and are gentle people but they are also said to have a quick temper and to be fast with a khukri without caring about the consequences. Similarly their relaxed attitude – spend and enjoy today, forget about tomorrow – is a minor cultural impediment to long-term development.

National parks

SAGARMATHA NATIONAL PARK

Set up to control the environmental impact of the increasingly large numbers of tourists visiting the Khumbu, Sagarmatha National Park was officially gazetted in July 1976. For the first six years, the New Zealand government, through the National Parks Service of New Zealand, provided training, management and guidelines. In 1979 it was declared a World Heritage Site by UNESCO in recognition of its rich cultural heritage and magnificent scenery. The park's area is around 1200 sq km encompassing the entire watershed of the Dudh Kosi with the boundary being a virtually impenetrable ring of mountains. The number of foreign visitors has been steadily increasing: from around 5000 people in the 1981-2 season (Nepali calendar year) to around 10,000 during the 1990-1 season. During 1996-7 approximately 17,500 foreigners visited the park and in the year 2000 the figure again jumped dramatically to approximately 25,000. The local Sherpa population numbers approximately 3500 and the national park staff around 60. There are more than 200 government civil servants and military personnel living in the park.

Policies

Initially, there was local resistance to the park owing to worries that the people might be forcibly resettled, as had happened when Rara Lake National Park (west Nepal) was created. To allay such fears village areas were excluded from the park. Inevitably, this has led to a clash of interests between villagers and park management: villagers are unhappy at not being able to farm new land or even work existing terraces that had previously been abandoned, while the park authorities take the view that land is a resource that is becoming more and more valuable, and as such that which can be protected, should be protected. In the Khumbu this clash has been less severe than in other parts of Nepal: the relatively well-educated people of the Khumbu have a slow rate of population growth, and the land that they are presently allowed to farm is already enough to generate a surplus of crops.

Many of the park authorities' other policies have also gradually been accepted by the villagers, particularly once they've been seen to show positive returns. The management of forest resources is a good example. Local forests were once protected by the collection of firewood in different sections on a yearly rotation. The nationalization of forests partially broke this system down, then the influx of starving Tibetan refugees escaping from the Chinese invasion took a heavy toll on the forests and the environment in general. After that, large expeditions turned firewood into a valuable cash crop, all adding up to a devastating result. To try to combat the rampant deforestation that was taking place, when the park came into being the authorities immediately placed a complete ban on the cutting down of trees. Though unpopular at the time, this ban has since been accepted by the villagers as the most sensible course of action, and although not proven definitively, it seems that overall there is now more forest cover in the Khumbu than when foreigners first visited in the 1950s.

Problems facing the park

For a number of years the national park functioned reasonably well. Then the central government cut the budget to a minimum and slowly the cancers of corruption and laziness began to permeate the park system, just as they had in almost every other park in the country.

The park today is also in something of a crisis when it comes to visitor numbers, which are growing alarmingly: in October 2000 more than 7500 trekkers entered the park. Although the problem has been studied and is understood, what to do about it is as yet undecided. Currently the International Centre for Protected Landscapes funded by the British Government has come up with a comprehensive strategy that involves developing a new management plan for both Sagarmatha National Park and the entire Solu-Khumbu district. Convoluted though their proposals may be, with so many parties taking an interest in the future of the park – including not only the park authorities and other relevant government bodies but also the United Nations Development Programme (UNDP), various other NGOs and, of course, the local people whose livelihoods depend on the park – a long-term solution that would satisfy everybody was always going to involve some serious and complex planning. Whether it will eventually prove to be successful, only time will tell.

Sagarmatha Conservation Area

This conservation area was still in planning at the time of writing but by the time you read this may well be a reality. The concept is to make a buffer zone for the national park: an area where, instead of going by a rules-based system, the managers work *in partnership* with the local communities, helping them to switch to a more sustainable form of development that will lessen the use of national park resources by those who live outside of the national park. Hopefully it will also strengthen local awareness of the limits of their own resources. Once again only time will tell whether the project is a success – though, as the next section shows, previous attempts at establishing a similar system leave much to be desired.

MAKALU-BARUN NATIONAL PARK & CONSERVATION AREA

Makalu-Barun National Park and Conservation Area (MBNPCA) was gazetted in 1991 and formally inaugurated in 1992 with a total area of 2330 sq km, of which 830 sq km was a conservation or buffer-zone area. Encompassing a region that stretched from near the Arun river all the way up to the Sagarmatha

National Park, including the Hongu/Hinku or Mera Peak area, the park was initially formed to set up an environmental protection system in case the planned 'Arun III' hydro-electric scheme went ahead. This truly massive project would require an access road that would open up a previously isolated area. The hydro-electric project has come close to being realized several times, including once by the now-bankrupt Enron corporation, but each time the proposals were cancelled in a storm of controversy.

There should also have been a storm of controversy over the ending of the buffer zone and the associated development work in 1999. Twelve years previously the **Mountain Institute** (TMI), using money provided by the UNDP, other NGOs and the governments of several countries, set up an ambitious management and development programme. This programme took a 'bottom-up' approach to protecting the park's resources, its primary aim being to teach the locals to become less reliant on the park area that they were no longer allowed to use, and to learn instead to utilize their own tourism potential. Its approach was broad and was definitely making a positive impact, at least with the people living in the buffer zone. Unfortunately, once the various institutes had departed, leaving the running of the operation in the hands of the park authorities, things began to fall apart to such an extent that the warden and senior staff (most appointed by a warden and from his home area in the Terai) simply didn't turn up for months at a time. At the time of writing the programme had all but collapsed, with the local villagers abandoning many of the initiatives implemented by the scheme in favour of traditional practices that rely heavily on the park's precious resources.

Facilities for the trekker

ACCOMMODATION AND FOOD

Our travels in Solu-Khumbu depended on Sherpa hospitality. When we arrived at a village where we wanted to spend the night, we would yell up at the window of any convenient house and ask to spend the night there. Permission was invariably given, whereupon we went upstairs to the main room, cooked our meal on the family fire, and went to sleep on whatever flat surface was available, usually the wooden floor. The host typically gave us any extra pillows lying around. We paid for food but, from Junbesi east, not for firewood.

James Fisher, in the 1970s.

The development of lodges

The hill peoples of Nepal have traditionally provided food and accommodation for the many travellers passing through their villages on the trade routes that cross the country. These small family-run establishments were nothing like hotels in the Western sense: guests were traditionally charged for food but not for their lodging, which was very basic. Not so long ago these teahouses were providing the same level of facilities as they had for the first foreign trekkers:

little more than dal bhaat or a plate of potatoes and a hard bed. As the flow of trekkers grew, however, it was soon realized that these foreigners were prepared to pay more for better accommodation and a choice of food.

Development was slow at first. In 1985 Kenja, Junbesi, Kharikhola and Monjo were the only places below Namche that had proper lodges. In the 1990s, however, many new lodges were built and teahouses upgraded in a building spree which continues to this day. Double rooms gradually replaced dormitories, showers and toilets were added and chimneys installed, so that the traditional smoky lodges are rare these days. Extensive menus catering to Western tastes are now provided too (most Nepalis have just two main meals a day, both consisting entirely of dal bhaat). Perhaps the biggest change of all, however, is that lodges are now run as businesses, very different from the teahouses of yesteryear with their hosts eager for news of the world beyond the village.

Nepal now has well-developed mountain lodge systems in the Solu Khumbu, Annapurna and Langtang areas, and on average the lodges of the Khumbu are the best in the country. This is, however, a developing country and still one of the world's poorest, so the lodges are not as grand as those you might find in the European Alps – but nor are they as expensive. Each lodge is, for the most part, owned and managed by a single family. Supplies are purchased or grown locally where possible, or carried in by porters if not; by staying in lodges, therefore, you are supporting the larger local economy. As long as you don't expect star quality facilities, you should be pleasantly surprised and happy with both the food and accommodation along the main trekking routes.

Hygiene

Once you could almost be guaranteed to get sick on a trek in Nepal. Now, although there is still a reasonable chance of a real stomach upset from Kathmandu, out on the trek there is a good chance you won't get sick at all. Remember, too, that if you do get sick there are a number of possible sources, including your own hygiene, so don't automatically assume that the lodge food is to blame.

Eating in well-established lodges is now probably safer than eating a cooked meal on an organized group trek, and getting sick from lodge food is becoming rarer, especially since Namche changed its water supply. Basic hygiene measures such as washing hands and boiling water have been learnt from courses in Kathmandu and while kitchens may lack stainless steel sinks and running water they are, nevertheless, cleaned frequently. The style of cooking (frying or boiling) renders much of the food safe and salads are rare. Hot drinks are safe, too, but local drinks such as *chang* are not always so hygienically prepared.

Lodges on the main routes

Food A typical lodge in this area offers an extensive menu (usually vegetarian except in and around Namche) based on noodles, rice, flour, potatoes, eggs and the sparing use of vegetables. Breakfast offerings include muesli, a variety of porridges, pancakes and bread with jam or eggs. Most meal choices are carbohydrate-heavy: exactly what trekkers require. Increasingly, apple pie, chocolate cake, pizza and toasted cheese and garlic sandwiches have found their way onto menus. All serve tea, coffee, hot chocolate, hot lemon and Coke etc. Canned beer can also be found along with *chang* (local beer), the respected Khukri rum and the infamous *rakshi*.

Bathroom facilities These are still developing. Many lodges now offer hot showers and the ones that don't usually have at least a bucket of water for you to use. Toilets are usually just a hole in the ground to be squatted over: no spotlessly white antiseptic auto-flush toilets here, so watch your ankles. The rural Nepalese have land that needs fertilizing so before foreign trekkers took to the mountains there was no need for toilets.

Rooms Sleeping arrangements vary. Older lodges have dormitories while most newer or larger places boast simple double rooms with thin partitions that rattle to a snoring neighbour: ear plugs can be helpful. Beds in the newer lodges have reasonably thick foam mattresses but in simple lodges the mattress is barely thick enough to disguise the knots in the wood below. These mattresses are covered by a single clean sheet and there's usually a pillow available, though it's often of granite consistency. Down jackets make great pillows.

Once bedbugs and fleas were a concern, now the majority of lodges above Lukla have a separate room and bedding for porters and guides – the major carriers of these parasites in the mountains – so there is virtually no chance of picking up unwanted bed companions. In the low country lodges if you use your own sleeping sheet and sleeping bag the risk is very low. Most lodges wash the sheets and air the mattresses frequently.

Seasons Lodges now remain open all year-round, even at Gokyo, Lobuche, Gorak Shep and Chukhung, so trekking options are no longer restricted during winter and the monsoon. They also never seem to suffer the problem of being full to the extent that trekkers are stranded without a bed, so you'll rarely be

---

❖ Choosing a lodge

Most trekkers tend to head either for the biggest and best-looking lodge or for the one where other trekkers are staying. Lodge-owners are well aware of this and will sometimes try very hard to attract the first trekkers arriving in the village, occasionally even trying to seat them outside (on seats provided for this very purpose) in order to attract more. Overcrowding can be a problem in the most popular lodges. At dinner there may be 15 trekkers ordering eight different dishes, all to be cooked on two fires, although most lodges do seem to cope remarkably well.

Look around at a few places before deciding where to stay. Except at the height of the season, you may find an empty lodge that is just as good as the one the other trekkers are crowding into. It's also worth trying out some of the smaller lodges and teashops, at least occasionally. This can be a rewarding cultural experience that gives you a better chance to see how the family lives. Expansion and competition with the big lodges is beyond the means of many of these small lodge owners, their money going to support relatives and pay school fees.

turned away. There are, however, a few busy places (Tengboche and Lobuche especially) that during October-November are filled almost to bursting. Sometimes this is because people on a group trek inconsiderately decide a lodge is more attractive and warmer than their tents. The national park has been reluctant to allow the building of new lodges or the expansion of old ones in this area so it pays to arrive early at these places during peak season. Elsewhere, the law of supply-and-demand seems to work well.

Off the main routes
In general, wherever there is a village, accommodation can be found. There may not be a lodge as such but people will often invite you to stay. If this does not happen try asking around (this is not considered rude by Nepalis) and something will turn up. Conditions can be extremely basic, however, and very different from the lodges on the main trekking routes. In strongly Hindu areas your presence may be considered *jutho* (polluting) so you may have to eat alone and perhaps even sleep on the porch.

Wilderness areas and base camps offer no shelter other than the occasional overhanging rock. You should also be aware that on detailed maps the dots marked in *kharkas* (high-altitude pastures) are usually just roofless stone buildings occupied only in the summer. Even then they are rarely able to offer food or shelter.

SHOPS, BANKS AND POST OFFICES

Most lodges also run a small shop offering canned drinks, Nepali and sometimes imported biscuits, chocolate, Mars Bars and some sweets. Often tins of fruit or fish can be found, along with noodles, coffee, drinking chocolate, tea, muesli, porridge, milk powder, jam and cheap batteries.

The Khumbu shops, especially in Namche, are well stocked and sell film (slide and print), batteries of all sizes including camera batteries, torches, socks, postcards, Swiss chocolate and Tibetan souvenirs. There's also a wide range of new and used mountaineering equipment for rent and sale.

Camping food If you're not choosy it's quite possible to assemble enough for a few nights' camping from the better shops in almost any village. The diet may be monotonous but it is light and cheap. In Namche there's a strange variety of expedition dried foods, usually little cheaper than in the West. Lobuche, Pheriche, Chukhung and Gokyo always have an interesting cheaper selection. Many of the locals are involved with expeditions and in little villages the weirdest collections of leftover expedition food can sometimes be found.

Banks and post offices There are banks for foreign exchange at Namche (reliable), Lukla, Salleri and Khandbari (currently closed due to Maoist problems). Post offices are also found in these three places, plus Junbesi. All are closed on Saturdays.

Internet Namche is the only place on the trek that is reliably connected; with one operator having their own satellite connection the service is surprisingly good.

Minimum impact trekking

Take nothing but pictures, leave nothing but footprints (Motto of the Sierra Club)

It is undeniable that trekking has had a significant impact on the environment, the culture and the economy of the Solu Khumbu, with effects both negative and positive. The opinions of experts as to the extent of the damaging effects of trekking on this region vary. Awareness of the problems has been raised, however, and solutions are being effected far more rapidly than elsewhere in Nepal. What is important to realize is that Lukla and north of there are at quite a different stage and in quite different circumstances to the Jiri and Arun regions.

It was most fortunate for the people of the Khumbu that the trekking industry started just as the vital trade links with Tibet were being severed by the Chinese. The industry has now developed into the single most important force in the economy and the Khumbu has become the richest area in rural Nepal. Many schools, hospitals and bridges, the obvious benefits of development, have been built.

Many people search for the negative aspects of the tourist industry before they begin to understand and balance the benefits. While tourism has negatively impacted the environment, perhaps the biggest damage to the forests of the Khumbu occurred when thousands of Tibetan refugees, fleeing the Chinese 'Great Leap Forward' and the continuing 'peaceful liberation' of Tibet, arrived and stayed in the Khumbu for months before moving down to other regions. However, the area seems to have recovered from the environmental damage this caused. Currently local villagers and lodges still use plenty of firewood but I have not read or been told that the current usage is unsustainable; after all, hundreds of tonnes of firewood still grow in the region each year. The biggest user of firewood was Namche-Khumjung-Khunde who now have enough electricity to cook with. The burning of juniper and moss has mostly stopped now too.

As far as trail litter goes, Khumbu villages are for the most part clean, with locals organizing clean-up campaigns, often several times a year. Mostly it is the porters brought by trekking groups that litter with abandon and there is still a need for an attitude change there. The other large polluters are trekking peak groups, and although the Nepal Mountaineering Association (NMA), who collect the fees, do organize clean-ups from time to time, it is the groups themselves who should smarten up. Glass was a major problem a few years ago, but since then the locals have resolved to use cans only. Probably the biggest litter problem now – aside from toilet waste – is the plastic mineral water bottles that trekkers insist on using. Admittedly it is bottled locally and so there are some benefits but there are more environmentally sound alternatives. It is paradoxical that the water in these bottles is in fact Namche town supply water, which is 100% clean.

Then there is the tricky question of the cultural impact that tourism has on the region. The question is, should the area be closed to avoid Western influences from seeping into the local culture, or should we let cultural 'imperialism' take its course? Personally, although I was apprehensive at first, I now know that the Khumbu Sherpas can handle the world with greater aplomb than most Western cultures. Theirs is a close-knit and united community, and the bonds that keep them together seem as strong as ever; indeed, in many ways it is us that have lessons to learn from them.

As a trekker you can still minimize your impact on the land and culture. Here are some suggestions.

ENVIRONMENTAL CONCERNS

Pack it in, pack it out
In national parks in the West, visitors are encouraged to take out all their litter when they leave (and indeed anything they bring into the park with them). In Nepal the situation is not so straightforward since many of the national parks contain villages and much of what you consume is purchased locally.

Litter
The most worrying and obvious litter problems in the Khumbu and Hinku (Mera Peak area) are directly related to the activities of expedition-style trekking and climbing groups. Tinned food and bottled sauces are served at every meal. The members may be careful with their litter, putting it in the bins set up in the camp, but what then happens to this rubbish? Sometimes it is burnt, with the remains left sitting in the embers. Sometimes it is buried in the toilet, covered by little more than an inch of dirt or it may be dumped at the nearest village or simply left in the snow. The problem goes virtually unnoticed by group members because the kitchen crew are the last to leave a camp or lunch spot. Despite constant clean-up campaigns, litter left by groups is still a serious problem. Park rules specifically state that all rubbish generated by trekking groups must now be packed out and not dumped in village garbage pits which were dug for the needs of the villagers.

The problem of litter generated by individual trekkers is not so serious. There is little non-burnable litter that is not recycled apart from plastic mineral water bottles which are a definite and unnecessary problem. Flour, sugar and rice come in sacks, the cardboard from egg-boxes is reused, oil comes in tins that are prized for roofing and, besides, very little tinned food is on menus. Most lodges now burn the burnables and villages have locally managed rubbish pits. Soft drink cans should be crushed flat.

● **Don't use mineral water** Since mineral water is sold in non-returnable, non-biodegradable plastic bottles and is now widely available in the Everest region (and the rest of Nepal) the empty bottles are becoming a serious litter problem. There are quite a few alternatives, of which using iodine compounds is the best, see p280.

> **A plea to group members**
> Please make voluble complaints to trek leaders and trekking company directors if any of the environmental recommendations noted in this section are not carried out. The entire group's unburnable litter must be taken out right to the end of the trek. Kerosene must be provided by the company not just for the trekkers but for porters' use also. They may not use any firewood either in the national park or en route to Mera Peak. The police of the area are lackadaisical and although the park staff have authority there are no penalties for contravening park rules. The trekking companies and sirdars do not yet care, seemingly motivated by personal gain only.

● **Put litter in bins** There is absolutely no excuse for dropping any litter along the trails, yet many trekkers are guilty of this, even if it's only the odd sweet wrapper. However, one piece of paper multiplied several thousand times becomes a significant problem.

Tissues, film cartons and biscuit wrappers are all easily stuffed into a backpack pocket for disposal in a bin at a lodge. You could also help by picking up a few bits of litter generated by other people.

● **Dispose of excess packaging before arrival** Today virtually everything comes wrapped in multiple, sometime unnecessary layers. Expeditions especially will find it more environmentally sound and more economic to plan packaging thoughtfully.

Other pollution
● **Use the toilet facilities provided** Most lodges have toilets which individual trekkers should use. Group trekkers should ensure that the toilets that are dug in their camps are of a sufficient depth and are properly filled in and covered with large stones when the campsite is left. With the large number of groups there are now so many holes that finding a new space to put a toilet tent can be a problem. This is particularly acute in Tengboche and Gokyo. Toilet blocks specifically for the use of trekking groups are now being constructed throughout the Khumbu.

● **Bury or burn used toilet paper** Nepalis use the 'water method' rather than toilet paper so all the pink streamers beside the track are generated by trekkers. Used toilet paper can easily be burnt, concealed under a rock where it will decompose, or put in a bin that has been provided specifically for this purpose. Some toilets double as compost heaps, their contents, when mixed with leaf matter, eventually being spread on the fields. As such, don't put tampons into these, but instead wrap them and put them into rubbish bins.

● **Don't pollute water sources** In the West the provision of clean drinking water has reduced the incidence of diarrhoea-related diseases to a negligible level. Nepal still has a long way to go but efforts are being made to provide villages with water from uncontaminated sources.

If bathing in streams, don't use soap or shampoo. Do not defecate close to the trail or a stream. If there is no toilet ensure you are at least 20 metres away from any water source and bury your waste and used toilet paper.

Fuel conservation

The total consumption of firewood by trekkers may be less than 0.1% of all the firewood consumed each year in Nepal but its effect is concentrated in a narrow ribbon along the main trails. Not only is wood used directly by lodges but also by all the porters who carry supplies for the markets. It is true that these porters would, like other Nepalis, use firewood anyway but the majority would do so in their villages away from these busy main trails. Depletion of the remaining forest cover compounds the already serious erosion problems.

For villages on the Jiri to Namche trail there is no instant solution. Kerosene has to be imported and is not entirely practical for lodge use. The micro-hydro-electric schemes cannot, so far, generate enough electricity for cooking and the establishment of an extensive national rural electricity grid is beyond the thinking of politicians. Tree replanting and community forests are, however, now well established and are showing returns.

The best news, however, is that Namche now has the most advanced hydro-electric system in rural Nepal, a 630kw medium-size hydro-scheme. The lodges and the local people of Namche and the surrounding villages are adapting to cooking on electricity because it is cheaper than a wood-fired stove. One hopes that this admirable project will serve as a pilot scheme for others.

● **Help conserve firewood** To help in a small way do not make open fires, use iodine to purify water instead of getting it boiled, coordinate meal times and limit hot showers to lodges where the water is heated in back boilers or solar panels.

Trekking companies deserve the harshest possible criticism for contravening park rules by allowing their porters to cook on open fires, although they do use kerosene for meals for the trekkers and main crew. If you're trekking with a group and see fires being lit for cooking you should make a complaint.

Accelerated erosion

Erosion is a natural phenomenon that creates river deltas and shapes mountains. In some parts of the world, however, it may occur at an accelerated rate that has serious consequences. The Himalaya are a young range of mountains, still in the process of formation, and erosion has always been considerable here. In the last few decades the problem has been exacerbated by rapid deforestation. The natural ground cover is being stripped away for firewood or animal fodder allowing rain to erode the essential topsoil. The problem is very serious: Nepal's forests are disappearing at the rate of 3% per year. One hectare of cleared forest loses around 50 tons of soil annually and approximately 400,000 hectares are cleared each year in Nepal.

● **Don't damage plants and stick to the trails** In the alpine areas, above the tree line, plants battle to survive in a harsh environment. Trekkers can have a negative effect on these areas. Big boots and yak hooves disturb the topsoil and sliding down a slope can leave scars that never heal.

CULTURAL CONSIDERATIONS

There is no return to the time of traditionality for those who have abandoned it because the first condition for belonging to a traditional culture is that one does not know it
Al Ghazale, 12th-century philosopher

One of the great attractions of Nepal for the first visitors was the fact that the cultures of the many different peoples living here had evolved independently of Western 'civilization'. Day-to-day life for most people had remained virtually unchanged. Sudden outside influence, however, has brought profound change, particularly in the rural areas popular with tourists.

There is no denying that the West is a technologically advanced society but its superiority over less 'developed' cultures does not, necessarily, extend beyond this. A visit to a country like Nepal can be a particularly rewarding experience, especially if you have not travelled much outside the West. Many things are done differently here but this does not make the methods any less valid and in some cases they may be better.

The Nepalese way of solving problems, for example, is to avoid confrontation which starkly contrasts with the head-on 'Rambo' style of the West. The incidence of murder, theft and rape (outside of the family) in Nepal is negligible in comparison to most nations, (although it is true that the Maoist revolution has dramatically altered perceptions of law and order here).

Although probably the biggest cultural influences are from Western television and Hindi movies, here are some ways that you can minimize your impact.

● **Dress decently** Dress standards are important despite the fact that they are overlooked by many trekkers. Whilst men may go around without a shirt in the West, this is considered indecent in Nepal. Women should not wear short shorts or singlet tops. See p46 for further information.

● **Respect people's right to privacy** Ask people before you take their photograph and be considerate when looking for subjects. Many people are afraid that the photo will later be thrown away, an insult and also a possible loss of karma and one of the many reasons that His Holiness the Dalai Lama will never appear on bank notes.

● **Don't flaunt your wealth** By lowland and normal Nepali standards, even the poorest foreign trekker is unimaginably wealthy. Nepalis often ask how much you earn; by all means tell them the truth, but qualify your answer by giving them some examples of the cost of living in your country. Don't leave valuables lying around as this is further evidence that you have so much money you can easily afford to replace them.

● **Respect religious customs** Pass to the left of mani walls and chortens where there is a good path. Prayer wheels should be turned clockwise. Remove your boots before entering a gompa and leave a donation; there's often a metal box provided.

● **Respect traditions** There are a number of other customs and traditions that
you should take care to respect. To not do so is to insult your hosts. The left
hand, used for washing after defecating, is not considered clean so you should
never touch anyone with it, offer them anything with it or eat with it. The head
and top of the shoulders is considered the most sacred part of the body and you
should never touch anyone there. Avoid pointing the soles of your feet at a person's head. If you're sitting with your legs outstretched and a Nepali needs to
pass, he or she will never step over you. Move your legs out of the way.

● **Encourage pride in Nepali culture** Express an interest in what people
are doing and try to explain that everything is not as rosy in the West as some
Nepalis might believe. In restaurants don't consistently shy away from
Nepalese food. Local people are being taught by insidious example that packaged sweets, biscuits, noodles and chocolate are more desirable than local
equivalents but in most cases they are actually less nutritious.

ECONOMIC IMPACT

The initial effect of independent trekkers using local lodges was an increase in
prices for many commodities along the major trekking routes. The villagers,
naturally enough, sought the best prices for their produce and the highest bid-
ders were the trekkers. In the short term this created a problem because villagers
were more willing to sell scarce commodities to trekkers. It should, however,
also be considered as a stage in the long development process: demand encourages production where previously there was no advantage in producing more. If
the commodity is not available locally then it must be carried in by a porter who
possibly comes from a remote village far from the trail, thus creating work in
areas where there may be few employment opportunities.

Teahouse trekking stimulates the local economy. Money from individual
trekkers enters the local economy via the shops and lodges but it can have an
effect on the whole area. Porters carry in the additional goods, new buildings
may need to be constructed requiring local resources and labour, staff are
required at the lodges and local producers have a new market. Collectively these
factors provide more jobs and can lead to a higher standard of living, not just
among lodge owners. This is immediately obvious from visiting areas frequented by trekkers and comparing them with villages without this stimulus.
Namche probably has the highest per capita income in Nepal, ahead even of
Kathmandu. It has often been said that only 10% of the money stays with the
lodge owner, but then the other 90% is spread between the manufacturer/local
growers, porters and middlemen, so there are many others who benefit.

The economic impact of expedition-style trekking groups is somewhat
different. Some of the money remains in Kathmandu for taxes and office
expenses. The secondary beneficiaries are the employees, who are rarely local
people and so their earnings do not as a rule stay in the capital, but instead
benefit their area. In fact, locals on the trekking routes receive little from these

THE MINIMUM IMPACT CODE

Developed by environmental groups in Nepal affiliated with the King Mahendra Trust for Nature Conservation, the Minimum Impact Code requests trekkers to:

● **Conserve firewood** Be self-sufficient in your fuel supply and make sure your trekking staff uses kerosene and has enough warm clothing. Make no open fires. Limit hot showers. If possible stay at lodges that use kerosene or fuel-efficient wood stoves and space heaters.

● **Stop pollution** Dispose of all trash properly. Paper products, cigarette butts, toilet paper, food scraps etc should be burned or buried. Bottles, plastics and other non-biodegradable items should be packed out or deposited in rubbish pits if available. Use the toilet facilities provided. If none exist, make sure you are 20 metres away from any water source and carry a small shovel to bury waste. Don't use soap or shampoo in any stream or hot spring. Supervise trekking staff to make sure they cover toilet pits and dispose of garbage properly.

● **Be a guest** Do not damage, disturb or remove any plants, animals, animal products or religious artifacts. Respect Nepali customs in your dress and behaviour. Women should not wear shorts or revealing blouses and men should always wear a shirt. Avoid outward displays of physical affection. Ask permission to take photographs and respect people's right to privacy. Begging is a negative interaction that has been unwittingly encouraged by well-meaning tourists – please do not give anything to beggars. Don't barter for food and lodging. Encourage young Nepalis to be proud of their culture.

Above all, remember that your vacation has a great impact on the natural environment and the people who live off its resources. By assisting in these small ways, you will help the land and people of Nepal enormously.

expeditions. Camping fees are modest and since the bulk of provisions are carried in, little food is purchased locally. Only firewood is used, and rubbish left.

● **Don't bargain for food and lodging** These prices are fixed and in most cases are surprisingly reasonable. Wisely, few Khumbu lodge owners will put up with hard bargaining and most will simply suggest politely that you look elsewhere.

● **Don't give to beggars** Some trekkers, embarrassed at the disparity in material wealth between their country and Nepal, have given money to beggars and sweets and pens to children. They may have thought that they were helping but the opposite is probably true. As well as fostering an unhealthy dependency attitude, begging can in some places be more profitable than earning money by portering or working in the fields. Giving sweets to children not only encourages them to see Westerners (and hence the West) as bringers of all good things but also leads to tooth decay, until recently quite rare in Nepal. On the trail you may encounter more creative forms of begging: teenagers asking for funds for their school. It's hard to judge how genuine many of the claims are but remember you don't have to give anything. You'll be shown a book with names and amounts donated; if the sums are unrealistically large, the solicitation probably isn't genuine.

PART 5: ROUTE GUIDE & MAPS

Using this guide

Route descriptions

All the main routes for the greater Everest region are described and each route description is accompanied by detailed trail maps. There is no day by day description; instead, all the lodges and possible stopping places are marked so that you can decide where to stay. To aid planning there are sample itineraries in the Appendix (pp273-5). Main route sections are as follows:

Jiri to Namche p145 (overview map p25)
Trekking from Lukla p165
Namche p178
To Lobuche and Kala Pattar p185
To Gokyo p204
Khumbu side trips and pass-hopping p218
From Bhojpur p248
Rolwaling p250
Trekking peaks p261

Village and feature names

Most of the Sherpa villages have both a Nepali name and the traditional Sherpa name; a few even have a name exclusively used by trekkers. All the familiar names of a village are mentioned in this guide, with the one most commonly used by trekkers and guides repeated in the text. For the purpose of this guide I have also tentatively named a couple of hills and passes that didn't appear to have a local name.

Trail maps

The main geographical features shown are major ridges, rivers and streams. Being the Himalaya, you are surrounded by huge mountains and steep gorges but the ruggedness of this terrain is not depicted. For working out which mountain you are admiring, a detailed colour topographic map is invaluable.

The maps are drawn to a scale of roughly 1:100,000 (ie one centimetre is equivalent to one kilometre). The maps of the Rolwaling Valley are at 1:250,000. Features have been stylised so that roads, rivers and villages appear larger (easier to read) than on a true topographic map.

Following trails

Unlike many tracks in developed countries the trails in Nepal are unmarked. Paths lead off the main route to grazing areas, firewood collecting areas and water sources. However, the main trail is usually larger and travels in a consistent direction so is easy enough to follow. If you think you have inadvertently taken the wrong path look carefully at the size of it: on a main path you don't usually brush against branches and undergrowth. Is it still heading in the right direction? If you must climb to the village and the path has been contouring for a while, don't be afraid to turn back. Occasionally trails divide and rejoin a little while later. This is usually marked on the trail maps.

The paths across glaciers and other difficult terrain often are littered with stone cairns (stone men). The majority mark the correct route but a few merely show that it is possible to climb a point. Occasionally cairns are toppled by snow, wind or animals. If you are sure that you are on the correct path, don't hesitate to rebuild these guides or add new ones. Locals take pride in the art of constructing ones that are surprisingly well balanced and in just the right spot so that they are visible from afar.

Walking times

The hills render measured distances in miles or kilometres virtually meaningless; walking times are far more useful. These are given along the side of the maps, with arrows indicating the villages they refer to. While I have tried to be consistent as to the times quoted, inevitably there is a high degree of variation. The walking times on the trail maps give a wide spread. Hiking briskly and steadily with few stops should approximate the lesser time while ambling along admiring the scenery and spotting wildlife should approximate the longer time. This is also the *group* pace.

The times are not meant to performance-orientate you: fast walkers, especially when heading downhill, could easily come in under the lesser times. In fact, my fervent hope is that trekkers mainly use them to help lunchtime and end of the day decision-making (for example, if it is half past three and you are wondering how far away the next lodge is and whether to stay or to go on).

The **group pace** is sedate with plenty of time for relaxation. Porters carry 30-35kg on group treks so the length of the trekking day is limited by this. On an expedition-style trek time must also be allowed for the kitchen crew who are the last to leave camp after cleaning up and must then race ahead to prepare the next meal. The need for adequate shelter for porters effectively prevents camping in unfrequented wild spots unless groups are well prepared. Groups may walk short days in order to stop in a camping place that is a traditional night stop. So the days are generally easy and lunch stops sometimes last half the afternoon. For people who are not used to exercise the pace is good but anyone who keeps fit by regularly playing sport will perhaps find the pace a little too leisurely after the first few days. **Individual trekkers** tend to cover more distance in a day than groups. Once at Namche the pace is solely dictated by the altitude gains and so involves rest days and half-day walks only.

When taking **day trips** uphill you can assume that the return will take you half to two-thirds of the time it took to ascend. Don't forget to allow for relaxing and exploring too. On a fine day there is no more satisfying place to bask in the sun than atop a glorious viewpoint.

Altitudes

These are given in metres on the maps and in the text they're also quoted in feet. Altitudes are approximate and rounded for villages since there are very few truly flat bits of ground. Altitudes have been quoted from the most accurate source available for the area: the National Geographic map for Pangboche and up, the Schneider series of maps and, where these were not available, Nepali topographic maps combined with an altimeter. In general, GPS measurements agree closely, although I have yet to double-check them all.

Don't get too worried about the sometimes huge differences in altitudes between some villages. Trekking in Nepal involves crossing mammoth ridges all the time. Simply go at a pace that suits, stop frequently and you'll soon get used to walking uphill and downhill. There is one absolutely flat stretch near Tumlingtar but, strangely, instead of being pleasant it's hell. You seem to be getting nowhere, the ground is hard and it actually seems tough walking.

Main ridges and mountains are shown as **thick lines** on the trail maps.

Facilities

The facilities available along the trail are indicated by symbols on the trail maps. **Large lodges** (❑) are the bigger and better establishments that will have a comprehensive menu and double rooms. Simple **lodges/teahouses** (❑) may not have a separate dining-room and may have only one dormitory but they're certainly more homely than the fancy places. Some are in locations where trekkers rarely stay, stopping at them only for tea or a meal. **Teashacks** (▽) are the simplest places. In the lower country they are often just a few bamboo mats over a wooden frame and generally don't look too hygienic. In the most basic, for example in the Arun Valley, there are no beds for guests, only room on the floor.

If there's just one lodge or teahouse it'll be shown as an **outline**, a few will be shown **half blacked-in** and if there are many lodges or teahouses they'll be shown with a **black symbol**.

For the majority of villages there is a village plan. This shows the names and locations of the lodges, with the words lodge, hotel, restaurant and guest house omitted. No doubt a few names will change and a few new lodges will be built too, so don't be surprised if the map is not entirely accurate.

Jiri to Namche

INTRODUCTION

Jiri to Namche takes most people seven to nine pleasant days walking, usually including a rest day at Junbesi and a shorter easy day or two. If you have more time and energy there are plenty of opportunities for side trips exploring little-visited villages and gompas. Several alpine valleys are also worth more thorough exploration by well-equipped parties. For the extremely fit in a hurry, walking from Jiri to Namche in four days is possible – just. There are good lodges along the main route and since these are usually only a few hours apart it's no longer necessary to plan a detailed itinerary as suggested by some guidebooks. Simply follow your instincts and the advice of other trekkers rather than sticking to a rigid schedule.

The walk is strenuous, following a route that goes against the grain of the land; all the rivers and ridges flow north to south and the trail runs west to east. Following the standard route (not including side trips)

by the time you reach Namche you will have climbed up almost exactly the height of Mt Everest, 8848m/29,028ft, and the corresponding descents to Namche total the height of Ama Dablam, 6828m/22,402ft. Since you have trekked the majority of the time between 2000 and 3000m this means you are well acclimatized to around 3000m and unlikely to feel the altitude at Namche. However, higher up you should take it just as cautiously as everyone else.

Leaving Jiri there is an introductory hill, then three higher major ridges: an unnamed 2700m/8858ft pass, the Lamjura Pass 3530m/11,581ft and Trakshindo Pass 3071m/10,075ft. Once across the Dudh Kosi (river), the trail climbs high up the valley sides skirting steep rock faces before descending to recross the river several times before the final hill to Namche.

Jiri has been the end of the road into the hills in this region for more than 15 years. Now, however, the road is being extended again, though it is unlikely to be completed particularly quickly. Currently there are sections being built as far in as Bhandar but it is only sometimes navigable as far as Shivalaya and currently there are no bus services; all buses still finish in Jiri. Doubtless this will change, so ask in Jiri for the latest details.

Route map key

☐ Simple lodge	☐ Large lodge	▽ Tea shack
☐ One lodge	◪ A few lodges	■ Many lodges
○ Other	╱ Trail	⟊ Pass
⊕ Difficult Pass	▲ Peak	△ Trekking Peak
⋰ Ridge	╱ Stream / River	⩫ Glacier

> **Jiri to Lukla route – less popular now**
> For perhaps a decade the Jiri to Lukla section remained more or less the
> same but in the last few years the route has been in a state of flux. A road is
> in the process of being pushed further in which will lessen the reliance of locals on
> trekkers for income. Despite the drop in popularity of the trail amongst foreigners
> there are, nevertheless, a lot more *lodges*, used mainly by locals en route to the
> road. The Maoists have recently been active in this area and this will further
> impact the region.

Services – Jiri to Lukla

There are a surprising number of medical
facilities, although Maoist activities have
temporarily disrupted services. Phaplu has
a bush hospital and there is usually a good
Nepali doctor at Kenja and at Kharikhola.
Between Jiri and Namche there are no functioning banks. Jiri has an unreliable and
busy phone and Phaplu has a telephone system, and beyond that there is Lukla.
Installation of new lines has been severely
hampered by Maoist activities.

KATHMANDU TO JIRI

This part of the journey is made by bus (see
p108) or taxi. Budget travellers take the
public bus while groups usually organize a
private bus or take taxis. Hiring a car and
driver is the most comfortable alternative
but you can go by bus for a fraction of the
cost. From the old bus station in the centre
of Kathmandu the first departure for Jiri is
at around 5.30am. Thieves are now working
the bus station and this route intensively so
take great care of your luggage. These
people are no mere opportunists, they are
professionals – many trekkers have lost
things from side-pockets, and occasionally
even a whole rucksack goes missing. It's
best to try to take your rucksack inside the
bus; the ticket office is helpful and will
often give you front seats or even a seat for
your rucksack (which you pay for) but other
passengers may object to this. Most buses
have a dusty boot at the back that can be
locked. If you're in a group ensure that all
the packs are stowed together on the roof
and at the first chance for passengers to ride
on the roof, go up and keep a close eye on
them. There are also occasional pickpockets at the bus station. Their favourite trick is

to watch where you put the change after
buying your ticket then hurry you onto the
bus while their hand delves into your pocket. The police have been unhelpful in all
cases.

The first part of this 10-12 (and occasionally up to 16) hour bus journey is to
Lamosangu (78km, 5 hours) along the
Chinese-constructed Arniko Rajmarg or
Kodari Highway that runs to the Tibetan
border and Lhasa. Leaving Kathmandu you
pass through the lower part of **Bhaktapur**
where, until the early 1960s, the trek to
Everest began.

There is a steep climb out of the
Kathmandu Valley and from **Dhulikhel**, at
the crest of the hill, there are views on a
clear day of the Himalaya from Manaslu to
Everest. The road drops to **Dolalghat** (*ghat*
means 'bridge') and crosses the Indrawati
River. The Chinese road had progressed
this far by 1967 so the first commercial
treks to the Khumbu started from here.

After crossing the Sun Kosi ('Gold
River') the road follows the river to
Lamosangu ('Long Bridge'), the buses
usually stopping by the scruffy stalls by the
bridge for dal bhaat. One only needs to
have a quick look around and sniff the air to
realize that hygiene is not even marginal
but there are biscuits, chocolate and soft
drinks available.

From the bridge it's a further 110km to
Jiri, marked by kilometre posts that start at
0km from the Lamosangu bridge. This road
was part of a Swiss aid programme, constructed as a model to demonstrate building
techniques for mountain roads using appropriate technology. Rather than employing
expensive machinery it was decided to
maximize the use of local labour. Rocks

were broken with hammers and a lot of sweat, and all the wire netting was woven by hand, providing a vast amount of work. In addition to wages, food was sold in set quantities at subsidized prices to reduce the local impact of the hungry workforce. The only heavy machinery used was a road roller. The result is a Swiss-quality road that will probably last longer with less maintenance than any other road in Nepal. Unfortunately the technique and attention to detail hasn't been duplicated for the rest of Nepal's rural hill roads.

From Lamosangu it can be pleasant to ride on the roof of the bus (theoretically illegal) but take a jacket or wind-cheater. At the top of the first major ridge is **Muldi** where there may be another stop before continuing to **Charikot** (km54) where trekkers are sometimes requested to register. The turn-off to the left here leads to **Dolakha**, a few kilometres away (see p257). On a cloudless day the monumental twin-headed Gauri Sankar stands out for the next half hour. The high peak slightly right is Menglutse in Tibet.

The descent to the Tamba Kosi ('Copper River') is steep. At the bridge the driver takes a break for a cup of tea or two. If you are on the roof it's a good idea to start putting on warm clothes because it is still several hours and 38km to Jiri. The plantations you pass are a Swiss reforestation programme. After another pass the gradual descent to Jiri begins and at a stop at **Kot**

you might have to register at the police checkpost. **Jiri** is ten minutes further on.

Note that in winter it's not unknown for a snowfall or sheet ice to block a high section of the road, which means a couple of extra days' walking.

JIRI (1935m/6348ft)

Nestling in a fertile valley beyond the ugly materialism of the road, Jiri is a prosperous and tidy village. The people are mainly of the Jirel caste who originate, so the legend goes, from a Sherpa mother and a Sunuwar father. There are also some Sherpas and with the road (which linked Jiri in 1984) came the merchant castes, mainly Newars.

There are many *lodges* but only a few that trekkers frequent. Most are four storeys high but look the same height as the three-storied buildings; inside, the low doorways are headbangingly obvious.

Electricity comes from Lamosangu, from the Chinese hydro-project there. The fact that it costs something means that the farmers cannot afford it so it's used mainly by the local businesses and lodges. Since firewood (for cooking) is still cheap, apart from a couple of refrigerators and a hot water cylinder electricity is only used for lighting.

With Jiri being the beginning or the end of a trek most people are anxious to be on their way and there is little to hold you here other than to inspect the various Swiss projects. Don't expect peaceful lie-ins in

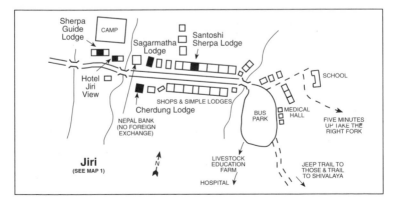

Jiri
(SEE MAP 1)

> ### Badminton frenzy hits Jiri
> Arriving in Jiri on a pleasant January afternoon, the place seemed to have gone badminton crazy. Over 100 people were playing with energetic enthusiasm and a similar number looked on as we wended our way between the makeshift courts, ducking to avoid shuttlecocks and erratic racquets in our search for candles. Several children aped their elders by improvising bits of card for rackets and hacky-sack balls for cocks. Was it all just for sport? Fun? Exercise? Or could this new-found enthusiasm for the game have something to do with the fact that the local women's group had banned the sale of alcohol ... ?   **Joel Schone**

the morning: you'll be woken at the crack of dawn by a cacophony of bus horns announcing the departures to Kathmandu. If you do have more time the hill above Jiri (at least a day's walk up) affords outrageous Himalayan views.

Planning the first day's trek
Walking from Jiri, groups generally stay at Shivalaya for the first night. This is only half a day's walk from Jiri but the first morning is busy with the porters and their loads being sorted out. This short, easy day is also ideal for gently accustoming the legs to the rigours of trekking. The facilities at Shivalaya are quite good so less fit independent trekkers may also consider spending the night here.

The next accommodation is in two simple *lodges* up the hill at Sangbadanda. Fit walkers can comfortably make the numerous lodges at Deorali although it is a long day. Reaching Bhandar is possible but your legs will suffer the following day.

Driving to Shivalaya is marginally quicker than walking, but probably less comfortable. You should be able to make Bhandar that day, and Sete the following day.

JIRI TO SHIVALAYA – STANDARD ROUTE   [MAP 1, opposite]
Each time this guide has been brought out the trail leaving Jiri has changed about a month later. Since there is now a jeep road on the point of opening no doubt this will happen again! Apologies to everyone. Currently, if trekking out of Jiri simply follow the porters, head along the jeep road before leaving it at an unmarked junction – though you'd be wise to ask your lodge owner for the latest.

The following assumes you are taking the standard route via Chitre:

Chitre An hour out of Jiri is Chitre, a shanty of primitive *teashacks*. The surrounding area looks horribly bare with goats having eaten all the vegetation and the people look decidedly poor. This is probably one of the most impoverished-looking areas on the whole route, although throughout Nepal there are many places similar to it. Around a bend lurks an unwelcome surprise: it's still a little way to the top of the small pass.

Small pass (2400m/7874ft) At the crest are a couple more *teashacks* and some new vistas. The path heads down; it's easy to

> ### Those
> This village is an hour's walk downstream of Shivalaya. Once it was the centre of an ancient iron mining and manufacturing industry that began to decline during the 1940s when Indian iron became readily available. Farming implements forged here were traded as far away as Tibet and this business was one of the first sources of wealth for Namche. A few iron products, particularly steel roosters, are still made here.

follow and in about ten minutes you pass a primary school. Around here is the usual spot for groups to have lunch. Another five minutes along the trail brings you to Mali.

Mali First there's a simple *teahouse*, then three *lodges* that look reasonable, one with a small shop in it. The facilities are basic and with it being so close to Jiri few trekkers ever stay here.

Leaving Mali the trail leads down, and down is the word. About one hour later cross a small stream; further on past a couple of buildings is the long suspension bridge over the Khimti Khola to Shivalaya.

Shivalaya (1800m/5905ft)
Resting on the east bank of the khola, Shivalaya ('Shiva's home' or 'Shiva's temple') was not much more than a sleepy

hamlet of eight or nine *lodges*. Now that the road has arrived, however, the pace of building is frantic, change is rapid, and lodges are far too numerous to list.

SHIVALAYA TO BHANDAR [MAP 2 p150]
The road is being pushed beyond Shivalaya and even at the time of writing sections of it went as far as Bhandar, though when it becomes navigable by car is anybody's guess. The following assumes you are walking.

The trail out of Shivalaya is steep from the first step, and will get the sweat flowing. The gradient relents only after the next village. The walking route is much more direct than following the road. There are a number of *lodges* under construction between here and Deorali.

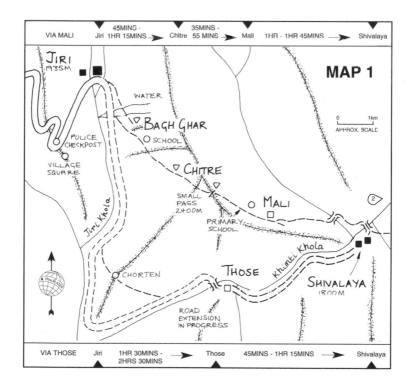

VIA MALI | 45MINS - Jiri 1HR 15MINS → Chitre | 35MINS - 55 MINS → Mali | 1HR - 1HR 45MINS → Shivalaya

JIRI 1935M

MAP 1

WATER

BAGH GHAR

O SCHOOL

POLICE CHECKPOST

VILLAGE SQUARE

Jiri Khola

0   1km
APPROX. SCALE

CHITRE

SMALL PASS 2400M

O MALI

PRIMARY SCHOOL

2

Khimti Khola

CHORTEN

THOSE

SHIVALAYA 1800M

ROAD EXTENSION IN PROGRESS

VIA THOSE | Jiri 1HR 30MINS - 2HRS 30MINS → Those | 45MINS - 1HR 15MINS → Shivalaya

Side trip to Thodung

For the energetic this route is worth the extra effort, providing you don't get lost. The views are good, especially on a clear morning when Gauri Sankar sparkles in the distance. In Thodung (3090m/10,137ft) there's one *lodge* set in the forest. The cheese factory here follows processes introduced by the Swiss, using similar technology to that in the small factories in the Alps. The idea was first introduced in the Langtang area after an FAO study (United Nations Food and Agriculture Organization) and spread throughout the region; the trekking route used to pass close to three more en route to Namche. Unfortunately, all were government-run – or rather mis-run – and in a rationalization all were closed. Now there is just one private cheese factory at Sallung.

Sangbadanda This is a mainly Sherpa settlement and has a couple of simple *lodges* with shops. Two minutes west is an important junction and a choice: the upper/left path leads to Thodung (see above); the right-hand trail is the slightly more direct and lower route to Deorali,

about a couple of hours away depending on your hill speeds.

Deorali (2705m/8875ft)

Meaning pass in Nepali, Deorali is a common village name. The actual village is slightly south where the water supply is bet-

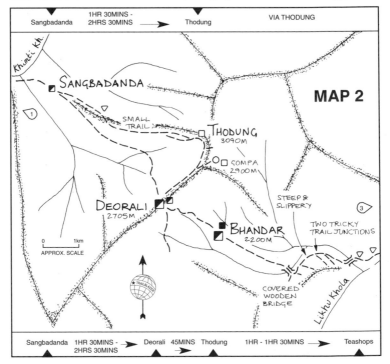

Sangbadanda — 1HR 30MINS - 2HRS 30MINS → Thodung — VIA THODUNG

SANGBADANDA

SMALL TRAIL

THODUNG 3090M

MAP 2

SOMPA 2900M

DEORALI 2705M

STEEP & SLIPPERY

BHANDAR 2200M

TWO TRICKY TRAIL JUNCTIONS

0   1km
APPROX. SCALE

COVERED WOODEN BRIDGE

Likhu Khola

Khimti Kh.

Sangbadanda 1HR 30MINS - 2HRS 30MINS → Deorali 45MINS → Thodung 1HR - 1HR 30MINS → Teashops

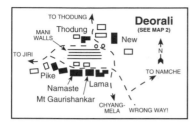

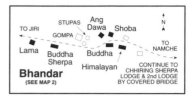

ter so again this is just a group of *lodges*. They are set in two neat rows divided by a set of mani walls (see map above), the first real sign of Buddhist Sherpa country. You should pass to the left of a mani wall or a wall of prayer wheels.

From some rocks immediately above the lodges there are superb views into the distance on a clear day; you can see much of the route ahead, and the scars of the new road. Below, the hillside stretches down to where the twin chortens of Bhandar are clearly visible. Take the left fork a couple of minutes below the pass; the descent is initially steep.

Bhandar (2200m/7218ft)
The Sherpa name for this area is Chyangma. Immediately above the chortens is a small gompa and below, a group of four *lodges*. The two main ones are *Ang Dawa Lodge* and *Buddha Lodge* but the others are also good.

A few of the lodges boast environmentally-friendly features that have become common in the better lodges along the route. 'Green' showers are provided by run-

ning pipes through the cooking fire, then into a hot-water tank which is sometimes connected directly to the shower-room. This produces essentially free hot water, using energy that would otherwise go straight up the chimney. It's a simple though effective system that has taken off not because of the green revolution but because there are numerous advantages for the lodge owners (the only way change can be introduced in an economy that generates virtually no surplus cash). Lodge owners are asked to cook a variety of meals and sometimes in huge quantities and trekkers also request hot water for washing. Heating water takes a long time so an instant source of hot water is invaluable. The system is cheap enough for the lodges to afford but beyond the reach of ordinary villagers.

BHANDAR TO JUNBESI [MAP 2 opposite; MAP 3 p152; MAP 4 p154]
From the chortens the descent is gentle with about seven simple *lodges* or *teahouses* evenly spaced a few minutes apart down the hill. There is a new, better trail to Kenja that locals will point out to you. Once back onto the old main trail you need to cross the Likhu Khola to Kenja.

✿ Solar cookers
Coming through Bhandar you will see what looks like a satellite dish on a wheeled trolley, with a pot in the centre. This is a solar cooker and Temba of the *Lama Lodge* told me that there are 36 of them in the Bhandar area, sponsored by the Rotary Club of Sweden. The reflector plates are made in Germany and the trolley made in Nepal.

But do they work? Temba pointed to two flasks full of hot water he had filled; apparently, he can boil ten litres an hour in full sunshine, with the trolley turned regularly to ensure the sun is kept on the pot. Of course, not all areas would benefit; but Bhandar, set on an east-facing plateau, is perfect. And all this without wiring or batteries. Prepare for tanning centres in Solu... **Joel Schone**

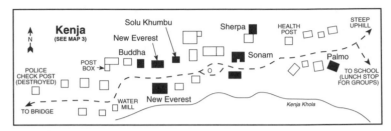

Kenja/Kinja (1640m/5380ft)

This is a thriving 'lodge town' with a few good *hotels* and no bad ones. It's a mixed village, mainly Sherpa with some Chhetri (a caste immediately below the Brahmins). Kenja is slightly unusual in this respect because, apart from Jubing, the trek from Bhandar to the Khumbu is through exclusively Sherpa country. The ruins here can be attributed to tourism. Once Kenja was nothing more than a couple of houses but people from up and down the valley were attracted by the rumours of fantastic wealth possible by setting up a lodge. By 1984 there were a couple of lodges and five houses but this has now grown to ten *lodges*.

In mid-1989 Kenja was linked to an electricity supply as part of a Japanese aid project. There are nine small generators and when they're all working (rarely) this generates 55kw which is enough power to provide electricity for cooking. Firewood is starting to become expensive but very few can afford the enormous cost of a stove. However, it was pleasing that the lodge owners I spoke to thought it entirely possible that if the project works well enough, lodge owners would begin cooking with electricity. Electricity would probably be a cheaper option than firewood in the near future. Stereos have already arrived here and one has to wonder how long it will be before there are video nights in Kenja.

In October you might see something that looks like a prickly pear dangling from leafy creepers. The local name is *iskus* and it must be cooked to be edible and tastes like a slightly sweet potato.

The side trail to Pike Peak (pronounced 'pee-kay'), the home of the benevolent spirit for this area, starts from the bridge over the Kenja Khola. The trail goes up the ridge to the south, then skirts the peak to a ridge heading north. It finally

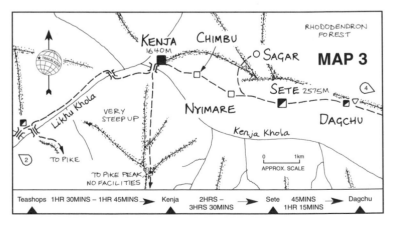

drops to the main trail after the Lamjura Pass. Since there are no facilities along the way, it is a camping route only. The panorama from the top is stunning.

Leaving Kenja

From Kenja it's an altitude gain of 1900m to the top of the Lamjura Pass and for this reason many people recommend staying in Sete to break the climb, although there are several lodges under construction in between too.

If you're reasonably fit, climbing over the pass in a single (tough) day from Kenja is quite possible. If you don't make it over the top there are some *lodges* where you can stay en route.

Sete (2575m/8448ft) This friendly Sherpa settlement is in two parts. First there are two *lodges*, one very spartan, then five minutes further on another three lodges with a few camping places. Sete is not a big village, with almost as many *lodges* as houses but it does have a small gompa.

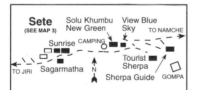

Dagchu When you've got your breath back, it's around an hour from Sete to Dagchu, a friendly settlement of six rather simple *lodges* atop the ridge. Out of the

forested areas there are some good views. To the south-east (right) you can see the twin tops of Pike Peak. The trail to the pass continues up the ridge; ignore all trails that lead off it. From some parts you can see the pass, well to the left of the ridge. Looking back you can see Deorali clearly with Bhandar below along with the new road from Jiri – the shape of things to come.

Goyem Another half an hour up brings you to Goyem with two groups of *teahouses/lodges* about five minutes apart. Apple juice, cider and apple brandy are all available here but the water supply is not clean so take particular care to purify water for drinking.

A minute out of Goyem is an important junction: continue up on the ridge through forest on a somewhat scrappy trail avoiding the good trail that begins contouring on the south side of the ridge. That is the direct, steep and rarely-used route to Salleri. The forest here is magnificent. Demand for firewood, however, grows with each new lodge built – a negative impact of the teahouse-style of trekking. In spring the rhododendrons put on quite a show with whole hillsides covered in blossoms that from late February spread upwards, reaching the crest of the pass by the end of April. The air is heady with their scent and with that of the many other flowering trees and shrubs.

Lamjura (3330m/10,925ft) Soon the trail becomes clearer and you reach three basic *lodges* scattered along the ridge that call themselves 'Lamjura'. This is the point where the trail starts contouring to the north of the ridge. There are several junctions but each trail rejoins the main route a few minutes later.

Further along in what was once pristine rhododendron forest three *lodges* replace the teashacks of yesteryear. Both settlements are above 3300m and so are quite high places to sleep. If would help if you slept at Deorali, but don't be unduly worried if you haven't. Although you are high and may have an uncomfortable night's sleep, you are descending the next day so there is little chance of worsening altitude sickness.

Passing a few mani walls, it's around half an hour to the top of the pass. Unless the weather is perfect this section can be very cold and windy, and in October even snow can fall with the patches shielded by the sun not melting for several days. In winter there may be quite a bit of snow lying around making the track muddy and even icy – real down-jacket weather. The difference to the temperature that altitude makes is really driven home to you as you head up this pass.

Lamjura La (3530m/11,581ft)
The prayer flags and chortens mark the gateway to the Solu (sometimes called Shorong) Sherpa area. It's common to suffer some altitude sickness, especially if you stay up here for a while to admire the view. This does not mean that you will not make it to the top of Kala Pattar, it's just a warning that ascending too fast has its consequences. You are in fact higher than Namche, where several nights are spent acclimatizing.

It's possible to climb the hill to the north of the pass. At first there is no trail but head along the ridge slightly on the western side and soon a small but definite path begins. This contours under the peak before finally doubling back with a stiff climb to the summit. It is a very strenuous climb and even if you felt perfectly well on the pass, the extra 500m gain in alti-

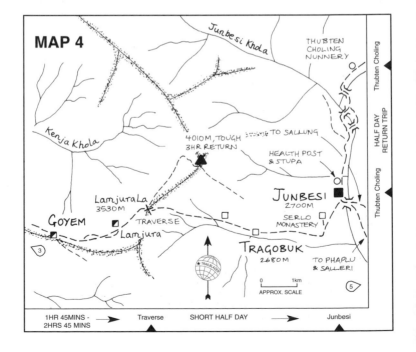

tude is often enough to induce a headache.

Heading down from the pass, there are many paths weaving through the forest but luckily they all head to the same place: a few well-spaced *restaurants* an hour below the pass. Occasionally you may see monkeys in the forest here.

Tragobuk / Taktok (2680m/9383ft) is proud to have a new gompa which you are welcome to look around. As with all gompas, it is customary to leave a donation when visiting: Rs100 is appropriate.

Continue straight through the long village and at junctions avoid trails that descend; these go to Salleri and not Junbesi. The scenic trail stays fairly high and rounds a major ridge and a large rock, with views of Junbesi and its distinctive yellow-roofed gompa. Take a look at the trail options immediately across the river from Junbesi while here.

A few minutes later at a signposted junction a trail leads off to **Serlo Monastery** where it is possible for a few people to stay. The local community have rebuilt the trail as it contours around the large rock, making it wider and walling it off from the valley below. Looking over the wall you can see the trail leading past the small primary school down to Salleri.

JUNBESI (2700m/8858ft)

This is one of the most pleasant Sherpa villages en route to Namche and it boasts some particularly good family-run *lodges* offering delicious fresh bread, pizzas, apple juice and cider. Apart from one large lodge built in the last few years Junbesi seems little changed from my first visit over a decade ago.

Although Salleri is the district headquarters, Junbesi has a primary school, high school and a **health post**. The high school has a particularly good reputation, largely due to the dedication of the headmaster. The health post has extension workers who are supposed to roam the surrounding hillsides offering vaccinations and health education programmes.

School education in Junbesi became available in 1964 when Sir Edmund Hillary helped construct a school house. It was quickly expanded and in 1972 a middle school was added. Both were run by the Himalayan Trust until 1975 when Nepal nationalized the primary and middle schools. In 1983, a high school was created with Himalayan Trust assistance and now the three schools (under one roof) muster nearly 300 pupils. High schools in Nepal are still privately-run, supported by student fees. In a country where the majority of the

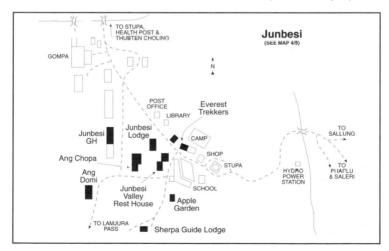

population has no money to spend on education it takes hard work and dedication to attend a high school. The costs (Rs2000-3000 for a year, including fees, books, bed and board) may not seem much but a village family, if they have any money at all, will need it to buy necessities and a little food around the lean time before harvest. Most of the pupils are boys and school fees, whether earned by father or son, will come from portering to Namche, low-paid agricultural work, or with luck a job as a porterguide or sherpa for a group where a month or two's work will pay for a year's schooling. For the even luckier few the Himalayan Trust offers three scholarships a year for the high school.

Development on a pleasant scale is evident everywhere in Junbesi. Agriculture is diversifying and a few lodges provide the majority of their vegetable requirements from their own gardens. The brandies, wines, ciders and jams are made with local fruit, as are the apple pies. Soybeans, wheat, corn, beans, potatoes and highly prized barley are the traditional crops. However, the altitude and problems with irrigation prevent the growing of rice which must be carried in from Jiri. There's a small hydro-electric scheme that provides lighting (with the odd hiccup). The gompa at the top end of town is old, perhaps founded in 1639. Ask your lodge owner if you want to see it.

A half-day trip to Thubten Choling

This is an active Buddhist monastery/nunnery with about 50 monks and over 200 nuns. Many are Tibetan; some are very recent arrivals. The murals were painted around 1970, a few years after the monastery was founded. The walk up is pleasant and, although it is little more than an hour away from Junbesi, with the friendly monks and beauty of the area do not count on being back for an early lunch.

From the monastery there's an **alternative route to Ringmo** over a 3476m/11,404ft pass. Unless you are confident about your route-finding ability, it is better to hire a lad from Junbesi who has been over this pass before.

Other gompas Around Junbesi are a scattering of gompas perched atop hills, good alternatives to visiting Thubten Choling. **Rumbak**, to the south above the track to Salleri, takes one and a half hours one way. Take something to eat and drink with you.

JUNBESI TO BUPSA
[MAP 5 opposite; MAP 6 p161]

Leaving Junbesi The Junbesi Khola is crossed on a steel bridge; from the other side, looking slightly downstream, you can see the hydro-electric plant. Note that after crossing the Junbesi Khola the main track divides twice. In each case take the upper/left path which should be signposted. The lower paths head to Phaplu and Salleri, a good half-day's walk away. The section around this huge ridge is one of the most pleasant walks so far. Although the trail climbs in places, it's not steep. The track is set high above the valley floor, at first through open forest. Later the view extends across the valley to picturesque villages surrounded by terraces and divided by sparse woodland.

Everest View Sherpa Lodge (3000m/9840ft)

This is an 'Everest View' lodge from which you can actually see Everest, the first point on the trek from Jiri where this is possible. Expanded in 1992 to provide dining with a view, it's perched on the end of a long grazing ridge that runs up to Numbur.

Naks (female yaks) are milked in the summer and autumn months and the rich milk is used to make just under 1000kg of pure nak cheese (although everyone wrongly refers to it as yak cheese) every year. The lodge owner manages the production using old Swiss methods. Delicious curd is often available too.

Early morning is generally the best time to spot Everest. If there's a single cloud in the sky a corollary of Murphy's Law says it will obscure Everest first, and it usually does. For the energetic even better views can be had by climbing part of the ridge behind.

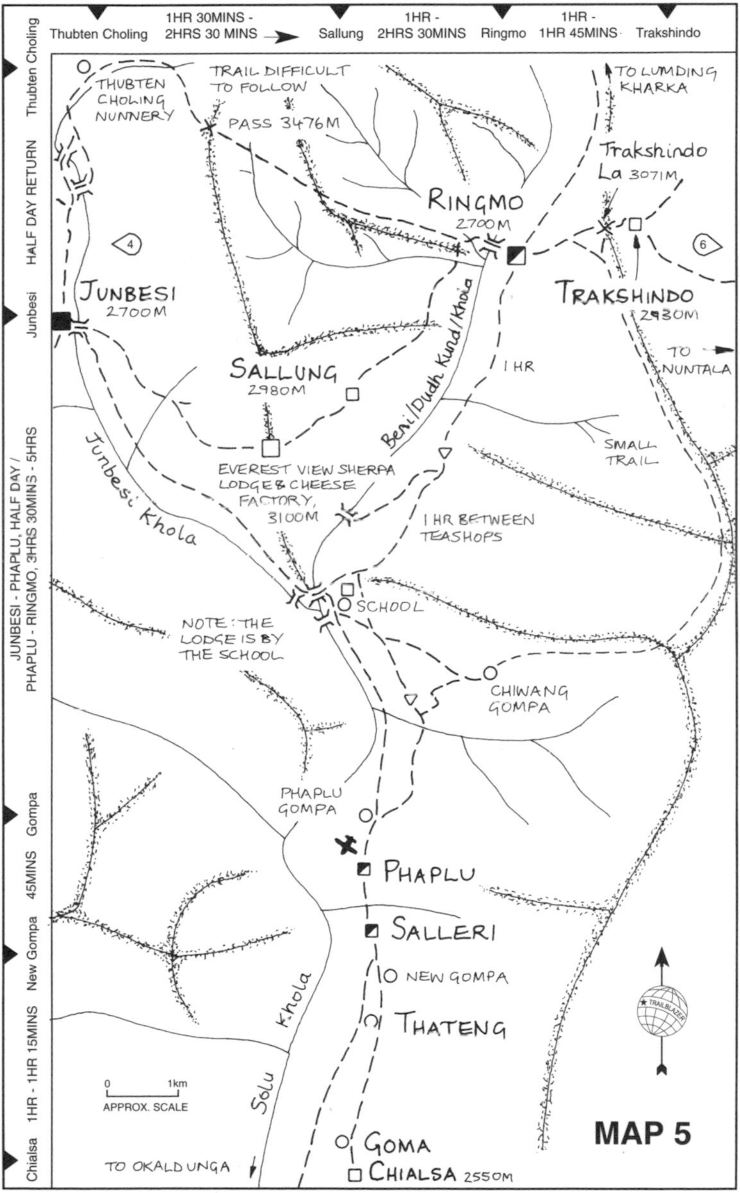

Thubten Choling
1HR 30MINS - 2HRS 30 MINS
Sallung
1HR - 2HRS 30MINS
Ringmo
1HR - 1HR 45MINS
Trakshindo
Thubten Choling
HALF DAY RETURN
Junbesi
JUNBESI - PHAPLU, HALF DAY / PHAPLU - RINGMO, 3HRS 30MINS - 5HRS
Gompa
45MINS
New Gompa
1HR - 1HR 15MINS
Chialsa
THUBTEN CHOLING NUNNERY
TRAIL DIFFICULT TO FOLLOW
PASS 3476M
RINGMO
2700M
TO LUMDING KHARKA
Trakshindo La 3071M
4
6
JUNBESI
2700M
TRAKSHINDO
2930M
TO NUNTALA
SALLUNG
2980M
Beni/Dudh Kund/Khola
1 HR
Junbesi Khola
SMALL TRAIL
EVEREST VIEW SHERPA LODGE & CHEESE FACTORY, 3100M
1 HR BETWEEN TEASHOPS
SCHOOL
NOTE: THE LODGE IS BY THE SCHOOL
CHIWANG GOMPA
PHAPLU GOMPA
PHAPLU
SALLERI
NEW GOMPA
THATENG
Solu Khola
0
1km
APPROX. SCALE
TRAILBLAZER
GOMA
CHIALSA 2550M
TO OKALDUNGA
MAP 5

Side route to Lumding Kharka

The path that continues straight ahead from the Ringmo mani wall leads to high grazing pastures below Numbur and several isolated high routes into the Dudh Kosi. There are **no lodges** or even villages until the Dudh Kosi, a two- to four-day walk away (depending on which route you take). The Lumding La route offers some good and unusual views of Everest, Lhotse and Makalu. Interestingly, it was used extensively by Tibetans who, because many yaks had died at Kharikhola in 1959, preferred this high route until the early 1970s. It was also the alternative route if the bridge across the Dudh Kosi below Jubing had been washed out; this was why the 1952 Swiss Everest Expedition was forced to use it. Two porters died of the cold which led to the Swiss providing the suspension bridge that now spans the Dudh Kosi. More than that, they set up and for many years funded HMG's suspension bridge division, the organization responsible for building many of the bridges across the country.

Sallung/Solung (2980m/9777ft) This hamlet also boasts magnificent views including a fraction of Everest and down the valley to the Phaplu airstrip. Once it had four *lodges* but they are in decline, although it is still possible to stay. These and the ***Everest View Lodge*** are convenient places to stay if you visited Thubten Choling monastery in the morning and had a late lunch in Junbesi. Leaving Sallung, the clear trail wanders gently downwards. After a few gullies you round another ridge for a change of view: the amazing knife-edge ridge of Karyolung whose ridge extends down to Ringmo and the Trakshindo La, the next pass.

The trail winds around ridges and streams to a wooden bridge across the Beni/Dudh Kund Khola, whose waters originate from the glaciers in the impressive basin formed by Karyolung (6511m/

21,361ft), Khatang (6853m/22,483ft) and Numbur (6959m/ 22,831ft). The twin peaks of Numbur and Khatang are the Shorong Yul Lha, where the Sherpa god for the Shorong area resides. It's possible to camp at the high grazing areas below their glaciers and stunning mountain faces; but this is virtually never attempted by trekkers.

Ringmo (2700m/8858ft) From the suspension bridge the trail climbs, steeply at first, to Ringmo and a major trail junction by the recently-built stupa. The south/right-hand trail heads to Phaplu and Salleri on a beautiful, wide path (see p224). Straight on is the route to the pass, Trakshindo La.

Ringmo is a spread-out settlement set among apple orchards and famous for all things apple. Try their apple pie, apple cake, apple juice, apple cider, and (or) their pink apple brandy. Apples, peaches and apricots are widely cultivated to such an extent that half the crop has to be made into delicious cider and firewater brandies. This is also the main source of fruit for the famous Namche apple pies.

At the top of Ringmo are two 50-metre mani walls. After correctly passing to the

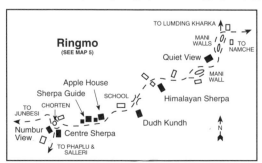

left of both do **not** continue straight on unless you're going to Lumding Kharka. The correct route (often signposted) is to the right. This is the beginning of the ascent to the Trakshindo La.

Immediately right after the Ringmo mani walls the trail divides after a few minutes at a well-signposted junction. Both trails lead to the pass.

Trakshindo La (3071m/10,075ft)
The pass, marked by a white stupa, divides the Solu (Shorong) and the Pharak Sherpa areas. There is a basic *lodge* and a handful of *teashacks* where porters stop for a welcome glass of tea. It's less than half an hour down to the gompa at Trakshindo, on wide stone steps, or what's left of them.

Trakshindo (2930m/9612ft)
There are two large but simple *lodges* in Trakshindo. If you arrive in cloudy weather and stay here be sure to have a look outside upon waking: the views are stunning. Trekking peak fans will enjoy the impressive pyramid of Kusum Kangguru. In the coldest winter months you may wake up in snow here and ice on the trail. The **gompa**, established in 1946 by the Tengboche Lama, can be visited and is usually open sometime early in the morning or around sunset. For a group of people the monk will often open up specially and you should leave a donation.

Nuntala is visible from the gompa and when leaving the path contours around immediately below the gompa fence and past a house or two before descending. The route down continues to contour in and out of gullies with a steep descent or two on the way. You pass some camping spots popular with porters heading for Namche.

Babu Chiri (see p119) was becoming a well-known mountaineer when, in 2001, he fell into a crevasse on Everest and died. A school is being built in memory of him.

Nuntala/Manidingma (2350m/7710ft)
Primarily a Sherpa village with a few Rai inhabitants, Nuntala (see plan) is pleasantly situated in a large valley. The bushes around and below the village are tea bush-

es. The views are better at the pass or gompa but the snowy tip of Karyolung can still just be seen, above a ridge to the north.

The wide paved street is lined with inns. Development here has been rapid since the first real lodge started operating around 1983. Environmentally-friendly water heating systems were installed in the fireplaces of some lodges in 1988 and electricity first lit the street lamps in July 1991. This mini hydro-electric scheme was set up privately by Pasang Sherpa, one of the many lodge owners, using a bank loan. The 'power house' is easily identified by the water pipe used to power the generator. If it's open take a look inside; Western concepts of a power station are of huge buildings and complex machinery but this system would fit in a Paris bathroom. It's all been well thought out for the needs of the village. By switching belts during the day the turbine is used to drive a circular saw or a flour milling machine. It had to be carried up here because an airlift by helicopter would have virtually doubled the total cost.

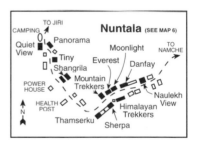

Leaving Nuntala the trail damage dates from the monsoon of 2000. There's a steep descent of at least a couple of hours to the suspension bridge across the Dudh Kosi. Early in the morning it can be slippery with dew. There's a couple of simple *teahouses* five minutes before the bridge but little else on the way.

Jubing (1700m/5577ft)
Half an hour uphill from the bridge, this is the only non-Sherpa village past Sete. It's a pretty Rai village, especially attractive in winter when the Khumbu appears brown and dry. Here

> ### Kayaking the Dudh Kosi
> In 1976 a group of British kayakers lead by Dr Mike Jones paddled part of the river. Lou Dickinson filmed it producing *Canoeing Down Everest*. The kayakers' summary was 'A steep rock-infested ditch with only fame to recommend it'. In 2000 it was kayaked again and found to be much easier, mainly on account of the development of kayaks. The plastic boats are much more manoeuvrable and tougher than the fibreglass boats used in 1976.

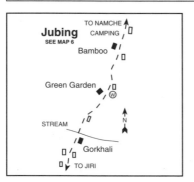

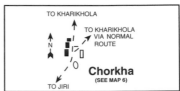

and is always used by porters. It heads over a small pass which offers good views up the valley. Khumbui Yul Lha is prominent, and with a map it is easy to figure out roughly where Namche, Khumjung and Khunde are, although they cannot actually be seen. The high snow and rock peak in the distance is Gyachung Kang (7922m/25,990ft), not Cho Oyu as guides will tell you.

plants thrive in the tropical warmth of the low altitude with flowers and vegetables growing year round. It is a rice-growing area, although the higher reaches of the village can support only millet and maize, the monsoon crops, and wheat plus barley in the winter. There are four *lodges*, each spaced a few minutes apart. Being warm year-round it's a good place to do a batch of washing – or at least a sock rinse.

Around ten minutes out of Jubing is a small but distinct trail junction. Continue upwards, **don't** take the path that cuts left through paddies and can be seen contouring around the next ridge. Another ten minutes up the hill is **Churkha** a group of three double-storied houses and another trail divide. Both forks head for Kharikhola; the left path is slightly longer in distance but not in time and is a little more gentle on the legs. The right fork is the 'Nepalese way' (the shortest distance no matter how steep)

Kharikhola/Khati Thenga (2050m/6726ft) This is a large spread-out village with houses dotted among the countless terraces. Among the Sherpas are a few Magars. There are thriving businesses, a boarding school and it's an agriculturally-productive area (though not nearly as productive as Jubing). Not only is it at a higher altitude (and so significantly cooler) but it also gets less sun, the terraces being north facing. Despite higher-yield crops, with the rapidly rising population there can be food shortages in the weeks leading up to the harvest. This is an especially difficult time for villagers as there is little trade from trekkers in the summer.

Kharikhola is developing into a focal point for the surrounding villages. This was started with the founding by Hillary and the

---

Opposite Top: The kitchen at a lodge on the trail. Most of the larger lodges now have energy-efficient stoves which incorporate a hot water system. **Bottom:** Inside an old-style lodge. Many lodges have a range of rooms, some even including attached bathrooms.

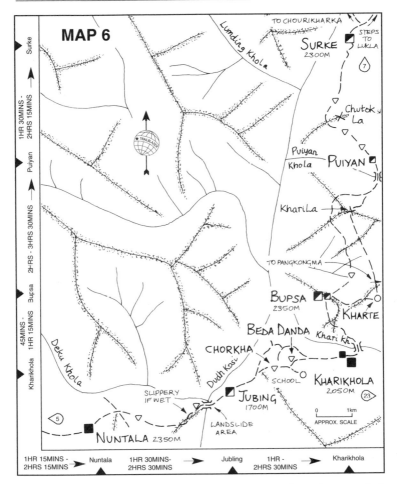

MAP 6

TO CHOURIKHARKA

SURKE 2300M

STEPS TO LUKLA

(7)

Lumding Khola

Chutok La

Puiyan Khola

PUIYAN

Khari La

TO PANGKONGMA

BUPSA 2350M

KHARTE

BEDA DANDA

Khari Kh.

CHORKHA

Deku Khola

Dudh Kosi

SCHOOL

KHARIKHOLA 2050M

(23)

SLIPPERY IF WET

JUBING 1700M

0   1km
APPROX. SCALE

(5)

LANDSLIDE AREA

NUNTALA 2350M

| 1HR 15MINS - 2HRS 15MINS → | Nuntala | 1HR 30MINS- 2HRS 30MINS → | Jubling | 1HR - 2HRS 30MINS → | Kharikhola |

Surke

1HR 30MINS - 2HRS 15MINS ↑ Puiyan

2HRS - 3HRS 30MINS ↑ Bupsa

45MINS - 1HR 15MINS ↑ Kharikhola

Himalayan Trust of a school and health post. The school grew rapidly, developing into a high school with an excellent reputation that has drawn pupils from villages several days' walk away. Now tailors and merchants have set up shop. Electricity

arrived in 1989, a private scheme organized by one of the lodge owners. In 1997 a foreign-funded **health post** staffed by a Nepali doctor was added to the list of facilities.

In late 1999 a small office began collecting a toll from trekkers. This money

---

Opposite Top: The crowds gather for Namche's popular Saturday market (see p174). **Bottom:** Lowland porters taking a break near Tumlingtar.

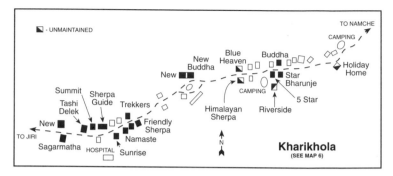

apparently goes to the VDC (Village Development Committee, the smallest administrative unit) and is used for development work. Supposedly it is optional, but that is not the feeling at the office. While it's not for us to comment on this particular VDC, it's a well-known fact that some VDCs use money wisely, while others are horribly corrupt.

The many *lodges* strung out along the main path for several kilometres are basically in three groups. Some are tidy, others falling apart. All are smaller and more homely compared to the Junbesi or Namche lodges. If you spend the night make an early start next day, leaving well before the sun actually reaches Kharikhola or the going gets hot and sticky. The chorten at Bupsa can be seen from Kharikhola but once over the small bridge there are several false crests that can be rather demoralizing on the slog up to Bupsa.

BUPSA TO SURKE
[MAP 6 p161; Bupsa / Gompa Danda/ Bumshing (2350m/7710ft) Perched on top of the ridge, this is a welcome refresh-

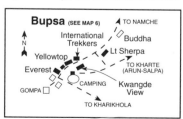

ment stop after the long climb. There are three *teahouses* in a cluster and, a few minutes further on, a couple more well-spaced *lodges*. Below, along the ridge, is a small gompa. You may be invited to visit – donations expected, of course.

Route to Salpa-Arun, Tumlingtar and Hille
Take the trail straight up the ridge behind the lodges in Bupsa (see plan).

Route to Namche
The trail between Kharikhola and Chourikharka was considerably altered in the early 1980s, levelling several small climbs. Despite the quicker trail porters haven't changed the stopping places so for groups this day is easier than it once was.

There's another trail that goes directly from Kharikhola to Surke but it's dangerous and therefore not recommended. It stays much closer to the Dudh Kosi and was used mainly by porters wanting to make a quick return down valley. Considered too steep for laden porters, it was never used for the journey up-river. Trekkers were never encouraged to go this way and now, since it has been neglected, it is dangerous involving some tricky traverses where the track has fallen away.

Khari The hills are not over yet: the trail continues steeply up, cutting into valleys, and there is a cluster of basic *lodges* where it is possible to stay.

After rounding more ridges you come to the **Khari La**, marked by a mani wall, a

The perfect flower
Home dull? Plant marigolds! Besides brightening up even the drabbest of mud houses, marigolds act as a natural pesticide to nearby kitchen (vegetable) gardens. Every Dasain, along with freshly whitewashed homes, a new string of marigolds adorns all entrances. It is also the preferred flower for *mallas* ('disposable' celebratory necklaces). Take a close look next time you pass a marigold: you'll notice two different types of flowers – one is male and one is female – and they don't smell too bad either. No wonder Nepalis consider the marigold to be the perfect flower.   **Suzanne Behrenfeld**

small *teahouse* and a rather smart new lodge, *Sonam Guest House*. This isn't as much of a pass as it once was, for the original trail used to be much higher. From here, at 2850m/9350ft, Khumbui Yul Lha and Gyachung Kang are visible. Looking down the valley you can really appreciate the scale of the middle hills. Continuing, the trail contour-climbs to a huge rock from where you can see Puiyan. There is a handful of *teashacks* on this corner.

Puiyan/Paiya/Chutok (2780m/9121ft)
The surrounding area was once heavily forested but many trees were cut down to make charcoal. This practice was banned in 1992 to try to save the remaining forests lining the Dudh Kosi here. There are several *lodges* and, ten minutes later, two more just before the climb to the pass.

Chutok La (Paiya La)
The new route passes 200m below the actual Chutok La, at 2780m/9121ft, but the views of Khumbui Yul Lha and Gyachung Kang are still good, though better just around the corner. The steep rock peak is Gonglha, above Lukla and the bigger mountain is Kusum Kangguru. Part of Lukla airstrip can also be seen but this is difficult to recognize: it's no use looking for a stretch of level ground.

On a corner further down at a place called Pakhepani is the aptly-named *Khumbu View Lodge*, and the smaller *Mountain View*.

Surke/Surkie/Bua (2300m/7546ft)
Local legend says that this area was once a lake; this would account for the fertile soil. Bua, the Sherpa name for the hamlet, means 'damp', no doubt from the lack of sun, but in fact it's a pleasant-enough place. Just around the corner from Surke are the first good views of Nupla (5885m/19,308ft) which forms part of the spectacular Kongde ridge that rears up above the Bhote Kosi by Namche.

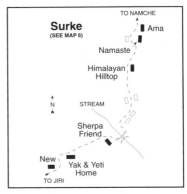

The good dal bhaat guide

In those early trekking days of the 1980s and 90s there was very little choice for a meal: roll up at a lodge at 11-ish and there would be dal bhaat and little else. Now you'll rarely see dal bhaat, at least in high season on the busy routes, with the lodges dishing out apple pie and pizzas instead.

Out of season, however – or if you're with a bunch of friends and happen to catch the owner at the right time – providing you can wait 40 minutes you might be in for a surprise. In the low country in January, for example, we got a delicious spicy tomato chutney and an excellent potato soup instead of dal, with some fresh *mullah* (radish) on the side. Our smiling *sahuni* (female business owner) then produced a tiny steel plate on which was lovingly arranged a green, orange, and red chilli, the idea being that you take a bite of the chilli then shovel the food in afterwards, local style. The next day we got sticky rice, black dal, and some pickled mullah from some jars in the kitchen that would not have looked out of place in Frankenstein's lab (you may have to ask for this as they rarely give such delicacies to guests). For extra protein ask for *sukuti* – slightly dried buffalo meat usually found hanging over the kitchen fire, which is then fried up with chillies and sometimes garlic and ginger – or even pork, which is usually reminiscent of British pork scratchings. **Joel Schone**

Route to Lukla About ten minutes out of Surke by a mani are some stone steps heading up; these lead to Lukla in about an hour. Although the trail starts off well-defined it breaks up into many confusing paths. You need to cross a bridge en route. If in doubt stay on main trails; going left at intersections usually works except around a carved mani rock. There are tracks up both sides of the runway. Note that it's not necessary to visit Lukla; to confirm a ticket, simply turn up the afternoon before your flight.

Direct route to Namche This continues straight ahead from the mani wall out of Surke. A little further on is an impressive waterfall, so high and close that it defies most camera lenses, although over the bridge and up the hill there's a more complete view. The trail traverses some impressively steep hillside. In the past, in tough country like this, the trails tended to be precarious and narrow but to cater for tourists this has been blasted out to a safe width. Stone steps and a few cunningly-constructed stone shelters herald Mushe, still a few minutes away.

Mushe/Nangbug This is a pleasant place with a few *lodges*; since it is overshadowed

by Lukla few people stay here. Many vegetables are grown in the area especially for the hotels in Lukla and Namche.

Chourikharka/Dungde (2760m/ 9055ft)

Meaning 'yak-herding area', Chourikharka is often mis-spelt Chaunikharka, although if you listen hard to a local person saying the name, the quietest of 'n's can often be heard. Dungde, the Sherpa name, means *dingma* or flat farming area: a more accurate name now. The village begins at the top of the short steep climb to the kani and has three well-spaced *lodges*.

Route from Chourikharka to Lukla

Thankfully Lukla is not visible from here but there are numerous small trails up. First head for the school, then from there a path leads up to join the main trail. The Hillary school was constructed in 1964 and has expanded to provide education to the final grade ten. There is also a **health post** founded by the Himalayan Trust. Alternatively walk to Chaplung and take the main trail.

Direct route to Namche If you're bypassing Lukla, the route description continues on p168.

Trekking from Lukla

INTRODUCTION

For the majority of trekkers and expeditions this is where the Everest trail now begins. Surprisingly though, Lukla wasn't built with tourists in mind. Sir Edmund Hillary and friends' intention when they constructed the airstrip in 1964 was to make it easier to bring building supplies in for the ever-growing number of projects they were undertaking. To this very day Hillary regrets that it was ever built, and (unfairly) blames himself for the volume of trekkers now arriving (assaulting, he thinks) the Khumbu. Undoubtedly the Lukla airstrip has made access easier and so, too, has the increasing standard of the lodges. Now the Khumbu isn't the exclusive domain of mountaineers and tough trekkers; instead it is enjoyed by a surprisingly broad spectrum of people.

With a sometimes alarming bump, you step out of a time capsule back into rural Nepal. It is no longer a huge leap back in time; instead the Time Lords have jumbled the modern world with the ancient in a confusing mess. Canned beer is drunk alongside *rakshi*, the most basic of spirits, Mars bars sit alongside *chirpee*, a dried cheese as old as yak herding itself, but from now on the only wheels you'll see are prayer wheels. It can take a few days to discover your trekking legs and settle into the rhythm of the days. It can even take a while before you begin to look around with a true appreciation of the surroundings, which is a

pity, because the trail to Namche sits in a magnificent gorge (beginning a day's walk to the south). The villages are a fascinating study of a strongly bonded community and the cultural side shouldn't be forgotten in the race to Chomolungma (Everest).

Services in the Khumbu

Lukla and Namche have a post office and bank each as well as moneychangers; if you are stuck the occasional lodge owner will also change US$ cash though at less than favourable rates. Visa and other plastics are **not** accepted anywhere. The Khumbu is well endowed with medical facilities. The Western-staffed Khunde bush hospital is open year-round, Western doctors staff the HRA clinic at Pheriche during the peak trekking seasons, while Lukla has a health post with a capable health assistant who can contact Khunde if needed, and there is even a dental clinic in Namche. There are telephones all over the Khumbu: most use a powerful radio system to link with telephones in Namche or Khumjung so amazingly enough you are rarely more than half a day from a phone; you can even make international calls.

LUKLA (2850m/9350ft)

It is a relief to escape the hustle and bustle of Kathmandu, not to mention the pollution, but initially probably the greatest relief is landing safely. Lukla means sheep corral, which is all it was before the airstrip was built. Now it's more like a tourist pen operated by a mish-mash of peoples: many Sherpas but also Rais, Brahmins and Chhetris. The sole industry is tourism but with 15–25 flights a day during the busy season, that's now a large industry.

Mountain madness

A number of lodge owners laugh at this phenomenon. We at Khunde Hospital cry over it. Some of our patients with serious AMS have been so goal-orientated that their trek, instead of being the experience of a lifetime, has turned into the journey from hell, with the one objective of seeing Everest close up over-riding all else. The Khumbu has so much more to offer than Everest. If your only focus is to see Everest, why not take a scenic flight instead?

Sue Heydon, ex-Khunde Hospital

Lukla airstrip

The airstrip was constructed by local Sherpas with Hillary's supervision. It took a month and cost US$2650. Being quite short, it could safely handle planes with only about eight passengers but it's subsequently been extended several times, the last time in 2000-01 when the runway was reshaped and tar sealed. Although it is still a tricky landing requiring a steep approach, it is much less hair-raising than it was and much smoother too, enabling not just the sturdy Twin Otters to land, but now the STOL (Short Take Off and Landing) Dorniers. The airport facilities were also expanded to cater for growing traffic. The Asian Development Bank financed the project. Despite the precarious nature of the landing, and although there have been a few snapped undercarriages, there have been no major accidents here.

For the children of the local people, Lukla boasts one of the few schools in the area that was not initiated by the Himalayan Trust. It's only a primary school so the middle and high school children must go to Chourikharka or to boarding school in Kathmandu.

Lukla now has a three-phase 15kw electricity system but charges are high so only the lodges can afford to be connected; even so, demand from the lodges outstrips supply despite the fact that that they don't use the power for cooking. This would require a supply of about 50kw more, necessitating the building of a small dam which might happen sometime – but probably not anytime soon.

Although Lukla is a well-developed and prosperous town by trekking standards, the community has never been able to solve its rubbish problem. Residents blame each other: some blame the poor, some the lodges' hired-helps, some the huge influx of porters and some the trekkers – in fact, they blame everyone but themselves. If you see rubbish in town, especially the stream which has turned into a rubbish pit and on the edge of town by the trails out, complain to your lodge owner and anyone else you can. Perhaps persistent cajoling may finally help to resolve a problem that's been plaguing the town for over ten years now.

Lodges

There's a wide variety of *lodges*. The most luxurious are *Sagarmatha Resort*, *Villa*

Sherpani and *Khangri*, where rooms with attached bathroom cost around US$20 a night. At the other end of the market are basic *lodges* for the porters and guides who hang around for another job; and, of course, there's everything in between. Despite the numerous comfortable places to stay, many trekking companies still provide accommodation in tents and group members who want a bed in a lodge must pay for it themselves.

Airline ticket reconfirmation

Flying Lukla to Kathmandu you are supposed to reconfirm your ticket the afternoon before you fly. Royal Nepal's (RNAC) office is open for reconfirmation only between 3pm and 4pm and these are the hours quoted by most other airline offices, but in practice tickets can usually be reconfirmed any time up to around 5pm; talk with your lodge owner if you have problems.

Should you reconfirm? It is probably wise to do so, and as such you should try to arrive in Lukla around 4pm. However, if you are out of peak season you can usually get away with seeing the airline staff first thing in the morning or enlisting the help of your lodge owner to track down the airline person (except RNAC).

Buying a ticket

You don't have a ticket and want to buy one? Amazingly enough, peak season or otherwise you stand a good chance of arriving one afternoon and leaving the next day.

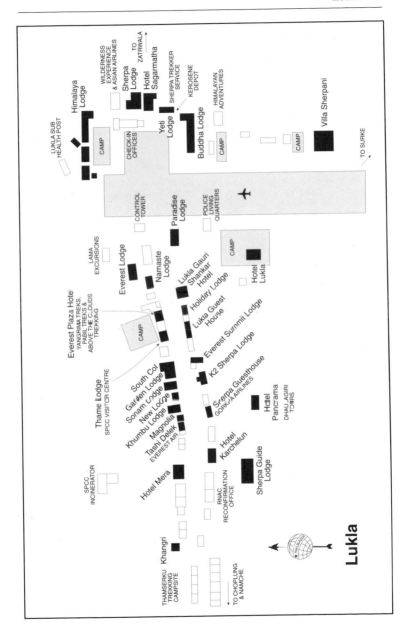

Lukla

Altitude awareness
The vast majority of people who fly into Lukla claim not to feel the altitude at all but many people seem to be afraid of admitting 'weakness' here on their very first night. People experienced with high altitude should notice the air feels sharper, fresher and drier, and this isn't just the lack of pollution. It is quite normal to get breathless climbing stairs and it is also common to have a (usually light) headache that evening. Even people who have been to altitude previously sometimes experience this, and it shows that your body needs to adapt, though it doesn't mean that you are particularly susceptible to AMS. However, be kind to your body, drink plenty of fluids and take it easy.

With the number of airlines flying in and the number of flights it is a bit unusual not to scrape a seat from somewhere, although sometimes it can be very last minute and on the last few flights. To make the process easier ensure that you have dollars to pay for the ticket, preferably the right amount, and don't have too much luggage.

Other services
Since national park rules prohibit trekking companies from using firewood past Jorsale a **kerosene depot** has been opened here. There's also a **health post**, set up with French aid and supported by the Himalayan Trust when other funds aren't forthcoming. Staffed by competent locals with a stake in the community, it is one of the best functioning health posts in the country.

Unlike Namche's **telephone** system, Lukla's has always had chronic problems, lines are frequently down and suffer interference from the airport control tower, but you can sometimes get through to Kathmandu.

LUKLA TO NAMCHE [MAP 7, opposite]
This is a trekkers' highway with *teashops* and *lodges* lining the route and, other than while ascending the hill to Namche, lodges are never more than half an hour apart. Although it is a busy and often a rushed hike up, there are many rewards for focus-

ing on the surroundings. There are several beautiful gompas en route and many smaller lodges where you can sit around the kitchen fire and chat with the owner. There are also alternative trails that are rarely used by trekkers.

Chaplung/Chablung/Lomdza (2660m/8727ft) Here the trail from Lukla meets the main trail from Jiri and Salpa-Arun. Coming down from Namche, the straight route up some gentle stairs out of Chaplung leads to Lukla, while a smaller trail drops for the real walk out, a little past the *Ama Dablam Guest House*.

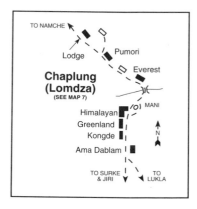

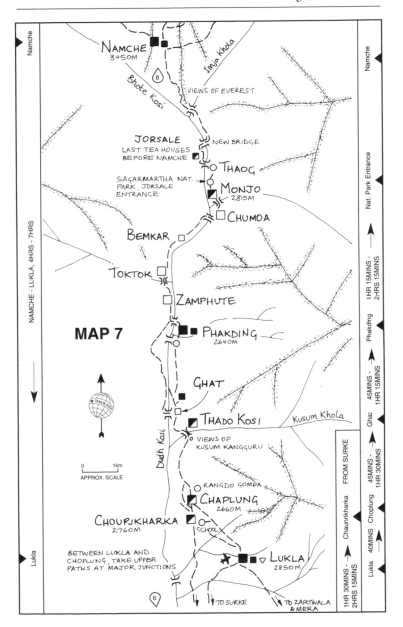

NAMCHE 3450M

Bhote Kosi

Imja Khola

⑧

VIEWS OF EVEREST

JORSALE
LAST TEA HOUSES
BEFORE NAMCHE

NEW BRIDGE

○ **THAOG**

SAGARMARTHA NAT.
PARK, JORSALE
ENTRANCE

○ **MONJO**
2815M

□ **CHUMOA**

BEMKAR □

TOKTOK □

□ **ZAMPHUTE**

PHAKDING 2640M

○

MAP 7

GHAT

□

0 1km
APPROX. SCALE

□ **THADO KOSI**

Kusum Khola

○ VIEWS OF
KUSUM KANGGURU

Dudh Kosi

○ RANGDO GOMPA

□ **CHAPLUNG**
2660M

CHOURIKHARKA
2760M

○
SCHOOL

LUKLA 2850M

BETWEEN LUKLA AND
CHOPLUNG, TAKE UPPER
PATHS AT MAJOR JUNCTIONS

⑥

↓ TO SURKE   ↓ TO ZARTWALA
& MERA

Namche

Namche

NAMCHE - LUKLA, 4HRS - 7HRS

Nat. Park Entrance

1HR 15MINS -
2HRS 15MINS

Phakding

45MINS -
1HR 15MINS

Ghat

45MINS -
1HR 30MINS

FROM SURKE

Chaunrikharka   Choplung

Lukla   40MINS

1HR 30MINS -
2HRS 15MINS

Lukla

Rangdo Gompa Stunningly set into the rock wall, this gompa is usually closed. Ask at the lodges for the key and usually a child will accompany you up. It is customary to leave a donation for the upkeep: Rs100 is appropriate, but any donation is appreciated. A village gompa promotes community spirit and pride and is a meeting point during festivals.

Thado Kosi Here an elegant bridge crosses the Kusum Khola. The tables outside the three *lodges* offer impressive views of Kusum Kangguru, a good place for a cuppa. This mountain is revered by local people; its name means the 'White (or Pure) Mountain House of the Three Gods' and indeed from around Namche three individual peaks can be seen.

Ghat/Nynyung This is the next settlement, just around the corner. *Ghat* means

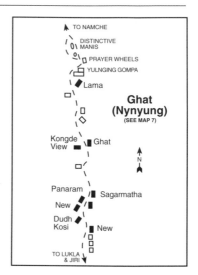

Ghat (Nynyung)
(SEE MAP 7)

TO NAMCHE

DISTINCTIVE MANIS

PRAYER WHEELS

YULNGING GOMPA

Lama

Kongde View

Ghat

Panaram

Sagarmatha

New

Dudh Kosi

New

TO LUKLA & JIRI

Sherpa do's and don't's

(Compiled with the assistance of **Urken Norbu** of Dole). You are now in Sherpa country. They are a relaxed people whose favourite pastimes include gambling with dice, drinking chang, joking and kidding around, then repenting in the gompa.

Do:
- Treat them as equals
- Smile, be friendly and take time to say hello or chat
- Joke with the right people, for you can't offend them
- If offered a drink with refills, accept a minimum of two refills
- Ask about culture and explain your own realistically. Once this might have been a delicate subject, but now it isn't: most sherpas aren't the least bit naive.
- Ask about caring for the environment, and mostly you will be surprised – they *do* care, do sometimes spend their own money on conservation and, furthermore, often complain that the government doesn't do anything
- Hand over money or things with your right hand or both hands
- Accept with your left hand or both hands
- If someone (usually a good friend) shakes hands with both hands, reciprocate

Don't:
- Sit in the head of the house's place by the fire (usually the right-hand side, the warmest spot)
- Stretch your legs out so that people have to walk over them
- Throw rubbish on the fire, unless you are told it is OK
- Put your feet or boots up on the fire
- Whistle inside the house
- Put your feet or bum on a table
- Touch anyone (children or adults) on the head or top part of the shoulders

'bridge' in Nepali and the bridge here was once important because it was one of the alternatives to the bridge at Jubing that was often washed away. With the advent of strong steel-cabled suspension bridges it has lost its importance.The direct route to Namche does not cross the bridge but instead follows a trail lined with *lodges* a few minutes apart. Few trekkers stay here but there are some friendly lodge owners, even if the lodges themselves aren't so fancy. It is often possible to have a look in the gompa at the top end of town.

Phakding-Rhanding (2640m/8661ft)

Welcome to lodge-city. A short half day's walk from Lukla, Phakding is the usual overnight spot for groups who've flown in to Lukla and as a result has a multitude of big, high standard *lodges*, which may come as a shock to Jiri and Salpa-Arun walkers.

Despite their size the *sahuni* are friendly, when not run off their feet. However, it is not necessary to stay here and there are plenty of alternatives further up, although the lodges are not quite as big.

If you arrive with time to spare there are two gompas on the west side of the river, half an hour from the main part of Phakding and visible from there. Another ten minutes further on is the village of Gomila, which is rarely visited by trekkers.

The long suspension bridge that joins Phakding and Rhanding was built in 1999, replacing a bridge that in recent years had rather more character than many trekkers cared for. Just beyond Rhanding the trail traverses a steep section that periodically collapses and falls away through erosion.

Toktok and Bemkar

Between Phakding and Monjo, a leisurely couple of hours' walk, are many *teahouses* (marked Zamphute on the map) and small shops and the occasional proper *lodge*. From Toktok the sheer face of Thamserku comes into view to the north-east. Bemkar has a developing set of *lodges* beginning above the waterfall pool.

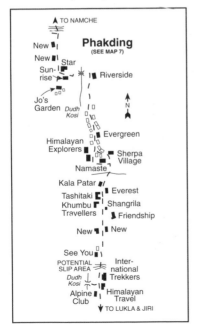

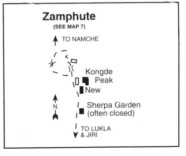

❏ **Timbore**
Beside the trail between Lukla and Namche you might notice a bush with large thorns similar in shape to rose thorns. In September this bears red berries, from which a black seed emerges as the berry dries. The flesh (rather than the seed) is crushed to make the spice timbore. It has a sharp distinctive taste and numbs the tongue and gums so it is widely used for toothache.

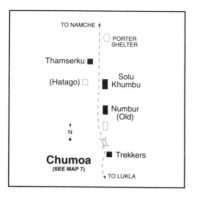

TO NAMCHE

○ PORTER SHELTER

Thamserku ■

(Hatago) □

Solu Khumbu ■

Numbur (Old) ■

N

Trekkers ■

Chumoa
(SEE MAP 7)

↘ TO LUKLA

Chumoa is a town that has moved with the times. Old Chumoa lies just south of the long 1997 cable bridge, so to catch the trekking business a couple of *lodges* have moved north to join the ruins of the Chumoa Lodge Hatago. This was one of the first high-standard lodges between Lamosangu (before the days of the road to Jiri) and Namche and was really a place to be looked forward to after the basic places on the long walk in.

Monjo (2815m/9235ft) There are a handful more *lodges* here, some quite large

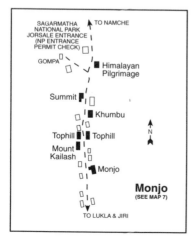

SAGARMATHA NATIONAL PARK JORSALE ENTRANCE (NP ENTRANCE PERMIT CHECK) □

TO NAMCHE

GOMPA □

Himalayan Pilgrimage ■

Summit ■ □

Khumbu ■

Tophill ■ ■ Tophill

Mount Kailash ■

N

Monjo ■

Monjo
(SEE MAP 7)

TO LUKLA & JIRI

and a few simple inns and **teashacks**. Signs welcoming donations herald the monastery, situated a hundred metres or so off the main trail. Strangely, despite ten years of donations, not much has materialized and locals now support another gompa. A minute later you reach the gateway to Sagarmatha National Park.

Sagarmatha National Park (Jorsale entrance) At the guarded entrance to the park your national park permit will be checked. If you don't already have a permit you can get one here. The fee as at August 2002 was Rs1000. Porters and guides must also register and have their loads checked.

From this point on no firewood is allowed to be cut so all groups must use kerosene for both themselves and their porters. Implied also is the universal 'Pack it in, pack it out' national park principle, a rule that most trekking companies flagrantly flaunt. The guidelines for rubbish are that whoever provides the goods or supplies should dispose of whatever rubbish they generate. This means that groups should pack out their rubbish, or at the very least dispose of it properly, but many don't.

For individual trekkers, it's the locals (who are, after all, getting the benefits of business) who are responsible for disposing of their rubbish. In practice this is a surprisingly small quantity of rubbish since egg cartons and sacks for rice are recycled, while empty noodle and biscuit packets are burnt. Mineral water bottles and soft drink cans (please crush cans), however, are a problem. Glass used to be the biggest problem but in 2001 lodge owners sensibly resolved to stop selling glass beer bottles and soft drinks.

Porters and camping group crews are by far the worst offenders when it comes to rubbish, though the problem of rubbish is better managed in the Khumbu than anywhere else in Nepal. There are two rubbish removal projects, one organized by the national park and the other by the Sagarmatha Pollution Control Committee, partly funded by the World Wide Fund for Nature (WWF) – although it must be said both appear to have been neglecting their

The Himalayan Trust and Sir Edmund Hillary

The Himalayan Trust is a charity that has helped local people set up almost thirty schools, several hospitals and construct many bridges and runways in the Solu Khumbu.

Many years on, the positive results are obvious and the region is far ahead along the development road compared with the rest of rural Nepal. Its phenomenal success is the result of sound principles and dedicated staff. Sir Edmund Hillary deserves the highest praise for his selfless efforts. Almost every Himalayan Trust school, bridge and hospital bears the stains of Hillary's sweat and he still returns to Nepal virtually every year to continue the work. Villagers soon saw him as the one person who could realize their local projects.

It is the fact that these were projects initiated by the people themselves (rather than imposed by the government or a distant aid agency) that has been the key to their success. Development has happened at the village pace. Involvement of the local people in their projects has been another reason for their success. As far as possible, villagers must provide land and labour although the Trust provides the bulk of finance required for materials. This degree of local involvement ensures that bridges, hospitals and schools are well cared for. In addition, more than 50 scholarships are awarded each year for further education, with priority for girls.

aims recently. In fact the locals have seen the tourism benefits of keeping their villages tidy and free of rubbish and generally do a good job, the Namche and Khumjung youth groups clean trails several times a year and lodge owners often sing in groups cleaning the trails too so if you do see rubbish, it is usually of fairly recent origin. If everybody picked up the occasional piece there would be none at all.

Jorsale/Tha Og Leaving the park entrance the path drops steeply to the long suspension bridge, built in 1995, across the Dudh Kosi.

The *lodges* and *teahouses* on the other side are the last lodges until Namche, as some of them indeed announce. Namche is still a minimum of 90 minutes away and closer to three hours if you are particularly slow so ensure that you have enough snacks to get you there.

High bridge over the Dudh Kosi Some boulder hopping and a couple of short but steep climbs bring you to this long, Swiss-built suspension bridge constructed in 1989 across the Dudh Kosi, the gateway to the

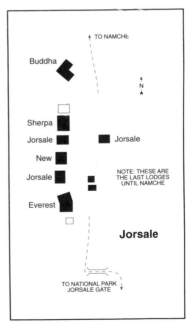

> ### ❖ Geography in action
> In September 1977 a huge avalanche peeled off Ama Dablam and crashed into a glacial lake. The lake burst and sent a great wave of water down the valley. A number of bridges which were normally unaffected by monsoon floods were wiped out as well as some sections of the trail.
>
> It has taken a long time, but the washed out bridges have virtually all now been replaced. The next calamity, however, cannot be far away. There are many forces that shape the landscape, and these waves of water are not only monumental in scale, but common too. Their causes are numerous: sometimes it is a lake that bursts; often it is a landslide that blocks a river, causing it to bank up before releasing a devastating wall of water that cuts into the river bed, undercutting the banks and providing the instability for yet another hillside to collapse and block the river again ... and so the process starts all over again.

Khumbu. Apparently designed with catastrophes in mind, it is indestructibly high above the river. After the steep concrete steps the path is broad and pleasant, having been widened and tidied up to lessen erosion. It is still quite a hill, especially hard on the legs if you flew in to Lukla, and the rapid gain in altitude may induce a headache. The halfway point is marked by a pile of rubble that was once a teashack (and hopefully will be rebuilt). From the ridge extending to the rear (now a bit of a toilet), are views of Everest, Lhotse and Nuptse.

As you near Namche, with occasional views of the town ahead and above, you reach a collection of *lodges* used by porters followed by a junction. The proper entrance to the town is via the lower path through a kani and up past the spring but local shopkeepers prefer that you take the upper route along the trail (which sometimes resembles a small stream and sometimes a rubbish pit) so that you pass their wares.

NAMCHE/NAUCHE (3450m/11,319ft)
Welcome to the Namche bowl. Looking across to the huge face of Kongde and with sharp peaks glistening above, you really know that you are in the mountains. Since all routes upwards pass through here, and it's an essential acclimatization stop, the facilities are well-developed and the village bustles with trekkers most of the year.

Called Nauche by all Sherpas and Naboche by Tibetans, the village is more widely known as Namche, a century-old Nepali mispronunciation. It's also long been referred to as Namche Bazaar, inaccurate since at the time all trading was conducted in private homes; the weekly market started only in 1965. The Sherpa name, Nauche, is in fact only a short form of an older name, thought to be Nakmuche or Nakuche, meaning 'big dark forest' – unfortunately now an inappropriate name. However, the couple of walled off areas on the hillside above the village are remedying this, and slowly but surely forests of pine are returning.

This thriving village has grown up around a magnificent spring in its centre though it was only recently realized that this spring water is not clean. Now the drinking water is taken from a clean source, another step in the ongoing development of the village.

Acclimatization
It is important for all trekkers to spend at least two nights acclimatizing here and, if fresh from Lukla, spending three nights may be advisable if you have spent only one night on the trail between Lukla and Namche. However, even if you do adhere to this advice it's not unusual to suffer mild altitude sickness at Namche and some people have trouble sleeping. If AMS symptoms do occur or are worse on the second night then staying three nights or taking Diamox is a good policy; you will only

---

Will this be you?

At the Khunde hospital we see too many cases of severe altitude sickness. Many people arrive close to death, and all need not have got so dangerously sick if they had followed altitude advice and guidelines. For example, a trekker in his early twenties arrived dying from HACE. From Monjo he had climbed to Gokyo in three days and had attempted Gokyo Ri. He said he knew there were warnings about altitude sickness – his English was excellent – but 'who ever reads them?' As you can guess, he did live to tell his story.

Our sickest patient who lived was a lowland porter but he was in a coma for five days. The Nepalese, especially Sherpas, have the completely untrue belief that Nepalese don't suffer from altitude sickness; they consider it a foreigners' disease, yet lowland porters are just as susceptible as foreigners, if not more so because of the load they carry. Ensure your sirdar is aware of this and ask the company to hire only altitude-experienced porters: it is false economy to hire young, inexperienced and therefore cheaper porters, as some will get sick and there have been cases of them being set down without companions and nearly dying. Watch your porters if you don't trust your sirdar, and if they ask for aspirin it may be because they haven't drunk enough fluids, but this is also a sign that they may indeed be suffering AMS.

One British trekker's porter became very sick at Lobuche. He had probably been suffering altitude sickness for a while but either didn't know what it was or didn't tell anyone. As soon as the trekker realized what was up, he helped him down but the porter died on the trail while still a day's walk from Khunde (Pheriche was closed). He was in shock and will suffer regrets for the rest of his life.

Sue Heydon, ex-Khunde Hospital

---

invite further trouble higher up if your body is not given a chance to cope adequately here. A sound alternative is to spend the third night at Phunki Tenga which is slightly lower and may give your body a chance to recuperate. The fact that the next night will be spent 600m higher should not matter if you have already spent two nights at Namche. See pp281-90 for more information on Diamox and AMS.

If you have plenty of time, an extra night's stop in Thame or Khumjung/Khunde/Kyangjuma/Phortse would be rewarding and further aid acclimatization. Since these villages are at an equivalent altitude to Tengboche they are also excellent alternatives to spending two nights there.

Note that it is possible, although rare, to develop serious altitude sickness at Namche: several trekkers have even died in Namche because people did not consider they could be sick with AMS. If you feel bad tell somebody responsible.

Lodges

In and around Namche there are about 20 lodges with the most popular being the group in the centre of town, simply because of their location, but all the lodges are good and a number are run by locally renowned sirdars and high altitude climbers.

Those who want the '70s authentic experience should try Namche's first lodge, a small unassuming building beside the fancy Khumbu Lodge.

As is common further up there is a two-tier pricing system. The bed charge is nominal if you eat breakfast and dinner at the lodge. If, however, you are in a group with your own cook or wish to eat at other lodge restaurants then the bed charges climb to cover this loss. The menus tend to be extensive and one of the Namche specialities is yak steaks. Sufficiently tenderised and with a fried egg on top, they are delicious. With the installation of electric ovens and microwaves new varieties of cakes and pies are appearing on menus.

Services

Although Namche feels important it isn't the district headquarters: that is to the south at Salleri. However, with a customs post, the National Park headquarters and army post there are still rather too many government officials and the imbalance of income is often a source of low-level conflict.

For your own safety you are asked to register at the **police checkpost**, which is up the hill from the post office.

Post office This is open from 10am to 4pm daily except Saturday, though it's really just a filing cabinet and a box.

Telephones Namche-Syangboche-Khumjung-Khunde now has a good telephone system and most lodges offer local and international call facilities with a few even offering fax services.

Dental clinic Namche boasts the only modern dental clinic out of Nepal's cities. Nawang Doka, the Namche Sherpani who runs it, is to be admired for staying in Namche because with three years training in Canada she could earn much more elsewhere. It was funded by the American Himalayan Foundation and money raised by the 1991 Everest Marathon. It's usually filled with local people: they treat roughly 70 patients a month, and are obviously doing a good job repairing the damage caused by the candy-culture, for which trekkers are partly to blame. Charges for foreign patients start from US$20. Visitors are welcome but running costs are high; donations are appreciated. They sell logo T-shirts and also basic medicines, which can save a trip to Khunde but is no substitute for a consultation. The clinic also carries out community work such as the distribution of fluoride tablets in schools, which help prevent decay and make teeth stronger.

Namche health post There is a government health post here but no doctor, indeed, often no staff at all. Partly the reason is the hospital at Khunde, an amazing facility, especially for being in the middle of nowhere; see p182 for details about Khunde Hospital.

Water Namche now produces its own mineral water. The seals don't always look professional but lodge owners are normally honest about these things. Amazingly enough for people that are used to the perception that even the water in the mountains is dirty in Nepal, Namche's town supply water is the same as the stuff they bottle, and has been tested many times. So why not save plastic and drink from the tap.

Bakeries *Hermann Helmers Bakery* and the companion *Namche Bakery* have great cakes, but try the pizza or apple strudel at your peril. The majority of the bread found in lodges higher up comes from the Namche Bakery. With 24-hour electricity several places offer cappuccino too.

Laundry services Some lodges offer this service and there are also several people in the centre of town who pile load after load through their machines and driers. Impressively, Namche had washing machines before I ever saw any in Kathmandu.

Internet and email You don't have to escape the modern world up here any more. There are several places but you are wise to ask how they hook up: some call Kathmandu so the connection is unreliable but the communications centre below the *Khumbu Guest house* has its own satellite connection and is amazingly fast. It is likely that other internet cafés will join their service too.

Tibetan market Down near the entrance kani are the encampments of Tibetans who sell cheap Chinese goods, mainly clothing. All these goods have been carried over the 5700m Nangpa La (pass) and the Tibetans simply sit there until everything is sold, so it is 'open' daily. There is talk of moving the market.

The Saturday market

At this popular weekly gathering, Sherpas meet friends, catch up with the gossip and of course trade supplies. Surprisingly, this famous market does not date back centuries

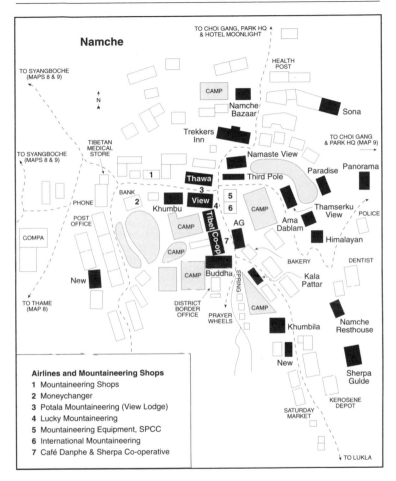

Namche

TO CHOI GANG, PARK HQ & HOTEL MOONLIGHT

HEALTH POST

TO SYANGBOCHE (MAPS 8 & 9)

N

CAMP

Namche Bazaar

Sona

TO SYANGBOCHE (MAPS 8 & 9)

TIBETAN MEDICAL STORE

Trekkers Inn

TO CHOI GANG & PARK HQ (MAP 9)

Namaste View

1

Thawa

Third Pole

Paradise

Panorama

PHONE

BANK

2

3

View

5

4

6

Khumbu

CAMP

Thamserku View

POLICE

POST OFFICE

CAMP

Tibet Co-op

7

AG

Ama Dablam

COMPA

CAMP

Buddha

SPRING

Himalayan

BAKERY

DENTIST

New

CAMP

Kala Pattar

TO THAME (MAP 8)

DISTRICT BORDER OFFICE

PRAYER WHEELS

CAMP

Khumbila

Namche Resthouse

New

Sherpa Gulde

SATURDAY MARKET

KEROSENE DEPOT

TO LUKLA

Airlines and Mountaineering Shops

1 Mountaineering Shops
2 Moneychanger
3 Potala Mountaineering (View Lodge)
4 Lucky Mountaineering
5 Mountaineering Equipment, SPCC
6 International Mountaineering
7 Café Danphe & Sherpa Co-operative

but only to 1965 when it was started by an army officer to cater for the increasing number of civil servants the village was attracting. Tough, sheepskin-clad Tibetans sell tsampa, dried meat, Chinese made clothes and perhaps a few souvenirs, while throngs of lowland porters offer food and goods arduously carried up to Namche. Most supplies originate from the roadhead at Jiri, with some reaching Lukla after being flown by helicopter from Jiri, but

there are also suntalas and rice from the Hinku, vegetables from Solu and eggs from Salleri. Lodge owners from up valley can often be seen with wads of rupees collecting yak-loads of goods.

Being one of the tourist highlights, the market determines many group schedules but especially in peak season it is actively worth avoiding the market time because of the trail congestion it causes. Porters begin arriving late Friday afternoon so the

Phakding-Namche trail becomes busy with both trekkers, their zopkios and heavily laden porters. Heading down from Namche on Friday can slow you right down.

By Saturday afternoon the trail down from Namche is busy with unladen porters racing down to warmer climes while the trails heading up out of Namche are clogged with trekking groups, their yaks and lodge owners' yaks all kicking up considerable dust.

AROUND NAMCHE   [MAP pp180-1]
Excursions
There are plenty of possible day trips. Visits to the picturesque Khumjung and Khunde villages can be combined with the pleasant walk to the Everest View Hotel.

A longer scenic trek is to Thame, with its gompa on the hill and the hydro-power station below. Closer and well worth visiting is the National Park Visitors Centre at Choi Gang. This is also easily visited the morning that you leave for Tengboche, though note that the centre is closed on Saturdays and Sundays.

Less strenuous is the walk to Namche Gompa which is better visited early in the morning or late afternoon, though it is open for tourists most of the day. A donation is expected. Other equally popular activities are clothes washing, apple pie feasting, chocolate bingeing and chang sampling.

Choi Gang and the National Park
Headquarters
With *choi* (or *cho/tsho*) meaning lake and *gang* meaning hill dropping into a valley or flats, the name com-

memorates the fact that there was once a lake here. Long ago it was the main trading area before Namche and Thame took over. Deserted until the 70s, it's now the Sagarmatha National Park Headquarters.

Built with New Zealand aid, the **Information Centre's** main building houses modest displays on the history and points of interest in the park. It's open 8am-4pm daily except Saturdays and public holidays.

There are superb views from the helicopter landing pad behind the centre. Early in the trekking scene this was a favourite camping spot offering from-the-tent views of Everest, the Nuptse-Lhotse wall, Tengboche and Ama Dablam. Even the addition of a toilet block in the foreground cannot detract from the magnificent views. With binoculars considerable segments of the route to Dingboche can be seen.

The pine trees that used to line the path up to the headquarters were planted in 1976 but chopped down in late 2001 so that the army had a clear view around their post there during the Maoist problems.

The **Sherpa Cultural Centre**, beside *Hotel Sherwi Khangba*, is also well worth visiting. The entry charge is approx Rs50.

Lodges   Several companies have bases at Choi Gang and there are four or five pleasant hotels. The huge traditional style building is the *Hotel Sherwi Khangba* (Sherpa's Old House), which is popular with expeditions and groups and is worth nosing around even if you are not staying since it has a library, occasional evening slide shows and educational plus historical photos.

Syangboche   (3900m/12,795ft)
Directly above Namche, although out of view, is Syangboche. The short airstrip here is capable of taking only the small single-engined Pilatus Porter planes (of which there are none left in Nepal) and helicopters.

The Everest View Hotel   This is a small upmarket hotel situated on top of a hill. Although it blends with the environment – and is hard to spot from most places in the valley – it boasts superb views, even from the bedrooms. This is fortunate, because

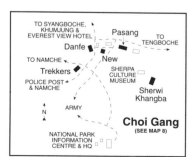

TO SYANGBOCHE,
KHUMJUNG &
EVEREST VIEW HOTEL

Pasang
Danfe
TO
TENGBOCHE

TO NAMCHE
Trekkers
New
SHERPA
CULTURE
MUSEUM

POLICE POST
& NAMCHE

Sherwi
Khangba

N
ARMY

NATIONAL PARK
INFORMATION
CENTRE & HQ

Choi Gang
(SEE MAP 8)

The Syangboche saga

From 1995 the new private helicopter companies began offering commercial flights to and from Syangboche, often flying cargo in and trekkers out. The region developed rapidly as a result with a handful of scattered hotels catering for the increasing number of flights. Then in 1996 the Lukla and Phakding (an area collectively called Pharak) lodge owners went on strike, blocking the runway just before the main trekking season. They complained that they were losing business and demanded that commercial flights to Syangboche be banned. Their arguments were flawed and driven only by shameless and short-sighted greed but, almost unbelievably, the government bowed to their demands. In addition to trekkers losing a valuable service that reduced crowding on the busiest stretch of trail, the people of the Khumbu also lost out, for many of them and their children used the new-found convenience. Their chance to retaliate came soon: The Khumbu Bijuli Company (KBC: electricity company), whose recent medium-scale project has worked so well, was approached by Pharak to provide high-quality electricity for them. The KBC, however, is managed by local groups who immediately stopped negotiations, demanding that Syangboche flights be resumed first, which of course they weren't. Then in mid-1997 the situation escalated when the forestry management committees of Pharak people decided that they would no longer allow any wood to be sold to Namche. Now all wood for new lodges is helicoptered in from Jiri, an extremely expensive exercise.

The latest developments mock much of the feuding. A study was undertaken and stringing an electricity line to Lukla was found to be plain uneconomic, so Lukla must now look at setting up its own system. However, the show isn't over yet: it is rumoured that the Syangboche runway will be extended to allow Twin Otter aircraft to land.

with the dangerously rapid gain in altitude this is where many people spend their time initially. Additional oxygen is provided and is very effective.

Even though the hotel often seems cold and empty, it is sometimes fully booked in high season, mainly with Japanese visitors on package tours. The cost is around US$200/£135 a night. On a fine day trekkers visit for tea on the terrace.

Khumjung (3790m/12,434ft)

This is a picturesque village set under the steep rock of Khumbui Yul Lha with many beautiful houses and grand views of Kangtaiga, Thamserku and Ama Dablam. Until recently the direct impact of tourism was low with few trekkers staying overnight, but with good lodges and a great bakery now located here, more people are staying.

Khumjung, however, has always looked wealthy because virtually every family has some involvement with the trekking industry. All bar four of the lodges from Dole to Gokyo are owned by Khumjung people and it is the home of a number of trekking company directors and well-known sirdars and climbers. In many ways it is a model village for Nepal with a good range of facilities, yet has coped with development well and still has a strong sense of community.

Khumjung's **gompa**, which was established around 1831, is at the top end of town amid a pleasant stand of protected trees. The other major set of buildings is the school on the flats. This was the first built by Hillary and friends and has subsequently been expanded several times and is now a thriving high school.

Leaving Khumjung The track to the Everest View Hotel begins by the chortens near the end of town and heads up the hill.

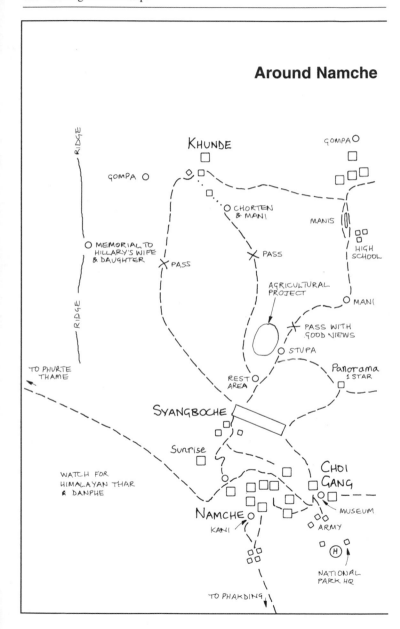

Around Namche

RIDGE

RIDGE

GOMPA ○

KHUNDE ▢

GOMPA ○

GOMPA ○ ▢

▢ ▢ ▢ ▢

◇ ▢

○ CHORTEN & MANI

MANIS

HIGH SCHOOL ▢ ▢

○ MEMORIAL TO HILLARY'S WIFE & DAUGHTER

✗ PASS

✗ PASS

○ MANI

AGRICULTURAL PROJECT

✗ PASS WITH GOOD VIEWS

○ STUPA

TO PHURTE THAME

REST AREA ○

Panorama 1 STAR

SYANGBOCHE ▭

▢ ▢ ◇

Sunrise ▢

WATCH FOR HIMALAYAN THAR & DANPHE

○ ▢ ▢ ▢

CHOI GANG

○ MUSEUM

NAMCHE ○

▢ ▢

KANI

◇ ◇ ARMY

□ (H) ↑

NATIONAL PARK HQ

TO PHAKDING ↓

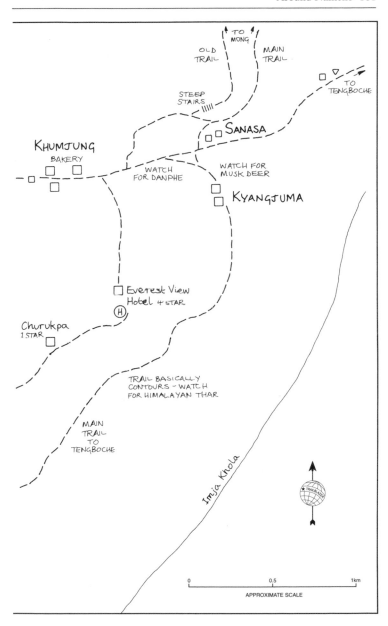

Khumjung
(SEE MAP 8)

GOMPA
Gompa Lodge
Khumjung Hill Top View
Nima
Thamserku View
Baudhamomo
TO MONG & GOKYO
Shangrila
EVEREST BAKERY
Himalayan
Mountain View
Ama Dablam View
Sherpini
TO KUNDE & KHUNDE HOSPITAL
Sherpa Land
Hidden Village
Hotel Khumjung (Konchok Chumbi)
Sherpa Cookhouse
STUPAS
TO SANASA & KYANGJUMA
TO EVEREST VIEW HOTEL

STUPA ○
MANIS
SCHOOL
N
ONLY MAIN TRAILS SHOWN

TO SYANGBOCHE & NAMCHE (MOST DIRECT ROUTE)

The trails to Sanasa and Gokyo are initially the same, before dividing by a house a few minutes down from the stupa.

Khunde/Khumte (3840m/12,598ft)

Although Khunde virtually adjoins Khumjung the two villages are actually quite separate communities. The Khunde villagers have traditionally been associated with the Pangboche Gompa, while people from Khumjung go to Thame for special occasions, despite the fact they have their own gompa. The village name is invariably pronounced Khunde or Kunde but originally it was Khumte: *Te* is upper, so upper Khum, while *jung* is lower flats. *Khum* means Khumbu and Khumjung is considered the middle of the Khumbu.

Khunde Hospital Built in 1966 as a Himalayan Trust project, this is staffed by dedicated locals and a volunteer doctor from New Zealand or Canada. It offers exceptional services for a 'bush' hospital: there's even an X-ray machine. It's also one of the few places in rural Nepal where contraception and pregnancy testing are readily and reliably available. Most patients are local people who have developed a great respect for the service. Patients are asked to pay according to their means – from twenty rupees for a destitute porter to US$40 (or rupee equivalent) for a foreign trekker. Additional charges for trekkers are $10 for medicine, $100 for an overnight stay, while out-of-hours or Saturday consultations are $80. It's open from 9am to 5pm but is closed on Saturdays and Wednesday afternoons except for emergencies. Previously fund-raising tours of the hospital were given but now the hospital is so busy that they prefer to take people with special medical interests only. Indeed, now the hospital is so busy that there is enough work for two doctors much of the time.

The Himalayan Trust has always wanted a local doctor instead of the volunteers and offers scholarships and other incentives. However, after training provided mainly by the Himalayan Trust the first hopeful, Doctor Mingma, decided that he preferred the USA. Currently one of the longest serving staff members is about to return from medical training and will stay in the community.

NAMCHE TO THAME [MAP 8, opp]

Thame is a pleasant village with a beautiful gompa three hours from Namche. Since it's 350m higher than Namche, groups often

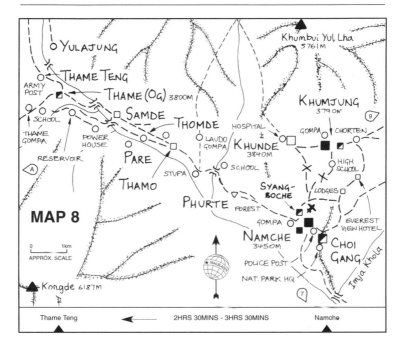

MAP 8

0   1km
APPRÓX. SCALE

Thame Teng ← 2HRS 30MINS - 3HRS 30MINS Namche

stay the night here as part of an acclimatization programme before trekking to Gokyo – a sensible idea. As a day trip it is strenuous but can help with acclimatization and the scenery is stunning.

Leaving Namche If planning to stay at Thame the latest you can leave Namche is about 2pm, walking at an ordinary pace. Head up to the gompa and continue traversing up on the same trail which rounds the ridge enclosing Namche. Soon you come to a forest, a favourite area for local women to collect *soluk* (leaves and vegetation that are mixed with dung and used to make fertiliser), singing as they work. It's also a good region to spot pheasant, especially the male danphe, the colourful national bird of Nepal. The female is a plainer spotted brown and similarly plump.

Phurte is the first village you come to. It has a forestry nursery funded by the

Himalayan Trust plus a few small *lodges*. The fields between Phurte and Samde are known as *gunsas*; they are owned by villages at higher altitudes and used by them to provide crops earlier in the season. The *gunsas* here belong to Thame Cho residents but several sons with their families have moved down here permanently, establishing a small village.

Between Phurte and Thamo, visible high above the main track, is a gompa. This is Laudo, a small monastic establishment built around 1970 as an arm of Kopan Monastery (near Bodhnath in Kathmandu). It is often used by foreign meditation groups.

Thamo/Thammu/Dramo In the centre of this village are the offices of the Khumbu Bijuli Company who manage the Thame hydro-electric scheme. On the opposite side of the valley is a reminder to them of the damage a glacial lake outburst can cause:

Thame Hydro-electric Project

The current project was set up with grant assistance totalling Rs124 million from the Austrian government and Rs14 million from the Nepal Electricity Authority (NEA), at the time a little under $2 million in total. An Austrian non-governmental organization (NGO) Eco-Himal carried out the installation and gave technical assistance and the project was officially opened in October 1995. The 630kw unit supplies around 500 households in Thame Cho, Namche, Khumjung, Khunde and the villages in between, plus enough power for all the lodges to cook with – a welcome attempt to counter the tourism related problem of firewood use.

The generators are housed in a traditionally decorated building well below Thame and the two small turbines are fed by a pool, near and visible from Thame village, which collects glacier run-off from up the valley. A 600mm diameter pipe, one kilometre long, drops 200m to provide the head. A local technician, trained in Austria, maintains the plant. Luckily, underground cabling for the villages proved cheaper than overhead wires though unsightly overhead cables still run from the plant to the villages.

For a private house there are several fixed cost payment schemes. Lodges use a meter system and for a large lodge during the busy months the bill may be Rs5000–10,000 a month.

One of the reasons for its overwhelming success is the structure of its ownership: each of the three main villages – greater Thame, greater Khumjung and Namche – own a 28.3% share while the Nepal Electricity Authority has the remaining 15%. The power is sold on a profit basis but the profits are then used for maintenance and development. By the end of 2001 there was approximately 7 million rupees put aside. As with most assistance projects, the government in the form of the NEA was involved to spread technical know-how. However, although it is a model scheme, no other imitations have been set up yet.

---

the first hydro-project was nearly completed in 1985 when a glacial lake burst and washed much of the river scheme away. The wall of water also engulfed many bridges and washed away farm land. The second attempt has been far more successful (see box above).

Scenic (normal) route to Thame

Immediately after the last houses of the village, climb the stone stairs on a track that slightly doubles back on itself. This climbs by a stream to the Khari Gompa, then crosses it. The trail continues to climb until suddenly dropping slightly to cross the Nangpo Tsangpo (river). A steel suspension bridge straddles a roaring tight gorge then the trail winds up and along to Thame.

Alternative route to Thame via the powerhouse Continue straight ahead and across a temporary bridge to the Austrian hydro-electric project.

Thame (3800m/12,467ft)

Thame is part of the group of villages called Thame Cho – Thame Og (lower), Thame Teng (upper) and Yulajung – and is an area noted for its potatoes.

These villages have traditional trading links with Tibet so when the Nangpa La is crossable Tibetans camp here and in Thame Teng. It is also home to a surprising number of Everest summiteers including Apa Sherpa who has climbed the mountain twelve times.

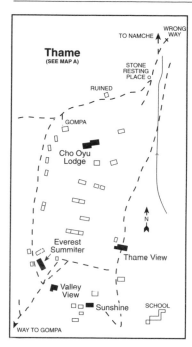

Thame
(SEE MAP A)

TO NAMCHE ↑ | WRONG WAY
✗

STONE RESTING PLACE ○

RUINED ▢

GOMPA

Cho Oyu Lodge

Everest Summiter

Thame View

Valley View

Sunshine

SCHOOL

N ↑

WAY TO GOMPA

Thame Gompa Thame has two gompas, the most frequently visited being a 15-minute walk up the track that begins on the ridge to the north and heads west. It was established around 325 years ago on the advice of Lama Sangwa Dorje, fifth reincarnate Lama of Rongphu/Rongbuk in Tibet, who played an important part in the spiritual history of the Khumbu. It's said that some of the books here are over 300 years old.

Recently the gompa has been partially rebuilt using the original materials and the interior has been preserved as it was. The result is stunning.

Lodges There are a handful of lodges who can offer lunch, snacks or a place to stay. They are mostly run by women since the menfolk are often away trekking or climbing.

The route description for the Nangpa La begins on p222.

To Lobuche and Kala Pattar

In this galaxy, which included a host of unnamed peaks, neither the lesser or the greater seemed designed for the use of climbers. HW Tilman, *Nepal Himalaya*

NAMCHE TO TENGBOCHE
[MAP 9, p187]
Leaving for Tengboche The trail that traverses from Choi Gang to Kyangjuma is wide and set high above the river. It's a beautiful walk where you are likely to see Himalayan tahr (goats).

Kyangjuma (3600m/11,811ft) This is the first set of *teahouses* you come to, about one to one and a half hours from the National Park HQ. There are a couple of good *lodges* with friendly owners and they also boast a decadent panorama.

Between here and Sanasa is virtually the only birch-rhododendron forest of the trek to Lobuche. Birch makes the best high altitude firewood (oak is the best in the low country) and since it doesn't split easily it is often used to make mortar and pestles and wooden bowls, especially the traditional and ceremonial silver and wood bowls used

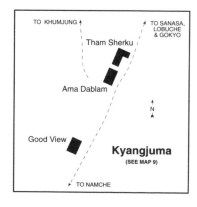

TO KHUMJUNG ↑

TO SANASA, LOBUCHE & GOKYO ↑

Tham Sherku

Ama Dablam

N ↑

Good View

Kyangjuma
(SEE MAP 9)

TO NAMCHE ↙

for serving Tibetan tea. Occasionally you will see Himalayan tahr, pheasants and even musk deer around here but it takes keen eyes to spot them.

Route to Gokyo or Pangboche via Phortse Past Kyangjuma and across the stream just before Sanasa is a small and usually signposted junction. The upper trail climbs in a couple of minutes to the main trail from Khumjung to Mong (see p204).

Sanasa (3600m/11,811ft) is five minutes beyond Kyangjuma. There's another couple of *teahouses* and more Tibetan souvenirs.

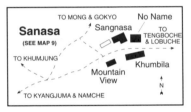

Continuing around the ridge are the *teahouses* of **Lawishasa** (Tashinga). There is also a forestry nursery established by the Canadian Sir Edmund Hillary Foundation. Here the descent to the suspension bridge across the Dudh Kosi begins.

There are a few *teahouses* suitable for lunch along the way.

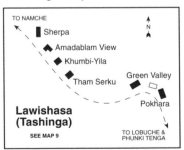

Phunki / Phongi Tenga (3250m/ 10,663ft) Down the hill just before you reach the bridge is the *Evergreen Lodge*. Sometimes you will see musk deer around

here, especially in the early evening. Across the beautifully situated old suspension bridge are more *lodges*. For those people suffering from altitude, this is the lowest place north of Namche to stay the night.

The walk up the hill to Tengboche is pleasant, if sometimes hot. You pass through a blend of forest and shrub on a wide trail with many shortcuts leading from it. It's also one of the better places for spotting pheasant, tahr and musk deer. They seem quite undisturbed by all the noise of passing trekkers. The end of the climb is heralded by a kani, an arched entrance with ceiling paintings of deities and forms of Buddha. Its function is to cleanse people of the many feared spirits before entering the sacred area.

TENGBOCHE/THYANGBOCHE (3860m/12,664ft)

True we were awakened at 4 am by the din of horns and the clash of cymbals, but we were not expected to rouse out for prayer or meditation, or indeed do anything beyond reach out for a wooden jorum thoughtfully left in readiness. In this, of course, lurked what we called 'lama's milk', which was raksi flavoured with cloves.

HW Tilman 1950

You may still be wakened by the clash of cymbals. And a snort of *lamas' milk* might still be in order. During the cold winter months most Sherpas will down a shot of raksi before breakfast, sometimes even Sherpas who profess to avoid the demon drink. They firmly believe in its warming properties.

Tengboche is a cultural and religious centre for the people of the Khumbu region. It is unique in that all the other gompas of the region are associated with a village but Tengboche isn't. The newly-reconstructed gompa is famous as the setting for the Mani Rimdu dance festival in late October or early November. It is a favoured overnight stop for all trekkers heading to Kala Pattar and, being an acclimatization stop, some trekkers, groups included, stay two nights; as a result, in the high season it is very busy. If it snows groups often abandon their tents

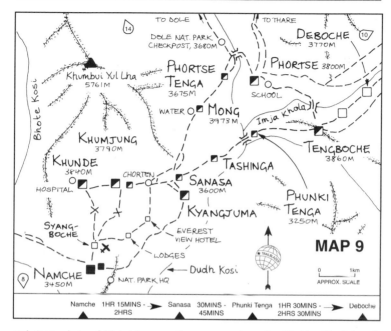

MAP 9

0   1km
APPROX. SCALE

Namche 1HR 15MINS - → Sanasa 30MINS - Phunki Tenga 1HR 30MINS - → Deboche
2HRS   45MINS   2HRS 30MINS

and (somewhat unfairly) take over the lodges. Good alternatives to a second night here are Pangboche, Phortse, Khumjung (stay on the first night here) or Deboche.

Behind the *National Park Lodge* is a ridge pointing to Khumbui Yul Lha that affords superb views. From this viewpoint and higher to Pangboche is the classic view of Ama Dablam. Notice especially the spectacular high trail from Pangboche to Phortse on the opposite side of the valley. There are several origins given for the name Ama Dablam (Amai Dablang). One says that it refers to the necklace of turquoise or coral usually worn by married women. With a little imagination it's possible to visualize shoulders and a head, and the pendulous lump of blue ice (a glacier) is roughly in the right spot for a necklace.

Rubbish and human waste are big problems at Tengboche. Each group used to construct a toilet (tent) leaving hundreds of unsightly half-filled holes. Toilet blocks constructed by the park to solve this problem

are now becoming dilapidated but it is park policy that all groups should use them. Your trekking crew might need a hint, and porters need to be instructed to use this facility. There are also rubbish bins provided.

Lodges

There are only five lodges, four of which are owned by the gompa and are rented out, providing further income for the gompa. The last is owned by the National Park. If the lodges seem full the three Deboche lodges are less than 15 minutes beyond.

Tengboche Gompa

This justly famous gompa is spectacularly situated under the mighty Kangtaiga ('horse saddle') and Thamserku ('golden door') mountains, in a commanding position with superb views up and down the surrounding valleys. You can see the Everest View Hotel and the National Park HQ down the valley, perhaps now more easily spotted at night. With these as mark-

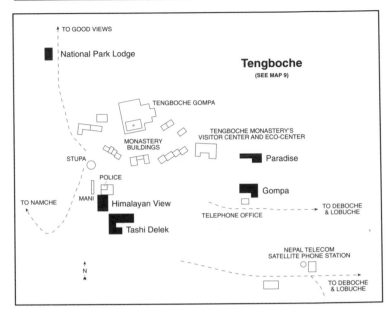

ers it's easy to work out where hidden Namche and Khumjung are, and the path that brought you up here.

The gompa serves as a spiritual and occasional social centre for the people of the region. The majority of the other buildings are the monastery's. Boys are sent here from all over the Khumbu to study Buddhism. For the period of study they must remain celibate but they may (and most do) get married when they have graduated.

Although the area has long been considered revered ground, the gompa was established only in 1916, by Lama Gulu at the request of the Abbot of Rongbuk. In 1934 a disastrous earthquake struck the area, causing considerable damage to the gompa. Lama Gulu died of shock. Rebuilt and headed by the present lama, Nawang Tenzing Zangbu. Tragedy struck again less than a year after electricity was installed: on 19 January 1989 a heater overturned burning the magnificent gompa to the ground. Not all was lost since some of what could be removed, including the priceless book

collection, was rescued. The construction of the grand new gompa was considerably aided by the American Himalayan foundation (set up by Sir Ed) and donations from wealthy locals. The library has now been put on micro-film, and the hydro-electric system has been revived. The gompa is often flood-lit at night to great effect.

The gompa is primarily a spiritual place and, so that the gompa itself is not disturbed too much, a modern-concept **visitors centre** was set up. It is all self-explanatory.

Excursions from Tengboche

The forests above and below Tengboche are protected and are still considered to be owned by the monastery. It is pleasant to wander through the trees and there is a reasonable chance of seeing deer and pheasant. The rhododendrons are spectacular in April. For a longer half-day trip, the rock peak above Tengboche, often called Hamugon, offers better views of the awesome Thamserku-Kangtaiga glacier. It's an easy but breathless scramble to the top of the first peak. The higher peak requires some more committed scrambling. Listen to your body though, while ascending.

TENGBOCHE TO PHERICHE / DINGBOCHE [MAP 10, p193]

Leaving Tengboche The route passes the water tap then takes the gully between the fields where groups camp.

Deboche (3770m/12,369ft)

Down through pleasant forest on a trail that is icy long after snowfall is a series of four or five *lodges*.

Deboche is five minutes further on and there are superb views of Khumbui Yul Lha which looks formidable from here. Behind a barrier of trees is the Deboche Gompa and nunnery, housing approximately 12 nuns. You are welcome to have a look around the gompa, which dates from 1925. The atmosphere is quite different from Tengboche.

After passing a few other hamlets you cross a spectacular little gorge on a steel box bridge. This is the junction for the trail to Phortse (see p215). Follow the main trail for Pangboche. About 20 minutes later the

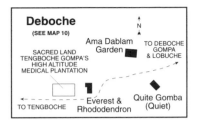

trail passes through a cleft in some rocks, with a mani wall virtually in the middle. Just after, the trail divides and is usually signposted, the upper trail heading to Upper Pangboche and the gompa, while the lower path takes a more gentle route through the fields to Lower Pangboche.

Pangboche (4000m/13,123ft)

This used to be the highest permanently occupied village until trekkers created a demand in winter for accommodation higher up the valley. However, both the upper and lower villages are now popular places to stay and consequently there are quite a number of new *lodges* in this pleasant place.

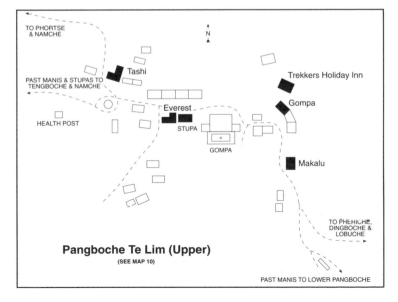

Pangboche Te Lim (Upper)
(SEE MAP 10)

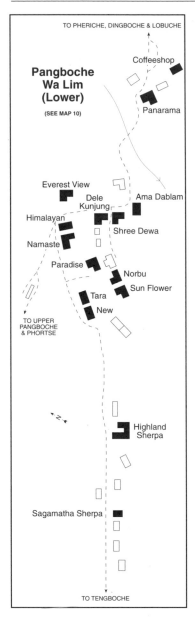

TO PHERICHE, DINGBOCHE & LOBUCHE

Coffeeshop

**Pangboche
Wa Lim
(Lower)**

(SEE MAP 10)

Panarama

Everest View

Dele
Kunjung

Ama Dablam

Himalayan

Shree Dewa

Namaste

Paradise

Norbu

Sun Flower

Tara

New

TO UPPER
PANGBOCHE
& PHORTSE

N

Highland
Sherpa

Sagamatha Sherpa

TO TENGBOCHE

From Lower Pangboche there's another trail which starts from the corner of *Namaste Lodge* and winds up to the upper village.

In **Pangboche Te Lim** (the upper village) the houses are clustered round the old gompa and there are five *lodges* here. The surrounding juniper trees have long been protected and are now very large. Legend has it that they were created by Lama Sangwa Dorje who tossed a handful of his hair into the air and it took root as juniper. Once the whole valley would have been thickly forested with trees this size.

The monastery is believed to have been founded around 1667, which makes it the oldest Sherpa gompa in the Khumbu. Many trekkers take the opportunity to have a look around; the lama (the 14th re-incarnate) or his wife are usually close by, and it is customary to leave a donation with them. This gompa was home to one of the Khumbu's famous yeti scalps until it was stolen under mysterious circumstances in 1991.

The lower village, **Pangboche Wa Lim** (3840m/12,598ft) was once just (big) grass fields, which is what the name 'Pangboche' means. It is now a settlement with at least ten *lodges* on the edge of the fields. Potatoes, radishes and a few vegetables are grown and there is often an abundance of wild mushrooms. Firewood collection in Pangboche is still well organized. Dead wood is collected from the opposite side of the valley from selected spots and when the supply thins another part of the forest is used. Yak dung, a valuable fertiliser, is now also used as fuel, something that started with the arrival of trekkers.

Leaving Upper Pangboche to **Shomare** (see village map opposite) you can see Everest peeking over the Lhotse-Nuptse ridge and you can also see it from the trail between the lower and upper villages, from where there is also a good view of Tengboche. At the last count there were 35 Everest summiteers from Pangboche.

Route from Pangboche to Phortse

The most direct route is a high and slightly wild trail that begins from near the gompa. From the top of the gompa take the trail

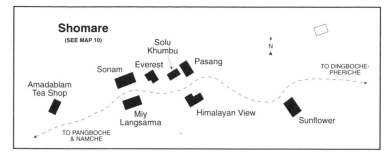

that contours west to two white chortens 100m away, then walk up to the bottom of *Tashi Lodge* and begin contouring. The path crosses fields and a stream. Once a little way out of Pangboche it is a large well-used trail. It takes a couple of hours to reach Phortse.

Route from Pangboche to Pheriche and Dingboche
There are several small *chhusas* (yak herding areas) en route. The first you come to is **Shomare** (see map above), owned by the villagers of Pangboche and used for growing potatoes. There is a growing collection of small *lodges* catering for lunch, although it is possible to stay. This is where trees fade away and the true alpine valley begins. The single *Orsho Restaurant* is at the next kharka; if this is closed, after the split for Pheriche or Dingboche there is another small restaurant, the *Dragon*, on the Pheriche trail, and a third, the *Ama Dablam*, on the Dingboche trail. Looking up, the massive Lhotse-Nuptse wall dominates; the black jagged ridge below is Pokalde.

From Pheriche/Dingboche Coming down the valley from Pheriche/Dingboche the turn-off to Upper Pangboche is by a small chorten, where the river widens and the first fields of Lower Pangboche can be seen.

For Mingbo and Ama Dablam Base Camp see p221.

To Pheriche and Dingboche
Route to Pheriche The track to Pheriche turns off perhaps five minutes out of Orsho. The trail veers left and climbs up to a small pass before descending on a wide trail to the bridge. It takes 30-40 minutes from the turn-off to Pheriche. Despite being marked on even the most recent maps, there is no trail immediately after the bridge to Dingboche.

Pheriche (4280m/14,042ft)
To combat the afternoon wind lodges here either have sun rooms or warm lounges. It is important to stop here or at Dingboche to acclimatize.

There are five *lodges*, most recently rebuilt bigger, better and warmer, and a few

---

The Garden of Eden
This was one of the 1977 vintage lodges in Pheriche: a pit dug into the ground, the excess dirt made into a wall around it. A plastic sheet was the 1.5-metre-high roof. People slept on turf around the edge. At night we put cardboard boxes in the open windows but it was still a fridge. After several days we made the mistake of asking the Sherpani how she made the chang. She explained that after the rice was first boiled she spread the mixture out on a blanket, then put another on top and slept on it for three days while it fermented, then it was thrown in a pot and water added for the final fermentation. **Russell**, Australia

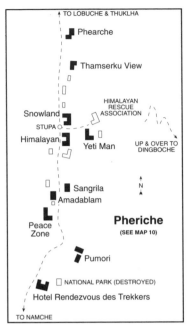

TO LOBUCHE & THUKLHA

Phearche

Thamserku View

HIMALAYAN
RESCUE
ASSOCIATION

Snowland

STUPA

Himalayan

Yeti Man

UP & OVER TO
DINGBOCHE

N

Sangrila

Amadablam

Pheriche

(SEE MAP 10)

Peace
Zone

Pumori

NATIONAL PARK (DESTROYED)

Hotel Rendezvous des Trekkers

TO NAMCHE

the Tokyo Medical College for research purposes and was expanded in 2000. Now it's staffed by two or three Western volunteer doctors who are available for consultations (US$40 or rupee equivalent in 2002; use of PAC bag $50 an hour, $10 per course of medicine) and who also give daily lectures on altitude sickness that are well worth attending (donations expected).

Recently lectures have been given every few days in Dingboche as well; look for a notice in the middle of the village. As part of the community service the consultation fee for Nepalis is less than a dollar, and group porters are encouraged to visit especially since they are the least likely to complain of medical problems and yet are most likely to be sick; they are also more likely to suffer altitude sickness than Western trekkers, partially as a result of the load they carry.

The Pheriche post opens only during the peak trekking seasons (October to mid-December and March to May) when the donations and consultation fees are able to cover the running costs. They also sell HRA patches and non-prescription medicines, lip balm and so on. It is an extraordinary service, please don't take it for granted. They treat numerous cases of altitude sickness (surprisingly, survivors often forget to donate) and provide many consultations. One of the most unusual was a yak that required a band-aid. Behind the scenes are Ang Rita and, about to retire, Namka, who have managed the place since virtually its inception.

houses spaced along the track that runs through the village. The lodge shops can be a good place to replenish camping supplies. Pheriche can get quite crowded during the high seasons.

Himalayan Rescue Association Medical Post This was built in 1976 by

Pheriche or Dingboche?

The villages are 45 minutes apart, separated by a ridge. Both have lodges and are at roughly the same altitude so it depends on your plans for the important acclimatization day as to where you stay. If the climb to Nangkartshang Peak (or Gompa) appeals, or you plan simply to relax it really does not matter where you stay. If planning a day trip to Chukhung then it is more convenient to sleep at Dingboche. There's a trail to Lobuche from either village, and they are of equal distance.

Opposite Top: Kala Pattar (see p 202) is the most popular viewpoint for Everest, here the slightly darker central peak trailing a plume of cloud. **Bottom:** Approaching Everest Base Camp (see p203).

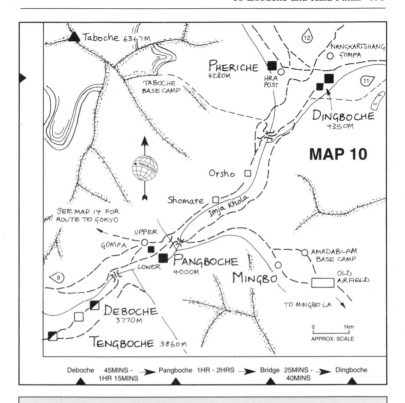

SEE MAP 14 FOR ROUTE TO GOKYO

Deboche 45MINS - 1HR 15MINS ➤ Pangboche 1HR - 2HRS ➤ Bridge 25MINS - 40MINS ➤ Dingboche

The latest AMS thinking

Previously the HRA recommended trekkers stay a minimum of two nights in Dingboche or Pheriche before moving on to Lobuche. However, even this relatively cautious approach led to many people suffering altitude sickness at Lobuche. Now that it is possible to stay at Thuklha the best advice is to spend one (or two) nights at Dingboche/Pheriche, then a night at Thuklha, then stay at Lobuche. Breaking the 600m jump in altitude into two 300m gains will considerably lessen the occurrence of mild altitude sickness: as always, gradual ascent is the safest approach. Note that if you have slept at Chukhung (or Dzonglha) without problems you should be able to trek directly to Lobuche rather than stopping en route. If you want to stay at Gorak Shep, unless you have already been to Gokyo or Chukhung, then staying a night at Lobuche before moving to Gorak Shep is the safest option.

Opposite: The Khumbu Icefall. **Previous pages:** From Mera (see p269) there are spectacular views. In this picture Mera La is to the left, Makalu just left of centre and Kanchenjunga on the right.

Dingboche
(SEE MAP 11)

TO CHUKHUNG & ISLAND PEAK

Peak 38 View

Island Peak View

Lhotse View

Tauche View

TO STUPAS ON RIDGETOP, LOBUCHE, PHERICHE & NANGKARTSHANG

Sonam

Friendship

Sagarmatha Garden

Himalaya

Tashi

Tramserku View   MANI

Mountain View

Amadablam

TRAILS TO PHERICHE

OLD STUPA

Dingboche Guest House

Snow Lion

TO PANGBOCHE & NAMCHE

Route to Dingboche From Orsho follow the straight trail that drops to the small *Ama Dablam Teashop* then the bridge across the Lobuche Khola.

Dingboche is still a hill and approximately 30–40 minutes away from the bridge. Approaching the village and walking through, the view of the Lhotse-Nuptse wall dominates.

Dingboche (4350m/14,271ft)

The houses of this summer village are dotted about the fields on land owned by people from Pangboche and Khunde. As Dingboche has become more popular than Pheriche, so too have the *lodges* grown. Although the *Snow Lion* looks the fanciest, there are friendlier lodges. Virtually all face Ama Dablam, big and fearsome from here. Most of the lodges are owned by people from Khunde, so although Khunde sees few trekkers, the village is still very much linked with tourism.

From Dingboche you can make the half-day trips described below or head to Chukhung. If you suffered mild AMS on the first night here it may be a better idea to rest here or, if you really suffered, trek slightly lower during the day. The bridge across the Lobuche Khola is the closest point that's easy to reach and often even this small drop in altitude can make a big difference.

Day trips from Pheriche and Dingboche

● **Half-day trip to Nangkartshang Peak**
For the amount of effort involved, this excursion from Pheriche or Dingboche offers some of the best views in this region – a perfect scenic lunch spot.

From Pheriche the path zigzags up directly behind the HRA buildings on the track heading to Dingboche. Some time before the steep descent, continue up the ridge past a stupa.

From Dingboche any track heading up to the ridge will do. Then, from the stupa on top is a small trail that follows the ridge up, and up, and up. The top is marked by prayer flags and you are brought up short by a sudden drop. The views here are magnificent with Numbur, Chukhung, Makalu and Ama Dablam visible.

In the hillside on the Dingboche face is a small gompa. It is usually locked and the trail to it is difficult to follow. Nearby are some meditation caves.

● **Half-day trip to the Ama Dablam lakes**
Among the moraine below Ama Dablam are two lakes at 4700m. Sometimes there's a bridge across the Imja Khola at the base of Dingboche and a track to Duroo, a small *yersa* (a summer crop-growing area, usually lower than the main village). The alternative is to cross the creek at the top of Dingboche and climb the steep hillside, or head upriver to Shangtso where there is usually a bridge and hook back on the trail heading up. The lakes are also a great place for lunch.

● **Half-day trip to Taboche Base Camp**
Opposite Pheriche is stunning Taboche. Atop the broad ridge are a couple of small rock peaks that can be climbed, or a hidden higher valley to explore. Cross the bridge to Pangboche and from Tsuro Teng follow small steep trails up. It is quite a grunt up there. Don't forget to take lunch and snacks.

TO AND AROUND CHUKHUNG [MAP 11, p197]
To Chukhung By the top lodges in Dingboche the track continues between the hill and the upper fences and is easy to follow through the low scrub.

Further up, the herding area of **Bibre** is above the main trail but below, beside the path, is a solitary one-roomed house where people from Dingboche sell cups of tea, biscuits and chocolate during the trekking seasons. From here Imjatse/Island Peak looks awesome, a triangle of almost sheer rock and incredibly steep snow faces, steep enough to bring a lump to climbers' throats. Yet strangely at Chukhung its magnificence fades. Chukhung is perhaps 20-25 minutes beyond Bibre but, until you are almost on top of it, it remains invisible.

Chukhung (4750m/15,584ft)
This is traditionally a Pangboche herding station (or phu) used as a base to graze the rich and extensive grasslands of the valley. It's nestled between two streams, which is what the name means. Viewed from above it is also surrounded by glaciers and their debris.

The views here are fantastic, even from the base of the valley, and they get even better the higher you explore. Looking down valley, Numbur, Khatang and Karyolung rise majestically above Kongde while Taboche (Tagouche/Tawouche literally means 'horse's head' but can be loosely translated as 'big ego') and Tsholatse ('Lake-pass Peak') are closer to the right. Ama Dablam is quite something to see from here and the fluted snow wall above Chukhung Glacier is stunning, especially at sunset.

With the number of trekkers and climbers passing through, the *lodges* at Chukhung have developed from the simple teahouses they once were. Now at least one lodge remains open throughout the year. The *phu* makes a good base to explore the huge valley system with its many 'small' peaks that can be fun to climb.

Hiring equipment Once the lodges here stocked enough equipment for trekkers to climb Island Peak. Now they generally don't.

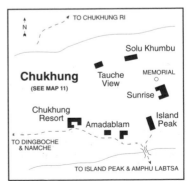

Half-day trip to Chukhung Ri (5559m/18,238ft)

This is an understandably popular excursion from Chukhung, involving an ascent of a ridge similar to Kala Pattar. The top cannot be seen from Chukhung but the paths are obvious scars ascending the side of the big pile of grass and dirt. At the saddle there's a choice: a lower peak (5417m/17,772ft) to the south or a trickier ascent on rock to the high peak (5559m/18,238ft). The views are staggering from both with Makalu dominating amongst a ring of mountains. It is possible to do this as a long day-trip from Dingboche but the altitude, for the unacclimatized (rather than the time), creates a problem.

Chukhung Tse (5857m/19,216ft)

This is the peak north of Chukhung Ri and is the highest hill in the Khumbu commonly scrambled by trekkers. The ridge between Chukhung Ri and Chukhung Tse is tricky to traverse in its entirety; take particular care on some short exposed moves and don't attempt if wet or snowy. The safer route is a steep gully scramble on the east side directly to the summit. The ablation valley to the east provides access and/or exit.

It is possible but strenuous to ascend both Chukhung Ri and Tse in a day, good preparation for Imjatse/Island Peak or the Amphu Labtsa. An ice axe, or trekking pole would be handy. Views are staggering and include Chomo Lonzo (the white ridge extending north of Makalu and the 27th highest mountain on the planet) and Gauri Sankar.

Island Peak Base Camp

This is an alternative to climbing the nearby hills. The rate of ascent is gradual, though it is quite a long way and often dusty. See p264 for further details.

Other routes: Island Peak and the base camp see p264; Amphu Labtsa see p220; Kongma La see p219; Pokalde and Kongma Tse see p271; Peak 5886m see p220. A map will reveal more possible side trips to little-explored valleys.

PHERICHE/DINGBOCHE TO LOBUCHE [MAP 12 p199] Route from Pheriche to Thuklha

Leaving Pheriche, the trail meanders up the open valley, beautiful when the weather's fine but muddy if snow or rain has recently fallen. It then cuts up a small but obvious valley. A smaller trail then branches off to the left and heads directly to the bridge over a few permanently slippery boulders, while the main path heads up to join the trail directly from Dingboche just a minute before the bridge to Thuklha.

Route from Dingboche to Thuklha

Climb the ridge behind Dingboche on one of the many trails to the higher plain. There are then several paths to follow, all leading to the two bridges across to Thuklha. Either will do, though the lower trail crosses an unstable slide area.

Thuklha (4600m/15,092ft)

Ram's (uncastrated male sheep) Corral is the translation; 'Tourist Corral' is perhaps a better name now. The three *lodges* here primarily used to make lunch for trekkers. Once poky and smoky, *Yak Lodge* now has lots of double rooms, a friendly owner and a large dining area. So it is possible to stay overnight in relative comfort and break the 600m gain in altitude between Dingboche or Pheriche and Lobuche.

The hill immediately beyond Thuklha is tough, especially if your pack is heavy. At the crest (4840m/15,879ft) are more than 20 memorials for Sherpas and a few foreign climbers who tragically didn't make it down again. From here the trail climbs gently in the ablation valley and it's just over an hour to Lobuche. At this altitude, even in October there's ice on the streams; by December they may be frozen over. Once on the west side of the khola, although it is not obvious, you can see the horribly steep summit ramparts of Lhotse past Nuptse.

Lobuche (4940m/16,207ft)

Lobuche is set on the slopes of a pleasant ablation valley which, possibly because of the altitude, is very little explored off the path to Gorak Shep.

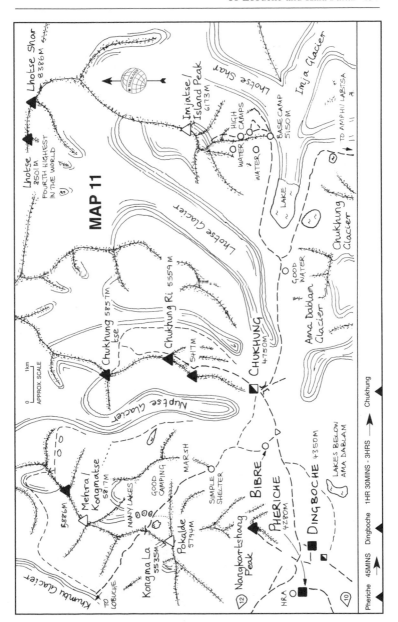

MAP 11

Lhotse Shar 8386M

Lhotse 8501M FOURTH HIGHEST IN THE WORLD

Lhotse Shar

Imja Glacier

Imjatse/ Island Peak 6173M

HIGH CAMPS

WATER

WATER

BASE CAMP 5150M

TO AMPHU LABTSA

LAKE

0   1km
APPROX. SCALE

Chukhung tse 5857M

Chukhung Ri 5559M

5417M

CHUKHUNG 4750M

GOOD WATER

Chukhung Glacier

Ama Dablam Glacier

Lhotse Glacier

Nuptse Glacier

Khumbu Glacier

TO LOBUCHE

5886M

Mehra/ Kongmatse 5817M

MANY LAKES

Pokalde 5794M

Kongma La 5535M

GOOD CAMPING

MARSH

SIMPLE SHELTER

Nangkartshang Peak

BIBRE

PHERICHE 4250M

DINGBOCHE 4350M

LAKES BELOW AMA DABLAM

12

HRA

10

◀ Pheriche   45MINS ▲   1HR 30MINS - 3HRS ▲   Dingboche ◀   → Chukhung ◀

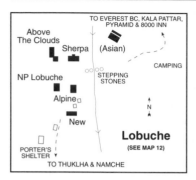

TO EVEREST BC, KALA PATTAR,
PYRAMID & 8000 INN

Above
The Clouds
Sherpa   (Asian)

CAMPING

NP Lobuche   STEPPING
                  STONES

Alpine

N

New

Lobuche
(SEE MAP 12)

PORTER'S
SHELTER

TO THUKLHA & NAMCHE

times creating accommodation problems for independent trekkers.

When heading out on day trips ensure that your gear has been stored securely: during peak season there are just too many people around to rely on honesty alone.

Supplies Lobuche is close to Everest Base Camp so many expeditions sell off their surplus food to the lodges here. So as well as the ubiquitous Mars and Snickers there's often an abundance of foreign delicacies, energy snacks and dehydrated foods for sale.

The environment Lobuche is in a sensitive alpine region. Please ensure that the water supply is kept clean and that your group's kitchen crew clean up after themselves properly, and don't let them chuck rubbish in the stream. The toilets are far too close to the water supply but at present nobody seems interested in rectifying this.

There is far too much toilet paper littering the trail to Gorak Shep and all dropped by trekkers. Just because you might be trekking up in the early morning when it is dark, this doesn't mean toilet paper remains invisible. Toilet paper can be put under a rock or in a plastic bag and tucked under a flap or in a side pocket. If you have got to go to the toilet make sure you are at least 10m off the trail and at least 30m from the stream and lift up a rock.

Lodges In 2000-1 three of the four lodges underwent long-overdue expansion. A new fifth lodge has finally shaken up the previously weak state of the others – now all they need is a crash course in environmental matters.

Asian Trekking's large *Eco-Lodge* is the best and given the location and the cost of building it, prices are still reasonable. It is often booked out by trekking groups in season.

Nights here from October onwards are invariably below 0°C and January temperatures are sometimes lower than -20°C/-3°F; only by April does it begin to warm up. The lodges are warm, however, if sometimes unhealthily stuffy. Once the sun strikes Lobuche mornings are pleasant though the wind gusts after midday throw the dust around and when the sun leaves in mid-afternoon it rapidly cools again.

Groups have a wide area to camp in but more often than not members decide that the lodges are rather more attractive than their cold tents and move in, some-

The Pyramid and the 8000m Inn The futuristic Pyramid was built in 1990 for research purposes, and in 1997 the facilities were expanded to include better accommodation for researchers and also, when not

---

How should you feel at 5000m?
The short answer is to expect to feel less than perfect. The air is thin and cold.
Many people suffer sleeplessness (often through worrying about Kala Pattar and altitude sickness), occasional breathlessness, mild headaches, anxiety, tiredness, disinterest in food or generally just don't feel 100%. And you thought you were on holiday!

These symptoms in mild form are quite usual. Minor suffering can often be relieved by drinking plenty, then drinking some more; alternatively, consider taking Diamox or mild painkillers. The full discussion on AMS is on pp281-90.

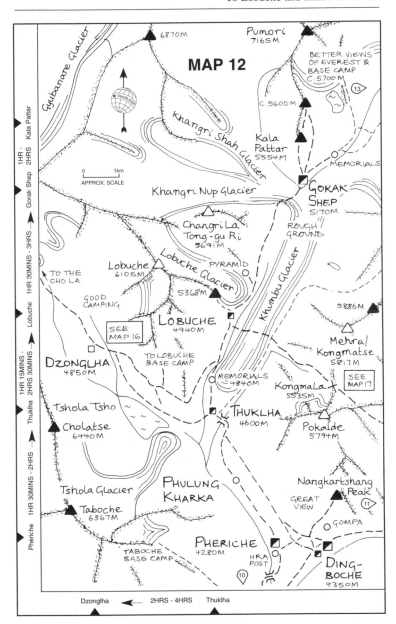

MAP 12

Gyubanare Glacier

6870M

Pumori 7165M

BETTER VIEWS OF EVEREST & BASE CAMP C. 5700 M

13

C. 5600 M

Kala Pattar 5554M

Khangri Shah Glacier

MEMORIALS

Kala Pattar
1HR - 2HRS

Gorak Shep
1HR 30MINS - 3HRS

0 1km
APPROX. SCALE

Khangri Nup Glacier

GORAK SHEP
5170M

ROUGH GROUND

Khumbu Glacier

Changri La Tong-gu Ri 5691M

PYRAMID

Lobuche
1HR 30MINS - 2HRS 30MINS

Lobuche 6105M

Lobuche Glacier

5368M

5886M

TO THE CHO LA

GOOD CAMPING

LOBUCHE 4940M

SEE MAP 16

Mehra/ Kongmatse 5817M

SEE MAP 17

Thukla
1HR 15MINS - 2HRS 30MINS

DZONGLHA 4850M

TO LOBUCHE BASE CAMP

MEMORIALS ~4840M

Kongma La 5535M

Tshola Tsho

THUKLHA 4600M

Pokalde 5794M

Pheriche
1HR 30MINS - 2HRS

Cholatse 6440M

Tshola Glacier

PHULUNG KHARKA

Nangkartshang Peak

GREAT VIEW

11

Taboche 6367M

GOMPA

TABOCHE BASE CAMP

PHERICHE 4280M

HRA POST

10

DING-BOCHE 4350M

Dzonglha ← 2HRS - 4HRS Thukla

full, some rooms for trekkers. The area is far more sheltered than Lobuche. Comfort costs around $15 per person. There is an inside toilet – only usable during the warm season – and even a real shower, as well as the only fax machine this high up. It even boasts room heating. This is the most environmentally sensitive lodge in the region, with no firewood used at all: instead they use kerosene for cooking, while solar panels and a mini hydro-project (at least, when the lake isn't frozen) provide the lighting.

The Pyramid is now a registered rescue organization with trained staff, a welcome addition to the region's services. They have a portable altitude chamber bag, portable oxygen, walkie talkie radios and are practised at using them. Expect to pay for any help you need and don't abuse the service.

The observant may notice 'K2' in the research post's real name; it was built at the time when K2 had just been remeasured and was thought to be higher that Everest. But then a mistake in the K2 calculations was found, and the old surveys were proved surprisingly accurate – indeed, staggeringly so.

Short excursions The small moraine towards Nuptse offers scenic sunset views if clouds have not rolled up the valley too far. The moraine immediately north of the *phu* is a stiff climb that's a little longer than it first looks but it also offers a few surprises: the Lobuche Glacier is close and spectacular. The grassy slopes behind Lobuche are also worth the climb. The sure-footed and energetic can attempt the three rock pinnacles, each harder than the last, for great views.

Changrila Tong-gu Ri Want to climb something other than Kala Pattar for great views? From near the top of the ridge that swings around above the Pyramid you can see Everest Base Camp, the summit, the west ridge and south summit and it almost looks like you are level with the Lho La

(though you aren't). Through the gap is Changtse (the peak north of Everest) and, temptingly, the smaller mountains seem to fall away to reveal a ring of serious peaks behind. It also appears that you are standing at a higher altitude than Kala Pattar although, as any surveyor will tell you, this is deceiving. The first peak is in fact a similar height.

This summit was shown to me by Peter from the Pyramid and not finding a name, I consulted with Sherpas there on something suitable and together we came up with Changrila Tong-gu Ri. Begin the walk at the turn-off to the Pyramid and simply climb the ridge between the main trail to Gorak Shep and the trail to the Pyramid. Somehow you have to gain height – which can be a little tricky – but once on the ridge line it is as pleasant as can be. Further along the trail steepens and turns a bit rocky and here, a little way up, there is a flat rock with a bolt (or a bolt hole) in it, and if you look up, you can just see the very top of Everest. This was one of the points used in 1992 to measure Everest.

Slightly further up, when you can see both the summit of Everest and Makalu, there is a memorial stupa for Benoit Chamoux, a famous French alpinist who died on Kanchenjunga with Rika Sherpa in October 1995.

From here the rock is substantially steeper and real scrambling is required. The first peak is roughly 5600m and a good place to stop. The farther peak requires scrambling that borders on rock climbing, and is more challenging than Gokyo's knobby view; however, it is a tempting 5691m high.

LOBUCHE TO GORAK SHEP AND KALA PATTAR
[MAP 12, p199; MAP 13, opposite]
Early in the season when it's not really cold many groups leave Lobuche well before dawn to reach the top of Kala Pattar for

❏ **Map key**
See p145 for a map key and information on the trail maps and route descriptions

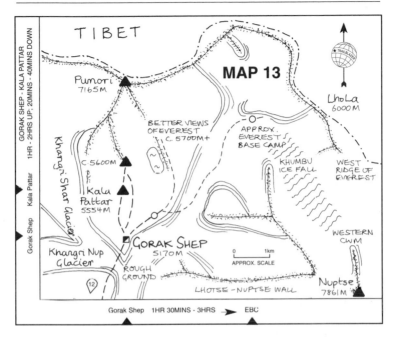

GORAK SHEP - KALA PATTAR
1HR - 2HRS UP; 20MINS - 40MINS DOWN

Kala Pattar

Gorak Shep

TIBET

MAP 13

Pumori
7165M

LhoLa
6000M

Khangri Shar Glacier

BETTER VIEWS
OF EVEREST
C. 5700M+

APPROX.
EVEREST
BASE CAMP

C.5600M

KHUMBU
ICE FALL

WEST
RIDGE OF
EVEREST

Kala
Pattar
5554M

GORAK SHEP
5170M

Khangri Nup
Glacier

ROUGH
GROUND

0   1km
APPROX. SCALE

WESTERN
CWM

12

LHOTSE - NUPTSE WALL

Nuptse
7861M

Gorak Shep 1HR 30MINS - 3HRS ➤ EBC

sunrise. This is a rare and usually rewarding experience, at least once you've got over the shock of the early start. By late November, however, the low night temperatures make starting with the sun a more reasonable and safer proposition. From Kala Pattar the surrounding mountains usually display themselves at their absolute best from mid-morning until sunset, if the weather has been stable.

For a good guide to the weather for your summit bid consider first the weather of the previous afternoon, and also ask lodge owners. Afternoon/evening cloud sweeping up the valley from lower down and **no** high cloud, or clouds hanging around lesser peaks, is a good sign. High cloud means the weather is harder to predict. In the spring season, during a patch where cloud forms regularly around or before lunchtime, a dawn start is advisable.

Some days a vicious cold wind picks up around 10 or 11am on the top while other days there is little more than a breeze on top for the whole day. Always take your warmest clothes (including a down jacket, if you have one), wind-proof clothing and a pack big enough to put it all in for the walk up. In winter, especially in snow, try to avoid getting your boots wet and beware of frostbite.

If the previous day was hopelessly cloudy don't despair. It could dawn perfectly fine the next day (but might not!). Being so far up a high valley system Kala Pattar is an unusually fine place and probably has one of the better weather records in Nepal. Even during the monsoon a day or two's patience will usually be rewarded with a stunning panorama. However, having two days set aside rather than just one will give you some peace of mind. Note that the majority of groups only allow a single day for Kala Pattar.

The walk to Gorak Shep takes only about one and a half hours for the fit and fast, or more than three hours for the less

fit. Kala Pattar is one to two hours above
Gorak Shep. Even for the slow, the round
trip should take less than eight hours. Look
out for furball pikas, the small Himalayan
mouse-hare.

From Lobuche the path is clear and
pleasant at first, gently wandering up the
ablation valley. Then it climbs, twisting and
turning, to thread its way onto the rough
moraine of the Khangri Glacier. Here it's
important not to lose the main track. The
rough walking ends suddenly and the trail
virtually falls into Gorak Shep.

Gorak Shep (5170m/16,962ft)

Here the Tibetan snowcocks are so tame
they will almost eat from your hands. For
trekkers from Lobuche the *lodges* at Gorak
Shep are merely places for a second breakfast or a late lunch after Kala Pattar but
many acclimatized trekkers stay the night.
The facilities have improved dramatically
and the lodges are warm and large as well,
with crowded dorms and many double
rooms. They stay open all winter – the only
time they may close is after a big winter
storm or during the monsoon.

If you intend staying here you must be
confident that you won't suffer altitude
problems so it pays to be well acclimatized
before arriving. A few people cope with two
nights at Dingboche/Pheriche, one at
Lobuche then one at Gorak Shep but a better plan is Dingboche, Thuklha, Lobuche
then Gorak Shep. If you have previously
stayed a couple of nights at Chukhung or
Gokyo then Dzonglha you are in a better
position to go direct to Gorak Shep and
bypass Lobuche. It is stupid to go directly
from Dingboche/Pheriche to Gorak Shep if
unacclimatized.

Ascending Kala Pattar

Kala Pattar, which means 'Black Rock' in
Hindi, is the most popular viewpoint in the
area for Everest and the Khumbu Icefall.
The first foreign ascent was in 1950 by
Tilman (who spoke with his sherpas in Raj
Hindi, rather than Nepali) and Oscar
Houston (father of the doctor, Charlie,
AMS specialist) who rated it a 'subsidiary
feature' without the extensive view of
climbing access to Everest they sought.
However, surrounded by a stupendous set
of faces, peaks and glaciers, it offers a
breathtaking arc of views.

Stop and look for the two trails up Kala
Pattar before crossing the sand. The one
that zigzags straight up leads to the slightly
lower and easier peak at 5554m/18,222ft
while the main trail that traverses around on
the right side gives the option of ascending
this easier peak or the more northern peak
(5600m/18,373ft). In snow use the longer
but less steep route. Between where the two
trails begin is a small spring with delicious
water.

From Gorak Shep a normal ascent time
is 75 minutes but some people take as long
as two laborious hours. Going fast but comfortably can take an hour, and a lung-burst-
ing 45 minutes is about the minimum, while
running down can take less than half an hour
though it's more usual to take about an hour.

A dizzying thought is the fact that to
climb Kala Pattar from Lukla you have to
ascend around 4800m/15,748ft, with a
modest 2400m/7874ft of descents in total.

Other points of interest
Two Glacier Rock (5529m/18,140ft)
Less imposing but virtually as high is the
hill marked 5529m on the National
Geographic Everest map and 5527m on the
Khumbu Himal map. The 360° panorama is
not as impressive as you can see more of
Everest. Pick up a trail of sorts at the north-
eastern end of Gorak Shep and head for the
square cairn on the skyline. Over the other
side is rough moraine and a small ridge,
behind which, near the lake, is a flat spot
often used as Pumori Base Camp. Pick up a
rough trail somewhere around here that
climbs to the eastern side of a minor rock

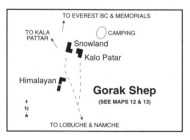

spur (in reality a big lump of rock). A small trail leads to where the rock meets Pumori and a way up onto the spur.

Pumori Advance Base Camp For a better view of the Khumbu Icefall you can climb another of Pumori's spurs. Pick up a faint trail at Pumori base camp (the lake mentioned above) then pass by the Two Glacier Rock, continuing a little north. Pick up, if you aren't already on, a small trail that soon begins climbing. The going gets steep and exposed but higher up you will come across a few tents/places for tents at an altitude of around 5700+m, Pumori advanced base camp. From here it is obvious that to get any higher takes some rope and perhaps a fair amount of stupidity. Don't attempt these view points in anything other than perfect, snow-free conditions.

Pumori was named by Mallory in 1921, it means 'Daughter Peak' or 'Sister Peak' (and is therefore pronounced 'Pumori' or 'Pomo-ri' rather than the more common 'Pu-mori'. Another mountain, incidentally, that is pronounced differently from when it was named is Everest: George's name was 'Eve-rest', not 'Ever-rest'.)

More memorials Close to Gorak Shep are some more memorials to mountaineers who died on Everest, in particular Rob Hall's and others who died on Everest in 1996. To reach them walk the length of the Gorak Shep flats and continue a little further in the same direction. They are on the obvious minor ridge.

Everest Base Camp

While many people rate this as a highlight, there are actually no views of Mt Everest. During the climbing season (late March, April and into mid-May) there are frequently yaks and sherpas on the trails but after fresh snow the trails can sometimes be hard to find or follow. To visit Kala Pattar plus the Base Camp in a single day is extremely tough – beyond most people. If you're going to visit one or the other, then Kala Pattar is the better choice.

In the past there were two trails to the Base Camp which both changed from one year to the next depending on conditions. Now the most frequently used route follows the top of the moraine past the Gorak Shep flats for a considerable distance before dropping onto the glacier. The route sometimes seems rather roundabout since there may be crevasses to avoid.

Some expeditions don't mind the occasional visitor (especially when from their home country) while others prefer no distractions and would rather not run the risk of having sickness brought into their camp. It takes between ninety minutes and three hours each way.

HEADING DOWN

From Lobuche most trekkers reach Pangboche, Deboche or Tengboche in a day. Groups tend to make for Deboche or Tengboche (making it more crowded). It's possible to reach Namche in a single long day – the Everest marathon is from Gorak Shep to Thamo and back to Namche.

Alternatively, after climbing Kala Pattar some trekkers head down immediately. Pheriche or Dingboche are only a few hours past Lobuche, but can be a tough end to the day. If you have been suffering from the altitude, descending the short distance to Thuklha may offer some relief.

Beginning from Gorak Shep reaching Pheriche or Dingboche is realistic so that means you should allow two full days to return to Namche.

To upper Pangboche Coming down the valley from Pheriche/Dingboche the turn off to Upper Pangboche and the gompa is by a small chorten, where the river widens and the first fields of Pangboche can be seen. Most people trek through or stay in Lower Pangboche.

A good alternative to the standard Tengboche route down is to go via Phortse and Mong, but allow more time – see p215. Trekkers with more time can walk from Lobuche to Chukhung easily in a day via Dingboche or the Kongma La (see p219). To Gokyo via the Chugyima La is covered on p216.

Namche to Lukla takes a day for the fit although many groups break this up: Namche to Phakding, then Phakding to Lukla. This then gives time for a special dinner and party in Lukla.

To Gokyo

INTRODUCTION
The Gokyo Valley offers great trekking and exploring but has always been overshadowed by the Lobuche, Kala Pattar and the Everest Base Camp area (discussed on p203). While Lobuche and Gokyo are both in ablation valleys, its many glittering lakes and silky streams mean Gokyo is far more beautiful and offers more day-trip possibilities to appreciate the impressive surroundings.

From Dole upwards the majority of the lodges are run by Khumjung people. The main places have many lodges but there are also some delightful single *house-lodge* settlements where a meal and a dormitory bed can be found. In years past most trekkers would stay only two nights at Gokyo. Now lodge owners comment that most independent trekkers stay three nights or more – sometimes many more.

Acclimatization
Planning a sensible acclimatization programme is essential if you're heading directly to Gokyo. The helicopter rescue pilots call it 'Death Valley' because many people go up too fast, unaware of the consequences. This is partly because the walking days are short, tempting trekkers to go on past their acclimatization limits.

The other reason serious AMS often results in death here is because there isn't the back-up of medical facilities that the Lobuche and Chukhung routes have with the Pyramid and Pheriche HRA clinic. The minimum acclimatization programme is two nights at Namche, and then one each at Khumjung (or Thame, Khunde, Kyangjuma, Mong, Tengboche or Phortse), Dole and then a night at either Luza,

Machermo or Pangka. You can still get AMS following this but it is definitely better than two nights at Namche and a night each at Dole, Machermo and Gokyo. A longer but rewarding itinerary would be Namche, Namche, Tengboche, Phortse, Dole, Machermo/Luza/Pangka, Gokyo. See pp274-5 for sample itineraries.

The route
The first section out of Namche is a high open traverse; its highest point at almost 4000m/13,123ft. The trail then drops abruptly through forest almost to the level of the river before climbing again. You may see deer and pheasant in this area. The countryside opens out offering great vistas of mountains on both sides of the deep valley and back to the stunning mountain wall above Tengboche. The climb up to the ablation valley beside the Ngozumpa Glacier leads you into a different world of azure lakes and golden alpine pastures beneath sparkling mountains overlooking the longest glacier in Nepal.

Facilities
Phortse used to be the last permanently inhabited village with only high *kharkas* higher up the valley. Now strategically-placed *lodges* stay open year-round, including during the monsoon and winter.

NAMCHE TO GOKYO
[MAP 14, opposite; MAP 15, p207]

Namche to Khumjung See p185.

Route from Khumjung This beautiful village – or Khunde – is a sensible place to spend the night at the start of the Gokyo trek. For Gokyo walk to the end of the village, then a minute down to a house with a blue roof by a junction, often marked with arrows painted on a convenient rock. Straight ahead is for Sanasa; the left path is the more direct to Mong.

Rounding a ridge you come to a small valley where the trail divides again; although the upper trail is easy to miss, this isn't a problem since you will still be on the main trail. That upper trail leads up to a

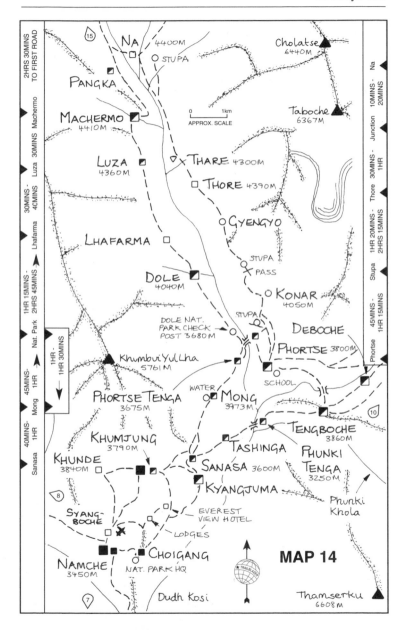

MAP 14

hair-raisingly steep stone staircase, the classic route. These days, however, it's more usual to contour on the better trail and head up the newer less steep stone stairs. Just beyond the main ridge the trail divides again, the larger trail for Mong, and the smaller trail to Tashinga.

Route from Sanasa

From Sanasa it's little more than 100m along the trail to Kyangjuma (ie towards Namche) to a small junction beside a rock. This trail climbs in a few minutes to the main trail from Khumjung to Mong. Turn right for the gentle stairs, or left then right a moment later for the classic route. Once through the rocks the trails cross the golden hillside gradually gaining height to a point overlooking Tengboche. It is well worth keeping your camera at the ready, and scanning the hillside, for it is common to see Himalayan tahr grazing here, and sometimes even musk deer in the gullies. Himalayan griffons and lammergeiers cruise the updrafts, and with a swoosh cruise often amazingly close. Close to Mong is a small stream: in dry times the only water supply for an hour in either direction.

Mong/Mohang (3973m/13,035ft) The

white chorten beckons and marks what is in effect a small pass. It is known to all Sherpas as the birth place of Lama Sangwa Dorje, the patron saint of the Khumbu and founder of some of the gompas. The views are stunning, especially of Ama Dablam, so if you haven't journeyed via the *Everest View Hotel*, this is a good substitute. In 1985 there were no lodges up here. Now, villagers from Khumjung and Tashinga have established four *lodges* with dormito-

ries, although mostly trekkers still use it as just a lunch stop.

The track to Phortse Tenga is rather steep but with great views over to Phortse and the spectacular river gorge below, including an inaccessible natural rock-bridge.

Phortse Tenga/Phortse Drangka
(3675m/12,057ft) *Tenga* means bridge but if heading to Gokyo you no longer need to descend to the river: a more direct trail contours from between the *Phortse Tanga Lodge* and the *Himalayan Lodge*.

There are now four lodges in the vicinity, all simple and with dormitories only. There are also many camping spots which are favoured by groups because there is plenty of wood around (despite the fact they are not allowed to use wood). *Drangka* means river in Sherpa, and if you follow the main trail, passing the *Himalaya Lodge* and camping area, this is where you will end up.

For the village of Phortse and the routes to it see p213.

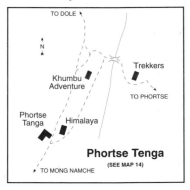

Phortse Tenga
(SEE MAP 14)

Dole National Park Post and army post/Newte 3680m/12,073ft) The staff here (if there are any), and at the army post a minute later, stuck in this horribly cold and miserable spot, play cards all day. They're here supposedly to protect the wildlife (especially the musk deer) and the forests. The village of Dole is one to two hours further on, up the long hill, through an area where you're likely to see colourful

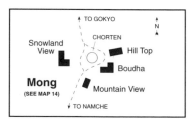

Mong
(SEE MAP 14)

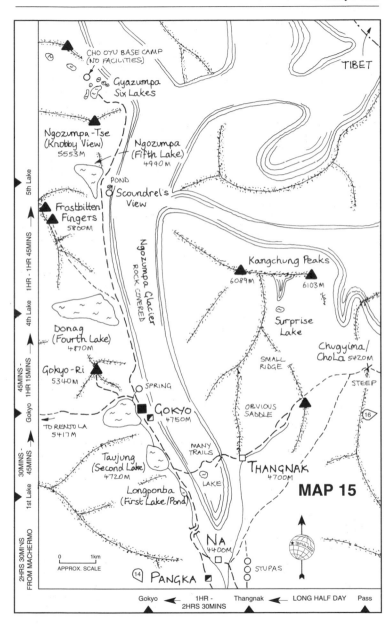

TIBET

CHO OYU BASE CAMP
(NO FACILITIES)

Gyazumpa
Six Lakes

Ngozumpa-Tse
(Knobby View)
5553M

Ngozumpa
(Fifth Lake)
4990M

POND

Scoundrel's
View

Frostbitten
Fingers
5800M

Kangchung Peaks
6089M   6103M

Ngozumpa Glacier
ROCK COVERED

Surprise
Lake

Donag
(Fourth Lake)
4870M

Chugyima/
ChoLa 5420M

SMALL
RIDGE

STEEP

Gokyo-Ri
5340M

SPRING

16

GOKYO
4750M

OBVIOUS
SADDLE

TO RENJO LA
5417M

MANY
TRAILS

Taujung
(Second Lake)
4720M

THANGNAK
4700M

LAKE

MAP 15

Longponba
(First Lake/Pond)

0   1km
APPROX. SCALE

NA
4400M

14 PANGKA

STUPAS

5th Lake

1HR - 1HR 45MINS

4th Lake

45MINS -
1HR 15MINS

Gokyo

30MINS -
45MINS

1st Lake

2HRS 30MINS
FROM MACHERMO

Gokyo ←   1HR -
2HRS 30MINS   Thangnak ←   LONG HALF DAY   Pass

pheasant and shy deer. In rain or snow this trail can be slippery and in winter the frozen waterfalls are impressive.

Dole (4040m/13,254ft)

The name means 'many stones' but despite this it's a pleasant kharka with six *lodges*. Here the yaks and naks are brought up in mid-June to graze and fertilize the soil with their dung, producing a rich crop of hay. If you arrive with time on your hands there are a couple of short exploration possibilities. Following the valley formed by the stream leads relatively gently up to a large grassy area in less than an hour. Alternatively follow the ridge from *Himalayan Lodge* up a steep trail to a rocky viewpoint, in an hour or so.

Dole, and Lafarma, Luza, Machermo get the sun early, making early starts easy, although there is little need with only a short day's walks between them.

The afternoon and sunset views of Kangtaiga and Thamserku from the hill behind Dole on the trail to Luza are most impressive. Up the valley are the first views of a high mountain wall, the left end of which is Cho Oyu, the sixth highest peak on the planet; the right hand side is Gyachung Kang, a name that few people have ever

heard of, though it is the 15th highest peak in the world and the highest below the 8000m mark, equal with Gasherbrum III in Pakistan.

The *Yeti Inn* (see box below) has a PAC bag, associated altitude medicines and people trained to use them. This bag is courtesy of Khunde Hospital and costs $50 per use. There is also a kerosene depot, although its future is uncertain.

Continuing towards Machermo the trail climbs out of Dole (past the Yeti Inn) and above the tree line to a chotar and small mani, and continues climbing up the ridge a short way before turning into a rising traverse with broad vistas.

Lhafarma/Lhapharma (4300m) has two

small *lodges* five minutes apart: the Mountain *View Top Hill Lodge* then the classically named *Holyday Inn*. The mountain views both up, down and across the valley are extensive. From here the trail contours, about as flat as it gets in the region.

While walking the fragrant smell comes from the small rhododendron plants. There are two types that look similar but only one, sunpati, is burnt at offerings. Approaching Luza is a mani and just below is a memorial to an Italian trekker who died here, and not surprisingly. He trekked from Lukla to Phakding, then one night in Namche, the next in Dole and arrived at Gokyo not feeling too well. A porter carried him down later that night but he died in Luza.

Luza (4360m/14,304ft) is an hour or so

from Dole and has several pleasant *lodges*. It is a good, and often less busy alternative to Machermo, and although it is 50 metres

Dole
(SEE MAP 14)

Cho Oyu

Yeti

Alpine Cottage

Himalayan   Dole Namaste

N
Trekkers ☐
Hilltop View

How the Yeti Inn was named

In 1990 eight of us passed through the very basic lodges at Phortse Tenga and pushed on to Dole. Arriving in the gloom and stumbling across the stream at the meadow bottom, we saw a light at what looked like a stable. This was the Yeti Inn, really just a basic sleeping platform and a kitchen area: you ate sitting on the beds. As we ate the excellent food Urkien, the lodge owner, showed us a book full of sketches of the yeti that a foreigner on a yeti hunt had left. Apparently the Gokyo Valley is full of them ...   **Joel Schone**

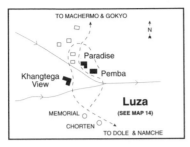

lower this difference is fairly significant: if you're feeling the altitude, staying here rather than Machermo and spending the next night at Pangka or Machermo is a good idea. When leaving, immediately after crossing the stream continue up through the fields rather than taking the left trail. In winter especially Tibetan snowcocks cackle in the fields.

Machermo (4410m/14,468ft) This is a relaxing spot with good views, especially of some little-known mountains. There's a sprawling fancy *lodge* (in season time double rooms are Rs300 or more) and a few smaller, friendlier hotels. Since Lhafarma, Luza and Machermo are so close together and at a similar altitude it doesn't matter which one you stay at.

Most people head directly from here to Gokyo but if acclimatization is causing problems it might be wiser to stay another night at Luza or Machermo. Alternatives are **Na** (4400m/14,436ft, see p213) where you can explore the surrounding area, or resting up at Pangka.

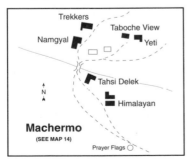

After an initial climb out of Machermo the trail is more or less level to Pangka.

Pangka (4480m/14,698ft)
This kharka has a chequered history. Two *lodges* opened in 1994. Then in 1995 one was hit by an avalanche during the massive freak November 8 snow storm. Thirteen members of a Japanese group along with their Sherpas were killed. Now there are three simple *lodges*, both built further away from the slopes above so that the same accident shouldn't re-occur.

There are trails around both sides of the fields. They rejoin by a small chorten then briefly drop-traverse out of the kharka before climbing closer to the Dudh Kosi. The massive slopes on your right (heading up) are the terminal moraine of the Ngozumpa Glacier, and less obvious, on your left are the remains of a smaller terminal moraine. You are now entering what is called an ablation valley, a usually narrow valley formed when a glacier lifts up moraine at its edges then retreats slightly, leaving this uplifted moraine to form a grassy valley.

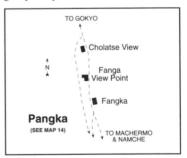

After passing a spot often used by camping groups and porters for cooking lunch the trail meets the rock wall and traverses the steep side on a reasonable trail. The views down-valley are magnificent but don't walk and look. The trail continues climbing, always staying above the river to a water source that only the paranoid would purify. In late winter this area is often quite icy. As you climb on the stone steps notice that there is one clear stream and one milky one. Unusually, the water draining from the glacier breaks through the terminal moraine here, rather than directly above Na. The clear stream comes from the first pond and is clear since much of the glacial sediment has settled in the lakes. A cold night, especially in winter, freezes the spray and sometimes even freezes the stream, diverting it onto the path which becomes treacherously slippery.

Longponba / the first pond A sudden change of scenery and hundreds of petite cairns introduces the first pond; it's really too small to be called a lake. It is beautiful up here, with a sparkling brook and tantalizingly close mountains. Between here and the second lake/pond, the trail to Thang Nak begins (ie for the Tso La) and, if you have time, walking up to the top of the moraine or just over the other side is simply spectacular.

Taujung / the second lake (4720m/ 15,485ft) *Taujung* means horse-grazing place and although now there are few horses, groups occasionally camp here and the spaciousness lends the area a measure of tranquillity, good preparation for the sudden views of the third lake.

In winter here I was berated for walking on the frozen lake: a sherpa said that I would anger the gods of the area, for the second lake is considered the holiest of the region.

GOKYO (4750M/15,584FT) & AROUND
On the shores of the third lake is the **Gokyo kharka**. Given the distance from anywhere, the *lodge* facilities are really very good, the lodge owners friendly and the prices reasonable, and they are certainly far better than most of the Lobuche lodges.

This standard of development was spurred on by the Gokyo Resort, a modified leftover of the film room built for the 1991 'Balloon Across Everest' expedition, and the fact that trekkers tend to stay here longer than previously. Although Gokyo has several shops they are simpler than the expedition-stocked lodges of Lobuche and

Pheriche; finding a variety of camping food is not so easy.

The Everest view from Gokyo Ri is only one of the many reasons for visiting Gokyo. Relaxing on the lodge patios or their sun rooms overlooking the rich turquoise, picturesque lake and the etched mountains above is considered reward enough by some; but it's the potential for far-ranging exploration that sets it apart from Lobuche. Climbing to the top of the Renjo/Henjo La is exhilarating and walking up to the fifth lake and beyond can only be described as 'out of this world'. Many of the peaks around here require some steepish scrambling or bouldering. Recognize your limits and take account of the weather; rocks are slippery when damp; otherwise enjoy!

With everyone heading off exploring at all hours of the morning don't expect to sleep in undisturbed. At the same time plan ahead if you are leaving early: the kitchen may not be open so stock up the evening before on boiled eggs and chapatis or plenty of biscuits and chocolate.

Gokyo is indeed a wonderful place but it does have its problems. The toilets are potentially polluting the lake – without visible impact yet, perhaps, but it is hard to work out how to improve this situation. To help in a small way at night you can pee outside, not in the toilets so that they don't fill the lake so quickly.

Less seriously, the lodges specialize in tacky posters with Indian sayings written on them: *Love is only chatter*
    friends are all that matter ...

Leaving, the **Na-Phortse alternative** is covered on p213.

Gokyo Ri (5340m/17,519ft) A stiff one and a quarter to three hour climb on an obvious track brings you to the prayer-flag bedecked top of this viewpoint. The panorama stretches well into the distance, a blend of glaciers and grass, sheer rock, snow and ice. The sunset on Everest and Makalu can be unforgettable here – as can be the descent afterwards if you forgot to

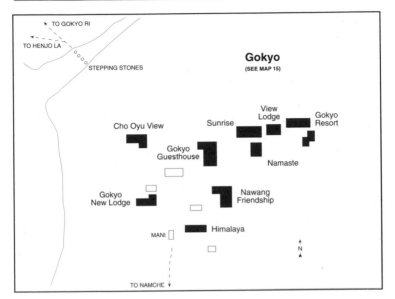

Gokyo
(SEE MAP 15)

TO GOKYO RI
TO HENJO LA
STEPPING STONES

View Lodge
Gokyo Resort
Cho Oyu View
Sunrise
Gokyo Guesthouse
Namaste
Gokyo New Lodge
Nawang Friendship
MANI
Himalaya
N
TO NAMCHE

bring your torch/flashlight. Sunrise is less worthwhile; only when it is fully light do the mountains look good, so there's rarely any need to start too early.

Renjo La/Henjo (5417m/17,772ft)

The trek to the top of this pass can be an exhilarating short day walk. In addition to some breathtaking new vistas, you end up in real alpine territory and pass within touching distance of a white glacier. Although it looks much further from Gokyo, it's only two to three hours to the top. A reasonable sense of balance and adventure is required as there are a few steep sections.

Begin by crossing the stream at the head of the lake, then follow the trail that contours, skirting the lake. At the head flats the views of Everest, Lhotse and, later, Makalu are interesting and quite photogenic. Cross the flats and stay to the right. There are some cairns once the rock scrambling begins but no real paths. The idea is to gain altitude up small stream gullies, eventually crossing the main stream that issues

from high above. At the first crest the view is quite unexpected and looks substantially different from the view from Gokyo. Again, stay to the right on the flat area. From here note the position of the pass above (it's marked by at least ten large cairns) and pick your own route up.

It's best to ascend following cairns over glacier-rounded slabs to the top of these then skirt south a short distance at a point that looks as if it could be tricky, to find the dusty steep track up. Alternatively, walk alongside the glacier on rough rock and later there is a steep loose scree slope to the dusty track. For the route over the other side see p222.

Donag/Tonak/the fourth lake (4870m/15,977ft)

A track leads up the valley but a more scenic way is to follow the crest of the moraine as far as possible. In about an hour you reach the fourth lake. This is large and beautiful, flanked to the south on one side by monumental cliffs. The most exciting features, however, are the unnamed peaks north of the lake:

Donag Tse/Frostbitten Fingers (5800m/ 19,029ft) It's well worth scrambling up to have a closer look at these tooth-like towers, and the views are fantastic, even if you can't reach the true summit. The climb can be made in a day-trip from Gokyo but with the altitude this is a trip for the fit and acclimatized only. The route up steepens over large boulders, getting quite tricky. It looks as if there is no way on but it's possible to climb over the boulders to the point where you reach a drop to the next tooth, at around 5600m: it is not possible, however, to reach the true tops.

The wall between Cho Oyu and Gyachung Kang defies description from this distance and the web of glaciers is fascinating. There's also the most extensive view of Everest you'll get anywhere in the Khumbu without resorting to serious mountaineering. You can see part of the Geneva Spur (but not the Hillary Step), the South Col, the stunning Lhotse face and Nuptse. To the north is the famous North Ridge and the First, Second and Third Steps where Mallory and Irvine were last seen. The perspective from this point, although not as close as from Kala Pattar, is more realistic than elsewhere.

Ngozumpa/the fifth lake (4990m/ 16,371ft) This jewel is about one and a half to three hours from Gokyo. Climbing the moraine, the pile of dirt to the east, to overlook the Ngozumpa Glacier also offers a 'scoundrel's view' of Everest that is more extensive than from both Gokyo Ri and Kala Pattar, and doesn't require climbing. Look out for furball pikas beside the trail. In the mid-morning light the view of Everest's formidable south face is the best there is.

Ngozumpa-tse (Knobby View) (5553m) From the true top this is simply the most outrageous trekking viewpoint there is; it is steep, however, and in places exposed so only attempt when the path is snow-free.

The only route that can be recommended is the spur that begins close to the fifth lake; when I first climbed this there was no trail but now a path guides you. Initially the

ridge is steep but soon eases off. Closer to the top is a steep boulder field so pick your route carefully: there still isn't much of a trail here. Once on the main ridge and at the top of what looked from below like the summit is a surprise: the real top is still a couple of knobs away, but well worth the extra effort if your nerves are up to the traverse.

From the real summit you overlook Gyazumpa (six lakes) and the exploration possibilities unfold below. With the Cho Oyu-Gyachung Kang wall to the north, the lakes under your toes, glaciers, snow and ice everywhere, this is as alpine a scene as it gets, without climbing a major peak. For some giddy excitement poke your nose over the edge, drop a stone and watch it as it plummets down an almost 300-metre, truly vertical drop.

You can even see Gokyo Lake and lodges and ridge after ridge of hills. The two Kangshung peaks are spectacular from here and this is the best view of Lhotse in the whole region.

It is possible to descend due east but this is dangerous. The terrain is very steep, there are a couple of places where you can be bluffed out, and there is a very real rockfall danger. In summary, don't descend on this route. Ascending here would be even trickier, and it isn't obvious where you should go.

Gyazumpa/six lakes/Cho Oyu Base Camp (5150m) The scenery up here is so spectacular it's overwhelming. It's a half-day trek from Gokyo but well worth camping/bivvying here so that you can have more time to appreciate the region. Northeast of the flat lakes area it is possible to climb several minor summits, only one of which is marked on the Schneider map, and there's a steepish (technical) ice route to the Sumna Glacier. Despite being labelled Cho Oyu Base Camp, very few expeditions have used this as a base; as you might notice from here, Cho Oyu presents a formidable challenge. Instead the standard route is from the Tibetan side, accessible from just over the other side of the Nangpa La. Cho Oyu is considered one of the least difficult 8000m mountains, if climbing on the stan-

---

The Nup La 5985m

Viewing the icefall that leads to this pass from the peaks above Gokyo, one has to wonder why this was ever named, and whether it has ever been crossed. The name means West Pass, and was named by the 1920s' explorers to Everest, who also named Lhotse, which means south peak (because it's south of Everest). Amazingly enough, the Nup La has been crossed, and by none other than Edmund Hillary and George Lowe, who in 1952, frustrated that the Chinese invasion of Tibet had stopped mountaineering attempts from the north, resolved to visit Everest's north base camp anyway. They also returned by the same route, without getting caught by the Tibetans or Chinese, which was better than Eric Shipton fared during the same period (see p115).

---

dard route, but, of course, any 8000m mountain is a major challenge.

Pass 5443m (17,857ft) Between Gyazumpa and Ngozumpa is a minor pass, marked as 5443m on the Schneider map. The glacier to the north has an even set of crescent crevasses so stay on the edge or on the rock. It is a bit of a scramble to the top but the descent on the other side is pleasant, passing a small lake that begs to be camped by.

Pass 5493m (Ngozumpa) West of the Ngozumpa, the fifth lake, is a pass that has long been known to Sherpas (in contrast the pass 5486m, west of Donag, is unknown to them and requires a rope, if it is passable at all). Conditions have changed since it was regularly used and now the east face is steeper than it used to be. The difficulties are less on the west side. I am unsure whether or not is is still easily crossable.

Chugyima La is covered on p215.

TO AND FROM PHORTSE [MAP 14, p205]
Route from Na to Phortse
The quickest route down from Gokyo is via Dole and Machermo. However, rather than back-tracking, there's an alternative trail on the east valley wall direct to Phortse via Na. Note that during the monsoon often there is no bridge between Pangka and Na. So the only way to take this route is to cross the Ngozumpa glacier to Thang Nak and descend from there.

Na/Nala (4400m/14,436ft) The tourist world of lycra and thermo-nuclear protection for your eyes has all but passed this place by. There is only one basic place where it's possible to stay and eat.

Leaving Na Aim for the small bridge. The trail is so faint that it can't be seen from the opposite side of the valley but it is there and it becomes clearer as you progress.

At **Thare (4300m/14,107ft)** tea and bikkies are served during the high season from the single simple *lodge* here. **Thore (4390m/14,403ft)** also boasts a quaint lone *teahouse* that is occasionally open. Joining the duo is a *teahouse* with a few beds at **Gyengyo**. I have arrived during January and February snow storms, a monsoon downpour, as well as during the normal trekking seasons, to find at least one of these places open. They are all run by women from Phortse, whose English (and Nepali) is little better than the yaks they look after, and who have no intention of clarifying which is Thore and which is Thare! A short climb leads to the chorten at 4278m/14,035ft with magnificent views.

Konar (4050m/13,287ft) is deserted during the trekking season but with the increasing number of trekkers using this side of the valley expect a lodge here sometime. In summer it's a large hay-growing area. Around the corner all the trails lead to Phortse.

Phortse (3800m/12,467ft)
Pronounced 'Phurtse' by the locals, *phurte* means flight, and it's supposed to have

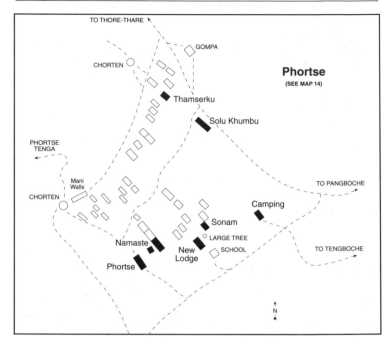

TO THORE-THARE

GOMPA

CHORTEN

Phortse
(SEE MAP 14)

Thamserku

Solu Khumbu

PHORTSE
TENGA

Mani
Walls

CHORTEN

TO PANGBOCHE

Camping

Sonam

LARGE TREE

Namaste

New
Lodge

SCHOOL

TO TENGBOCHE

Phortse

N

gained its name when the Khumbu saint, Lama Sangwa Dorje, landed here after a trance-induced flight. Apparently it was here that he attained enlightenment. It's a picturesque village, magnificently situated and defended by steep hillsides. The area is famous for its buckwheat but potatoes are also grown in large numbers.

The forests to the south-west and the north are protected by a ban on wood cutting that was made over one hundred years ago by the lama who lived in the forest. In other areas, notably Namche, Khumjung and Khunde, when the government took over control of the forests and redefined the areas that could be cut, the pattern of use changed quickly. Here, the old lama's edict seems to have proved more effective. It is also a shelter for innumerable danphe, other pheasants and deer.

Late afternoon is good spotting time: only the blind would miss seeing a variety of wildlife and they would be likely to trip over them.

Phortse is reputed to be one of the most conservative villages in the Khumbu and previously suffered a lack of reasonable *lodges*. Now *Namaste* and *Phortse* guest houses in the centre (with their names written on their roofs) have filled this gap. There are several other simple but pleasant lodges at the top of the village and another on the way to the two bigger lodges. Phortse is also home to a number of Everest summiteers, including Panuru (Phortse Guest house) and Tshering Lhakpa (Thuklha).

Phortse to Na From the *Khumbu Lodge* at the top of the village head north (left) on a path that follows the walls but stays above the fields. There's another trail that starts from the middle level of the village but it's harder to follow. If in doubt take upper trails.

Phortse to Phortse Tenga The trail starts behind the mani walls at the lower northern part of the village. It's a wide but sometimes slippery track passing through forest where there's a good chance of spotting pheasant. It continues down until you reach the wooden bridge. Close by is a protected stand of trees that is set aside exclusively for bridge repair.

Immediately after the bridge is a junction. Straight up a small path leads up to the main trail to the **Dole checkpost** (p206). The route to the left goes to some reasonable camping spots and Phortse Tenga (p206).

Phortse to Pangboche or Tengboche Walking without watching where you're going could be hazardous on this trail. If you're scared of heights and not happy walking along trails with steep drops beside them avoid this route.

The track starts from the top of the village on a gentle gradient with excellent views of Tengboche.

For the **gentle route to Deboche/ Tengboche**, the turn-off for the bridge that crosses the gorge is immediately after the first small rock cleft. The path heads down steeply before continuing at a more gentle rate of descent. It's not always obvious, sometimes little more than an imaginary trail, and divides many times but it is not easy to become totally lost. Once close to the bridge the path heads up 100m or so to climb over bluffs below, crosses a stream, then drops to join the main Pangboche-Tengboche trail immediately above the bridge.

For Pangboche At the first rock cleft continue straight on the main trail as it winds and climbs in and out of bluffs. It finishes in Upper Pangboche.

For Tengboche direct From the southern corner of the village a trail drops to a small bridge for the steep climb to Tengboche.

From the bridge above Tengboche to Phortse The old path skirting around the bluffs immediately west of the bridge is now disused, for obvious reasons. You must now climb up about 100m on goat tracks until you reach a point where it's easy to

cross the little creek to your left. Follow the tiny trail on the other side down to the fields. Work your way across, taking the upper paths where possible until you reach the main Pangboche-Phortse trail.

THE CHUGYIMA LA/TSHO LA/CHO LA [MAP 16, p217]
Safety
Although the crossing of the Chugyima La (5420m/17,782ft) has become popular, it does cross a glacier which could be dangerous; note the general information on glaciers on p263. If it has snowed recently either avoid the pass or take great care descending/ascending the smooth slabs on the Gokyo side of the pass and the steep section on the Dzonglha side. If it has snowed heavily or the weather is unstable **avoid the pass** altogether.

The rock approaches are steep and exposed but present no real problems *in good conditions*. However, the glacier is sometimes icy and treacherously slippery. Porters are never provided with crampons, instead they tie thick string around their shoes at the ball of the foot. This concentrates the load at that point and provides more grip, a handy trick that everybody without crampons should adopt if it is icy. String can usually be found at Lobuche and Gokyo, as well as discarded near the pass.

Crossing between Gokyo and Lobuche in one day is tough; it's more pleasant to break it up and now that there are lodges in Dzonglha and Thangnak (Tagnag) there are possibilities to suit everyone. Fit trekkers should, in good conditions, be able to make Dzonglha from Gokyo or vice versa, or Thangnak (Tagnag) from Lobuche. Note that Dzonglha to Gorak Shep is a relatively easy day, and if you stayed at Gokyo for a few days, Gorak Shep's altitude shouldn't be a problem. For people equipped to sleep outside there are good camping spots between Dzonglha and the pass, and on the Gokyo side there is a huge area worthy of exploration.

Route from Lobuche
Follow the track towards Thuklha but do not continue across the creek: stay on the

right (west) side. After a flat area (an ice sheet in winter) there's an obvious track that contours up around the huge spur to another flat area about an hour away. Up this broad gully is the route to Lobuche Peak Base Camp. Continue straight ahead for the route to the Cho La, climbing to the top of the ridge and then dropping down to an area with many streams. After jumping across the biggest the path heads gently up a tiny valley to hidden Dzonglha.

Dzonglha (4850m/15,912ft) This is a summer yak herding station on the left, or south, side of the miniature valley. There are two *lodges* here, at least one of which is normally open year-round. In difficult conditions or the monsoon check at nearby lodges that a lodge is open. If camping, there are suitable watered spots from here up to the beginning of the steep climb.

The approach There are two routes up the pass but one is disused now. Leaving Dzonglha the area is incredibly photogenic with Cholatse as one backdrop and the ridge extending from Lobuche Peak another.

Rounding a slightly rocky ridge, cross a stream and a small flattish area to the broad valley. Further up as the valley tightens the path crosses the main stream, which can sometimes be a little tricky to negotiate, then climbs a ridge on the southern side on a clear path. At the rock face the trail virtually disappears. Head right or north and climb up big boulders and slabs staying close to the wall on your left (west). There are a few cairns to look out for and eventually a heavily cairned flattish area is reached. The route continues to climb still staying close to the rock wall which is now to your south since the trail has taken a 90° turn.

If you have crampons head for the glacier as soon as you can see a way onto it, otherwise continue up to where the rock meets an almost flat snowy area. From here the tip of Everest is just visible and down-valley Baruntse begins to look formidable. Little of this wild mountain is normally visible.

Take great care around here: when it is warmer rockfall can be a problem, when colder it can be dangerously icy.

The glacier Stay to the southern edge of the glacier on the trail (assuming there is one). Never cross to the middle. Sometimes the footprints stay high on the south bank and at other times they drop down a little. It's very important to keep a good look out for crevasses. Often there are none visible, though if you do have to jump across one, be extremely careful. The highest point of the pass is at the far end of the snow/ice.

CHUGYIMA LA/TSHO LA TO GOKYO
[MAP 16, opposite; MAP 15, p207]
Down to Thangnak (Tagnag) Before continuing down, have a look at the route possibilities in the valley below. The main valley descends gently to the south to Charchung and Tshom Teng while the route to Gokyo crosses a couple of ridges via a shallow saddle with a large boulder with a cairn on top, the correct route. This saddle is apparently called Tar-Kure or perhaps Targula, meaning like a horse's back.

The descent is via rounded rock ledges, wide but often slippery. Staying on a track, or sometimes even finding one, is hard. Stay close to the southern rock wall. There are several vague trails and plenty of cairns around/over the rocky ridge to a camping place occasionally used by groups (called Base Camp). Once over the shallow saddle it's down, down, down, mainly on the north side of the khola.

Thangnak (Tagnag) (4700m/15,420ft) This collection of yak sheds has grown in the last couple of years to include two real *lodges*, which are normally open while the Chugyima La is passable, and extensive tent platforms. Gokyo is still an hour or two

TO CHOLA & GOLYO

Green Valley

TO LOBUCHE & THUKLHA

N

Dzonglha
(SEE MAP 16)

Himalaya

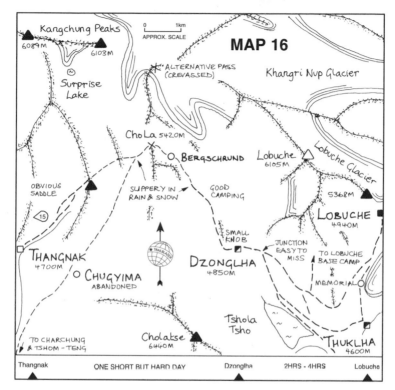

MAP 16

Kangchung Peaks 6089M 6103M

0 1km APPROX. SCALE

Surprise Lake

Khangri Nup Glacier

ALTERNATIVE PASS (CREVASSED)

Cho La 5420M

BERGSCHRUND

Lobuche 6105M

Lobuche Glacier

OBVIOUS SADDLE

15

SLIPPERY IN RAIN & SNOW

GOOD CAMPING

5368M

LOBUCHE 4940M

THANGNAK 4700M

CHUGYIMA ABANDONED

★ TRAIL BLAZER

SMALL KNOB

DZONGLHA 4850M

JUNCTION EASY TO MISS

TO LOBUCHE BASE CAMP

MEMORIAL

Tshola Tsho

TO CHARCHUNG & TSHOM-TENG

Cholatse 6440M

THUKLHA 4600M

Thangnak   ONE SHORT BUT HARD DAY   Dzonglha   2HRS - 4HRS   Lobuche

from here over rough ground. Several guidebooks (mine included) and maps have called this place Dragnag, Tagnag and other variations; the correct name is Thangnak.

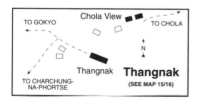

TO GOKYO
Chola View
TO CHOLA
N
Thangnak
TO CHARCHUNG-
NA-PHORTSE
Thangnak
(SEE MAP 15/16)

Crossing the Ngozumpa Glacier
Follow a thin trail; up a little around the corner is a prominent cairn on the crest of the moraine which you should head for.

Scan the glacier and look for signs of the most direct route. The path across is well used but not always obvious and there are older paths further down (glaciers move!). Don't attempt to cross in thick cloud. The walking is tough for tired feet, but after climbing the moraine on the opposite side you drop to just below the second lake (see p210).

Route from Gokyo to Lobuche
If you're beginning from Gokyo to cross the pass that day, start early. Just past the second lake pick up a thin trail contour-climbing to cairns that overlook the glacier. It is essential to find this point. Just before you descend onto the glacier there is a superb view up to Cho Oyu and directly

below the summit is a black rock peak, ('knobby view', see p212) and to the left with its broad slopes but jagged summits are the Frost-bitten Fingers. Closer in you will also recognize Gokyo Ri, best seen exactly from the notch.

Beyond Thangnak (Tagnag) Ascend the valley on the north side. After 30-40 minutes follow the trail up a smaller valley on the left. After 15-20 minutes recross the main stream, leaving it behind, and head up to a minor saddle, another 12-20 minutes away, to a large rock. There are new views, including the Cho La, the steep rock face with thin snowy saddle which looks particularly formidable from here. Descend on the trail, crossing streams, and traverse to a camping area sometimes used by groups and called Cho La Base Camp. From here the rough rock begins. There are several rough cairned paths, easy to lose, that lead to a flat area with a pond above it. Pick up a trail ascending a debris cone to the southern rock wall. This ascends moderately steeply and the trail is quite exposed. In deep snow this can be impossible or at least highly dangerous as this is in fact an avalanche cone. Thirty to seventy-five minutes later you reach the pass cairns and prayer flags and the glacier. Clamber onto the glacier and stay high on the southern side, and beware of it is icy as it can be *very* slippery, and ice is very hard! Many people have bruised themselves. Traverse the glacier, always staying on the southern side and once you reach the rocks descend on difficult but short slopes to a set of cairns in a semi-sheltered area. Continue down on difficult ground, staying close to the rock wall to your right and look for the trail below. Once off the difficult ground at the ridge a clear path descends to the open, almost flat valley. The walking in this valley is pleasant and incredibly photogenic. Cholatse's face is utterly dramatic, Ama Dablam's triangle is stunning and Lobuche East peak looks particularly formidable and even surreal in some lighting. As the valley makes a bend towards Cholatse cross the stream and briefly climb-traverse to the trail. Don't descend further.

Dzonglha
A few desultory buildings sit in a sometimes swampy hollow not quite sheltered from the huge mountains surrounding it. There are two *lodges* and it is worth consulting departing trekkers of their opinion of them.

If you have reached Dzonglha and are contemplating continuing, Thuklha is about an hour away but involves a descent that would be tricky in half-light. Alternatively, one and a half to two hours of hard walking will bring you to Lobuche.

Heading out of Dzonglha to Lobuche (or vice versa) Cholatse steals the show with its awesome face. As you round the spur with your first views of Nuptse there is one of the best views of the uppermost parts of Lhotse's fearsome upper reaches that you will get in the Khumbu.

Khumbu side trips and pass-hopping

Some of these routes are distinctly adventurous so come mentally prepared. On one route, a couple of days from anywhere and on dicey ground, Tom and Vanessa's sherpa said 'I know a shortcut – did you bring a ladder?' Wisely, they decided to turn back.

KHUMBU TO MAKALU
Crossing between the Everest region and Makalu Base Camp is a route that requires serious planning (see the 1988 National Geographic Mount Everest map) and real mountaineering experience. The route is via Sherpani Col (6146m/20,164ft) or East Col (6183m/20,285ft) over the large, almost flat, snow field to West Col (6143m/20,154ft) which drops down a glacier to the 5200m/17,060ft head of the Hongu Basin. There are several ways out of this. You can go over the Mingbo La (5866m/19,245ft), or over the Amphu Labtsa (5780m/18,963ft) with its steep (or vertical, if your route-finding isn't spot-on) descent and couple of big open crevasses at

the base. The third option is down the Hongu Valley to Mera La and one more pass to Lukla. These routes should only be attempted by well-equipped, seasoned mountaineers. The survival rate among the inexperienced does not make nice reading.

Makalu Base Camp
There is some information about this on 🖥 www.project-himalaya.com.

THE KONGMA LA [MAP 17, below]
Meaning Pass of the Tibetan snowcock, the Kongma La (5535m/18,159ft) provides an interesting high route between Chukhung and Lobuche. It takes a tough day to walk and is longer than the lower route via Dingboche. If free of snow, it's a non-technical pass. It requires only a little confidence and steady feet for the last short section to the crest. A trekking pole may be handy. It's more pleasant to do in the Chukhung-Lobuche direction because the

walk up is on grass, leaving the rock-hopping and loose scree for the descent. It's really worth camping by the high lakes or even slightly above the pass itself (views in both directions) for the stunning sunset and sunrise.

Route from Chukhung to Lobuche
Contour and cross the large stream issuing from the ablation valley just west of the Nuptse Glacier. Then there's a long climb up the huge grassy ridge. There are faint trails; aim for the point where the high, sharp rocky spur peters out into the grass. Pick up the track on the western side of this ridge at a high kharka which has some rock shelters and a water source. There are several ways up and the main track from here is easy to lose. It stays above the marshy/icy grass flats, then heads left (north-west), parallel to some bluffs where you may see Himalayan tahr nimbly cavorting over the sheer rock faces. The track then

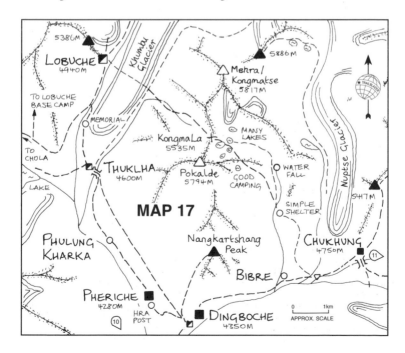

curves and ascends right to round a big knob of rock (on the right side of it).

The lakes After a couple of climbs and short descents, the lakes are the next stage with the highest being the most beautiful. The sun arrives around here wonderfully early in the morning which makes up for the night temperatures (usually well below 0ºC). Even when the lakes are frozen there's a tiny spring by one of the smaller ones.

The Kongma La The track to the pass goes to the right (north) of the highest lake to start the diagonal traverse of the steep face. The pass itself is littered with cairns up each ridge, and 50m to the north up the ridge is a small ledge perfect for a single tent. Bring a block of ice up from the lake as there's no water.

The route down drops only a little while heading right (almost due north) for a long way before beginning a slide down scree. From the ablation valley, crossing the Khumbu Glacier takes another tiring hour before Lobuche appears.

Route from Lobuche to Chukhung

To locate the trail across the glacier from the Lobuche side, head downstream about 200m to a large rock right beside the stream. Perpendicular to the stream at this point there are a couple of tracks on the moraine that head for a small notch. Once across the glacier, climb grassy slopes on a small trail and once in the rock stay on the right-hand side of the valley. There are a few rocky stretches near the top without a trail across.

PEAK 5886M (19,311FT) [MAP 17, p219]

This peak is marked as 5880m on the Schneider map; the lakes below are unmarked. Accessed via the short north summit ridge from east or west sides, it could also be used as a possible glacier pass-hop. There is the odd hole and step in the ice, and a sling plus 10m cord would aid retreat off the scenic lunch spot. Since there are lakes on either side, camping here is easy. A good nose to follow and adventurous, steady feet are required.

AMPHU LABTSA (5787M/18,986FT) [MAP 11: p197]

Shipton was the first person (foreign or Sherpa) to cross this col in 1951. The Amphu Labtsa is a tough and dangerous mountaineering proposition, nothing akin to the Tsho La or Thorong La (Annapurna area) and it leads into some particularly isolated country. You need a climbing-experienced guide who has crossed the passes many times, good equipment and a rope. Each year several porters get frost-bite and ill-prepared trekkers have died here; it is no place for porters unless perhaps you have a Western guide who can assist them.

The pass is well concealed, visible only as you near it or from Imjatse/Island Peak Base Camp. It's best attempted early in the morning to lessen the danger of avalanche and rockfall so this means camping below at Amphu, a short half-day's walk from Chukhung. Unfortunately this grass/stone area gets very little sun, making it one of the coldest parts of the entire valley, and it also lacks water. The nearest easily accessible water is a clear spring just west of where the trail joins the Imjatse/Island Peak Base Camp path. Other possible sources are two small lakes above the faint trail and there's also glacier runoff or ice.

Routes to the top of the pass

There are two routes each with a sub-route or two. From both sides both routes look sheer but on climbing the route unravels. For the snow/ice route begin in Amphu and head up the glacier and across the big crevasses to the avalanche-smoothed diagonal gully – the route up. It is possible to stay mainly on rock for the first part even if at first this does not appear to be the case. Then there is a short exposed traverse before the final petit basin to the crest. If you're coming over from the Hongu it's difficult to reach the top of the pass in the correct spot and many lengths of rope testify to the number of parties that decided it was easier to simply abseil down a vertical wall than attempt to find the easiest crossing point. From a distance look for the two low spots. In the centre is a small notch that is slightly higher – the pass.

If snow-free, the higher **rock route** (5900m/19,357ft) is an alternative. Pick up the trail on the way up; near the top one steep section often requires a short rope pitch. From the summit there is a tricky rock trail down. Sometimes it is possible to descend partly on the glacier beside, staying near the rock.

To Mera

Along the shore of the larger lake of Panch Pokhari is a small trail that descends to the other lakes. The trail crosses briefly to the east bank of the Hunku/Hongu Khola to skirt the lake marked 5004m on the *Shorong Hinku* map. Otherwise the trail remains on the west bank. See p266 for the Mera La.

MINGBO VALLEY [MAP 10, p193]

Just above and opposite Pangboche, the Mingbo Valley is an infrequently explored but spectacular valley. Reaching a satisfying distance into it requires an overnight camp and perhaps some acclimatization.

Leaving Pangboche descend to the bridge, then follow the trail accurately marked on the National Geographic and *Khumbu Himal* maps to the stream just before Mingbo. Here a trail branches off to roughly follow the stream to Ama Dablam Base Camp. The path straight ahead leads to Mingbo with its *goths* which are usually locked. Over the ridge from the Base Camp or ten minutes north of Mingbo is the outline of the old Mingbo airstrip which was used to ferry supplies to the Tibetan refugees leaving Tibet after China invaded. A glance at the approach will reveal why it is disused now. It was another 'Hillary job'. Several small paths continue up the valley and the keen can scramble to around 5700m on the larger of Ama Dablam's southern ridges.

Mingbo La (5800m/19,029ft)

Groups occasionally use this pass rather than the more standard Amphu Labtsa after climbing Mera (p266). The approach from the Hinku Valley up the Hunku/Hongu Nup Glacier is straightforward although crevassed. Conditions on the Mingbo side

vary: sometimes the fluted face drops off at perhaps 60° and requires at least two pitches to reach the glacier proper, sometimes it is tamer, and occasionally it is virtually impassable.

From the pass look for the small trail on the ridge descending from Ama Dablam. Once off the glacier you will have to cross some rough terrain and climb up to this.

THE BHOTE VALLEY

The upper Bhote Valley was officially opened to trekking only in 2002, although in fact nobody ever stopped you going up there previously. Currently there are no lodges above Thame and no year-round occupied villages above Thame Teng but there is some great wilderness trekking and several valleys deserve exploration.

Whatever you do though, don't cross the border, ie the top of the Nangpa La (pass), into China. Over the border you are in China and since you have just broken Chinese law, Tibetans have no problem with robbing you because you can't go to the police, and they will hassle you. Second, there are border guards patrolling the area, normally situated past the end of the glacier, and to save getting blamed for assisting foreigners, many Tibetans will tell the Chinese patrol if they see anything unusual. If you are caught then expect some real trouble. One story concerns two German brothers who were caught. The police simply locked one up and told the other to go back and return with $10,000 as payment for his brother's release.

Although the Chinese border police are now strict, until about 1995 this wasn't the case. Beginning with Shipton in 1952, Cho Oyu was attempted from the Nepal side by crossing the Nangpa La into Tibet. But even at that time Shipton was wary, and this is probably the reason the expedition failed: because of Shipton's concerns, their base camp was still in Nepal, just a little too far from the mountain. Herbert Tichy in 1954 had no such scruples and set a base camp up in Tibet. This pattern was followed by many expeditions who, strangely, usually had permits issued by the Nepal Government. Suddenly in the mid-90s

China realized that the border was being crossed illegally and sent armed soldiers to confront a Spanish expedition, and the route was closed. Instead the multitude of expeditions that now head to Cho Oyu travel officially through Tibet to get to the mountain from the north. Note that most maps don't actually mark the border and feigning ignorance with the Chinese does not work.

Note, too, that Nepali law also forbids crossing the border, for the moment anyway. At the time of writing the other regulations were unclear: it may be that you are supposed to get a special trekking permit for the trek, perhaps only available to trekking companies, or perhaps it will be regulation-free. Not that it matters in the current situation anyway.

Facilities
Past Thame Teng there is a simple *teahouse* at Marulung that is only sometimes open, and past that there are **no lodges, shops or teahouses**. Don't underestimate how much you might eat on this trip, nor the number of days that you might take. You will need to be self-sufficient for at least a week even if you are already acclimatized, and this does not allow for side trips.

If travelling with a company, ensure that they understand just how rough the last section is and that there are **no facilities for porters** up there; furthermore, it is savagely cold.

Security
Part of the attraction of this trek are the wild Tibetans, who mostly are lovable scoundrels. Many of them will try to appropriate things from your pack or tent. Be careful.

From the Renjo/Henjo La
From Gokyo to the top of the Renjo/Henjo La (5417m/17,772ft) is described as a day-trip from Gokyo. On the Bhote Valley side the descent isn't easy and with snow or ice could be quite dangerous. The pass itself is long. You can descend in two places to head left (south) along smoothed, slightly exposed slabs close to the bluffs above.

Beware of yetis throwing stones down. Then, when you can, head for the lake, aiming to go around it on the northern shore. The overflow stream leads to another lake area where there's a *phu* (herding station) with a good small rock shelter.

To Thame Continue to another *phu* where there's a real track down to the valley floor. Sometimes there is a simple *teashop* open at Marulung. Check with Gokyo lodge owners what the situation is. Note that Gokyo to Thame isn't possible in one day, unless you leave very early, are fit and fast; even then, it is a tough day. So count on spending one night out.

Heading north Once you hit the grassy slopes swing north and descend to the valley floor.

To the Nangpa La
Despite the fact that yaks are used for the crossing of this pass into Tibet, it is no ordinary trek. It's tough, even for yaks, judging from the number of carcasses along the track; the trek from Gorak Shep to Everest Base Camp is a trifle compared to the slog up to the Nangpa Glacier.

Lunag/Lonak (5070m/16,634ft) There's shelter and a spring here, the only roofed buildings in either direction for a long way. From here the ground begins to get rougher and water can be hard to find. The scenery also becomes wild.

At **Dzasampa** the ablation valley ends and it's time to cross into the middle of the glacier. Conditions are quite variable and it's not difficult to turn an ankle on the rocks which look firmly fixed to the slopes of verglas (glass-ice) but aren't. As you work your way up, concentrating on finding a safe route, the surrounding mountains begin taking on mythical shapes. The rubble gives way to a smooth white glacier with contouring hair-line cracks every 10m or so. Crevasses have, on occasion, swallowed a yak or even a person. The pass is marked in true Tibetan fashion and the view of the purple-brown hills is enough to inspire any explorer. The nights up here are even colder than at the six lakes/Cho Oyu Base Camp area and the sun doesn't hit the pass until mid-morning.

From late April to May and September you can see the colourful patchwork of tents of Cho Oyu expeditions on the other side of a glacier.

KYAJO

The Himalaya and Tibet have many legends about mythical valleys accessible only to flying lamas. This is the real thing, a hidden valley that is an absolute delight to explore. The ability to fly at least for short sections would be appreciated: the routes into and out of this valley are adventurous even in the best of conditions. In poor visibility it is easy to lose the trail while in snow the thin trail with big exposure could be lethal. Yaks do occasionally graze up here but that says a lot about how tough yaks are rather than the quality of the trail. They are the sort of trails that unless you are standing directly on them you would have difficulty believing there is a trail at all.

Without climbing gear take three to four days food; otherwise take supplies for at least five days, or seven would be better. Increase your chances of success by camping as high as possible.

From Laudo Gompa Continue directly up the ridge. This turns into more of a steep valley that passes between some rock faces. Then head right (at about 4200m) under one rock face on a more distinct trail and follow this up. From around 4300m the small trail begins traversing in and out of ridges to a minor pass at 4525m from where the route becomes more obvious, although is still small and little-used and there is little or no water along this stretch. The consolation is its location on the sunny side of the valley.

Finally traverse and descend to the valley floor at 4450m. Here the valley reveals its glacial heritage: impossibly sheer sides with a crystal creek meandering through. Looking back it feels as if you are looking over at the edge of the world.

The rock wall at the valley head looks formidable but a steep gully does lead to the next flat step. Not much lingers here except snow and ice. Ahead is the last step, topped by a glacier.

Exit via Khunde If you thought the trail in was fun you'll be happy to know the surprises don't end. A couple of short sections of this route follow little more than your imagination. If coming from Khunde you might want to use a rope but heading up you can escape without one – just – if you have steady nerves.

If you are wondering if there is a trail down the valley; at first it looks like it might go, but later it is obvious that there is no way down without a rope.

The route drops under bluffs then climbs a short slippery gully at around 4230m, which is sometimes icy. It looks as if a ledge above this might go but it is even more difficult. These sections are the reason this trail is now barely used.

Traverse around then head up on a real trail up to a pass, 4410m, with views of the civilized world below. Pass by the water supply tank and piping.

PHAPLU START   [MAP 5, p157]
Beginning a trek from Phaplu is a great way to experience the middle-hills Sherpa culture. The main difference is that flying in rather than beginning from Jiri saves all but one hill and two days.

Phaplu
The short runway describes a gentle 'U' shape, a real 'Hillary job'. It was constructed to help build the Himalayan Trust hospital here. The hospital, now government-run, sits a few minutes' walk below the runway.

Phaplu is the airport that services Salleri, the district headquarters of the Solu-Khumbu district. It has a collection of dal bhaat hotels, houses and offices that could more properly be described as mansions and some shops that even stock chocolate. RNAC and the helicopter companies have offices here. It has a strange atmosphere with the large buildings and a rubbish dump in the middle of it all. There are a string of *bhattis*, simple hotels where you can stay. The biggest and most comfortable hotel is the *Hotel del Sherpa*. It is set slightly off the main trail through a *kani*. Ornate dragons guard the main door. Apparently it boasts a sauna but when I visited the hotel there wasn't a soul around.

Leaving north The main trail passes beside the airport. At the Phaplu Gompa the lower trail leads to Junbesi while the higher leads to Chiwang Gompa.

Chiwang Gompa On the path up it is common to see langur monkeys, squirrels and deer. The gompa is particularly old, being originally built at the time of Lama Sangwa Dorje, and is of an interesting design. Although there is no real lodge monks will generally invite you in to stay with them and expect a donation for the service. There is also a good camping place a little below the gompa.

Salleri

This is the hustling, bustling district headquarters of the Solu-Khumbu Jila (or district). It has a strange atmosphere, lackadaisical almost to the point of being unfriendly. They aren't used to trekkers but there are several Nepali-style *lodges* and *restaurants*. The path running through town has been widened with the expectation that the Okaldunga road will be extended to here. It is many years off though.

The **Pemba Thuben Choeling gompa**, slightly south of Salleri is worth a visit. It was in part funded by the Himalayan Trust and was only completed in 1998.

Route from Phaplu to Ringmo

From Phaplu you can either walk directly to Ringmo or make a worthwhile detour to Junbesi. For Ringmo, take the wide trail beginning just above the end of the airstrip. There are a couple of basic places en route that could provide lunch, some snacks and even a simple bed. For Junbesi, head north and down to the valley floor. Follow the valley to cross the suspension bridge. This leads to the trail on the northern bank of the Junbesi Khola.

Route from Ringmo to Phaplu

The junction for the path to Phaplu is obvious at Ringmo but don't believe local assurances that Phaplu is only a couple of hours away. It'll take more than three hours and probably almost five.

The trail is well constructed and passes though some pleasant forest. An hour or so out of Ringmo another path branches off the main trail. This descends to the river and the bridges below to join the track from Junbesi to Phaplu. However, it's better to continue along the main trail, the branch that contours leading to Phaplu without any serious climbs. After many more bends the airstrip at Phaplu comes into view.

To/from Bung direct Although little used by trekkers, the direct trail between Bung and Salleri is a main local route. Between the two is the Dudh Kosi, which must be descended to, and a high ridge close to Salleri, which must be crossed. It is normally a two-day walk.

From Bung Near the Makalu-Barun National Park and Conservation area post ask for the trail to Sotang. From there keep asking for Salleri.

TO CHIALSA

Chialsa is commonly called a Tibetan refugee camp, implying a temporary nature. Now it is perhaps better called a sanctuary. Although the people are distinctly Tibetan they have adapted and more or less integrated with the surrounding region. For the trekker with energy or time and a desire to learn a little more on Tibet it is well worth a visit.

The route Slightly above the main trail leading through Salleri is a parallel trail that

---

Opposite Top: The lodges and frozen lake at Gokyo (see pp210-1). Some late winter and early spring snow occurs but these times are mostly snow free. **Bottom:** The Chugyima La (Cho La, see p215): Gokyo-side approach (left – the snowy area in the centre top of the photo is the pass itself) and Dzonglha-side approach (right).

Pivotal Salleri

On 23 November 2001 the Maoists attacked the army base in Dang, West Nepal. It was their first move directly against the army, for previously they had only shot up police posts. The army barracks was caught completely by surprise and overwhelmed with the loss of many lives and weapons.

Two nights later the Maoists attacked Salleri, the district headquarters of the Solukhumbu region. However, this time the army was prepared and fought back ferociously, at one time calling the Maoists to surrender. Eleven soldiers died and nearly double the number of police but it is thought that something like 200 Maoists died, around one in ten attackers. It was a major setback for the Maoists. It was the first skirmish or battle that they decisively lost.

No tourists were killed, injured or even threatened. I met two women who were in a lodge at Sete when it suddenly filled with armed Maoist soldiers, still grimy and devastated from the experience. The women were ignored. Several other tourists met Maoists on the trail in the following days without problems.

The Maoists took a while to recover from the experience. It wasn't until 16 February 2002 (Democracy Day) that they attacked the Achham army post. With the use of machine guns, mortars and grenades looted from Dang, all except two of the 59 soldiers were slaughtered in under an hour, demonstrating that the Government and army had utterly failed to understand the situation and the strength, size and organization of the Maoist opposition.

---

goes to Chialsa, among other places. Perhaps the easiest place to pick up the Chialsa track is to trek south to the new Pemba Thuben Choeling gompa and climb immediately above that. The trail passes above a higher education college then passes through Thateng. About 40 minutes from the gompa climb to and pass another gompa. A further 20 minutes along, where the power lines end, is a stupa with prayer wheels – the entrance to Chialsa.

Chialsa

The people are friendly here, although not much English is spoken. The *hotel* is simple and only has one double room. The food is whatever you can think of that they can make: momos, thukpa (Tibetan soup), fried and boiled potatoes, sukuti (fried dried meat), roti, tsampa and the inevitable Tibetan salt-butter tea.

There's an extensive mountain panorama from the top of the ridge, an hour or so up. Apparently even Everest is visible. For less breathtaking views visit the gompa that is ringed by flags. This gompa is one of four that His Holiness (HH) the Dalai Lama commissioned to face Tibet. The others are in India at Zanskar, Ladakh, Deurali-Gantok in Sikkim and Bumdila.

Heading south Okaldunga is around 36km away, a long day's walk for locals but two days for loaded porters and trekkers. A road from the Terai to Okaldunga is under construction and will perhaps be completed by the time you read this. Once the new Eastern Highway out of Kathmandu is finished as well, this could provide an alternative trekking route to Jiri and the Salpa-Arun. Those that hope that this route might involve no hill-climbing, however, will be disappointed: there is still a 3000m ridge to cross between Okaldunga and Salleri.

Opposite: Climbing Island Peak (Imjatse, see p264). Fixed ropes are normally used to climb the bergschrund at the beginning of the headwall (top right).

Tibetans in Nepal

Beginning in 1949 the Chinese built a road to Lhasa so as to 'peacefully liberate' Tibet. (They have also built friendship highways into Nepal and Pakistan, while with India they were more brazen, building a road through India's Aksai Chin that led to a border war in 1962.) This Peaceful Liberation, the Great Leap Forward and the Cultural Revolution resulted in the deaths of around one million Tibetans, perhaps a quarter of the population. In 1959 they plotted to kidnap the Dalai Lama, Tibet's leader. He escaped but the consequent fighting, in which the Chinese displayed merciless brutality, set off an exodus of Tibetans. It was estimated by the International Red Cross (IRC) that between 7000 and 10,000 fled over the Nangpa La alone. The IRC set up ten transit camps throughout Nepal but many Tibetans still died of hunger and disease. In 1961, using thinly veiled threats, the Chinese forced the Nepalese to kick out the IRC, so the Swiss Red Cross stepped in (the IRC is based in Geneva), buying 40 acres of land in the name of the Nepal Red Cross. Tibetans scattered throughout Solu-Khumbu trekked there to establish new, hopefully temporary, lives. During the 1960s and 1970s over 1000 Tibetans lived there. SATA helped with agricultural and handicraft programmes: carpet-weaving, established in 1961, boomed and by the late 1970s some workers migrated to Kathmandu and set up business there. With intense competition from imitators in the Kathmandu Valley, however, Chialsa's carpet sales declined to next to nothing by the 1990s.

In 1993 the Germans dealt a further blow by banning Nepalese carpets because of concerns over child labour. Carpets are still made in Chialsa, however, and the quality is excellent, being 30% Tibetan and 70% New Zealand wool.

To make up for the loss of income five orchards have been planted. After selling in the surrounding area the surplus will be dried, and what is left after that will no doubt be made into brandy!

In 1989 the Nepalese Government no longer allowed Tibetans to seek refugee status in Nepal, although existing Tibetan are allowed to remain. Chialsa has been expanded to 100 acres and around 250 Tibetans remain.

Salpa-Arun to the Khumbu

INTRODUCTION

On the walk between the Khumbu and the Arun Kosi the differences between ethnic groups are probably more striking than any other teahouse trek. Although the Sherpa and Rai peoples are both of Mongolian stock and speak Tibeto-Burmese languages, the fact that they live at different altitudes influences many areas of their lives. The self-assured Buddhist Sherpas (see p122)

inhabit the higher regions, growing potatoes and barley or wheat, and have herds of cattle. Throughout the year they wear heavy dark woollen clothing. In contrast the ancient Animist Rai people (see p127) occupy land at a lower level, growing rice, millet and maize. It's warm enough for cotton clothes and they often harvest two crops a year in the frost-free climate. Although they mostly keep to themselves they are a pleasant, polite, community orientated people with egalitarian views. Also living in the perpetually warm low country are the traditional rice farmers, the Hindus: the lean Brahmins, Chhetris and other castes, a land of bodice tops, singlets and umbrellas. In the lazy heat there is a listless feeling in the small shops and the ways of the buffalo.

Rafting the mighty Sun Kosi
This is a fantastic six- to eight-day rafting expedition, at least during the September to November season. The rafting ends roughly where the Arun and the Sun Kosi merge so why not begin the Salpa-Arun immediately afterwards? Either hop on a bus to Hille/Leguwa or Basantpur or head to Biratnagar and fly to Tumlingtar or Bhojpur.

The walk is described in the Tumlingtar–Namche direction. In the third edition Suzanne Behrenfeld, who worked in the region for 18 months, added substantial input and for this edition I have built on this.

The route

Less experienced trekkers planning to walk in and out (rather than fly from Lukla) should still consider walking in from Jiri then out to Tumlingtar/Hille/Leguwa/ Basantpur. The reason is the Salpa-Arun route is tougher than the Jiri to Namche section – the hills are steeper and the facilities simpler. Tumlingtar to Namche involves somewhere around 10,000 vertical metres of ascent (as well as 7000m of descents) and being fitter and more used to the trekking lifestyle definitely makes the going easier.

The most sensible place to begin this trek is from Tumlingtar airport. Other possibilities are Hille/Leguwa, Basantpur or Bhojpur (p248). The traditional Hille start was due to be shortened with the long ridge descent/ascent replaced by a road to Leguwa Ghat in the Arun Valley sometime in 2002. Although the road is heading on to Bhojpur, completion is still many years off, so beginning in Bhojpur is still best accomplished by flying in. Once the road is open this means the Basantpur-Chainpur-Tumlingtar walk will be longer than the new Leguwa route but the cooler ridge route and the chance to visit historic Chainpur still has appeal. At present Hille-Leguwa and Basantpur are approximately 18-hours' drive or so from Kathmandu; perhaps in 2005/6 the new East–West highway from Kathmandu will nearly halve this time.

From the flats of Tumlingtar the trail crosses the mighty Arun river then climbs over a spur to follow the Irkhuwa Khola up to Phedi (which means bottom of the hill). From here it is a long climb to the top of the first pass, the Salpa Bhanjyang (3349m/10,987ft), the highest pass en route. The Surkie La (3085m/10,121ft) then the Satu La (3173m/10,410ft) follow in quick succession but between them, of course, are deep valleys. The route joins the main Dudh Kosi trekking route from Jiri between Puiyan and Kharikhola and it is a further two to three days to Namche.

The route description below follows the trail in the Hille/Tumlingtar to Lukla direction. At the end of each section there are notes for trekkers walking in the opposite direction (Lukla to Tumlingtar), marked '▲'.

The first trekkers
The first foreign visitors to the Khumbu were Tilman, Oscar Houston and his wife, Dr Charles Houston and a couple of other companions. This was perhaps the first true trek undertaken in Nepal; it was purely for pleasure rather than science or mountaineering. They trekked from Dharan to the Khumbu and back during November 1950. Their trek-in via Salpa Arun was considerably more pleasant than the Everest reconnaissance of 1951, led by Eric Shipton, who trekked in during the monsoon. His party had great difficulty in recruiting porters, had to avoid villages struck by bubonic plague, suffered leeches and was even attacked by hornets.

The time needed

The amount of time required for this walk varies considerably. From Tumlingtar to Namche takes nine or even ten days at a moderate pace; faster, fitter trekkers are still likely to take eight days in, although doing it in seven days is possible. Using the Basantpur or Hille/Leguwa routes and including a leisurely drive, allow eleven or twelve days, although nine is possible.

On the way out Namche to Tumlingtar is likely to take eight days at a moderate pace, although seven is also possible. Feeling strong? The fit and hill-hardened could reduce Namche to Hille to five and a half tough days, though a week is more realistic.

Facilities

Between the Arun and the Dudh Kosi there's a scattering of *lodges* and family homes masquerading as lodges that offer food and a bed. Their varied standards add to the pleasure of trekking along this route. Don't expect apple pie or pizza here; in fact, don't expect even a menu, just a share of what the family is eating. Prices are mostly very reasonable and often ridiculously cheap, and barely reflect the true costs of running a small lodge that sees only a low volume of trekkers. The majority of lodges have at least a dormitory and simple double rooms are becoming more common.

The hot Arun Valley itself still has few facilities specifically for trekkers. Instead there are many bhattis and teashops catering for the multitude of porters that transport goods up and down the valley. Usually there is a cool open area above the kitchen, occasionally with beds.

Camping There are a number of stone shelters, mainly used by porters who cannot afford to pay for accommodation, and plenty of open spaces so camping is an alternative, although along the Arun camping makes less sense because of the heat. However, you are better off pitching a tent outside a lodge.

During peak seasons lodges are modestly stocked with supplies for trekkers: muesli, porridge, packet soups, chocolate,

beer, rum and the like. Trekking off season you might find little more than biscuits, noodles and beer in the way of supplies. Luxuries like Mars bars and coffee are better bought from Kathmandu.

Planning

There are *lodges* or simple places to stay a couple of hours apart on this route but some facilities are better than others so planning/asking ahead still pays. Always carry plenty of snacks, too, for when you get caught out. Change has been slow, so don't count on finding extra facilities that aren't already marked here.

Maps

There are few accurate trekking maps of this region, but do take a good look at the Himalayan Maphouse series.

GETTING TO EASTERN NEPAL

Flying to Tumlingtar is by far the quickest way into the region but if you have more time there are many more options involving long bus rides across the Terai with many breaks possible.

By flight

Tumlingtar There are several flights a day into Tumlingtar, the cost $67. The description begins on p232.

Biratnagar Nepal's second largest city is the air hub and trading centre for the east. Calling it a city is rather an exaggeration, rather it is a town trapped in the 1950s, and not worth a detour if you have visited another Terai town. Flying here is an option if you want to avoid the long journey out of Kathmandu but still wish to see the Terai and the middle hills by road. The airport is well out of town, the bus station is in town and the few *hotels* are scattered randomly. There are frequent 14-hour night buses to Kathmandu and day buses to Dharan, perhaps two hours away.

By land

Until the new eastern road out of Kathmandu opens getting to Hille/Leguwa/Basantpur is still a bit of a mission, but if you have time it can be fun and great travelling. Sadists can take a 14-hour night bus from Kathmandu to Dharan and then, the same day, a grinding bus to Hille or Basantpur.

Splitting the journey up, however, the most interesting overnighting point is Janakpur, a surprisingly pleasant Terai town. From here you can take day buses to Itahari/Dharan and change there. If you arrive before lunch in Dharan you may be able to get to Dhankuta, Hille or Basantpur that day.

Dhankuta is another pleasant place to break your trip. If you overnight in this town you can still catch a bus the next morning and be on the trail before lunchtime.

As a glance at a map will show there are other alternatives. You could stop at Chitwan (Sauraha) then after a few days there move on. Still on the wildlife theme the road passes Tappu Kosi Wildlife Reserve, recently set up for bird-watching. Dharan is also a possible stopping point and, beyond the bustle of the bus station, is a pleasant introduction to Terai towns.

The new eastern highway out of Kathmandu, when complete, will dramatically change the time taken to reach eastern Nepal by road (see map on p107). At present it is under construction with Japanese assistance, and begins from Dhulikhel.

Currently all buses to east Nepal go via Mugling, halfway to Pokhara, ie west for four to five hours, before dropping to the south (the Terai) and heading east. The road is scheduled for completion around the year 2005.

It is almost unfathomable why this road, probably the third most important in the country, had not been built previously.

New road extensions Past Hille new road tentacles are rapidly being pushed through but are real boneshakers. From Hille the extension to Pakribas has been reworked so that it is again 'jeepable', and from there it descends to Leguwa Khola – on the way to Tumlingtar – and so up to this point is useful for the trekker. Once across

the Arun the road veers out of the valley towards Bhojpur, but it will be many years before it gets there. From Leguwa the road will be pushed through to Tumlingtar and Khandbari, which means it will also link in a loop with the road from Basantpur via Gupha. A road goes as far as Terathum, which is rough but during the dry seasons has a regular bus service.

Janakpur

This is an agreeable Terai city. Being off the main East-West highway it is a quiet place that is still a long way off the twenty-first century. There is a new bus park and a new square, plus closer into town, the old bus park. Rickshaw drivers will take you to the better *hotels* almost without asking. The *Welcome* and the *Ram* were full so we were taken to the *Kathmandu Guest House*, which had a friendly owner. Attached bathroom and mosquito nets (necessary) came in at under US$2 each. As you are so close to the border, Indian cuisine should be the choice, but it will be drenched in ghee.

The main temple, the **Janaki Mandir**, is well worth a visit and there are several more temples for the dedicated. Especially if you haven't been to India, wandering the streets is also reward enough. The occasional person speaks English.

There is a day bus that leaves Kathmandu around 6am from the new bus park and arrives in Janakpur around 3pm.

Itahari is little more than a major intersection where the road from Dharan-Basantpur crosses the East-West Highway to Biratnagar. There are mosquito-ridden *hotels* if you get stuck, or you could jump on a passing night bus heading to Kathmandu (or Kharkadvitta) – just check you are getting a comfortable seat.

Dharan

Although roads now push well into the hills, this bustling plains town is still the gateway to the eastern Himalaya. Immediately north the dramatic Chure barrier of hills begins, so rugged that only small areas are cultivatable – indeed they would be labelled mountains elsewhere.

Hotels away from the central bus station may be quieter. It is also the base for Eastern sector cargo helicopters and a number of aid programs.

▲ The first view of Dharan and the plain is wondrous, but the true dimensions of the plain is almost unimaginable: it extends south several hundred kilometres to the sea in the Bay of Bengal, and west past Delhi, nearly a thousand kilometres away, and into Rajasthan, with barely a hillock in-between.

Dhankuta
This pleasant hill station lies slightly off the main road but all buses stop at least briefly at Dhankuta's bus park. Once the road ended here, now merely the tar seal.

The *Suravi Hotel* is perhaps the best without being budget-breaking. A double room with attached bathroom featuring a warm shower goes for approximately US$5 and there are cheaper rooms available. The menu is extensive and the Indian food, at least, surprisingly good. There is little that you should see but a walk up the main trail is relaxing.

Heading down, it is around two and a half to three hours to Dharan. The road crosses the Tamur and another big range of hills; only then do the plains dramatically become visible and the heat begins to build.

BASANTPUR TO TUMLINGTAR
Until recently this was a stunning walk along a high ridge followed by a descent into the Arun Valley past picturesque villages. Now a road is being built along the trek and while it will take a long time to become driveable, already the harmony of the walk has been compromised.

Basantpur
There are a few dal bhaat *hotels* and many shops, but nothing as substantial or historic as Dhankuta or Dharan. The trail, now a road, traverses up the ridge to a collection of buildings half an hour out where it is also possible to stay.

Deorali is 45 minutes further on and has a few *bhattis*. **Panch Pokhari** is anoth-er 45 minutes to one hour along. From here you can see Chamalang (the long flat-topped mountain), Makalu (right) and, left of Makalu, the huge snowy face is the rarely seen Kangshung face of Everest.

Phedi is 45 minutes away and has more simple *bhattis*.

Chauki is 45 minutes past Phedi. Chauki is a growing settlement and is the better place to stay, offering reasonable views of the mountains. From here pass through **Manglaybare** (45 minutes to 1 hour), **Lamu Pokhari** (1 hour) and it is a further 60-90 minutes to **Gupha**.

Gupha
The people of Gupha are Tibetans who moved from Olangchung Gola sometime in the 1970s. They are hospitable and some lodges cook good food and even have double rooms. Groups generally stay here to catch the views. The settlement is in two parts with the southernmost perhaps the better for views. For even better views the locals recommend taking the Milke Danda trail and ascending to the top of the hill, which takes perhaps an hour to an hour and a half from Gupha. The very keen, willing to carry enough water, could bivvy or camp out.

To Nundaki Initially traverse out on the beginnings of the road then join a smaller trail and contour-descend. Once at the fields ask the way, for there are many trails. A little way down is the village, with the shop down below the gompa. There are many stone resting areas; descend through these onto what becomes a ridge and a set of good, wide stone steps and a trail that, lower down, passes many graves.

Nundaki stretches the whole way down to the side khola with a suspension bridge across it, one hour down. This is shortly followed by another, newer suspension bridge with the main trail running below it. Leaving, 45 minutes later is the village of **Chitlung**. **Mayum** is a further 60-75 minutes; there are **no lodges** there although you may be able to stay with a family.

Pokhari, with several basic *hotels*, is 30-45 minutes on, and is a large, regular stopping place for porters. It is a messy place but pleasant enough. You are now on top of a considerably smaller ridge, and the trail follows this. (If walking in the opposite direction, veer right at the junction in the centre of town.) You can see Makalu from around here if it is clear.

Leaving Pokhari, the trail used to follow the ridge top but now the new road-trail contours around, an easy trail. Chainpur is 60-75 minutes away, initially seen only almost once you are upon it.

Chainpur

This pleasant ridge top town is famous throughout Nepal for the brass pots, pans and dishes that are made here. The brass comes from Singapore (and has done for the last 70 years or so) and is worked by local craftspeople. Since brass is valuable and not the lightest material to transport every effort is made to recycle old and dented objects, with some salvaged from villages up to five days' walk away. Now there are only a couple of brass workshops (ask locals where) but the town is still pleasant; initially a series of proudly tidy houses followed by some well-stocked shops. The *hotels* are further down.

To Tumlingtar Leaving Chainpur the trail traverses particularly pleasant middle hills countryside. Ninety minutes to two hours along is Kharang (1360m), with a few shops and *bhattis*. At the end of the village is a chautara; turn right here, rather than going straight on to the school. The descent begins gently at first. Forty-five minutes to one hour later is Lhuakot (1000m) and a few shops. Gaire Gaon (720m) is 45 minutes further and from there the descent is

steep, 30-45 minutes down, to the ferry across the Sabai Khola at an altitude of perhaps 400m. The fare is Rs5 but you will probably get charged more. It is a short but stiff and hot climb (100m vertical gain) to the plain that Tumling sits on. *Tar* means plain. The last section takes 35-45 minutes, and half way along this there are a couple of simple but pleasant *lodges* with cold drinks. Here the trail divides: left for Tumlingtar, right for Khandbari.

Tumlingtar and the route onwards is covered on p232.

HILLE-LEGUWA TO TUMLINGTAR [MAP 18, p233]
Hille (1850m/6069ft)

Perched atop a prominent ridge, once this was the all-important end of the road, a distinction that turned it into an ugly pseudo-modern bazaar town. Among the ribbon of shops are several simple *hotels* with double rooms to stay in, but don't expect a peaceful lie-in. Once it thronged with porters but now they (and you) are spared trudging the long hill to Pakribas and Leguwa. This road turns off from near the top of the town.

▲ Buses leave hourly for Dharan, taking two and a half to three hours, with the last one down leaving at 3pm or 4pm. If you've missed the last 5pm Dharan to Kathmandu bus, head for Itahari (see p229). An alternative is to stop half way at the pleasant hilltown of Dhankuta and spend the night there.

Pakribas The open road now extends at least as far as here. It is a simpler and perhaps uglier version of Hille but there are some simple *restaurants* and *hotels* where it is possible to stay. As with all roads into the hills it takes a while to walk out of their

---

A healthier diet

The British-established Pakribas Agricultural Research and Development Project is modestly famous throughout Nepal for it is largely as a result of their work that the concept of kitchen gardens for growing vegetables and herbs has been established. Much of their work also concentrates on developing new high yield and disease-resistant crop strains. The project is now run by the Nepal government.

influence. If the weather is clear, the views of Makalu and the surrounding peaks are inspiring.

Mangmaya (250m/746ft) This small mainly Brahmin village is where the road reaches the valley base. It is pleasant enough with a few simple *bhattis*. Leguwa Ghat is about an hour away if you have to walk and, in the opposite direction, Pakribas is three and a half to five hours up, including stops.

Along the Arun Kosi to Tumlingtar
The trail mainly follows the river; some sections are carved into the rock banks, others follow the shore. It is hot, low country with little shade – an umbrella can be useful and an early start – but there are plenty of opportunities to cool off in refreshing streams or the chilly, silty Arun itself.

From **Mangmaya** or **Leguwa** it is a long day's walk to Tumlingtar, probably longer than a normal trekking day. In between there are simple *teashacks* only. It is normal to wade across the tributary streams but there are suspension bridges too. The exception is the Sabbaya Khola which is a deep wade and using the bridge (Rs5 tax) makes more sense.

From the bridge it is an hour to Tumlingtar but there are simple *lodges* before the airfield. If you are feeling the heat it might be worthwhile hiring a porter.

TUMLINGTAR (515m/1700ft)
Approaching Tumlingtar by plane, the endless terraced hills, pretty villages and the distant Himalayan peaks are staggeringly beautiful. Arriving is mellowing. The runway is very 1950s, grass-covered with a simple fence to keep the cows and goats out. One day this will change; it is destined to be the eastern air hub once an all-weather road reaches here.

Hotels
The two main hotels, *Kanchenjunga* (☎ 029 69120) and *Makalu* (☎ 029 69057) are immediately opposite the gate, and *Arun* (☎ 029 69062) is a few minutes north. They mainly cater to the locals arriving and leav-

ing by plane but the dal bhaat is excellent and the beer cold. If buying a ticket you are perhaps better off staying at the lodge concerned (see under Flights below).

The best hotel is *Makalu Resort*, which opened in November 2000. It is a five-minute walk north and doubles with their tiled attached bathrooms are $20 with breakfast. There are even two self-contained cottages. Amazingly enough all the fittings, reinforcing and concrete was carried from Hille. You might wonder what such a fancy hotel is doing here, and how could it possibly make money? The answer is Japanese clients: around here as you may have already noticed is some of the most beautiful hill country in Nepal, and of course you can see Makalu. Bookings for Makalu Resort should be made via Sherpa-Nippon Treks, ▭ nippon@ecomail.com.np, ☎ 01 412744 (Kathmandu) or direct on ☎ 029 6904.

Flights
There are at least two flights a day by at least two airlines; these generally arrive at lunchtime or after, and are rarely ever cancelled due to bad weather. If you arrive early you could walk south for a swim, wander up the main track to the east to a modestly higher plain and scattered houses or begin trekking. If leaving by plane track down the airline representative (Makalu Hotel for RNAC and Kanchenjunga for Gorkha) and reconfirm. If you don't have a ticket, you will usually be able to get out that day or the next, with luck. There are flights to Kathmandu and to Biratnagar. Tumlingtar is one of the few rural airstrips that is long enough to handle any prop plane.

TUMLINGTAR TO BALAWA BESI
[MAP 19, p235]
Assuming you are staying the night at Tumlingtar, **Chewa Besi** is the place for lunch although the quick may make Kartiki Ghat. There are several choices for where to stay. The first real lodge set up for trekkers is *Sagarmatha*, on the ridge. The villages after the spur are Marduwa and Charlissay, where commonly you will be invited to

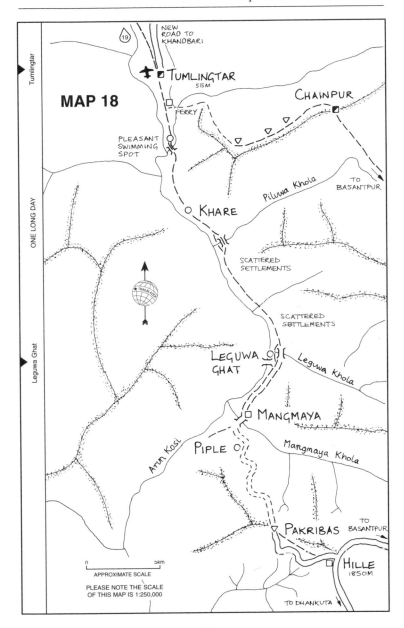

stay. Reaching Gothe Bazaar (pronounced Goatay) is for those keen to put in a harder day.

If you flew in and made it to Kartiki Ghat or Balawa Besi that evening then the next day aiming for Dobani, or for the fit, Tallo Phedi or Phedi, is realistic.

Leaving Tumlingtar On a clear day mountains rise surreally out of the heat haze. Chamalang is the left-most peak and Makalu is to the far right, often with a tell-tale cloud spinning off it, jet stream turbulence. Beat the heat by starting early and **drink lots**.

The main path heads north from the hotels and passes to the left or west side of the brick pits. Follow the electricity poles. The track is straight, passing the occasional house and shop/teashop.

After an hour is Gidhe and the simple *Irkhuwa Arun Hotel*, with another hotel beside it. The trail drops close to the river bank (but no swimming for a while) and uses every opportunity to follow the shore.

At **Kartiki Ghat** a suspension bridge (Rs2 bridge tax) crosses the Arun, a short half-day's walk from Tumlingtar. There are a few simple *restaurants* and it is possible to find a rough bed but the place, and Balawa Besi, are not particularly endearing, with a sometimes rude, laughing indifference that's thankfully found nowhere else.

▲ **To Leguwa-Hille** If you're not flying out cold beer is the only compelling reason to stay at Tumlingtar.

To Khandbari This is a completely different trail: at the brick pits and the sign for the *Arun Hotel* turn right (east) then left to put you on a main trail on the other side of the pits.

Vehicles began running between Tumlingtar and Khandbari in 2001, flown in because there was no other road.

The Dingla alternative The standard trekking route (as described in the following) is the shortest trail. In fact the main trail detours via Dingla, a historic bazaar town. Although it is a main route, the Dingla to Salpa trail (see p249), isn't straightforward trekking.

BALAWA BESI TO JAU BARI
[MAP 20, p237]

Balawa Besi is a bridge across a sparkling khola plus a few houses and a shop that sometimes puts up trekkers. Leaving, cross the sturdy frame bridge and head right past **teashacks** and homes then head left climbing up and up. At first the trail is clear, but then climbs steep, slippery clay. There's a Nepali saying 'Rato mato, chiplo bhato' or 'red mud, slippery trail', and more appropriately in English, 'red mud, land with a thud'. Up the steep section, take a traversing right at a chautara with a small, off-centre tree.

You are beginning a 600m traversing climb with many trail junctions, although heading up most are obvious in the first stretch and locals point the way. If you reach *Sagarmatha Lodge* you are doing OK. From here it is better to follow some porters or ask frequently for Phedi and Salpa Bhanjyang.

Marduwa From the top of the spur Marduwa is approximately 20 minutes

---

> ◈◈◈ **The chautara – 'the coolies' joy and the travellers' bane'**
> 'In this pleasant land where all loads are carried upon men's backs, where the tracks are rough and steep and the days hot, various pious and public-spirited men – of which in my opinion there have been too many – perpetuate their names by planting two fast-growing shady trees and building round them a rectangular or sometimes circular stone dais with a lower parapet as a seat...
>
> There is a Nepali proverb – or if there isn't there should be – that the sight of a chautara makes the coolie's back ache.' **HW Tilman**

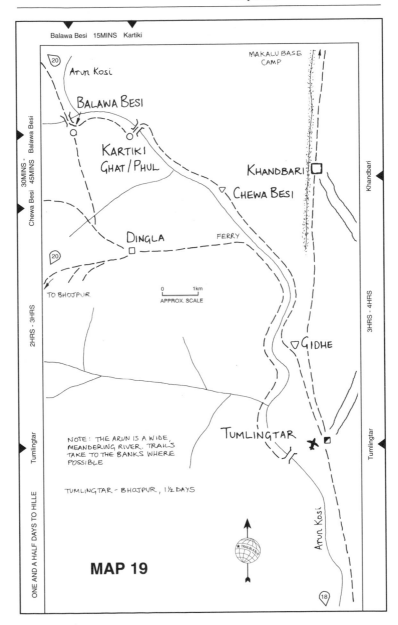

Balawa Besi   15MINS   Kartiki

20 Arun Kosi

BALAWA BESI

MAKALU BASE CAMP

KARTIKI GHAT / PHUL

KHANDBARI

▽ Chewa Besi

DINGLA

FERRY

20

TO BHOJPUR

0   1km
APPROX. SCALE

▽ GIDHE

30MINS - 45MINS - Balawa Besi

Chewa Besi

2HRS - 3HRS

Tumlingtar

Balawa Besi

Khandbari

3HRS - 4HRS

Tumlingtar

ONE AND A HALF DAYS TO HILLE

NOTE: THE ARUN IS A WIDE, MEANDERING RIVER. TRAILS TAKE TO THE BANKS WHERE POSSIBLE

TUMLINGTAR - BHOJPUR, 1½ DAYS

TUMLINGTAR

Arun Kosi

★ TRAILBLAZER

MAP 19

18

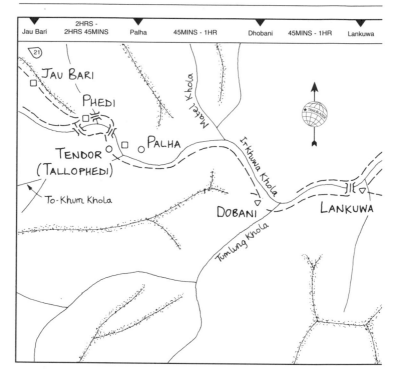

beyond. Follow the most worn track (ask too!) through terraced fields. Between Marduwa and Charlissay contour around a small bowl.

Charlissay is the name of a Chhetri caste that lived in these areas generations ago. It is said that they now mostly live in the Kathmandu Valley. Villagers, usually older women or children, invite you in to eat or stay.

From here the real main trail (ie the old one from Dingla) is around 20-25 minutes away. Contour and cross a small ravine. Once out of this head for two large pipal trees with a chautara and rejoin a larger clear trail here.

From the pipal trees Descend through dense semi-tropical forest to the Irkhuwa

Khola. A few minutes along the bank is a **teashack**, *Tabutar*. Between here and Gothe Bazaar the trail – and the point where it crosses the Irkhuwa Khola – changes regularly: ask the locals for directions!

▲ About half an hour after leaving Gothe there is a steel bridge across the Irkhuwa Khola. Above this is a pleasant, rising traverse through some forest. You want to be on this trail, no other; it leads to the two trees and chautara with the fields of Charlissay in view. You are now well above the khola. At the pipal trees people usually offer tea, dal bhaat and, during the right season, suntala (mandarin oranges). About 100m past the trees the trail divides properly, the upper trail going up to Nepali Danda then Dingla while you want to head across the fields on a trail that then drops very

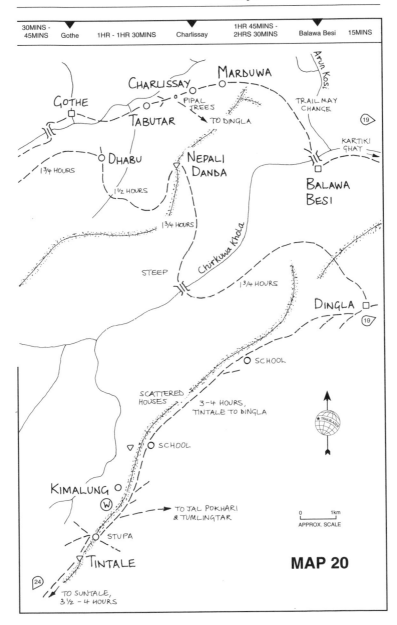

| 30MINS -
45MINS | Gothe | 1HR - 1HR 30MINS | Charlissay | 1HR 45MINS -
2HRS 30MINS | Balawa Besi | 15MINS |

Arun Kosi

CHARLISSAY

MARDUWA

GOTHE

PIPAL TREES

TABUTAR

TRAIL MAY CHANGE

TO DINGLA

19

KARTIKI GHAT

DHABU

NEPALI DANDA

1¾ HOURS

1½ HOURS

BALAWA BESI

1¾ HOURS

Churkuwa Khola

STEEP

1¾ HOURS

DINGLA

19

SCHOOL

SCATTERED HOUSES

3 - 4 HOURS,
TINTALE TO DINGLA

SCHOOL

KIMALUNG

W

TO JAL POKHARI
& TUMLINGTAR

0   1km
APPROX. SCALE

STUPA

TINTALE

MAP 20

24

TO SUNTALE,
3½ - 4 HOURS

> ### Cardamom
> Look out for cardamom (*elaichi*) plants in small fields in the cool shaded forest. In early October they are distinctive for having a red fleshy-flower at the base of a 1-1.5m stem with well spaced leaves around 30 cm long. By the end of October the stem withers and all that's left is the thick red flower with mainly white seeds. Thousands of kilos of these valuable and fragrant seeds are grown in East Nepal then dried and carried down to roadheads. Kashmiri tea relies on the seeds' distinctive flavour, as do many masala-flavoured Indian dishes, and the plants are also valuable for soil conservation.

---

briefly before passing through the village where dal bhaat is on offer and continues on its climbing traverse through fields to another pipal and bhodhi tree chautara. Soon after this you have to climb a stone wall, walk through the fields past a house and over a crude stile by a water tap, then head up. Finally, within sight of the Arun, take the main trail up; rounding this ridge, you'll find three chairs with a view at the highest point. Heading straight, and flat rather than down, sets you on the main way to another large chautara and porters shelter, and just below, the well-placed simple *Sagarmatha Lodge*.

Gothe Bazaar Tintamang/ Membahang (775m/2550ft)
After crossing the Irkhuwa and climbing a small hill you come to the delightful settlement of Gothe (pronounced Got-hey). There is one *lodge* and a camping place beside the khola, Tintamang side, and a *teashop* on the Membahang side, and after a hot day's trekking the best place is in the middle, the sparkling khola. With the bamboo, airy lodgings and the sound of water, one could almost be in Thailand. The people here are apparently a mix between Gurung from the Pokhara region and local Rai.

Lankuwa (875m/2870ft)
Things haven't changed here for at least ten years. If you do have an urge or need to stay check the quality of the tea first, and then the price and arrangements. It is a curious place – some of the inhabitants even think they are still in Gothe.

Dobani / Thunglung Doban (975m/ 3200ft)
Doban means Confluence of Two Rivers. The 1999-built new bridge and trail bypasses the small cluster of buildings including a simple *lodge*, although there might still be a bamboo bridge heading there. Around this region paper is made by hand, destined for Kathmandu. Here and at Tallo Phedi you may be able to watch the process and buy some of the finished product. Leaving Dobani, the trail stays above the Irkhuwa Khola for a while.

Tendor/Tallo Phedi (1400m/4600ft)
Don't confuse Tallo Phedi (Lower Bottom of the Hill) with Phedi (which merely means Bottom of the Hill). There is a paper factory and immediately above, the *Irkhuwa Rai Lodge*. Leaving, traverse into the gully and cross near, or on if you are game, the dodgy bridge. At the next village, Tendor, there is a choice of two trails. One climbs the ridge to Chole then contours and descends to the suspension bridge. The other, more usual route stays low in fields, passing the school and crossing the river, before climbing a bit on the opposite bank to recross to Phedi.

Phedi (1700m/5575ft)
Virtually at the confluence of two rivers, Phedi boasts three simple but developing *lodges.* Trekking up through the village, if in doubt take two lefts and follow the stone steps. By this stage of the trek you have already gained 1400m, perhaps barely noticing it. But from here the real climb begins: the attack of the killer stone steps, sweatier and more real than any B-grade movie. At the same time

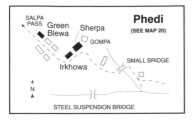

as cursing the never-ending steps one has to wonder who built them. Was it a labour of love? Was it for money? Or for penance? And how old are they? It's a very tough day from Phedi over the pass so an early start is useful. It's not a bad idea to see if you can find a porter to help for this stretch.

Jau Bari/Thulofokte (2300m/7550ft)
The trail to this spread out small settlement is relentlessly steep and brutal at the end of the day. There are two simple *teashops* then, further up, two simple *lodges*, also well separated: the *Saelpa Seharpa*, where donations for the gompa are sometimes collected (they can open it for you too) and, the higher lodge, *Kalo Patthar*.

▲ Prepare to fall off the end of the world.

JAU BARI TO SANAM [MAP 21, p241]
Guranse (2920m/9580ft)
After cresting the sharp ridge there is a flattish area with a sometimes dry pond and a stone shelter. The trail to Guranse (pronounced Gurasé, light on the 'n') stays on

the south side of the main ridge and starts about 20 minutes past the pond. The other trail up the ridge goes directly to Salpa Pokhari.

This is a rhododendron region, *laligurans* or *laliguras* in Nepali, but it is a somehow miserable place with tree stumps littering the cleared area. There are a couple of buildings, both *lodges*, although only one is generally open year-round, and they are set up for porters rather than trekkers – although it is possible to stay.

▲ The thin track passes though untidy grazing land to pass by a pond with a stone shelter then climbs to the crest of the obvious razorback ridge and descends steeply.

Salpa Bhanjyang / Khulophongko (Danda) (3349m/10,987ft)
A weathered chorten graces the top of the pass. Slightly better views can be had by climbing south a little way. The pass also marks the boundary of the Bhojpur district, which you have been in since Kartiki Ghat or Bhojpur, and Solukhumbu, which you stay in for the rest of the trek. You are now entering a Sherpa region.

The top part of the pass receives snow during the winter and the locals may wait several days after a fall before crossing. If snow-covered, the trail can be slippery and challenging to follow.

The path down soon follows a small stream and passes a few old mani walls. There are three rock shelters before Whaka but none is particularly dry. In the main val-

Paper-making Nepali style
A number of paper-making set-ups are found along this part of the Salpa-Arun trek. A plant called lokto is harvested from the forest; the outer layer is pulled off and the fibrous heartwood is carried down for the processing. After boiling the lokto for two hours, it is then smashed into a pulp with a rock and mixed with water. A wood-framed piece of mesh is then dipped into the soup which helps to evenly distribute the pulp. This frame is then set out in the sun to dry for a day. The finished product is 'transportcred' to Kathmandu, Hetauda and Biratnagar to be sold at approximately Rs10 per sheet. Once all official government documents had to be printed on this special paper but the advent of type-writers and – anytime in the next hundred years – computers, means this practice is changing, and now it is the export and tourist market that are the main consumers.

❖ Side trip to Salpa Pokhari (3460m/11,350ft)

A long, long time ago a local Rai king and queen went for a vacation in the local hills. Unfortunately, at the time the queen was suffering from a mental sickness, though upon reaching the lake the queen recovered – only to then be consumed by a large serpent living in the lake. The king spent the rest of his weary days looking for his beloved wife.

It's said that if a person comes to praise the lake, she/he will be successful in the future. So naturally enough to take advantage of this there are four main *mellas* (festivals) a year, each lasting four days and attracting thousands of people from the Solu Khumbu, Kotang, Bhojpur and Sankhwasaba districts. It is a time to eat, drink and be merry and many of the local *dhamis* (holy men) perform sacred ceremonies by the lake to ask the lake god (the snake) to protect all. During their long trance, it is said that the dhami are able to see both the snake and the queen. Both Buddhists and Hindus visit the lake.

In the Hindu religion, the God Shiva is related to the snake with the snake being the symbol of water. So to worship the lake is to worship the element of water, and therefore the snake and therefore Shiva. In Nepali, *salp* means snake.

This trail begins on the right side of the large boulder, to the north of the chorten on the pass. Traverse north-east, gradually ascending for 30 minutes and walk through a flat open area. A large stupa marks the beginning of the holy area.

---

ley, well down, the track crosses to the north bank of the Lidung Khola. Later, where the trail emerges from the forest, there's **Whaka/Orkobug**; here there are two *teahouses*, of which one is usually open, and a camping place. The usual place to stay after the pass is Sanam but all the places can now support trekkers.

▲ Going down the other side is easy. Follow the stone track that curves left, and continue roughly in the same direction, eventually to Guranse.

Side trip to Silingchuk (4156m/13,630ft)

This is a difficult scramble on narrow, steep, almost non-existent trails. Don't attempt this climb in winter with snow lying around. There are no possible camping spots on or near the top.

Locals swear there is a route from Silingchuk to Sanam and Gudel but the only way to find this would be to take a local guide, otherwise you will be bluffed out.

❖ Nature is God

In essence the Rai people worship nature, perhaps more so than any other ethnic group in Nepal. They work in a co-operative, community-based way unlike, say, the Brahmins and so development agencies find they are easy to work with, but there are a couple of projects that have been notably unsuccessful for cultural reasons. The design for more efficient cooking stoves was demonstrated but there was zero uptake since the three cooking stones are the holiest part of the house. It is hoped that a new design incorporating these three essential stones might be more successful. The new designs are much more efficient, using less firewood, and produce less smoke. A chimney can also be added. Many of the health problems throughout Nepal are caused by smoky homes.

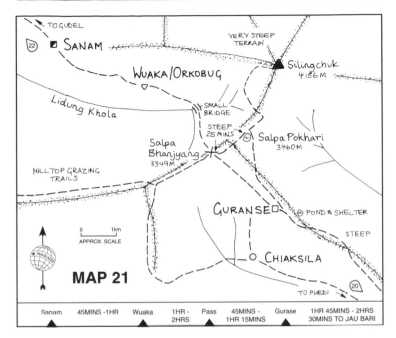

Sanam	45MINS -1HR	Wuaka	1HR - 2HRS	Pass	45MINS - 1HR 15MINS	Gurase	1HR 45MINS - 2HRS 30MINS TO JAU BARI

Sanam (2650m/8700ft)

Land of the Sky is the Sherpa translation of Sanam. The locals are keen for trekkers' business and all the houses there seem to be turning themselves into *lodges* or *homestays*, and some even have double rooms, although only the *Gumba Lodge* has a signboard. As you may be able to guess, it is next to the gompa. Delicious dairy products are often available here. At the end of the row of houses descend through the vegetable garden to the new house/lodge.

▲ **In reverse** The pass is a half day's walk from Sanam and is not at the obvious head of the valley but up a small valley to the right or south. Note that in dry conditions the Lidung Khola is often the last source of

water until well over the pass. En route to the pass are three rock shelters but all leak to some degree in rain.

SANAM TO NAJING DINGMA [MAP 22, p243]

Tiu/Duire (2600m/8500ft) Meaning Horse Mare, the name commemorates the fact that once someone was silly enough to bring one up here.

There are a couple of simple *lodges*, the *Tiue* and the *Arun Valley*.

Nimtsola/Gompa The monastery here gives tutelage to a number of boys from the surrounding villages. Several of the people here offer tea and it is possible to eat/stay, although there are no signboards. From

❏ **Map key**
See p145 for a map key and discussions on the trail maps and route descriptions

For dreadfulness nought can excel
The prospect of Bung from Gudel
And words die away on the tongue
When we look back at Gudel from
Bung   **HW Tilman**

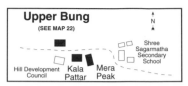

Upper Bung
(SEE MAP 22)

Shree
Sagarmatha
Secondary
School

Hill Development Council   Kala Pattar   Mera Peak

here the trail widens – maintained by Gudel VDC – and Sherpa country ends; lower down are Rai people.

Gudel (1950m/6400ft) The main trail leads to a mani (visible from afar) on the ridge that overlooks the large Rai village of Gudel. As well as Gudel and Bung the panorama includes the Naulekh mountains and, with good eyes, the Khiraunle-Chambaling (Boksom) Gompa. Only in 1998 did the first lodge open, now there are three, all basic: the **Kulung** is right at the base of the village, the **Namaste** is sign-posted in the middle and just above it is the **Kopila**. Ask around to find them.

Leaving From Gudel you can see the trail from the bridge zigzagging up to Bung. Follow the stream on a mainly stone path for a while. The trail then veers right (or north) away from the stream, and down towards a beautiful waterfall before cutting back south-west to the bridge that crosses the Hongu Khola at about 1280m/4200ft. Bung begins approximately ten minutes up. The *Dudh Kosi* Schneider map marks the trails in and out of Gudel inaccurately.

Note the large stream north of Bung: for several hours the trail above Bung stays approximately parallel to this about half to one kilometre away.

▲ Gudel to Sanam Climb on one of several trails to the mani walls above Gudel on the spur to the south. From here the wide trail climbs gently but steadily, hugging the steep valley wall. The trail abruptly narrows at Nimtsola.

Bung
Jid Bahadur Rai, the VDC chairman of Bung provided sincere hospitality and much of the information given here.

Meaning Beautiful Flower in Rai, this is the largest village of the Maha Kulung (great Kulung Rai) region. It spreads over a huge hillside. There are two *lodges* close to the bottom of the village (Bung, lower; 1420m/4650ft) with a second cluster around the old, Makalu-Barun Conservation Area Bung Sector Headquarters (Bung, upper; 1800m/5900ft), which is now the Hill Development Council.

Bung is a particularly pleasant middle hills village, clean and spread out, and the kids barely beg either: joyful 'namastes' and 'hellos' are the norm. It has seen a sur-prising amount of development over the last decade, although perhaps only the regularly spaced water taps are immediately obvious. It is surprising that there isn't a telephone: there was, but it was partially destroyed during a VDC (Village Development Committee) chairman election. The health post is one of the few in the country that works well, mainly because it is staffed with locals and also gets assistance from the Himalayan Trust's Khunde hospital. The hope is to have electricity here by around late 2002, which, in the quest for funding etc, has been a longer process than expected. All in all it is a pleasant place.

▲ Just before Bung is a white three-sided porters' shelter; the village is heralded by clumps of huge bamboo. Soon there is a trail junction: contour following the wall

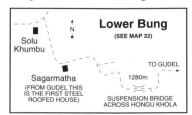

Lower Bung
(SEE MAP 22)

Solu Khumbu

TO GUDEL

Sagarmatha
(FROM GUDEL THIS IS THE FIRST STEEL ROOFED HOUSE)

1280m

SUSPENSION BRIDGE ACROSS HONGU KHOLA

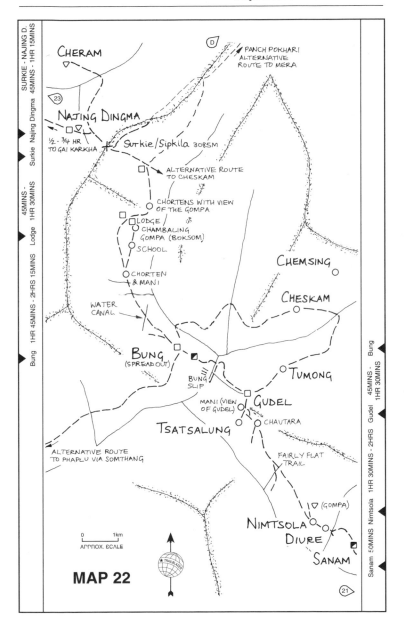

CHERAM

PANCH POKHARI
ALTERNATIVE
ROUTE TO MERA

23

NAJING DINGMA

SURKIE - NAJING D.
45MINS - 1HR 15MINS

Surkie Najing Dingma

1/2 - 3/4 HR
TO GAI KARKHA

Surkie/Sipkila 3085M

ALTERNATIVE ROUTE
TO CHESKAM

45MINS -
1HR 30MINS

CHORTENS WITH VIEW
OF THE GOMPA

LODGE
CHAMBALING
GOMPA (BOKSOM)

SCHOOL

Lodge

CHORTEN
& MANI

CHEMSING

CHESKAM

WATER
CANAL

Bung 1HR 45MINS - 2HRS 15MINS

BUNG
(SPREAD OUT)

BUNG
SLIP

TUMONG

MANI (VIEW
OF GUDEL)

GUDEL

Bung

TSATSALUNG

CHAUTARA

45MINS -
1HR 30MINS

Gudel

ALTERNATIVE ROUTE
TO PHAPLU VIA SOMTHANG

FAIRLY FLAT
TRAIL

1HR 30MINS - 2HRS

(GOMPA)

NIMTSOLA

Nimtsola

0   1km
APPROX. SCALE

DIURE

SANAM

Sanam 50MINS

MAP 22

21

Bung

This region is known for its *tungba*, an alcoholic brew served in a tall wooden vessel and drunk using a bamboo straw. Boiling water is poured over fermented millet to make this warming drink. If there's a really big celebration it's served in a barrel, everybody using their own straw. The more mature the millet, the smoother the taste with a special vintage (rarely served to tourists) being about a year old. The villagers are also big chang drinkers (usually a mix of corn (more) and millet (less) and raksi, distilled from the chang. The Rai culture has been surprisingly durable, and occasionally you will see the men wearing the traditional *phenga* sleeveless jacket made from *allo* (see box opposite). The *phoria* or *lungi* wrap skirt is what the women wear, and, if it is raining, the *ghum*, which is a folding bamboo mat with either banana leaf or plastic sandwiched between to cover both the person and the *doko*.

Many women still wear the traditional double nose piece, the *dhungri* which is round, and the hanging piece, the *jhamke*. Earrings (*maluwari*) complete the picture. Prior to marriage girls usually wear a *phulli* – a nose stud – and if they marry wealthy then all the pieces will come. However, love marriage without the trappings of wealth is also totally acceptable, and in this case no gold or anything else need be given. It used to be that most marriages were arranged, over lots of drinks and discussion, but now mostly the trend is for love marriages. Once married all work is generally shared.

The houses are all still made from traditional adobe mud and, although steel roofs are arriving, most are either wooden shingles with bamboo mats over the top or thatched. Inside, the fire is always in the middle of the room so that in winter everyone, especially the guests, can all sit around it. As you can imagine, the Rais know their wood, and in many houses there is a wooden frame that sits over the fire to dry the wood but prevent it, one hopes, from burning. Most houses have a *janto* stone for grinding corn and millet. Although there are no chimneys and the ceiling is shiny and smoke-blackened, usually the interior is not too smoky, at least as long as you sit on the floor. Neatness seems to come in threes.

The region exports ghee, eggs and quite a bit of meat to Namche, where the money and demand is. Bung, although a pleasant place, is a long way from any road, something that makes life less than easy for the locals.

---

rather than descending through the fields. This leads to a pleasant bamboo-lined gully. Once in the open again it is five minutes to the top set of lodges.

To Phaplu The trail starts at the top set of lodges. The path to Sotang basically contours and is easy to follow. See p224.

To Cheskam Locals here are keen to attract trekkers to this large Rai village although it is somewhat off the usual route. There is one small *lodge* run by sherpas. Bung to Cheskam takes two hours, perhaps a little more at a slower pace. The trail from

Bung starts at the top set of lodges. It is also possible to trek from Gudel and from a little below the Surkie La.

▲ **In reverse** From Bung it's a short day's walk to Sanam or one very long and tough day to Guranse. It's possible to camp after Sanam but not on top of the pass since there is no water there. Leaving Bung, there is a maze of paths, hopefully signposted. After some clumps of bamboo there are many tracks and slips but most lead to the suspension bridge. Take the left fork after crossing the bridge for the steep ascent to Gudel.

> ### Allo
> Nettle fibre, called *allo*, was once the main source for cloth. A few items, such as vests, are still worn though the importance of allo weaving has greatly decreased due to the intensive labour required and the ready availability of cotton clothes.

Khiraunle-Chambaling Gompa (Boksom)

After an initial steep ascent out of Bung the trail eases to a continuous gently ascending traverse. It's easy to get lost as there are numerous trails, but all lead close to Khiraunle-Chambaling Gompa (several hours away) and its distinctive ring of large trees. The main trail is perhaps half a kilometre above this.

The friendly owners of a small new *lodge* close to the gompa are intent on creating a new trail that passes through a school then on to the gompa and themselves. It isn't necessary to take this new trail; the lodge is only five minutes off the main trail higher up, and is signposted. However, once the new path is finished it may prove marginally quicker. The gompa is being rebuilt and you are welcome to look around. Once on the main trail, just a little before the chortens is a new, simple *teahouse*.

Over the Surkie La/Sipki La/Betoma Cha (3085m/10,121ft)

Above the gompa on a ridge are some chortens followed by some mani walls and a beautiful, mainly old and moss-encrusted rhododendron forest. At two *teahouses* there is a major trail junction: go up for the pass. This is an uneventful pass but for better views climb the trail to a sightseeing platform where you can see Khatang and Numbur, collectively called Shorong Yul La, the holy mountains of the region around Junbesi. The descent is initially quite steep (and icy in winter) through bamboo groves.

Najing/Naji Dingma is on a flat grassy knoll at 2650m/8694ft. Here, among the few houses are two *teahouses* and a small shop. These are run by people, often kids, from the Sherpa village of **Cheram** (Chereme on the *Shorong/Hinku* Schneider map). Although most trekkers take the

> ### Cheram
> The history of Cheram/Chereme (meaning Quiet Place for Meditation) sheds light on a very resilient and determined community. About 35 years ago this village was home to 45 families who were confronted with three consecutive years of frigid weather, destroying crops and leaving most with inadequate amounts of food. Struggling for survival, most families fled to Sikkim in the hope of a better life, leaving fewer than ten households. Slowly the remaining villagers were able to recover with sustainable food productions and the number of households grew to 18. In 1994 disaster struck in the form of a large forest fire which forced wild animals into the forest close to Cheram. Once again the locals lost their crops, this time in the form of hungry critters. Unable to sufficiently guard the crops, the locals are now looking for alternative income-generating activities. They are seeking support for a 6km hydro-electric project in the hope of producing rhododendron and juniper perfume, nettle fabric, handmade paper and incense.
>
> Cheram is a worthwhile side trip as the locals are hospitable and the new gompa (which serves as both a religious and a community centre) radiates with the commitment of locals meeting and working together to make life better. The gompa has partly been funded by the now defunct MBNPCA (Makalu-Barun National Park and Conservation Area) as part of its cultural preservation policies.

shorter Gai Kharka route to Shubuche it is possible to go via Cheram – see the box on p245. You can stay there, although there are **no real lodges**. People from Najing Dingma can show you the way.

GAI KHARKA TO PUIYAN
[MAP 23, opposite]
Gai Kharka
This means Cow Pasture but now the area is under cultivation. Apart from a new water tap there are no facilities for trekkers and it is easy to lose the way. At first stay right on the trails then, once well down, join a path leading across a small stream that heads up. Three metres after crossing the stream another trail, only now visible, heads down. Take this down a minor ridge. In all it takes approximately 15 minutes to descend through Gai Kharka.

Bridge across the Inkhuwa/Inukhu/ Hinku Khola (1850m/6069ft) The bridge was built in 1993 by the Himalayan Trust with money provided by Canada International development Association (CIDA). It is an impressive height above the river, and even more impressive are the hills on the western side. This is one brutal, unrelentingly steep hill.

Shubuche/Shiboche The fields begin as the hill relents in gradient, but it is still perhaps half an hour to the main *lodge* of Shubuche. This lodge is occasionally closed: either temporarily while the family work the fields, or sometimes completely closed while the family goes shopping. One other family sometimes offers to put up trekkers. There are great views of the Inkhu Valley and the peaks of Mera.

▲ **In the opposite direction** The trail continues straight to the end of the ridge, crossing a fence or two before dropping off, turning slightly south. It's a very steep, knee-jerking descent.

Over the Satu/Pangum La (3173m/ 10,410ft) Atop the pass on the far side of the valley you may perhaps be able to make out the trail heading up to the Trakshindo

La on the Jiri route. Looking behind you across the valley it's possible to see Najing Dingma, about two-thirds of the way up the previous ridge.

Pangkongma/Pangum (2850m/ 9350ft) The village has a wonderfully-located 1970 Hillary school and a gompa. There are two *lodges* and, being close to the main Jiri route, they use the menu system.

Leaving Pick up the trail at the parallel mani walls just below the lodges and head north-west. Bupsa can be seen on the ridge slightly north and Kharikhola below on the southern wall of the valley. At first the trail is straightforward but further on are several junctions that can be confusing. Think about which trail you want (Bupsa, Kharte or the old trail to Puiyan: in Nepali 'purano Puiyan ra Khari La bhaato') then ask the locals for directions.

▲ **From the main trail to Pangkongma** The main Namche to Kharikhola trail can be left at Puiyan, Bupsa (possibly the best option) or Kharikhola. It is about half a day's walk to Pangkongma (sometimes called Pangum) from these places. At the beginning of Pangkongma after two approximately parallel mani walls walk to the left and head up to a group of houses and *lodges*.

If you're very fit you may be able to reach Najing Dingma from Bupsa in a day, or make Bung from Pangkongma or Shubuche. For most people, from Pangkongma or Shubuche to Najing Dingma is a long day. Carry lunch and snacks.

Route from Puiyan Ten minutes north of Puiyan is a big boulder that makes an attractive viewpoint. From here the several trails south of Puiyan are visible. You can also see the rocky gully that the main Namche trail traverses. Just visible above is a trail which can be reached by a short scramble up the rocks and a slip to the path. This is part of the old route between Puiyan and Kharikhola, via Kharte; the present direct trail to Bupsa was constructed in the

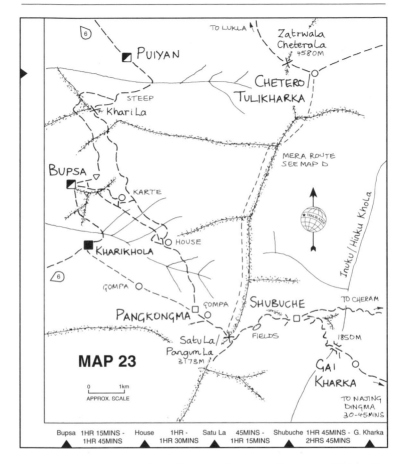

MAP 23

0   1km
APPROX. SCALE

Bupsa 1HR 15MINS - House   1HR -   Satu La   45MINS -   Shubuche 1HR 45MINS - G. Kharka
       1HR 45MINS   1HR 30MINS   1HR 15MINS   2HRS 45MINS

early 1980s. Head over the ridge and the **Khari La (3081m/10,108ft)** and down to the distinctive two-storey white house (a couple of hours in total). Five minutes below is the main trail leading to Pangkongma, heading up the valley.

Route from Bupsa Go straight up the ridge behind the *Solu Khumbu Trekkers' Lodge* on a mainly mud trail. At the mani wall further up, just before the two-storey white house, turn right and contour or drop

to the main trails ahead and below. The Bupsa-Pangkongma trail is narrow but well-used and contours with some real ups and downs. A couple of days before the Namche Saturday market the trail is crowded with heavily laden porters heading for the bazaar.

Route from Kharikhola The locals recommend going via Bupsa, although there is a direct trail from Kharikhola after the maze of fields. You pass by a gompa along the way.

From Bhojpur

This is the real tourist-free Nepal. Since there aren't the trekkers' lodges this route to Salpa Bhanjyang is better attempted with a Nepali-speaking guide or by the most adventurous of trekkers. Occasionally groups begin from here. The advantages of a Bhojpur beginning over Tumlingtar are that this mainly ridge route is cooler during the Arun's steamy months of October and April to May. There are RNAC passenger flights from Biratnagar and Kathmandu.

The Maoist situation
Bhojpur is the district headquarters and should be in government control, however, Maoists move freely in the surrounding countryside.

The airport
The short runway is nestled amid paddies and you are dumped rather suddenly into rural Nepal. It is a pretty region and reasonably developed. Bhojpur is approximately 45 minutes' walk away; there are several trails, all easy enough to lose so follow locals. Bhojpur is at an angle of approximately 25° east from the direction that the plane landed.

Bhojpur
Among Nepalese, Bhojpur is famous for khukris (Gurkha army knives) and suntala, Nepali mandarin oranges. The bazaar stretches along a ridge and is almost big enough to lose your way. There are a few *restaurants* (called hotels) where it is possible to stay but be warned: the accommodation is less than basic, grungy even. They aren't the least bit set up for teahouse trekkers. Dal bhaat is the staple but samosas, momos, noodles and omelettes are also available.

The whitewashed shops stock a surprising array of goods to soak up salaried workers' wages. The bazaar is pleasantly busy with goldsmiths working gold, barbers shaving and cutting and blacksmiths hammering out khukris. Goats cavort around and roosters crow. Stereos and heaters take advantage of electricity. There is also a telephone system and occasional TV aerials and satellite dishes. The large field sees football games and a surprising range of other sports such as tai-kwondo and volleyball. Because it is a district headquarters (Nepal is made up of 75 districts) there is a full set of government offices including forestry, *kani pani* (drinking water), soil conservation and watershed management, women's development, agricultural and horticultural development, district court, district police headquarters and even a prison.

Bhojpur is also an education centre. The several boarding schools have been joined by a college offering complete two year commerce and arts courses.

Saturday market Saturday morning features the *Hat* or *Hati*, an open market. A fascinating melange of sellers, some of whom have walked a day or two to get here, sell mainly foodstuffs. This is the only place where vegetables and meat are sold. Bazaar merchants and hopeful porters sell sweets, biscuits and snacks. *Sakaar*, raw sugar, comes from Chainpur. A surprising variety of dals, rices, spices, black pepper, chillies, salt, eggs – both duck and chicken – feature. You can even buy whole tobacco leaves to make your own.

BHOJPUR TO DINGLA / NEPALI DANDA [MAP 24, opposite; MAP 20, p237]
At the top of the main bazaar veer right up a steep stone staircase through the rest of ribbon Bhojpur. Houses turn red-washed with tile or thatched roofs as the trail climbs more or less along the ridge.

Kafle has a school with a community forestry plantation opposite and a couple of shops that can make dal bhaat. Terraces dotted with trees extend further than the eye can see. Occasional prayer flags reveal that this is a Tamang region.

Half an hour past Kafle is a well worn shortcut going right while the main stone-paved trail continues ahead. If you are lucky Kanchenjunga rears on the horizon at the beginning of a large pine plantation that the locals are proud of.

Dhap Kharka, which you pass, has its Japanese-financed school, hence the unusual architecture.

Suntale

This is the first real village after leaving Bhojpur. It appears around the corner as views of the ridge extend into the distance. There are some dal bhaat *restaurants* and it is possible to find rough places to stay. If the atmosphere is clear, to the north is Makalu; the long white summit ridge slightly left is Chamalang. Slightly further left part of the Lhotse-Nuptse ridge is visible. Perhaps it is possible to just see the tip of Everest. To the east is the huge Kanchenjunga massif.

Tintale   This is also a Sherpa village. Meals are available but expect to sleep on the kitchen floor if staying. Until this point the ridge has been more or less level but now it begins falling off. Parts of the trail are wide and deeply incised. There are magnificent views of Makalu along here. Across the Arun River valley the flat area is Tumlingtar and along the ridge you can pick out Khandbari.

Dingla

This is a bustling bazaar village nestled in a saddle. Unlike ribbon Bhojpur it is a rough circle of houses, shops and simple *restaurants*. There are several simple places to stay. *Suntala* are usually available. Dingla also features a Saturday market. The village's claim to fame is that the first public school in Nepal was founded here in approximately 1876. The Ranas established Nepal's first school after a visit to Europe in 1854. It was only for their children. However, it is only now, in the last 15 years, that public schooling has become widely available in Nepal and considered a right rather than a privilege.

Leaving, the trail gently drops and contours but isn't straightforward to follow. At a water pipe, chautara and small cattle

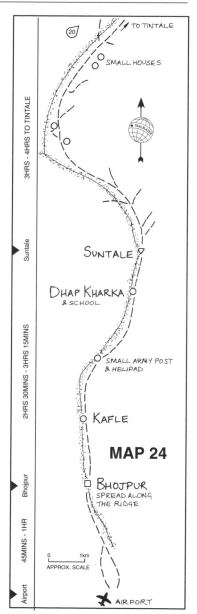

shelter take a left. If you go straight the stone steps take you to a bridge across the Arun. Mountains tantalise in the distance.

Nepali Danda is recognizable by the solar panels for the telephone, which occasionally rings. Not a lot happens here on the ridge top but food is available. Head west along the northern side of the ridge. Eventually descend to the river at Lankuwa where the trail meets the more usual route in from Tumlingtar. The description continues on p232.

There is also a regularly used trail between Dobani and Bhojpur. From Dobani it passes through Kuda Kaule, Khartham Cha and Kimalung before joining the trail mentioned above at Tintale. Taking a local guide would be wise.

Rowaling

INTRODUCTION
Rolwaling means 'the furrow left by the plough', an appropriate name for this steep-walled valley. It's a rugged yet beautiful area inhabited by friendly Sherpas. Unlike their Khumbu cousins, they form a single isolated community with just one main village. Above the inhabited area the valley divides into several little explored glaciated valleys dominated by formidable 6000m/19,685ft peaks. The highest mountain in the area is the holy Gauri Sankar, an ice-castle that can be admired even from Kathmandu.

Despite the dotted line marking the route on many trekking maps, the Tashi Labtsa (5755m/18,881ft) is a mountaineering challenge not a teahouse trekking route. It's far more dangerous than the Kongma La, Tsho La or Annapurna's Thorong La.

Safety
It would be insane to try to cross the Tashi Labtsa by yourself and several climbers have disappeared while alone in this area. Crevasses are a real danger and there are some areas in the icefall that may need an abseil. From Thame or Beding you will need at least three days' food and should carry reserves for two more days, plus enough fuel to melt snow or ice for water. For small parties ice axes and crampons are needed by all, plus a rope with a few ice screws and slings and gear for a short abseil. Conditions have changed considerably on the glaciers in Nepal: as recently as 1972 yaks were taken across this pass.

There is one section of the route that could quite possibly change, making traversing around the Tsho Rolpa even more challenging than it already is, if the lake isn't frozen. **You must** consult with someone who has crossed the pass that season to find out the exact situation.

The Maoist situation
The Dolakha district, ie the section of trail between Dolakha and Simigoan and the section to Barabise was, as of 2002, controlled by the Maoists. Although trekking groups were still occasionally using the routes, often they were asked to donate to the Maoists. Trekking as a group of for-

---

♦ **Tsampa**

The process of making tsampa (barley flour) is quite complex. Dark high-altitude barley is dried in the sun, then mixed with white barley. The grains are soaked in water and dried three times before being stored for a few days. Next the barley is roasted in sand. The grain explodes like popcorn and is ground up into a light fluffy flour. It can be eaten dry and washed down with *chang*, mixed with *solja* (salt-butter tea) to make a thick porridge or rolled into a doughy ball to be chewed. For trekkers, ordinary tea is used for tsampa porridge, rather than *solja*.

Are you prepared for the worst?

Where is the place that you would least want to be when it snows? I can't think of many worst places than on the Drolambao Glacier between the pass and Noisy Knob. We set up camp in the icefall slightly off route and awoke to find snow completely covering our two tents. The three guys in the other tent were actually suffocating. It was a marathon three-hour job to completely clear around the tents (always take a snow shovel!) and they needed clearing again in the afternoon.

The next night the tents were completely covered again but this time we stayed awake keeping the air vent clear. Enough snow had fallen that the crevasses, some more than ten metres deep, were completely filled and in all probability we waded over a few. It wasn't more than 1.5km to Noisy Knob but it took us a whole day of laboriously breaking a trail then packing down enough so that the guys following wouldn't fall through to their waists too often. We crawled across many patches too. To cut a long story short it took us a further four days of the most torturous trail-breaking imaginable to make Beding, and that was taking a shortcut over the frozen lake. Everyone suffered frost-nipped toes and had wasted away but luckily we all lived, and with no permanent damage.

We survived the worst; but will you?

eigners without Nepali crew seems to invite less attention. Check Trailblazer's website for the latest.

Route planning and acclimatization

The Rolwaling Valley is a destination in its own right but most trekkers combine it with a visit to the Khumbu. Commercial trekking groups usually approach the valley from Dolakha or Barabise, attempt the trekking peak Ramdung-Go for acclimatization, then cross the Tashi Labtsa. For proper acclimatization 12 nights should be spent between Simigoan (2000m/6562ft) and the first night above 5000m/16,404ft. Since the highest village (Beding) is at 3700m/12,139ft this means many days camping.

Independent trekkers will find crossing from the Khumbu to the Rolwaling makes more sense logistically than the other way around. From Thame (suitably acclimatized) it is possible to reach Dolakha/Barabise in just under a week and taking 8-9 days would be quite leisurely. Extra time will allow exploration of the valleys that head the Rolwaling and the wall of mountains to the south.

There are two route possibilities for starting (or finishing) the trek (see Map B:

p258; Map C: p259). Dolakha (near Charikot) is a few km off the Jiri road and the walk to Simigoan takes two to four days following the Tamba Kosi. Barabise is on the Arniko Highway and from here to Simigoan takes four to six days. Between Simigoan and Beding there is also a choice of routes.

Note that the route is described crossing the pass from Thame to the Rolwaling and on to the roadheads at Dolakha/Charikot and Barabise. Information relevant to travelling in the reverse direction is also given, marked by '▲'.

Facilities

Since it's usually groups with tents that pass through here, there's no organized system of lodges but finding basic food and a place to stay at villages en route isn't difficult.

However, there are a number of nights where camping is unavoidable and camping supplies are far more difficult to find than in the Khumbu. Don't expect them to stock things like muesli and milk powder, except perhaps in Beding. It's best to carry in all you need and it's worth considering employing porters unless you're approaching from the Khumbu.

THE ROLWALING VALLEY
[MAP A: opposite]

Leaving Thame The trail leaves from the little *lodge* beside Thame Gompa (visible from Thame village). Take the upper tracks at each of the main junctions and you pass several small *chhusa*, deserted except during summer.

Tengpo (4350m/14,271ft) is a couple of hours from the gompa. This large *chhusa* has a number of minuscule two-storey houses. It's overlooked by the spectacular south faces of Teng Kangboche. There's ample spring water year-round and plenty of places to camp. If, however, your party is well acclimatized then it's a better idea to camp closer to the pass.

The track continues but is smaller now. Looking back there's an unusual view of Ama Dablam with the fluted cirque and glacier of the Mingbo La clearly visible and with Makalu almost hidden behind Ama Dablam. There are good camping areas around the point from where the views of Ama Dablam start to disappear. Further up the track stays above the valley base and heads to the black rock spur (north-western side of the valley), where there are more camping places but these lack water after a spell of dry weather. Over and slightly down the other side of the moraine (the route does not follow the valley by the black rock ridge) there are several more rocky sites.

To the north is an icefall and to the left of this are several rough moraine ridges. Partially ascend one and head up, keeping to the left of the icefall. There should be a rough track to follow. Above are another two groups of campsites called **Ngole/Mgole** (5100m/16,732ft) with windy and very cold overhanging rock shelters.

▲ Crossing in the reverse direction

Note that when coming down from the pass to these camps you must keep to the left and avoid descending to the obvious and large valley floor.

The Tashi Labtsa / Tesi Lapcha (5755m/18,881ft)

Access to the pass involves passing areas of frequent rockfall so an early morning start is best. In the early morning the rocks may still be frozen in place but as the sun hits them they expand, loosen and come thundering down. On a winter's day things might be stable but on a warm October afternoon it's like Russian roulette. It's said by the Sherpas that Lama Sange Dorje crossed this pass and the name Tashi Labtsa bestows a certain protection on travellers.

Onto the glacier There are two obvious routes. You can head left, down and under an icefall close to a large avalanche cone from Parcharmo. However, the quicker and more popular route is simply to stay on moraine-covered ice and head up the ice valley. This could also be totally snow covered. Once up here the lay of the land becomes clearer. To the left, almost on Parcharmo's flanks, is a small diagonal icefall that fails to meet the smooth, white, almost flat glacier below. The upper part meets a rock wall that stretches from the right of the glacier to above you. Make for the point where the icefall and the wall meet, which involves an ascent of the steep unstable scree slope below the wall. Beware of heavy rockfall here. Sometimes stepping onto the icefall is easier. Groups often use a rope here although with crampons and good glacier conditions it may not be necessary.

Alternatively, right of the small icefall is a large avalanche cone which leads to a rock shelf that runs between it and the top of the small icefall. Consult locals as to which route might be easier and safer.

From above the small icefall the going is easier and it's a simple plod to the top of the pass. Crevasses are not normally a problem but if there has been a lot of snow recently then use a rope. Parcharmo's snow bulges rise to the left and you should watch out for falling rocks from Tengi Ragi Tau (6940m/22,769ft) to the right. Just before the pass is Tashi Phuk (Tashi's Cave), a few daringly placed camping spots sheltered by a slightly overhanging rock wall. These

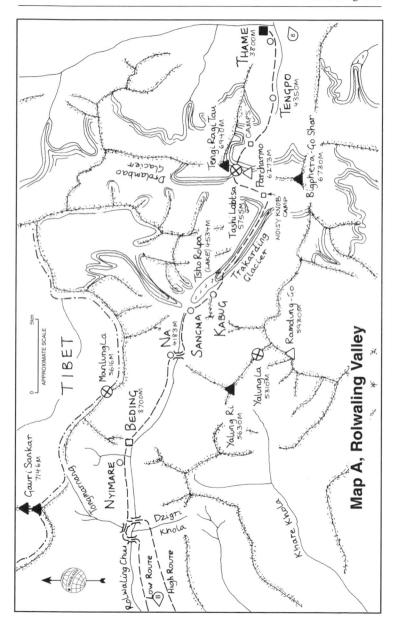

Map A, Rolwaling Valley

make a good base for an attempt on Parcharmo.

The pass (5755m/18,881ft) New vistas unfold at the pass which is a small flat rock rib running out from Tengi Ragi Tau/Kangi Tau marked by cairns and a few prayer flags.

The descent is steeper than the ascent and requires care – there are several crevasses and a bergschrund. Head directly down, to where the glacier flattens out and meets the white Drolambao Glacier, divided by a line of moraine rubble. Once down stay close to, or on, the nearest medial moraine. Most groups camp somewhere around here (Tolungbawe Nang) but if you're making good time you may be able to reach the next camp. Don't cross to the far side of the glacier – the route marked on the *Rolwaling Himal* Schneider map is the 1950s route, now out of use, considered too dangerous and impractical.

From this point several routes have been used. Some trekkers have crossed the Drolambao Glacier before it starts to break up (and off!), then descended against the wall of Dragkar-Go but this requires some abseils and appears to descend a very dicey ramp. On my explorations, after descending some distance, I could not find a practical way down that did not need several ropes. Much better is to continue following the moraine, then cross over the broken ice to the left to another line of moraine debris formed by a glacier entering from Bigphera-Go Shar. This begins under a distinctive striped rock face. It leads, sometimes easily, sometimes hazardously, off the glacier/icefall onto solid rock. Conditions vary tremendously just here and at times it may require an abseil of up to 25m. Below, perhaps slightly to the right, is a massive lump of rock with obvious camping spots perched on top of it.

Dza Bua/Dzenasa/noisy knob camp (5000m/16,404ft) To reach this camp, either drop to an obvious wide rock ledge below or bear right and drop into it further along. Then drop down the small diagonal

gully within view of noisy knob. Depending on conditions and your skill, a rope may be necessary here. The camp is a classic, perched almost under the falling seracs and above the Trakarding Glacier. A warm night will surround you with the roar of avalanches, the crash-tinkle of seracs and continual groans of the glacier ghosts.

▲ Crossing in the reverse direction
This camp is situated on the large blunt knob of rock clearly visible projecting at the far end of the Drolambao Icefall, dividing it and the next icefall. It's shown on the *Rolwaling Himal* Schneider map. The route up the knob is from the Bigphera-Go Shar side.

The Trakarding Glacier
Continuing on, the most frequently used route is on the north side where there's a definite track but moving down on the south side is equally feasible. You could perhaps even head for the ablation valley early. If on the north side then once you're well down, the glacier cairns lead to the south side, while a vague path continues. Don't follow this path unless the lake is frozen. You must cross to the south to traverse around the lake. The old northern route is extremely dangerous. Some of the steep moraines extend to sheer rock faces and are shelled with a virtually continuous hail of stones and rocks.

Once on the south side of the glacier, climb up on a rough track, eventually reaching the steep crumbling moraine (groups use a rope down here). Binoculars will help you spot a large cairn well above. There's grass and a big flat dust bowl with a track across it here. Then it's up again to avoid the huge bowling alley that drops into the side of the lake.

At the top, walk south-west a little before crossing among the boulders. The descent is steep but with great views of the Tsho Rolpa (4550m/14,927ft) and the mountains towering above it. This section of trail is getting more and more precarious each year. It is possible that the hillside might fall away meaning this route is no longer possible.

Down the ablation valley is **Kabug** with its small cave, water and pleasant camping area. **Sangma** and the areas below the lake are also pleasant camping areas, especially for a day or overnight trip up to Bombok (or higher) beside the Ripimo Shar Glacier. The bridge below Sangma is sometimes dismantled for winter.

Na (4183m/13,724ft)

After a few hours of pleasant walking down the valley, cross the bridge to **Na**. This is a large *chhusa*, a summer village set under an incredible wall of mountains on the sunny northern side of the valley. It's deserted soon after the potatoes have been harvested, the fields left for the yaks and naks to pick over and add their dose of fertiliser.

It's a short half day's walk above the north bank to Beding, still with the spectacular Chobutse/Tsoboje (6689m/21,945ft) rising behind. The forests en route are striking for the size of the trees, even in areas that get very little sun. This is how the area around Namche, and even as high as Dingboche, must once have looked. As Beding becomes visible it is framed against one of the twin peaks of Gauri Sankar (7146m/ 23,445ft), or Jomo Tseringma (Chomotseringma) as the Sherpas call it.

Beding (3700m/12,139ft)

Beding is a picturesque cluster of buildings centred around the gompa, with a well-kept stupa in the river bed. Although it's the only real village in the upper Rolwaling Valley, it's not permanently occupied. During the coldest winter months the entire population huddles down in the *gunsas* Gyabrug to Nyimare. In the summer, some villagers move up to cultivate potatoes at Na and others roam higher with their grazing yaks.

The people seem to manage their village well without outside interference or government offices but there's no health post. There is a school opened in 1972 by Hillary and bridges erected with Japanese aid. The way of life here has changed less than for the Khumbu Sherpas in recent years. Trade with Tibet has been replaced with trekking-related jobs here too but since

only groups pass through, there are no trekking lodges. (Nevertheless almost every resident will more than willingly put a few people up in local style.) Locals find employment as sirdars, cooks and especially as high-altitude sherpas on expeditions. Lots of Everest summiteers live here. Lowland porters sometimes quit en masse on the Tashi Labtsa so there's often lots of portering work for local people. The Rolwaling Sherpas are not as poor as Sherpas in non-tourist areas and the relative wealth has manifested itself in modernization of many houses, expanding them to Khumbu proportions.

Trading with Tibet has virtually died out now that Indian iodised salt is so cheaply available. Previously salt, tsampa, yaks and naks, dried meat and Chinese-manufactured goods were traded. The route was over the Manlung La (5616m/ 18,425ft) which is reached up the impossible-looking slabs a little to the north of Beding. The glaciated pass affords amazing views of the mountain known to the Sherpas as Jomo Garu (Chomogaru: 7181m/23,559ft). This beautiful peak is more commonly known as Menlungtse, the name Shipton gave it in 1951.

Routes to Simigoan There are two routes: the direct lower winter route via Gyalche, a short day's walk down but tough coming up, or the high scenic Daldung La route for which it's best to allow two days. Snow in winter virtually precludes using the high route because the track is mostly in shaded areas where the snow is slow to melt. In addition, except in the early part of the season, this route is uninhabited until Simigoan.

To the Dzigri Khola, the boundary of the high Rolwaling Valley, both routes follow the same trail. The path is sunny and pleasant, always on the northern side, sometimes through forest, and, lower, sometimes in stunted bamboo. Prayer flags mark the wooden bridge (3200m/10,499ft).

The low route The trail, narrower now, continues on the north bank to cross the

Tongmarnang, the stream with a view up Gauri Sankar's stunning face.

A little further down, the trail crosses to the south bank and starts its long roller-coaster ride to Simigoan. There are infrequent small campsites and perhaps one *teashack*. The trail is different from that marked on the *Rowaling Himal* Schneider map but is wide, well-used and easy to follow. It leads directly into Simigoan Gompa rather than heading via Shakpa.

▲ **Trekking in the reverse direction**
The high route is especially rewarding on the way in, with stunning views of Gauri Sankar and perhaps even a glimpse of Menlungtse. It's also an introduction to altitude, and a rather harsh one for many people, but relief should come when crossing the Rolwaling Chhu. For this reason it is preferable to stay at Shakpa (2650m/8694ft), rather than Simigoan, and it reduces the climb the next day over the Daldung La (3976m/13,044ft).

SIMIGOAN TO DOLAKHA/ CHARIKOT [MAP B: p258]
Simigoan (2000m/6562ft)
This is a large agricultural village, spread way down the hillside: Sherpa in the higher parts and Tamang in the lower section. There are a couple of *campsites* (where it is also possible to stay inside and get a meal) but signs giving directions for them are only along the route coming up to Simigoan. Camping by the gompa offers superb views (but rubbish left by groups is a problem here).

To leave Simigoan descend through the village, pass the small police checkpost with its tiny sign in English and continue down. At the edge of a flattish cultivated area is a junction almost overlooking cliffs. It's worth asking someone around here to check that you're on the correct trail. Go right (north) here on what may look like the slightly less used trail. This descends steeply, writhing down a steep wide gully to the suspension bridge across the Bhote Kosi at 1520m/4987ft.

On the west bank, the trail to the north leads to Lamabagar/Chhogsham and the police post controlling traffic to Tibet. The trail to the south leads (in just a minute) to Chetchet and a *teashack*. The route down follows the impressive Bhote Kosi (Tibetan River) with the path, in places, held together by concrete. The tide marks on the river rocks show the height of the torrent that rages through during the monsoon. For this reason there's a second river route to Gongar, used when the river is at its most dangerous, which branches up half an hour below Chetchet. Around here the waterfalls and the gorge are particularly impressive.

Gongar (1400m/4593ft)
This is just a small village but lodging is available. Around the corner, a few hundred metres upstream, is the new bridge across the Gongar Khola. On the main part of the far bank the trail divides: the lower path passing a huge house just below is for Charikot, while the upper path goes to Barabise (see trail description on p259).

The trail roughly follows the river, sometimes traversing and sometimes with short climbs to avoid bluffs.

Jagat is approximately the half-way point to the old suspension bridge at **Manthale**. Here, particularly on the east bank, are some shops, and frequently fruit, usually suntala (mandarin oranges) can be found.

The valley starts to widen out although en route to Suri Dhoban there are still some narrow traverses that preclude the use of animals instead of porters.

Suri Dhoban/Dhovan (1020m/3346ft)
has *teashacks* and *bhattis* and is a normal overnight stopping place or lunch spot for Rolwaling Sherpas heading to or from Kathmandu. Across the fine suspension bridge up-valley is one of the trails for the route over the Yalung La, up the Khare Khola. The route down passes a post office little bigger than a postage stamp. The trail continues more or less along the river bank and after a cluster of houses crosses to the

west bank on a suspension bridge. At the Sangawa Khola is a small but often busy village with a *bhatti* or two. The trail that zigzags up the hill goes to Laduk and is heavily used. Take the suspension bridge across the Sangawa Khola instead and continue south.

Somewhere around here the name of the Bhote Kosi (Tibetan River) changes to the Tamba Kosi, or Copper River. The Tamba Kosi and the Sun Kosi, or Gold River are said to issue out of water spouts, one made of copper, and one of gold.

Piguti (Singi Ghat) On the west bank of the river, this trading town has a few Nepalese-style *lodges*. The trail continues south, staying on the west bank of the river (not marked on the Schneider map). A little before Bong Khola is a reasonable camping place.

Bong/Bongu Khola (Malepu) (880m/ 2887ft), an hour further on, is a second large trading village with *hotels* and shops. It's a regular overnight stop since, with tired legs, the climb to Dolakha and Charikot can be soul-destroying in the afternoon sun.

The path widens (it's more like a road here) and runs through fine forests for a short time.

Ratomate Continue for one and a half to two and a quarter hours to the hamlet of Ratomate (red mud) where the climb actually begins. The *accommodation* and *restaurants* are simple but it is possible to stay.

By the khola is a camping place and across the bridge the haul up to Dolakha begins.

The ridge is tough and unrelenting for the climb of almost 800m; count on a two-hour haul. There are several paths leading off to villages but the trail heading up is usually the correct one and the volume of traffic heading to the town means you're unlikely to get lost.

Dolakha (1650m/5413ft)

This is a beautiful and historic town with a few stupas and some flagstone-paved streets.

Once it was a main town on the trading route from Tibet to the Indian plains and it still has a Saturday market. Becoming a roadhead has increased prosperity here but not ravaged the town, except by the bus station, as has happened elsewhere. There are at least three **buses** a day to Kathmandu at 6am, 8am and 10am.

Dolakha, sometimes also called Charikot, and the new Charikot further up the ridge share the title of headquarters for the Dolakha District, which stretches from here to the Tibetan border. Consequently there are a number of government departments. The latest addition is a modern **hospital** funded by Korea. The view alone is worth the visit.

▲ **Starting at Dolakha** If the bus you were on was heading to Jiri you'll be dropped off at Charikot. Depending on the time, you can either start trekking along the 3.5km dirt road to Dolakha or stay in Charikot. Both have simple Nepali-style *lodges* and great views of the dominant Gauri Sankar and Menlungtse slightly to the east.

At the group pace, Simigoan is about four days' walk away, or a quicker two to three days. Returning in a hurry, two days is plenty of time. For the first expeditions, walking from Kathmandu to the Khumbu or Rolwaling, Dolakha was six days into the trek.

Charikot If you arrived too late for the last bus out of Dolakha walk up the road to Charikot and catch one of the buses passing through from Jiri. The last one leaves Charikot at approx 2pm.

The atmosphere here is quite different from Dolakha. It is a relatively new town and has grown rapidly. There are a few *hotels* and *restaurants* that look fancier than they really are.

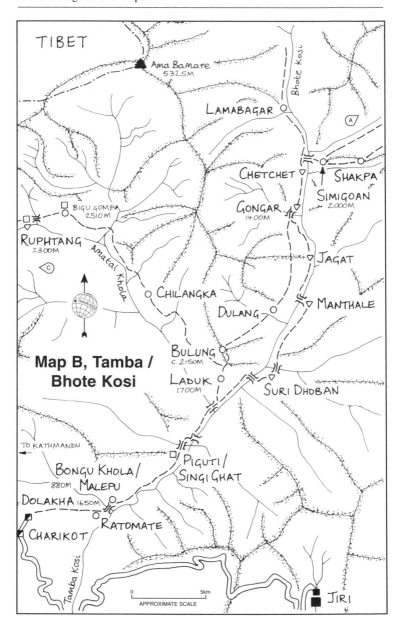

TIBET

Ama Bamare
5325M

LAMABAGAR

Bhote Kosi

A

CHETCHET

SHAKPA

SIMIGOAN
2000M

BIGU GOMPA
2510M

GONGAR
1400M

RUPHTANG
2300M

Amatal Khola

C

JAGAT

CHILANGKA

DULANG

MANTHALE

**Map B, Tamba /
Bhote Kosi**

BULUNG
C. 2150M

LADUK
1700M

SURI DHOBAN

TO KATHMANDU

BONGU KHOLA /
880M MALEPU

PIGUTI /
SINGI GHAT

DOLAKHA 1650M

CHARIKOT

RATOMATE

Tamba Kosi

JIRI

0   5km
APPROXIMATE SCALE

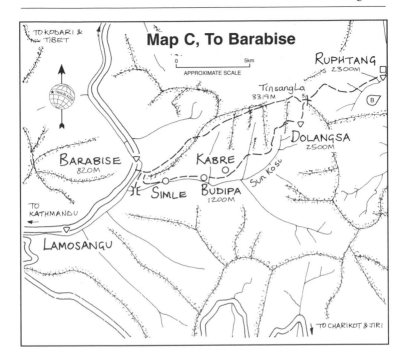

GONGAR TO BARABISE [MAP B: opposite; MAP C: above]

This is one of the classic routes which has been superseded by the Jiri road. As a route into the Rolwaling, it still has advantages because it offers a degree of helpful acclimatization. It's also little changed since the early days of trekking and is very much a route suited to the expedition approach or to individual trekkers happy to eat dal bhaat and learn some Nepali. Simigoan to Barabise is a pleasant four-day walk including perhaps a half day rest at Bigu Gompa. It could be shortened to two-and-a-bit days by strong legs in a hurry.

Routes There are several possible routes from the Bhote/Tamba Kosi to Bigu Gompa and on to Barabise. See the *Lapchi Kang* Schneider map. The route described here leaves the Bhote/Tamba Kosi after crossing the Gongar Khola on a good trail that is not marked on the Schneider map.

Leaving Gongar Take the upper of the equal-sized paths, heading up and around on the south bank of the Gongar Khola. Shortly after a stupa is a small but interesting Hindu shrine. Although virtually nothing is marked on the Schneider map, this is a well-populated, mainly Tamang area.

The trail passes through several villages during the several hours to Dulang (1900m/6234ft). Around here, since there are so many small trails, it pays to repeatedly ask the way. Ask for Bigu or Bigu Gompa, otherwise villagers tend to direct you to Laduk and the slightly shorter route out to Charikot.

Bulung (2150m/7054ft)

This sprawling village is a few hours further on. You may meet the pleasant high school teacher or some of the friendly children, many of whom are more interested in practising their English than in the usual begging. Bulung has some **shops** but since few visitors pass through they are not obvious. You'll need to ask a villager where they are and, if you need accommodation, asking around will soon turn something up. On leaving the village there are superb views of Gauri Sankar.

All the main trails lead to **Laduk** (1700m/5577ft) which, once out of Bulung and around the major ridge, is visible below. Stay high on the terraces and look for the large high school that sits above Laduk. The main trail continues directly from the school and is the one that contours and descends slightly. Laduk is a large centre with many shops. The porters prefer to walk here from Charikot rather than Barabise since the Tamba Kosi route is considered shorter.

Continue contouring and descend, then drop to the Thuran Khola. After climbing steeply, head around the ridge on an easy-to-follow trail.

Chilangka (1900m/6234ft) This little village spreads above and below the main trail with little to offer except a shop beside the path. Contour, staying fairly high, and cross the Jorong Khola on a log bridge. Then head up and out onto the hillside and a pretty forest. Contour to **Loding/Lading (1800m/5904ft)** and after it reach a prominent viewpoint. Look for Bigu Gompa: a mass of prayer flags. The best route from here is to wander upstream along the east bank of the Kothale Khola and cross on a major suspension bridge although there are some temporary bridges.

Numerous trails lead through the villages stacked up the hillside so ask for the gompa, sometimes also called Tashi Gompa. It is also possible to bypass the gompa – although it's one of the main reasons for taking this route – by dropping to Amatal and continuing up the valley on the south bank of the Amatal Khola.

Bigu Gompa (2510m/8235ft)

This nunnery is impressively-located amid prayer flags and huge juniper trees at the top of the village. The gompa is an island of Buddhism in the surrounding Hindu area. Many of the nuns are Tibetan refugees, and some are very recent arrivals. There are some beautiful paintings in this gompa and the setting is very pleasant. It's possible to stay at the tidy, smoke-free *guest house*. Below, in Bigu village, there's a **paper factory** that sells its products in Kathmandu.

Leaving the gompa, it's a fairly gentle descent passing through an area ravaged by forest fires, to the distinctive roofed bridge across a tributary. There are many water-driven flour mills above and this heralds **Ruphtang (2300m/7546ft)**. It boasts a *teahouse* just up from the bridge and more *teashacks* a little further on. These are the last facilities en route to the pass, still a 1000m/3281ft haul away.

The Tinsang La (3319m/10,889ft)

The sometimes eroded and elusive trail stays on the north bank of the Amatal Khola. In the kharkas and forests of tall firs maintaining your sense of direction may not be easy. Just before the crest of the Tinsang La is beautiful flat pasture used for grazing in summer, and dotted with roofless huts in the fall and winter. It's a good place to camp with a reasonably good water supply.

The panorama here stretches from Gauri Sankar (7146m/23,445ft) and the closer rock cone of Jomo Bamare (Chomobamare: 5927m/19,445ft) on the Tibetan border to Numbur (6959m/22,831ft) in the east, the Yul Lha (holy mountain) of Shorong. Unlike the gentle ascent, the route down to Dolangsa seems unrelentingly steep though it takes only an hour or less.

Dolangsa (2500m/8202ft)

This is an extensive village resting on a large flat area. There are a few *bhattis* and *teashacks* above and below the gompa. Winter here is a time of crafts: knitting and weaving bamboo mats and dokos.

There are numerous ways down to Barabise but more widely used is the route on the northern side of the Sun Kosi via Budipa. Once across a few streams, down a ridge and across another stream you come to the village of **Kabre**. Stay on the large well-defined trail on the north bank and cross a large tributary to Budipa.

Budipa (1200m/3937ft) There are some *teahouses* and shops in this village. You can stay either here or in **Simle**, the next village, so as to avoid having to spend the night in Barabise. The trail from Budipa contours above the river and around a sharp ridge before descending into Barabise, and the mess of modern civilization.

Barabise (820m/2690ft)
Big, dirty and crowded, Barabise is a trading post for many Chinese goods that have found their way over from Tibet via the Arniko Highway or been smuggled in along the older trading routes.

▲ **Starting from Barabise** Route-finding for the first few hours is difficult so it's a very good idea to hire a local porter. As well as acting as a guide, he (or she) will enable you to start with a light load in a hot area with a 2400m/7874ft climb to the Tinsang La. Note that if you camp just below this pass (a few days later) you're likely to feel the altitude as a result of the rapid ascent. By the time you reach Bigu Gompa, however, all symptoms should have cleared.

Trekking peaks

INTRODUCTION
In 1981 the government of Nepal streamlined group climbing permit applications for 18 mountains which it calls 'trekking peaks'. The name is not well-chosen: 'limited bureaucracy' peaks is more accurate because some of these peaks are actually challenging technical climbs but a handful are 6000m or 20,000ft peaks within the ability of the experienced hill-walker/hiker with a guide. This form of recreational

mountaineering took off at the end of the 1980s and expeditions can now be organized at a similar cost and within a timeframe similar to less adventurous treks.

The idea behind the rules is that the expedition should be organized through a guide or better, a trekking company, and unless you are particularly independent and an experienced climber this is the better way. For many people the decision is whether to go cheaply with a Nepali company or pay more for a Western-guided trip through an overseas operator.

Basically, unless you are an experienced climber who would prefer to lead and be responsible for safety you are better booking with a competent home-country adventure trekking company. The standard of Nepali mountain guides, even the NMA certified, is generally poor; few 'guides' understand Western-standard safety practices and amazingly enough the vast majority of Nepali guides, qualified or not, can't even belay, although they are generally skilled sirdars (organizers).

The best professional operators offer full expedition-style treks with experienced mountain guides and staff with medical training to ensure a safe trek. Expedition peaks are now also on a few company programmes: Ama Dablam (6856m) is popular and so are the big peaks: Cho Oyu and Everest.

To climb or to explore
For climbers on a budget and on their first journey to Nepal the expenses of permits, getting gear over and getting it all to the base of the mountain add up. Realistically a climb with permits will add at least another $500 per person, and more like $800 if you are a smaller team. Then there is how to organize it. You will probably want someone to haul all the gear to the last village and join you there but very few trekking companies will do this; naturally they prefer that you book a full trekking tour with them, sometimes lodge-based except for the climb, but mostly camping style. Even though the cost will be around $900-1300 their service has a high chance of being very ordinary. All this takes some setting up too.

> ### Expedition peaks – changes and charges
> In January 2002 the cumbersome expeditions permits system was partially overhauled and more changes in the future are expected, too. As well as 103 'new' peaks, there is no longer the requirement for a liaison officer for peaks under 6500m, a welcome change. Currently for peaks under 6500m the **standard peak fee** is $1500 plus $200 per person above seven members, so these peaks are now a possibility for a normal budget expedition with five to seven members.
>
> There is only one peak in that list which compares to say Island Peak, and that is **Kyajo Ri** (Kyazo Ri) 6186m. There are a bunch of peaks around Sherpani Col-West Col that are fun climbing and people who cross the pass occasionally try even without a permit. Out Makalu way on the Tibet border **Pethangtse**, at 6710m, is interesting, although a slog is required to get to the base. In the 1930s a survey tripod was carried to the top.
>
> There is also a set of **'discounted' expedition peaks**, ones that have had few or no expeditions on them. One set is discounted by 75% and includes Lobuche West (which now costs only $225 and some paperwork). The peaks in West Nepal (where the Maoists are concentrated) are all free, although the paperwork requires some effort to process. For full details see the Trailblazer website.
>
> These changes have been made with good intentions but the cynical will still say that the lining of pockets won't be affected in that nobody ever took out permits for these anyway; a cynic will also say that the Liaison Officer's don't, and still won't do their jobs honestly.

For many people going exploring – rather than mountaineering – is a better option. There are lots of 5500-5800m peaks to scramble on and without climbing gear you can travel lighter. A few budget mountaineers get a permit and simply take a porter or two from a company. To do this you should be confident of your organizational and climbing ability.

Permits and costs

The procedure for obtaining a permit is streamlined in comparison to the peaks under the expedition system. It's possible to arrive in Kathmandu, organize a trekking-peak trip from scratch and be on the trail in only a few days. The rules last changed in 2001 but they are still biased towards groups because the larger the group, the smaller the fee per person. The fee is a flat rate for up to four climbers of US$350 or US$350 plus US$40 per extra person for groups of five to eight people. For a group of 9-12 the rate is US$510 for 9 members plus US$25 for every person above nine. The permit is valid for a month only and

either the leader or one of the team members must pick it up from the NMA office. The distinction between lower 'B class' and higher 'A class' peaks has gone.

An NMA-registered sirdar must accompany the group for the entire trek and if you wish he can act as guide rather than overseer. This is to ensure that every climbing trip is organized as a fully-guided group trek, involving porters (who must all be insured) and tents and costing at least US$20/£13.50 per person per day. Some trekking companies are willing to waive this rule.

The noticeboards at the HRA, KEEP Trekkers' Information Centre and the Kathmandu Guest House are the best places to advertise for climbing partners in Kathmandu. Unfortunately, there doesn't seem to be a good place on the web yet.

Without a permit The new permit system means one or two people on a tight budget are hit for more money per person, yet joining another group of people who are probably also inexperienced is not the safest way to climb a mountain. The fine for

> ### Glaciers for the uninitiated
> When falling snow doesn't melt quickly enough, it accumulates, consolidates and is compressed to ice. Its weight forces it slowly downhill, literally bull-dozing its way down to a warmer area where it melts.
>
> The névé is the glacier's accumulation area, (the Western Cwm below Everest, for example) where snow falls in avalanches from the steep walls to the basin below and is squashed to ice.
>
> Next, as it moves down, it bends and catches on the valley walls, the uneven pressures forming cracks or crevasses. In the Himalaya these may be hundreds of metres deep, and in Greenland and Antarctica more than a kilometre. When snow falls, rather than fill the bottom of the crevasse it often sticks to the top of the sides forming cornices. Instead it can also, dangerously, cover the crack, sometimes with a snow bridge little stronger than a playing card.
>
> Sometimes the ice drops down a steep slope and completely breaks up into a mess of building-sized blocks of ice, known as seracs. The infamous icefall above Everest Base Camp is a good example. Here the danger is not so much the huge cracks but of being squashed flat by them as they fall. The Drolambao Icefall on the Tashi Labtsa route is particularly risky.
>
> The big glaciers shovel rocks up on themselves, especially where they meet another glacier. These rocks appear to be held in gravity-defying poses – that is until you put your weight on one whereupon it shoots away. Rocks tend to protect and extend the life of a glacier.

climbing without a permit is double the climbing permit fee (so total $700). Half of this goes to the sirdar who catches the illegal climbers, half to the NMA, so there is a powerful incentive for them to ask to see a permit. For a peak like Island Peak or Mera you will stand out from the other teams if you have just a porter or two; the climbing sirdars mostly know each other and know the companies everyone is working for. Climbing out of season on other peaks you are less likely to encounter trouble.

Ethically, lots of climbers disagree with a permit system, but you are guests in another country and they, of course, make the rules. The NMA's 'trekking peak' system is, however, at least better than India's and Pakistan's, where you have to take a liaison officer (LO) for any peak over 6000m. The money collected, too, has been put to good use; currently it is financing the Pokhara-based mountaineering museum, and in the past they have contributed to building shelters and cleaning up base camps. There is little or no corruption in the organization.

Nepal's **expedition peak system**, on the other hand, is run through the Ministry of Tourism and has similar rules to India and Pakistan. But whereas in India and Pakistan an LO does his/her job, in Nepal they don't, and the system is rumoured to be very corrupt.

Equipment and safety

One man's prudence is another man's poison. HW Tilman

If climbing as part of a trekking company group headed by a climbing guide, then harnesses and ropes will be used on every one of the following peaks, whether for crevasse danger or steep slopes. If climbing without a guide, recognizing your personal limits is important. Some of these peaks are 'straightforward' but what this really means is that to be safe you don't need a shop's worth of karabiners, ice screws, snow-stakes and rock racks – just a partner, rope, a few bits of protection, experience using this gear, good weather and an overriding urge to live.

Routes described below cover the least difficult way up some of the main trekking peaks in the region. For proficient technical alpinists none of the routes is particularly challenging under good conditions. For safety-conscious amateurs, they have potential to provide satisfaction and experience without excessive danger.

Walkie talkie radios The officials involved with the permit system have always insisted that the procedures behind permits was for climbers' own safety, yet two of the best tools for increasing safety, walkie talkies and satellite phones, have ridiculous paperwork and fees surrounding their use. Small cheap handheld radios are rarely noticed by the wrong people, especially in X-ray checked luggage.

Itinerary planning
Heading straight up to high altitude for the first time, even if following the recommended guidelines, is usually a shock to everyone's system. The effort required for walking, let alone climbing, uphill at 5000m is much greater than you might think. By far the best approach to climbing trekking peaks or the high passes is to warm up first by heading high, say to Kala Pattar or the Gokyo viewpoints then down, sleeping a night or two much lower, eg Namche. Although this advice is not yet scientifically proven and the technique little-used, many climbers will attest to how much easier the next slog to high altitude is.

Glacier preparation
Everyone on the rope should always carry prussik loops/jumars and be familiar with their use. If you fall in a crevasse and do the job properly, knocking yourself out, then rescue, particularly by only one partner is an arduous, sometimes impossible, business requiring a pulley system and some gear. Crevasses can be completely invisible, especially in spring. Practise rescue moves and reacting quickly before entering dangerous territory and that worst-case scenario is very unlikely to occur.

Avalanche danger
Just as the Himalayan mountains are the largest in the world, so too are some of the

avalanches. They should be treated with similar respect. Debris cones are a tell-tale sign that avalanches are frequent. Try to avoid going within 300m of these. One of the most dangerous times for avalanches is late winter when there is a massive dump of snow. Parts of Island Peak Base Camp can be hit in these conditions. However, most of the avalanches in Nepal are not from snow, but from ice seracs and hanging glaciers collapsing and worryingly, these can and do occur at any time, whether it has snowed recently or not. One would think that once a section has fallen, it is unlikely to fall again. This is usually wrong.

Technical climbing
Although some of the peaks are regularly climbed by groups many of the peaks are delightful technical mountaineering propositions. For an introduction see Apa's *Insight Guide to Nepal*, and for more detailed information there's Bill O'Connor's dated and often less than accurate *The Trekking Peaks of Nepal*.

Trailblazer's new *Nepal Mountaineering Guide* (due mid 2003) has full coverage of 25 peaks including most of the trekking peaks described here plus more technical climbs and even including Everest.

IMJATSE/ISLAND PEAK (6173m/20,252ft)
The name was coined by Shipton, who thought this peak looked like 'an island in a sea of ice'. Finding a route to the top could be a challenge in itself were it not for the fact that as many as 25 people a day reach the summit during the busy season, October to November. This does not, however, detract from the fact that it's a hard climb that many people fail to complete, either because of a badly-planned acclimatization itinerary, or because they set off too late in the morning or the winds become too strong. Occasionally deep snow makes even reaching the Base Camp difficult.

Suggested itinerary
Before attempting this peak it's essential to include an acclimatization trip (eg to Lobuche and Kala Pattar or any of the other

❏ **IMJATSE PEAK ITINERARY**

Day	Altitude guideline	Overnight stop	Actual altitude
01	2-3000m	Phakding/Monjo	2650m/2850m
02	2-3000m	Namche	3450m
03	3000m	Namche	3450m
04	3000m	Tengboche/Khumjung	3860m/3790m
05	3300m	Tengboche/Pangboche	3860m/4000m
06	3900m	Dingboche/Pheriche	4350m/4280m
07	3900m	Dingboche/Pheriche	4350m/4280m
08	4200m	Thuklha	4600m
09	4500m	Lobuche	4940m
10	4800m	Lobuche (Climb Kala Pattar)	4940m
11	4800m	Dingboche/Chukhung	4350m/4750m
12	5100m	Base Camp	5150m
13	5400m	Climb Imjatse	5150m
14		Extra day for safety	
15		Pangboche	
16		Namche	
17		Lukla	

Chukhung Valley peaks). The table shows the absolute minimum number of days required to allow for relatively safe acclimatization for most climbers. Night stops are shown. Note that it is better to spend more time in the region than this, if possible.

Chukhung to Base Camp (5150m/16,896ft)

This walk takes a short afternoon on the well-defined track, accurately marked on the 1988 National Geographic map. The long thin Base Camp area is a real cesspit despite being cleaned up occasionally. Other problems here include the frequent howling winds and a lack of water in December and January, with only a trickle available a ten-minute walk above the camp near a couple of cairns on the rock fan south and above the Base Camp. As well as this it's not safe to leave a tent unattended, not so much because things will be stolen (although this is starting to happen) but because of the birds. They seem to enjoy ripping through even the toughest of tents so leave them packed up and, with all your other gear, well covered with rocks or, much better, leave someone to mind the camp. The high camp suffers from this

problem as well, and so does the 8000m South Col on Everest.

The route up

As early a start as possible is best: before dawn or at dawn at the latest. It can be a long day and the wind sometimes arrives just before lunch. From the high camps, leaving just as the sun hits may be sufficient.

A trail heads clearly up the hill and then branches into direct and zigzag yak routes up to the high camp which is a series of tent platforms in several groups. From the high camp beside the steep stream, ascend the dry gully immediately to the left of the stream. After about a 50m ascent (measured vertically), cross the gully with the (frozen) stream in it and traverse on one of several cairned trails continuing around to the right. It's important here to find one of the correct routes. Do not continue ascending the gully or you'll come to a tricky white rock wall that is difficult to solo. Beware, also, of many misplaced cairns, some in the oddest of places. You should traverse around and continue ascending on black and brown rock to reach a further gully that steepens, bringing you onto the spur which shortly leads to the glacier.

There is a convenient spot to put on crampons but take care where you sit – it's amazing where some people have the audacity to shit. (If you really need to go here, do so on a rock and toss it off the north-east side, ie away from your water supply.) Well-acclimatized groups have occasionally set up a camp just on the snow. From here there should be a track threading through the maze of gaping holes and crossing snow bridges to the flat, but still lightly crevassed, glacier above. If there's no clear track, route-finding can be difficult and possibly fatal without a rope. Head up the smooth, sometimes crevassed glacier and look for a line of weakness where the snow extends to the summit ridge. Beware of the bergschrund; often it is only barely visible and messy, ie easy and dangerous to fall into. The two general routes are either straight up (120-200m of fixed rope) or a diagonal traverse away from the summit. Groups always fix a rope although careful crampon and axe work alone may be enough in perfect conditions. The wind can be savage on the ridge.

The summit ridge presents the last surprise. Once it was straightforward, but in the last few years a dangerous crevasse has opened up and it is tricky to get around. It is essential to rope up for this section because what is underfoot can be loose and rotten. In total around 250m of fixed rope are required for this section. As of Jan 2002 getting around this serac-crevasse took some gutsy climbing, swinging around the break to a relatively steep face that must have a rope fixed up it. This last section has rendered the climb of Island Peak much tougher than it once was.

The north ridge

Lots talk about it but few ever do it. Firm snow would make it a nice proposition with a rope and a few screws, stakes and a piton. Getting on/off the ablation valley by the Lhotse Shar Glacier can be tricky.

MERA (6476M/21,246FT)   [MAP D]

Mera is one of the most popular of the trekking peaks and, despite being considered little more than a walk to the summit,

it is also one of the most dangerous. It's often attempted by people who have flown in to Lukla and not given themselves adequate time to acclimatize. Several people each year pay for their lack of awareness (or their foolhardiness) with their lives.

Itinerary planning

As with all climbs to 6000m or more careful acclimatization planning is critical but the hard reality is many companies, foreign and Nepali, use an itinerary that is bound to cause altitude problems. The added danger in the Mera area is that descent and a rapid exit are not always possible.

The ignorance of the trekking companies that sell expeditions based on the table on p267 is hard to believe but many groups approximately follow this itinerary. Typically, out of a group of ten members two to four might make the summit, perhaps eight or nine will feel sick and two or three might not even make the Mera La. In most large groups at least one person will get ataxia and without immediate descent death is only a day or so away.

If you do consider an expedition using this itinerary ensure that a PAC/Gamow bag, ie a portable altitude chamber, is carried and the guide is trained in its use. The Hinku and Hongu/Hunku areas are particularly isolated and all exits mean crossing a pass.

There are many itinerary alternatives that provide better acclimatization preparation. If time is at a premium then consider visiting Namche first or flying in to Phaplu and taking the alternative Pangkongma routes. While superior to the shortest itineraries these still bring you to altitude at a rate that is slightly too quick for some people (a course of Diamox may help). With more time why not walk in from Jiri (the bulk of the crew need only join you at Lukla) or for more adventure try the Salpa-Arun route via the Surkie La and Panch Pokhari. For better preparation first trek to Kala Pattar then over the Amphu Labtsa. There are many more variations, the only limits are time and your imagination.

Once you have summited the peak it depends on where you get to that day as to how many days it will take to get back to

❏ Recommended itinerary

Day	Altitude Guideline	Overnight stop	Actual altitude	
01	2-3000m	Phakding 2650m	Fly Lukla	2850m
02	2-3000m	Namche 3450m	Chutenga	3050m
03	3000m	Namche 3450m	Chutenga	3050m
04	3300m	Lukla 2850m	Mid/H. camp	4100m/4200m
05	3600m	Chutenga/H. camp 3050m/4200m	Tuli Kharka	4300m
06	3900m	Tuli Kharka 4300m	Kothe	3500m
07	3900m	Kothe 3500m	Tuli Kharka	4300m
08	4200m	Thangnak (Tagnag) 4350m	Thangnak (Tagnag)	4350m
09	4500m	Thangnak (Tagnag) 4350m	Thangnak (Tagnag)	4350m
10	4800m	Khare 5000m	Dig Kharka	4750m
11	4800m	Khare 5000m	Khare	5000m
12	5100m	High Camp/Mera La 5800m/5400m	Khare 5000m	
13	5400m	Summit, Mera La/Khare 5400m/5000m	H. Camp/M.La	5800m/5400m
14		Thangnak (Tagnag)	Mera La/Khare	5400m/5000m
15		Kothe		
16		Tuli Kharka		
17		Lukla		
18		Fly Kathmandu		

Dangerous itinerary

The following is a dangerous acclimatization planner as followed by many groups. Do **not** book on such a trek.

Day	Altitude guideline	Overnight stop	Actual altitude
01	2-3000m	Fly Lukla, stay Chutenga	3050m
02	2-3000m	High camp	4200m
03	3000m	Tuli Kharka	4300m
04	3300m	Kothe	3500m
05	3600m	Thangnak (Tagnag)	4350m
06	3900m	Thangnak (Tagnag)	4350m
07	3900m	Khare 5000m	
08	4200m	Mera La	5400m
09	4500m	High Camp	5800m
10	4800m	Khare	5000m
11	4800m	head out 3-4 days	

Lukla. There are plenty of alternative places to that mentioned above.

The Hinku and Hongu/Hunku areas are particularly isolated so groups planning to go faster than the recommended acclimatization rate MUST carry a Gamow bag and should have trained Western medical personnel with them who have altitude experience.

To Mera over the Chetera La/ Zatrwala La (4580m/15,026ft)

Note that the Chilli La/Zatr Teng (4943m/16,217ft) is infrequently used, being steeper and higher and impractical for loaded porters. A number of groups have got into trouble trying to use this trail, although it is occasionally used to exit the region. Some

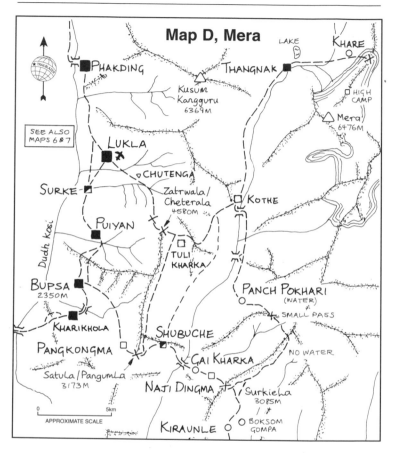

place names on the *Shorong/Hinku* Schneider map are incorrectly placed according to locals: Gondishung is often referred to as Orshela, Dupishung is Gondishung, Lungsamba is Dupishung and Lungsamba is the name for the whole region, not a single place name. Got it?

The first camping place is often Chutenga. Although only three hours out of Lukla it's a sensible choice for the purposes of acclimatization. The second camp (or the first if the group is acclimatized) is at 4200m/13,780ft where there's the last reli-

able water source until well down the double pass. This area can be entirely snow-covered in March-April. The trail traverses steep terrain but is straightforward if snow-free. In snow, however, it gets icy and several hundred metres of handline for porters in a couple of spots is advisable.

Chetero/Tuli Kharka camp (4300m/14,107ft) is marked by a huge boulder that offers fine weather shelter for porters, and there is a simple porters' lodge as well. Beyond the views open up spectacularly.

Which Mera?

Recently there has been some debate and confusion as to which peak exactly is the real Mera Peak. A discrepancy was noticed by a Finnish climber in the details given by the NMA; the latitude and longitude plus the altitude (which was noticed by many) didn't match the commonly climbed peak. Rather they pointed to another peak, labelled 'Mera' on Nepali maps, 8km to the north with a height of 6650m. The alternative name for this peak is Peak 41.

After further research it turns out that the people who suggested and researched the peaks that became the NMA's 'trekking peaks' always meant Mera to be the 6476m peak: however, when more details were added to the list, the wrong details taken from the Nepali district maps were transferred. And that is how the error crept in.

It appeared as of mid-2001 that the Mera Peak 41 had not been climbed, yet technically you should be able to attempt it with a mere $350 permit; however, in January 2002, Peak 41 appeared on the list of newly-opened expedition peaks.

Half an hour on is another camping place, part of the same kharka and also with a huge boulder. The exposed trail is usually cairned although it descends several streams. The next camp and a usual stopping place is Kothe (Kothé). The trail (in October, the expressway) alongside the Hinku Khola is small and confusing in a few places, follow porters who will know the most direct route. At first, views here on either side are not very inspiring – rough, barren country – but ahead is the awesome Peak 43 (6769m/22,208ft) a real eye-catching pyramid and also a sacred mountain (and recently opened for mountaineering). Then the west face of Mera comes into view, sheer and horrible, but climbed once via a buttress by a Japanese expedition.

Thangnak/Tagnag (4350m/14,271ft) is

a summer grazing area with the simplest *lodges* and shops beginning to develop. It has been mis-named by myself and others as Tagnag for years. An acclimatization day is essential here and a visit to the Sabal Tsho or the cairn (5271m) on the flanks of Kusum Kangguru can be rewarding, if the views are not reward enough already.

It's a slog to **Khare 5025m/16,486ft**, a regular camping spot, where another acclimatization day or short trekking day is necessary. For the energetic there are plenty of exploring possibilities. Alternative

camping spots are Dig Kharka or near the snout of the Hinku Nup Glacier. There are two trails on the western side of this glacier, a higher one (for the lake) and a lower trail that both lead around to near the Kangtaiga Glacier.

Conditions on the climb to the Mera La 5415m/17,766ft are variable. When the glacier is dry and the crevasses open, it presents few problems but in new snow a rope (at the very least for the leaders) is essential. A camp may be made either on top of the savagely windy pass, or slightly the other side, but even with a slow ascent it's likely that you'll suffer the effects of the altitude. Porters without crampons should be watched and assisted; indeed, it is better they are not up there at all.

Climbing Mera Peak

It is particularly important for the climbing leader to assess the crevasse dangers for the climb to the Mera La, to the high camp and to the summit. The majority of Nepali guides are far too gung-ho. If the glacier ice is hard and with a packed trail over it, the risk of falling in a crevasse is low, but not quite zero. If it has snowed recently or there is soft snow without a trail you **must rope up**; quite a number of people have fallen into crevasses here.

The standard route up is through a potentially dangerous crevassed area – note that the *Shorong/Hinku* Schneider map does not mark crevassed areas – to the top of the rock band, marked by a large cairn. Here it's possible to establish a high camp either in the snow or on the rock at 5800m. From here the views are outstanding, with Everest, Makalu, Cho Oyu and more piercing the skyline.

In recent years especially as the season progresses into November and December, the snow has almost completely melted off the glacier leaving hard bare ice. Even with crampons caution is required as they don't always grip, especially if the points are blunt.

Mera has two summits. The easier one attempted by most groups is accessed by taking a higher line to the eastern 6461m/21,197ft peak, with its steep last 20m or so. The true 6476m/21,246ft summit can either be reached by a drop and traverse – beyond many people by this stage – or by initially taking a more westerly lower line out of the high camp for a steep haul to the true summit. Note that both of these routes are crevassed.

Approaching Mera from the Surkie La
There are two routes to the Surkie La: from Hille/Tumlingtar via the Arun Kosi, or via Bupsa from Jiri or Phaplu. The trail junction, a little east of the Surkie La, is by a crumbling mani wall and soon leads on to the high and pleasant ridge, passing through pastures. A couple of these are suitable for camping if water is still available. The holy lakes of **Panch Pokhari**, where there is a Hindu shrine, also offer good camping but from the Surkie La they would be a rapid ascent to do in one day. Finding your way out of the lakes area is a little tricky. The trail now contours in and out of numerous gullies where, if the monsoon run-off has dried up, there is no water until the Mojang

Khola/Drangka and quite a descent to the Hinku Khola. You can cross the bridge to Tashing Ongma or go up the valley to Mosom Kharka, where there's another bridge and a camping area. The trail then crosses the Hinku on temporary bridges, joining the regular route from Lukla.

Approaching Mera from the Pangum La
This is an alternative to the standard route over the Zatrwala if coming from Jiri or Phaplu or even from Lukla. Although the route from Lukla is longer, it would give useful acclimatization time. The route to the Pangum La is covered on p246; from here, just east of the pass is a trail that follows the ridge. This route is used occasionally but it is not always obvious. It joins the Lukla-Chetero La/Zatrwala approach around Chetero/Tuli Kharka.

The new trail from Shubuche
Between 1998 and 2000 a new trail was constructed from Shubuche to Kothe (Kothé) making it easier to supply Thangnak (Tagnag) from the south, and easier to enter or exit. Lyn Taylor provided the following information.

From Shubuche ask the way to the beginning of the new trail. In sections the trail is narrow and steep, difficult in rain. Nungsar, a kharka surrounded by rhododendrons and magnolia trees, is a good camping spot with water. It is a couple of hours away on a trail that winds around big spurs. It is best to stay here and plan with that in mind because the next reliable camping place, Chautra Khola, is perhaps seven hours' walk. The trail climbs switchbacks on a rocky and sometimes narrow path to a height of around 3250m before undulating through the rhododendron forest. After approximately one and a half hours there is a steep, sometimes treacherous descent to a

---

Bring your mother-in-law
Panch Pokhari (meaning five lakes) is a holy area where pilgrims gather on the holy days of Baisakh Purne and Rishi Tarpani. There are five holy lakes in the area, believed to be father, mother, two sons and a daughter-in-law. The mother pond is believed to seek sacrifices from those persons who come near it.

waterfall and landslide area, a good spot for lunch. The trail now winds around to a steep climb up stone steps. At the top of the ridge is a sign stating three hours to Chautra Khola; there is a small campsite here with enough room for perhaps three tents. Three hours of slogging and climbing does indeed bring you to a small waterfall and bridge. Approximately three minutes after crossing is a small turnoff that leads to the campsite, which has enough room for a single group. Alternatively by the waterfall there are a few small spots and some caves. From here it is approximately four hours at a group pace to the main trail from Lukla and a further three hours to Kothe.

After Mera

Some groups backtrack or head to Lukla for a quick exit. The more daring head east down the Mera La then north to reach the Khumbu via the Mingbo La (5866m/ 19,245ft; see p221), or into the Chukhung Valley via the Amphu Labtsa 5787m/ 18986ft. The trail is unmarked on the Shorong/Hinku map but descends from just before point 4919 near the lake and joins the valley floor roughly where the 270 45' line intersects the Hunku Khola. Note that the logistics of getting fully-laden porters over the Amphu Labtsa early on in the expedition are difficult. It's easier later in the trip when the majority of the supplies have been consumed and packs are lighter.

LOBUCHE (6105m/20,029ft)

This is the hardest of the trekking peaks that ordinary commercial groups attempt and while many clients attain the worthwhile false summit, very few make the real summit.

Base Camp

There are two routes to Base Camp. If you're coming down from Lobuche, where the track to Thuklha crosses the creek, stay instead on the west bank. From the first flat area, that valley ascends to the Base Camp area via a short rope pitch. To reach Base Camp without using a rope continue around the huge spur between Tsola Tso and Thukla and at the large, roughly flat area a cairned

track heads up the valley. The Base Camp is pleasant with lots of snow for water.

The climb

Good conditions and a dawn or pre-dawn start are essential. The average angle for the entire climb is not steep but there are some areas of messy seracs that require two axes, front pointing and belaying. The ridge route is sometimes easier. Many people stop at the top of the ridge thinking this is the false summit. It isn't; continue on the knife-edged ridge (groups fix a rope) to the false summit.

PARCHARMO (6273m/20,580ft)

There is some confusion over the height of Parcharmo. The height given on the Schneider maps is 6273m, the Nepal Mountaineering Association state the height to be 6187m/20,298ft and surveyors on the first expeditions calculated it to be 6318m/20,700ft. However, it's over the magic numbers 6000m and 20,000ft.

There's a reasonable view of the least difficult route up as you approach Parcharmo and from the Tashi Labtsa but a cursory glance here may lead you to underestimate the difficulties. Although of modest angle, the access to the ridge is crevassed and, further up, seracs tower. Basic equipment should include a rope (or two) with a few stakes and screws, and two tools (at least for the leader).

POKALDE/DOLMA RI (5794m/19,009ft)

When snow-free and with clear weather, the top of Pokalde is a great place to have lunch. Although below 6000m or 20,000ft, the view is reward enough for a few hours' scrambling.

East ridge route There's a splendid base camp by the lakes below the Kongma La. From this large lake pick up a small trail that leads to the small lake to the east, which isn't visible until you have climbed a bit. Then scramble over glacier-smoothed rock to a trail up the east ridge. Approaching the top of the peak the going gets more difficult and less experienced climbers may want a hand line or other help. Rather than climbing directly up it is easier to swing around the top pinnacle and approach from another side.

The north ridge route runs directly up from the Kongma La and is a little more hazardous. There are some exposed moves, requiring steady feet and nerves, that prudent climbers would not attempt solo. Safer would be to take 10m of cord, a sling harness, a couple of slings and a tool or two.

If there's no snow lying around then both routes are solid rock, but beside a section of the north ridge is an ice/snow slope that is convenient to climb with crampons and axe. If there is snow, the conditions are infinitely more variable, requiring a real rope.

OTHER TREKKING PEAKS IN THE REGION
Kongma Tse (5817m/19,084ft)
Once called Mehra, this can be climbed from either the east side or from the south. The south route from the superb camping spot below the Kongma La goes up beside the glacier, at times on slippery rocks, then continues on steep rock to the summit ridge. A rope (plus limited gear) is widely considered necessary.

Ramdung-Go (5930m/19,455ft)
This is usually climbed from the north and combined with a crossing of the Tashi Labtsa. The southern approach is long, difficult to follow and crevassed but otherwise isn't technical.

Kongde (6187m/20,298ft)
This peak is seldom attempted. It's more of a climbing than a scrambling peak and requires a stocked rock rack and bivvy gear.

Kusum Kangguru (6369m/20,895ft)
Rarely climbed, its razor ridges provide a challenge for the serious and well-prepared.

Kangchung Shar/Pyramid (6103m/20,023ft) and Kangchung Nup (6089m/19,975ft)
The twin peaks of Kangchung are eye-catching from all the high points around the Gokyo region, sticking up like islands from the surroundings. The Sherpa name means 'small mountain'. The Schneider map marks a pass between the peaks and approaching from the south is fairly straightforward up an icefall. The north side, however, is impossible, not a pass at all.

The eastern Kangchung (Shar) is, if viewed from knobby view, a steep pyramid. Camping on the col will give the best chance of success. The angle of the snow on the face changes season to season, perhaps depending on wind loading. However, expect the steepest pitch to be around 60°, and an average of 40° or so.

The west (Nup) peak is best attempted from a rock saddle south-west of Surprise Lake. This rock ridge meets the snow summit ridge and in good conditions is a fairly straightforward climb, possible to solo by the brave. The whole area is fun to explore. These peaks are not yet on the trekking or expedition peak lists.

Changri Lho (6189m/20,304ft) and pass (5690m/18667ft)
Slightly north of the Chugyima La/Tso La is another pass, one that was used for crossing with yaks until the snow level dropped. It is considerably higher, but except for variable conditions for the last 10m, is quite straightforward. The approaches are gentle although crevassed. From the Gokyo side access the glacier by skirting under the Kangchung Shar peak. On the Dzonglha side the route is lightly cairned to the glacier. From the pass itself it is possible to ascend Changri Nup (unnamed on the Schneider map). The ridge is a series of seracs and under most conditions requires some ice-climbing gear.

APPENDIX A: ITINERARIES

The preceding trail guide was deliberately not written on a 'Day 1, Day 2' basis to encourage trekkers to travel at their own pace and not stop all in the same places. Some guidelines are, however, necessary for overall planning. Overnight stops are given in the tables below.

ACCLIMATIZATION PLANNER

Awareness of the time taken for your body to acclimatize is the key to planning itineraries in this region. Although the process of acclimatization begins even at altitudes as low as Kathmandu (1400m), planning only becomes important if heading above 3000m. The usually ignored medical recommendation is that a minimum of two to three days (and better four to five days) should be taken to reach 3000m or 10,000ft, followed by a daily altitude gain of 300m or 1000ft with a rest day every 900m or 3000ft, as shown on the table below.

Some people acclimatize slower than others but you should find that your body will tolerate deviations of plus or minus approximately 300m from these figures. Larger deviations may bring on symptoms. For example, if after Night 8 at 4200m/13,779ft you spend Night 9 at 5000m, this may cause some symptoms, although sometimes a night later. Spending Night 8 at 4800m/15,748ft, however, is much less likely to bring on mild AMS especially if you stay a further night there to synchronize with the table again.

Night			Night		
	00	below 2000m/6562ft		07	3900m/12,795ft
	01	2-3000m/6562-9842ft		08	4200m/13,779ft
	02	2-3000m/6562-9842ft		09	4500m/14,764ft
	03	3000m/9842ft		10	4800m/15,748ft
	04	3300m/10,827ft		11	4800m/15,748ft
	05	3600m/11,811ft		12	5100m/16,732ft
	06	3900m/12,795ft		13	5400m/17,716ft

GETTING TO NAMCHE

	Jiri (sedate*)	Jiri (rapid)	Phaplu (medium)	Tumlingtar (sedate/medium)
01	Ktm-Jiri (bus)	Ktm-Jiri (bus)	Ktm-Phaplu§ (plane)	Ktm-Tum (plane)
02	Shivalaya	Bhandar	Jubing	Balawa
03	Bhandar	Sete (short day)	Surke	Phedi
04	Sete	Junbesi	Monjo	Sanam (long day)
05	Junbesi	Kharikhola	Namche	Bung
06	Junbesi(rest)	Chourikharka	Najing	Naji Dingma
07	Nuntala	Namche		Pangkongma
08	Kharikhola			Surke
09	Puiyan			Monjo
10	Phakding			Namche
11	Namche			

* or group pace   § overnight at Ringmo

Note that it's possible to get from Jiri to Namche in four days but only if you are extremely fit. To walk from Kathmandu to Tumlingtar takes three to four days. For Tumlingtar to Namche, whether you are fast or slow, allow 10 days.

LUKLA TO NAMCHE

The table below shows the safe rate of ascent if you have flown from Kathmandu (1400m) to Lukla (2850m). The recommended maximum altitude for each day (as laid down by AMS specialists) is indicated. Ascending above Namche in four days, which is the schedule followed by most trekking companies, has been shown to cause troublesome mild AMS in about 50% of trekkers.

	Altitude guideline*	Itinerary 1	Itinerary 2	Unwise option
01	2-3000m	Phakding/Monjo 2650m	Lukla 2850m	Phakding/Monjo
02	2-3000m	Namche 3450m	Phakding/Monjo	Namche
03	3000m	Namche	Namche	Namche
04	3300m	Namche	Namche	(higher)
05	3600m	(higher)	(higher)	

NAMCHE TO LOBUCHE/GOKYO

For acclimatization, you should spend two nights at Namche (or three if you flew to Lukla), two nights at Tengboche or similar altitude and two nights at Dingboche or Pheriche, before reaching Lobuche and attempting Kala Pattar. Note that an alternative to spending three nights at Namche is to spend just two nights there and an extra night at somewhere near Lukla.

Studies have shown that spending one night at Phakding, two nights at Namche, one at Tengboche, and two nights at Dingboche before reaching Lobuche causes mild AMS in about 50% of trekkers.

	Altitude guideline*	Itinerary 1	Itinerary 2	Itinerary 3
00	(additional night at Namche for people who flew to Lukla)			
01	3000m	Namche 3450m	Namche	Namche
02	3300m	Namche	Namche	Namche
03	3600m	Tengboche 3860m/ Khumjung 3790m	Tengboche/ Khumjung	Namche/Khumjung or Thame
04	3900m	Tengboche/Pangboche	Pheriche 4280m	Phortse/Phortse T
05	3900m	Dingboche/Pheriche	Pheriche	Dole 4040m
06	4200m	Dingboche/Pheriche	Duglha 4600m	Machermo§ 4410m
07	4500m	Lobuche 4940m	Lobuche	Gokyo 4750m
08	(day)	up Kala Pattar	up Kala Pattar	up Gokyo Ri
08	4800m	Lobuche	Lobuche	Gokyo
09	(down)	Tengboche	Pangboche	Phortse T/Namche
10	(down)	Namche	Namche	Lukla
11	(down)	Lukla	Lukla	

This acclimatization plan seems to work quite well for most people but obviously the more time spent acclimatizing, the better you will feel. Conversely if you cut out just one of the nights listed above the risk of minor altitude sickness greatly increases.

* The altitude guideline shows the fastest recommended rate of ascent.

§ or Pangka

GRAND TOUR – NAMCHE TO CHUKHUNG, LOBUCHE & GOKYO

	Itinerary 1 (long)	Itinerary 2 (short)	Itinerary 3 (reverse)
00	(additional night at Namche for people who flew to Lukla)		
01	Namche	Namche	Namche
02	Namche	Namche	Namche
03	Tengboche/Khumjung	Tengboche/Khumjung	Namche/Khumjung/Thame
04	Pangboche/Tengboche	Pangboche/Tengboche	Phortse/Phortse Tenga
05	Dingboche	Dingboche	Dole
06	Dingboche Chukhung Ri	Dingboche ↓	Machermo/Pangka ↓
07	Chukhung ↓	Lobuche Kala Pattar	Gokyo Gokyo Ri
08	Dingboche/Duglha	Lobuche	Gokyo
09	Lobuche Kala Pattar	Pangboche/Phortse ↓	Gokyo Gokyo area
10	Lobuche	Machermo/Gokyo	Gokyo
11	Pangboche/Tsho La	Gokyo	Phortse/Cho La
12	Machermo/Gokyo	Gokyo	Pheriche/Dingboche
13	Gokyo Around Gokyo	Phortse/Dole ↓	Lobuche Kala Pattar
14	Gokyo	Namche/Monjo/Phakding	Lobuche
15	Phortse/Dole	Lukla	Tengboche
16	Namche		Namche/Monjo/Phakding
17	Namche		Lukla
18	Lukla		

RETURN – NAMCHE TO JIRI OR TO THE ARUN

	Itinerary 1 (medium)	Itinerary 2 (rapid)	Itinerary 3 (sedate)	Itinerary 4 (rapid)
00	Namche	Namche	Namche	Namche
01	Surke	Puiyan	Surke	Puiyan
02	Nuntala	Trakshindo	Pangum	Shubuche
03	Junbesi	Tragdobuk	Najing Dingma	Bung
04	Kenja	Bhandar	Bung	Salpa/Thulofokte
05	Shivalaya	Jiri	Sanam	Balawa Besi
06	Jiri		Phedi	Past Tumlingtar
07			Balawa Besi	Leguwa Ghat
08			Tumlingtar	
09			Leguwa Ghat	

BHOJPUR START

00	Kathmandu	05	Phedi	10	Puiyan
01	Bhojpur	06	Gurase	11	Chaurikharka
02	Suntale	07	Sanam	12	Monjo
03	Dingla	08	Bung	13	Namche
04	Lankuwa	09	Shubuche		

APPENDIX B: HEALTH

Special thanks to Dr Helena Swinkels at CIWEC Clinic, Kathmandu for thoroughly reviewing this section, but there is of course no liability implied.

STAYING HEALTHY WHILE TREKKING

In developed countries we take for granted treated drinking water, hygienically packaged food and comprehensive sewage systems, none of which exist in the villages of Nepal. New arrivals to Asia will be lucky to escape a visit to Nepal without some form of upset stomach, although in some cases this is relatively mild and can clear up of its own accord. Trekking for a long period and in extreme conditions involves new challenges, particularly with the high altitude nature of the trek. This comprehensive section has been thoroughly researched to help you cope with these environments.

Given the high likelihood of getting sick you should be prepared with your own small personal drugs kit. Most of the drugs are prescription medicines and some are expensive; it is much less hassle to put together a kit in Kathmandu where you can buy most of them directly from a pharmacy.

DIET

The food you will eat in the mountains is generally nutritious and healthy. The diet is carbohydrate-weighted and, intriguingly, a high carbo diet seems to slightly reduce AMS. Protein comes mainly from eggs, nuts, beans and dal and on a long trek getting enough protein becomes important.

The diet is short on fibre, which comes mostly from fruits, vegetables and legumes, and many people get constipated while they are trekking. Bringing dried fruits as snacks and focusing on vegetables when ordering can help avoid this. Some people who have a tendency to constipation should bring some metamucil with them. Walking every day, breathing harder and the cold at higher altitudes all mean that you'll burn far more calories than normal. Don't be afraid to eat as much as you like! A vitamin tablet every day or two will do no harm and women may want to take an iron supplement too.

Snack frequently to avoid hypoglycaemia (getting low on energy); always carry some spare energy bars with you. Be sure to drink plenty too. Alcohol should be drunk in moderation, if at all at altitude, and while a good cup of tea or hot lemon is refreshing, drinking a good volume of fluids means drinking plain water; a glass of hot water can also be surprisingly pleasant, as can swigging icy cold mountain water.

DIARRHOEA

This is a common problem in developing countries, especially Nepal, and few trekkers escape without contracting some stomach disorder. Ideally, you should visit a good doctor for a stool test if it doesn't clear up in a few days. While trekking, however, this is impossible so some self-diagnosis may be necessary.

The causes are many, only some of which are in your control, so even people who are particularly careful still sometimes get sick. While on the trail it seems to make little difference whether you trek with an expedition-style group package or stay in lodges. Most group cooks working for the bigger agencies have completed a basic hygiene course. Their assistants, however, usually have not and the conditions under which food is prepared are far from perfect. Most lodge owners have attended basic hygiene courses, their working conditions are better and they attempt less adventurous dishes and their hygiene has improved significantly in the last decade. The last often overlooked factor is your own personal hygiene and contact with paper money and other items that harbour bacteria.

During the winter months there is much less sickness; April, May and June are probably the worst months because of the more numerous flies; even if you eat only in the best restaurants that are serious about cleanliness at this time, you may still get sick.

In Kathmandu it pays to be particularly cautious with water. The normal town supply water comes through pipes that are uncomfortably close to sewage pipes, and sometimes both are broken. Some hotels use water pumped from the ground, which is becoming increasingly contaminated too.

Many people over-react and start taking medication at the first loose stool. Diarrhoea will not normally kill you so urgent treatment is neither necessary nor always recommended. If not too troublesome it's better to wait a few days and see if it goes away on its own. Do drink lots of water and listen to your body: if you feel hungry, eat, and if you don't then take soup and light foods. If the diarrhoea is particularly severe or still troublesome after a few days and you are fairly sure what type it is you may want to treat it. Unless the diarrhoea is particularly severe there is no need to stop trekking

The bugs that cause diarrhoea can be divided into a few categories: parasites (amoebas and giardia which travel as cysts), bacteria and viruses. Giardia and amoebic dysentery are caused by a protozoan that survives outside the gut in a tough protective shell, and are vulnerable to similar drugs. Similarly the many different bacteria that cause bacterial diarrhoea are all killed by a separate class of drugs. Surprisingly the exact cause of over 20% of cases of diarrhoea is as yet unknown. So first decide if the diarrhoea fits one of the descriptions then consider whether you want to treat it. Even when treating with drugs you can expect only about an 80% chance of being cured rapidly. If the drugs don't work then the diarrhoea will normally clear by itself with time.

Precautions

There are two basic schools of thought: one is that you may be able to avoid an upset stomach if you are extremely careful. This involves only drinking purified/boiled/bottled water (including for brushing your teeth), avoiding salads and other uncooked food and only eating fruit that you have peeled. Only eat meat that has been well cooked. Eat only with cutlery (not your hands), and off plates and glasses that were served dry. Wash your hands carefully or, better still, use the water-free hand cleaning gels. You should only eat in the best restaurants in Kathmandu. This can be an appropriate strategy for a shorter visit, but even taking all of these precautions you still might get sick.

For a stay of more than a few days in Kathmandu, though, this becomes impractical but it would still be a good idea to eat salads sparingly, use only purified/boiled/bottled water, and eat at the cleaner-looking restaurants.

If trekking with an expedition-style kitchen crew, the sirdar or leader should give a good pre-trek hygiene briefing to the crew and regularly check that the kitchen is clean. Many less educated Nepalis don't realise that there are germs that you can't see. Towels should be cleaned regularly or everything air-dried. The best solution is the new gel hand cleaners that don't require any water but don't expect the trekking company to provide it.

Once you are hit

Take it easy and drink oral dehydration solutions or less fizzy soft drinks. Some people subscribe to the idea that your should 'starve' diarrhoea. From a scientific point of view this is wrong, though if you do feel like eating, do so in moderation; if you don't feel like eating, then don't – but do drink enough. Certainly plain food seems easier on the stomach, but that doesn't mean you should limit yourself to bananas, toast or plain rice, just avoid food that is spicy or oily. Occasionally if you're afflicted with a stomach bug, eating or drinking will induce an immediate run to the bathroom. Don't worry about this, it is a normal reaction and if you eat after this, normally your body will accept food.

Stoppers

All the drugs that fix the root cause of diarrhoea are prescription medicines so doctors commonly hand out Imodium or Loperamide (Lomitil), drugs that simply stop you up, but don't fix the root cause. These drugs can be useful if you need to take a long bus journey but in a lot of cases by following the instructions, you might be stopped up for a week. So either avoid them or use them carefully. Don't use them in case of dysentery (diarrhoea with blood and mucus in it).

Travellers'/bacterial diarrhoea

If you are new to Asia you will have to be lucky to escape a bout of "Travellers' diarrhoea". The onset is often preceded or accompanied by a fever and/or chills, nausea and cramps followed by fairly sudden, frequent, watery diarrhoea. It is this reasonably sudden onset that distinguishes a bacterial diarrhoea from others. Sometimes people feel off-colour for a day, usually with a light fever or chills; then only a day or so later, the diarrhoea strikes.

The cause is usually eating food or drinking water that is contaminated with strains of bacteria different to those that your body is used to, or simply plain nasty bacteria, and is responsible for roughly 80% of diarrhoea cases in Nepal. It could be from flies, dirty money, your own habits, the cooks' habits, dirty water, a less than spotless kitchen – there a multitude of possibilities.

Treatment The sooner you take drugs, the quicker you will be better – assuming that you do actually have a bacterial diarrhoea. And this is the reason to consider taking drugs to cure it. The alternative is to wait for your body to fight it off: the diarrhoea should lessen in a few days, and after another few, be gone. Occasionally if you are weakened or at high altitudes bacterial diarrhoea can take a long time, 7-10 days, to go away by itself. The most effective treatment is to begin a short course of Norfloxacin or Ciprofloxacin.

Dosages For Norfloxacin, 400mg, every 12 hours, for 3 days. For Ciprofloxacin, 500mg every 12 hours for 3 days. In most cases you will begin to feel better in around 12 hours, and should be back to normal after perhaps 24-36 hours. If you are not better after 36 hours then you don't have bacterial diarrhoea (or the bacteria was drug-resistant).

It is possible to use these drugs prophylactically but while this strategy can work against bacterial diarrhoeas, as with all drugs longer term use often has real side effects and so is not recommended except in special cases.

Food poisoning

Symptoms 'I don't feel so good' or turning white and then 'uh-oh, I need the bathroom **now**'. This comes on suddenly and severely about two to eight hours after eating contaminated food. It is more usual to vomit repeatedly first then sometimes spout both ends but occasionally it can be explosive diarrhoea only. Often it strikes at night; you'll be thankful if you have an attached bathroom. Luckily, the misery usually lasts 4-12 hours and recovery is quick, though you will probably feel weakened.

The classic cause is pre-cooked food that has been infected when allowed to sit. It is also sometimes thought to be from contamination in the fluffy egg-white-based cake icings. Sometimes it can strike all the eaters of a meal, but sometimes only one person is affected, ie there is only one small area of contamination on the food.

Food poisoning is not an infection of the body so there are no drugs that can help – the body just has to eject all the contaminated food and rid itself of the toxin. Resting and drinking plenty of fluids helps. Oral rehydration solutions and soft drinks (shaken after opening to reduce the fizz) are helpful.

Irritated bowels

The payback for eating chilli the night before is to wake up early the next morning for a long dump; once the offending chillies are flushed out, however, relief quickly follows. Rich curry gravies, too, are made with plenty of ghee or oil that sometimes lubricates the bowls rather too well, especially with a few too many lagers.

There are many other causes for mildly irritated bowels that can cause some uncomfortableness or diarrhoea. Many drugs, even the ones to fix diarrhoea, can cause loose stools. A change in diet, time zones and stress all can affect your body unpredictably.

After a bout of diarrhoea has ended, whether by drugs or by time, your system can still be sensitive, gassy and not particularly regular for quite a period afterwards. In other words if you are back to defecating roughly once a day but your movement isn't quite normal, don't, in general, worry. Sometimes staying off coffee helps.

Giardia

This generally takes 7-10 days to develop and does not come on suddenly. The classic often-quoted symptoms are sulphurous (rotten egg) smelling farts and burps but this does not necessarily mean giardia: these are just as common in bacterial infections and are therefore not useful whatsoever in coming to a diagnosis.

Distinguishing symptoms are a churning, upset stomach, bloating, cramps, and on-off diarrhoea. Nausea (without vomiting) and fatigue are normal. There is usually no fever, chills or vomiting. Frequently the sickness follows a pattern: an uncomfortable stomach or mild diarrhoea after food, often in the morning, for a few days, followed by a day or two of feeling relatively better. This pattern alternates, sometimes with a bit of constipation in between, but gradually the trend is to worsening symptoms.

Giardia can also be virtually symptomless: just a slightly rumbling stomach with occasional soft stools or even constipation. Some forms may go away on their own after several weeks but treatment is usually required. If you have been in Nepal (or India) for less than a week, then it is extremely unlikely you have giardia.

Giardia is caught from infected water, especially from washing salads in Kathmandu and from high mountain streams near areas where yaks graze.

Treatment There's a choice of two drugs: **Tinidazole** (Tiniba), of which the dose is 2 grams, ie 4 x 500mg, taken all at once. It's better taken in the evening because the usual side effects (nausea and a strong metallic taste in the mouth) may be slept off. Do not mix with alcohol: other medications in this class of drug are used to get alcoholics off. Take the same dose again 24 hours later.

Alternatively **Flagyl/Metronidazole** may be used but is harder on the body. The dose is 250mg, three times a day for 5 to 7 days. This should also not be mixed with alcohol.

Amoebic diarrhoea

Amoebic infection usually has similar symptoms to giardia, with a low grade diarrhoea alternating with days of being normal or even constipated – symptoms that can almost, but not quite be ignored. Fatigue and weight loss are common over time. Most infections with amoeba are actually without symptoms, but the illness can vary greatly in severity – though the sudden onset of bloody diarrhoea, like some bad bacterial diarrhoeas, is rare. It can also be dormant for a time and recur months later. Only about 1% of all diarrhoea cases are caused by amoeba. Amoebas are easily confused with other things that are commonly found in diarrhoea and so is highly overdiagnosed at most clinics in Nepal (except CIWEC!). You will often be recommended to take treatment for amoebic infection (Tinidazole 2g daily on each of three days) by drug store owners and doctors, even though it is unlikely that you have it. Proven infection needs to be followed by a second medication called Dilamide to completely clear it from the system.

Viral diarrhoea

At least 10% of diarrhoea is caused by viruses. Similar to the common cold, drugs can't fix the root problem, instead your body just has to fight it, and after a couple of days you should begin to feel better and after perhaps five days it should have cleared up.

Cyclospora

Any diarrhoea between April and September that doesn't clear up with the above drugs could be cyclospora. You should consult a doctor in Nepal. The cure is cotrimoxazole.

WATER PURIFICATION

Part of avoiding diarrhoea is drinking clean water. All water from taps, streams and rivers in Nepal (even at high altitudes) could be contaminated to some degree and should not be considered safe to drink without purification. Only spring water and water made from clean snow is safe without being treated. There are several methods of purifying water but first it helps to know who your enemies are. The most difficult to kill of the various pathogens are the cysts that cause cyclospora, giardia and amoebic dysentery; even just one or two cysts can cause disease. These can survive in very cold water for several months and can even survive when the water freezes. High concentrations of chemicals are required to penetrate their protective shell. They are, however, killed immediately by bringing water to the boil. Bacteria and viruses are less resilient. Larger numbers are needed before infection occurs and they are destroyed by very low concentrations of chemicals.

Boiling

Water that has been brought to the boil, even at 5000m/16,404ft, is safe to drink. It need only be pasteurized (heating to 75°C/162F or 68°C for 10 minutes), not sterilized (boiling for 10 minutes). At 5800m/19,000ft water boils at around 81°C/177°F so hot drinks, like tea, coffee and hot lemon etc, are all safe.

Iodine-based methods

Iodine tablets The active ingredient is tetraglycine hydroperiodide. If the water is very cold allow 30 minutes rather than the usual 10; if it is cloudy double the dose (ie 2 tablets per litre). These tablets are convenient and easy to use but only sometimes available in Kathmandu. The recommendation for water that is possibly giardia-contaminated is two tablets per litre, but I have never met anyone who has got giardia while using only one tablet. The two main brand names are: Potable Aqua and Coghlan's Drinking Water Tablets.

Polar Pure This method relies on dissolving a small amount of iodine directly in water. It is effective and cheap. The iodine crystals come in a glass bottle with a system to prevent the crystals from falling out of the bottle and there's a temperature sensitive strip on the side to determine the dose needed.

Betadine/Povidone This method uses a non-iodine based molecule to bind free iodine. For a 10% solution use 8 drops per litre of water. If the water is 20°C wait 15 minutes before drinking; if very cold, one hour.

Lugol's Iodine Solution Unless purchased in the West, the solutions come in different concentrations that are often not indicated on the bottle: the solution could be 2%, 4% or 8%. In addition, the free iodine (the active ingredient) is dissolved in potassium iodide so the total amount of iodine consumed is much higher than necessary. However, if you have no choice, it's definitely better than nothing. For 2% solution use 5 drops per litre of water and leave for 15 minutes before drinking. If the water is very cold, or cloudy, then it should be left 30 minutes or 10 drops should be used.

Iodine solutions are messy, so put the bottle in several plastic bags, and the iodine (except Betadine) should be kept only in a glass bottle.

Chlorine-based methods

Sierra Water Purifier This uses super-chlorination, a high dose of chlorine that is later neutralized by adding hydrogen peroxide. It is effective.

Chlorine based tablets (Steritabs, Puritabs) If used alone, they aren't effective against giardia. However if used with a fine filter (to remove the giardia), half a tablet is adequate. Note that standard **Micropur** tablets are not effective for trekking conditions. Having said that I have met trekkers that have used only Steritabs or Micropur and none have got sick. There's also a new system called **Pristine** which is chlorine dioxide based. It needs to be mixed and left to sit for five minutes before being added to the water and is therefore a bit finicky. After adding to the water, it needs to be left for 30 minutes. It leaves no aftertaste and claims to be effective against protozoa including giardia and cryptosporidium (but no word on cyclospora).

Water filters

There is quite a variety on the market. Follow the manufacturer's instructions carefully, especially with regard to cleaning and maintenance. Filtering water requires more effort than many methods but if you can develop the habit it's a good method for longer trips. The drawbacks with filters are that they can freeze plus their size, weight and cost. Also, most filters are not considered adequate for removing viruses from the water and therefore should be used only in conjunction with chemical methods.

Using bottled water

This can be obtained along the trail almost everywhere. Because it must be carried in, its price rises dramatically. The leftover bottles are also unsightly and difficult to dispose of so using purifying methods or buying boiled water is a far better solution.

ALTITUDE AND AMS – ACUTE MOUNTAIN SICKNESS

Going to high and extreme altitudes is exceptionally hard on the body and it is a testament to the complex adaptability of body chemistry that humans can usually survive the experience.

Commonly called altitude sickness, AMS can affect all trekkers in Lukla and above. It's caused by going up too fast to high altitude and can be fatal if the warning signals are ignored. Your body needs time to adjust to the smaller quantity of oxygen that is present in the air at altitude and this involves dramatic changes in your body chemistry. At 5500m/18,044ft the air pressure is approximately half that at sea level, so there is half the amount of oxygen (and nitrogen) in it (see table below). For treks below an altitude of about 2500m/8000ft, AMS is not normally a problem.

Altitude sickness is preventable. Go up slowly, giving your body enough time to adjust. The 'safe' rates of ascent for 95% of trekkers involve spending 2-3 nights between 2000m/c6500ft and 3000m/c10,000ft before going higher. From 3000m you should sleep at an average of 300m/c1000ft higher each night with a rest day approximately every 900m/c3000ft. These rates are marked on the sample itineraries on p273. Be aware of the symptoms of AMS and only ascend if you are symptom-free.

The process of adapting to higher altitudes is called **acclimatization**. Firstly, you want to go up at a pace slow enough that you acclimatize and not get altitude sickness. Secondly, the longer you stay at altitude, the more you acclimatize and the stronger you become.

Note that the altitudes attained while trekking in the Khumbu are more extreme than virtually anywhere else, requiring a more cautious approach than, for example, skiing at 3000m/c10,000ft in Colorado, USA.

❏ Barometric pressure table

Altitude	mmHG	Pressure	O₂ sat
Sea level	760	100%	99%
1000m/3281ft	670	88%	
2500m/8202ft	554	73%	
3000m/9843ft	520	68%	93%
3500m/11,483ft	489	64%	
4000m/13,123ft	460	60%	88%
4500m/14,764ft	431	57%	
5000m/16,404ft	404	53%	80%
5500m/18,044ft	380	50% *	
6000m/19,685ft	356	47%	75%
7000m/22,966ft	314	41%	
8000m/26,247ft	277	36%	
8848m/29,028ft	249	33% **	

* (Kala Pattar) ** (Everest)
Pressure is the air pressure relative to sea level

O₂ sat is the average level of oxygen saturation in the blood at rest. Readings +/- 5% are still within the normal range.

NORMAL SYMPTOMS

Don't expect to feel perfect at altitudes of more than 3000m. These are the normal altitude symptoms that you should expect but **not** worry about. Every trekker will experience some or all of these, no matter how slowly they ascend.

● Periods of sleeplessness
● The need for more sleep than normal, often 10 hours or more
● Occasional loss of appetite
● Vivid, wild dreams especially at around 2500-3800m in altitude
● Unexpected momentary shortness of breath, day and night
● Periodic breathing
● The need to rest/catch your breath frequently while trekking, especially above 4000m
● runny nose
● beer and soft drinks don't taste so good until you have been at altitude for a long time
● Increased urination while moving to/at higher altitudes – a good sign

Many people have trouble sleeping in a new environment, especially if it changes every day. Altitude adds to the problems by inducing periodic breathing (see further on) and the decrease of oxygen means that some trekkers experience wild dreams. This often happens at Namche, on the way up. You need to sleep well most nights so ensure you are warm enough – a hot water bottle is luxurious – and if you have persistent problems certainly consider taking some drugs. When you are ascending day after day there comes a point where suddenly you pee an unexpectedly large volume and many times and every night you have to pee a few times. After this you find water moves thru you quickly. This is your body making changes and is an excellent sign that you are adapting to altitude. At Gokyo, Sean from Canada's record was 18 times in one day. A really large pee will be almost a litre! If you are ascending and are not peeing more than normal you need to drink more. After you have stayed at the same altitude for a day or longer or begin descending this extra urination stops.

MILD AMS SYMPTOMS – NEVER GO HIGHER!

Many trekkers in the high valleys of the Khumbu get mild AMS; admit or acknowledge that you are having symptoms. You need have only one of the following symptoms to be getting altitude sickness.

Mild symptoms

● **Headaches** are very common among trekkers. A headache is usually frontal, all over or simply all-round pressure, and often comes on during the evening, remaining into the night until you fall asleep. Raising your head and shoulders while trying to sleep sometimes offers partial relief. Ensure you have drunk enough fluids and then consider taking something for it. At the point of getting mild AMS a slight headache may come and go, sensitive to the difference between exercising and rest, or even simply breathing less or more.
● **Nausea** can occur without other symptoms but usually develops with a bad headache. If you are better in the morning, take a rest day; if you still feel bad after breakfast descend.
● **Lightheadedness** or mild dizziness If this occurs while walking, stop out of the sun and have a rest and a drink. Stay at the closest teahouse.
● **Appetite-loss** or generally feeling bad is common at altitude after too rapid an ascent.
● **Sleeplessness** or generally feeling lazy
● **Dry raspy cough** This may sometimes be painful, use throat lozenges.

In other words, anything other than diarrhoea or a sore throat could be altitude sickness and you should assume that it is. If, for example, your headache is due to dehydration ascending further is not dangerous but if it's due to AMS the consequences could be serious. You cannot tell the difference so caution is the safest course. Don't try to deceive yourself. Accept that you body needs more time to adapt. The basic AMS rule is: **Never go higher with mild symptoms**.

> **If Mild AMS doesn't go away**
> If mild AMS symptoms continue descent for a few hours may be more beneficial than staying at the same altitude. The following case is a good example. A climber bound for Island Peak experienced mild AMS in Pheriche (4280m/14,042ft) and wisely decided not to go higher. Three days later he had improved and continued to Chukhung (4750m/15,584ft). Here, his mild AMS returned and he was advised to go down to Dingboche (4350m/14,271ft) for the rest of the day. On arrival, he immediately felt better, had lunch and for good measure spent the rest of the day by the bridge below Dingboche. He returned to Chukhung late that day, had the best sleep since Lukla and suffered no problems the next night at the Base Camp (5150m/16,896ft).

What to do about mild AMS symptoms

There are two basic choices: the natural way and the drug way.

● **The natural way** If you find mild symptoms developing while walking, stop and relax (with your head out of the sun) and drink some fluids. Drink frequently.

● **The drug way** If mild symptoms develop while walking, stop have a rest, drink some fluids and take 125-250mg Diamox. Diamox generally takes one to four hours to begin alleviating symptoms. Drink more water and consider staying close by.

If symptoms develop in the evening take 125-250mg Diamox and drink plenty of fluids. If you have a headache/nausea perhaps take some Ibuprofen. Be prepared to make many toilet journeys or obtain a pee bottle. If symptoms partially go away but are still annoying it is safe to take another 250mg Diamox 6-8 hours later. If similar symptoms return consider taking 125-250mg of Diamox every 12 hours until you begin descending in sleeping altitude.

In both cases If the symptoms (including a headache) do not go away completely then stay at the same altitude. If symptoms get worse, go down. Even a small loss of elevation (100m/328ft or so) can make a big difference to how you feel and how you sleep. You should descend to the last place where you felt fine.

If symptoms develop at night then, unless they rapidly get worse, wait them out and see how you feel in the morning. If the symptoms have not gone after breakfast then have a rest day or descend. If they have gone, you should still consider having a rest day or at least only an easy day's walking. Continued ascent is likely to bring back the symptoms.

Note that there can be a time lag between arriving at altitude and the onset of symptoms. In fact, statistically it is just as common to suffer mild symptoms on the second night of staying at the same altitude.

Altitude sickness must be reacted to when symptoms are mild: going higher will definitely make it worse. You trek to enjoy, not to feel sick.

SERIOUS AMS SYMPTOMS – IMMEDIATE DESCENT

● **Persistent, severe headache**
● **Persistent vomiting**
● **Ataxia** – loss of co-ordination, an inability to walk in a straight line, making the sufferer look drunk.
● **Mental confusion and/or hallucinations**
● **Losing consciousness** – inability to stay awake or understand instructions.
● **Liquid sounds in the lungs**
● **Very persistent, sometimes watery, cough**
● **Difficulty breathing**
● **Rapid breathing or feeling breathless at rest.**
● **Coughing clear fluid, pink phlegm or blood (a very bad sign)**
● **Severe lethargy/fatigue**
● **Marked blueness of face and lips**
● **High resting heartbeat** – over 130 beats per minute.
● **Mild symptoms rapidly getting worse**

Ataxia is the single most important sign for recognizing the progression of cerebral AMS from mild to serious. This is easily tested by trying to walk in a straight line, heel to toe and should be compared with somebody who has no symptoms. Twelve hours after the onset of ataxia a coma is possible, followed by death, unless you descend. Take note of the second basic AMS rule: **Immediate and fast descent with serious symptoms.**

That is the basic rule but here are more details. Firstly, remain calm. If there is a doctor consult them first and show them this guide. If there is bottled oxygen available use before descending or, if they are unconscious, while descending. If there is a PAC bag (see below), use this for at least an hour before descending.

If far away from expert care and these tools consider carefully which type of AMS – HACE or HAPE (see below) – give the appropriate drug treatment and begin descending. The patient must be taken as far down as possible, even if it is the middle of the night. Ensure the descent party is well equipped and there are enough people to carry the patient if they collapse since his or her condition may get worse before getting better. Exercise makes HAPE worse: carry the person. Later the patient must rest and see a doctor, even if well recovered. People with serious symptoms may not be able to think for themselves and may say they feel OK. They are not.

If you are at or above Lobuche head to the Pyramid. If at Chukhung or higher, or Thukla or Dingboche or Dzonglha head to the Pheriche HRA post, if open, otherwise head further down. Ask at the Gompa Lodge in Upper Pangboche (ask for Namka) or the Rhododendron lodge in Deboche. Note that the HRA and Khunde doctors are frequently called out to sick people. Normally their first action is to get them back to the clinic where there is light and all the tools. So if you are considering calling a doctor out, it may be wiser to begin descending towards the clinic first. If at Gokyo, head down to Dole Yeti Inn and the PAC bag there. In all cases you have to pay for services.

Medical conditions at altitude

● **High Altitude Cerebral Edema (HACE)** This is a build-up of fluid around the brain. It causes the first five symptoms on the mild and severe lists previously. Coma from HACE can occur in as little as 12 hours from the onset of symptoms, but normally takes 1-3 days to develop. At the first sign of ataxia begin treatment with medication, oxygen and descent. Usually 4 to 8mg of dexamethasone is given as a first dose, then 4mg every 6 hours, Diamox every 12 hours and 2-4l/min oxygen. Descent is necessary, but a PAC Bag will be often be used first if available. This can make an unsteady, uncooperative, difficult to manage patient into one that is more able to assist in his own evacuation. An O_2 sat reading is an unreliable indicator of HACE.

What happens if you ascend too quickly?

Many people say that the 300m a day guideline is too cautious; some people consider 500m a day more realistic. Certainly a few people can handle 500m a day, but many people cannot – a very few cannot even handle 300m a day. Consider this French group. They followed this itinerary on the advice of a less than professional Kathmandu trekking company.

Night stops at: Kathmandu (1400m), Namche (3450m), Tengboche (3860m), Dingboche (4350m), Lobuche (4940m), the HRA Pheriche clinic. On reaching Lobuche the group immediately turned back: 3 out of 12 had cerebral edema (HACE) that would have killed them if it wasn't for the HRA doctors, and two still had to be helicopter evacuated. The rest came down with moderate AMS (not mild) but felt better at the Pheriche clinic after taking Diamox. Nobody made it up Kala Pattar.

Using a portable altitude chamber

Increasingly trekking companies/groups rent a PAC/Gamow/CERTEC bag and occasionally there is nobody trained in their use. Each of these is basically a large plastic tube that you can put someone in then pump up the pressure thereby simulating a lower altitude. Used properly they are very effective. For moderately severe HAPE/HACE one or two one-hour sessions may be enough; for more severe cases, longer periods or more sessions will be required.

If there are instructions, follow them; the PAC bag has instructions printed on the side. Briefly:

● Pumping up and releasing the pressure should be done slowly, patients may need time to equalize their ear drums: when pumping up they can hold their nose and blow, when deflating the bag, swallow with the mouth wide open.
● With severe HAPE use a sloping surface, the head being 30-40cms higher.
● Put a sleeping bag in with the patient, or if in the sun, shield the bag.
● Maintain eye contact and communication.
● Pump regularly otherwise CO_2 can build up to dangerous levels in the bag.
● Never sit on the bag.

● **High Altitude Pulmonary Edema (HAPE)** This is an accumulation of fluid in the lungs and is very serious. It is responsible for all the other mild and serious symptoms and it is often accompanied by a mild fever. By far the best treatment is oxygen at 4 litres a minute but PAC bag treatment is a good substitute. If there is no oxygen or a PAC bag then descent will be life saving. Drugs are of limited necessity in HAPE because oxygen and descent are such effective treatments. However, if oxygen is unavailable and descent is delayed, it is reasonable to give 10mg of regular (fast-acting) Nifedipine (swallow the gel capsule intact) or, if unavailable, Nifedipine 30mg slow-release tablets; in both cases, descend as soon as possible. Asthma medications (Salbutamol, Ventolin, Asthalin) help in mild cases although this has not been studied in detail. It is common to suffer some HACE as well so Diamox should be given. It is far more common for serious HAPE to strike while sleeping so with mild HAPE during the day descent or treatment is essential. HAPE patients have low O_2 sat readings. Administering medication and waiting for a helicopter is **not** adequate treatment.

Before much was known about AMS, HAPE was often misdiagnosed as pneumonia and since the treatment was antibiotics rather than descent, most people died.

While the symptoms of AMS are usually clear, occasionally the symptoms don't follow the usual pattern or other problems show up in conjunction. This could be because of complications or in rare cases, it is not altitude sickness at all. The patient may have suffered a heart attack, a stroke, a blood clot in the lungs or kidney failure and there are many other possibilities.

● **Periodic breathing (Cheyne-Stokes respiration)** Less oxygen in the blood affects the body's breathing mechanism. While at rest or sleeping your body seems to feel the need to breathe less and less, to the point where suddenly you require some deep breaths to recover. This cycle can be a few breaths long, in which after a couple breaths you miss a breath completely. Alternatively it may be a gradual cycle over a minute, appearing as if your breathing rate simply goes up and down regularly. It is experienced by most trekkers at Namche, although many people are unaware of it while asleep. At 5000m/16,404ft virtually all trekkers experience periodic breathing, although it is troublesome for only a few. Studies have so far found no direct link to AMS.

If periodic breathing wakes you sometimes during the night seriously consider Diamox an hour before bed; this usually works very effectively.

● **Swelling of the hands, feet, face and lower abdomen** An HRA study showed that about 18% of trekkers experience some swelling, usually minor, and women are more susceptible. It is a sign that you are not acclimatizing as well as you could, but is not a cause for concern unless the swelling is severe. Continued cautious ascent is OK. Rings should be removed. People who have experienced swelling should not push themselves hard on the trail.

● **Altitude immune suppression** At base camp altitudes, cuts and infections heal very slowly. You body is unaffected in its ability to fight viral infections but is much more susceptible to bacterial infections. For serious infections, especially bronchitis, descent to Namche level is recommended.

● **High Altitude Flatulence Expulsion (HAFE)** This is commonly known as HAF (High Altitude Farts). The cure – let it rip! You're not a balloon that needs blowing up.

Re-ascent after severe AMS
This entails risk, but is not impossible; you should discuss carefully with an AMS-experienced doctor.

Useful drugs at altitude
● **Diamox (Acetazolamide)** This is a mild diuretic (leads to increased urination) that acidifies the blood to stimulate breathing. It also reduces cerebrospinal fluid formation. Often, it is not recommended to take it as a prophylactic (ie to prevent AMS, before you have symptoms) unless you ascend rapidly, unavoidably (eg flying to a high altitude – Lhasa, for example – or on a rescue mission), or unless you have experienced undue altitude problems previously. However there is no harm in taking it as a prophylactic. Once you have some troublesome symptoms it is a good drug to take.

It is a sulfa drug derivative, and people allergic to this class of drugs should not take Diamox (sulfa allergy is uncommon). You could test your reaction to this at home prior to being in the mountains. The normal side effects are increased urination (you should drink more when this happens), and tingling sensations in the lips, fingers or toes but these symptoms are not an indication to stop the drug. In rare cases it causes a rash or other allergic symptoms and it can soften the eyeball to the point that vision is affected. In that case don't take Diamox again.It can ruin the taste of beer and soft drinks. It should not be used at the same time as full-strength aspirin (this also acidifies the blood slightly).

The recommendations are to carry Diamox and consider using it if you experience mild but annoying symptoms, especially periodic breathing if it continually wakes you up. The dosage for prevention and treatment of mild symptoms is 125-250mg every 12 hours until you descend in sleeping altitude or after 2 days at the same altitude. For aiding sleep try 125mg about an hour before going to bed. It is not necessary to take it in the morning as well, although Diamox does appear to assist more effectively if taken for several days. In case of real altitude sickness and HACE the exact effective dosages have not been established so the guideline is as follows: the sicker you are, the bigger the dose you should consider taking. This could be up to 500mg three times a day.

Diamox actually goes to the root of the problem, it does not simply hide the problem. So if you feel better, you are better. However this does not mean that you can ascend at a faster rate than normal, or ignore altitude sickness symptoms since it is quite possible to still develop AMS while taking Diamox. If you are experiencing altitude sickness problems the further away you are from medical care, the sooner you should consider beginning Diamox. Note that if you are going high rapidly then Diamox can be used to best effect by beginning a course 24 hours before. If you are already at altitude and are going to take a large jump in sleeping altitude, ie greater than 600m, Diamox begun one day before should help significantly.

● **Gingko biloba** Two controlled trials revealed that Gingko at 80-120mg a day begun before going to altitude and continued at altitude reduced the incidence of AMS. It also assisted circulation to the extremities. The mechanism of how it works is not understood and while it does help some people, subjectively Diamox seems to be slightly better. More work is needed on this. Many people believe that homeopathic/ayurvedic/herbal medicines are somehow different from the other drugs listed here. Remedies are still drugs; remember that Aspirin comes from willow bark.

● **Dexamethasone (Decadron/Dexasone)** This is a potent steroid but taken for periods of only a day or two has few side effects. It should only be used in treatment and should **not** be used prophylactically, ie to prevent AMS before it happens. It does not aid in acclimatization and therefore there is a potential rebound effect, ie once the drug wears off, you may feel worse than before, particularly if you haven't descended in the meantime.

● **Aspirin (Dispirin/Bufferin/Ascriptin/Ecotrin)** The usual dose is one to two 325mg to 500mg tablets every six hours (to a maximum of 8 per day). In some countries 650mg tablets are also available and only one is taken at a time. Even small amounts reduce the ability of the blood to clot, useful on extreme altitude expeditions where dangerous blood clots can occur. Aspirin reduces inflammation of the joints, a common affliction among long distance trekkers. It can also reduce fevers, although doesn't fix the underlying problem. Plain aspirin is hard on the stomach lining but most preparations add a buffer to minimize this. It is, however, still better taken with food. It should not be taken at the same time as Diamox.

● **Ibuprofen (Advil, Nurofen, Motrin, Nuprin, Midol)** Tablets come in 200mg, 400mg or 600mg. The maximum daily allowance is 2400mg, usually divided into four or five doses. This is probably the best drug for tendonitis and inflammation of joints. It is also considered the best drug for high altitude headaches. It also decreases fever.

● **Naproxen (Aleve, Naprosyn)** The usual dose is 220mg. It is similar to Ibuprofen but its effects are longer lasting so you need only one tablet for 12 hours or more of relief. No studies have been conducted about how well it works for altitude headaches but it is probably less effective than Aspirin or Ibuprofen.

● **Acetaminophen (Tylenol Paracetamol, Panadol)** The usual dose is one to two 325-500mg tablets up to four times a day and it can be combined with Ibuprofen or Aspirin. It is a good painkiller (but doesn't reduce inflammation) and has fewer side effects than anti-inflammatories like Aspirin. It reduces fevers, although it does not fix the cause of the fever It should not be used by people who regularly consume more than about three alcoholic drinks a day.

● **Nifedipine** comes in two forms, quick-acting gel capsules and the more normal slow release small tablets (Nifed, Adulat, Retard). For HAPE the capsules are preferable and the dose is 10 mg, swallowed whole. If the person is still sick another 10mg can be taken 1 hour later and then every 4-6 hours. If only the slow-acting form is available the dose is 20-30mg, and this is effective for approximately 12 hours. Nifedipine should only be taken if no other treatment is available for HAPE. Smaller doses can be useful for warming up fingers or toes in an extreme situation, providing your core is warm and you are exercising.

● **Sleeping tablets** The majority of sleeping tablets depress the breathing instinct and the effect on trekkers at altitude has not been studied in depth so generally they are not recommended. Also tablets can leave you drowsy the next day. Identifying the cause of the sleep

Aspirin, Ibuprofen and Naproxen – caution
At altitude many people end up taking far more drugs than normal. Aspirin, Ibuprofen and Naproxen are all related drugs (and therefore should not be mixed) and because of the way they work they are hard on the stomach and so are better taken with a snack, meal or at least a drink. They should not be taken continuously for extended periods, ie more than a week without consulting a doctor to help determine what is causing the problem and to discuss potential side effects. If a lower strength tablet works, take a lower strength.

problem, such as periodic breathing or aches and pains from trekking, may mean taking Diamox or Ibuprofen is a sensible and effective option.

The acclimatization process

When you move to a higher altitude your body quickly realises that there is less oxygen available and its first reaction is to get you to hyperventilate (breathe more). More oxygen (O_2) is inhaled but more carbon dioxide (CO_2) is breathed out and with the O_2-CO_2 balance upset the pH of the blood is altered. Your body determines how deeply to breathe by the pH level (mainly the dissolved CO_2 in your blood). If you exercise hard at sea level, your muscles produce large amounts of CO_2 so you breathe hard and fast. While resting, your body is using little energy so little CO_2 is produced. When this balance is upset your body may believe that it needs to breathe less than it really does. Over several days it tries to correct this imbalance by disposing of bicarbonate (carbon dioxide in water) in the urine. (Since it's not very soluble you need to drink plenty.) Diamox assists by allowing the kidneys to do this more efficiently thereby enhancing many people's ability to acclimatize. In addition, after a day or two, the body moves some fluid out of the blood thus increasing the haemoglobin concentration. After several days more new red blood cells are released than normal. A changed blood pH also affects how oxygen sticks on the red blood and other chemical changes take place to compensate for this.

Intentional hyperventilation, ie consciously breathing harder for several minutes is potentially harmful. Less oxygen is the main reason the body needs to adapt, but less air pressure alone also has effects on the body.

Rates of acclimatization

Individual rates of acclimatization are dependent on how fast your body reacts to compensate for the altered pH level of the blood. For slow starters Diamox provides a good kickstart but for people already adapting well its effect is minimal.

Interestingly it is this reaction of breathing more when there is less oxygen (Hypoxic Ventilatory Response: HVR) that is most important initially; being fit or having a higher lung capacity has nothing to do with it. A quicker reaction (ie higher HVR) means that while ascending you will feel better – acclimatize more quickly – and feel stronger than someone whose reaction is slower. However once you are acclimatized, ie stayed at a similar altitude for 3-7 days then overall fitness matters and the fitter will be stronger. So people who do not acclimatize easily may still perform well at altitude if given time.

Your HVR is mainly genetic but importantly the mega-fit, ie marathon runners and people who train regularly for long periods at a similar work rate, have a depressed/blunted HVR, often very significantly, and can have a tough time acclimatizing initially. In some cases pushing yourself harder and using a stop-start pattern can assist in developing a lower HVR. In other cases pushing hard can be detrimental, in the worst cases bring on HAPE.

Sherpas have genetic adaptation to altitude but they can still get sick. Sherpas who live in Kathmandu occasionally get AMS upon returning to the Khumbu. Studies have shown that people who live at moderate altitudes (1000m-2000m/3281ft-6562ft) are acclimatized to those altitudes. They are much less susceptible to AMS when ascending to around 3000m/9842ft (ie going to Namche). However the benefits decrease once higher and they should follow the same acclimatization programme as others.

Trekkers who fly from sea level to Kathmandu and then almost immediately fly to Lukla are more likely to suffer AMS than people who have spent a few days in Kathmandu (1400m/4593ft) on the way. Unfortunately it is usually these people who are in a hurry to go higher. This is why group trekkers are initially more susceptible to troublesome AMS than individual trekkers, who often walk from Jiri or spend time in Kathmandu first.

Opposite: Yaks carrying group equipment above Pangboche, after some winter snow. From Namche to Dingboche and Thukla, Ama Dablam dominates the skyline.

Climb high – sleep low?

This often quoted dictum is partly correct in some situations, plain wrong in others. If you are already well acclimatized then climbing higher and returning to a similar altitude may help further with acclimatization.

If you are still in the early stages of acclimatizing process, ie still ascending to a higher altitude each night, then be careful. If you feel any symptoms of AMS at all you are probably better taking light/moderate exercise only with little or no increase in altitude. If you feel really good you could consider climbing a bit higher (200-400m), but climbing significantly higher, ie 1000m or more higher will almost always result in a headache on the way down or upon returning to the lodge. You may have had a good day but it is not so sure that you have actually helped acclimatization.

Effects of long-term exposure to altitude

If you stay at altitude for several weeks there are more changes: your muscles' mitochondria (the energy converters in the muscle) multiply, a denser network of capillaries develop and your maximum work rate increases slowly with these changes. Expeditions have run medical programmes with some interesting results. Climbers who experience periodic breathing (the majority) at base camp never shake it off and have great difficulty maintaining their normal body weight. Muscles will strengthen and stamina is increased but not the muscle bulk. Sherpas who have always lived at altitude never experience periodic breathing and can actually put on weight with enough food.

How long does acclimatization last?

It varies, but if you were at altitude for a month or more your improved work rates could continue for weeks so you'd still feel fit upon returning to altitude. You should not, however, ascend faster than normal if you return to sea level for a few days since you can still be susceptible to HAPE. If you have been up to 5000m/c16,500ft and then go down to 3500m/c11,500ft for a few days, returning rapidly to 5000m/c16,500ft should cause no problems. Thus, having been to Lobuche and Kala Pattar, then rested for two days in Namche, you should be able to ascend to Gokyo or a trekking peak fairly quickly.

Appetite

Altitude causes some people to lose an interest in food but you should try to eat as much as you can since your energy consumption, even at rest, is significantly higher than normal. Your body needs to generate heat to combat the constant cold, especially while sleeping. Very energetic trekkers, no matter how much they eat, will barely be able to replace the huge quantities of energy used.

The pill and fertility

The risk of a blood clot at high altitude while on the combined oral contraceptive pill is theoretically slightly higher, but no studies have been undertaken to see if there is significant risk. However, no problems have been reported while trekking or at the medium altitude ski resorts in the States. It is important to keep hydrated. For an 8000m expedition more caution is suggested. There is no increased risk of thrombosis with the mini-pill.

A common trick while trekking to avoid the mess of a period is to take two cycles of the combined oral contraceptive pill back to back. There are no special altitude-related reasons not to do this. Prolonged exposure to altitude does reduce men's fertility, although this returns to normal after a few weeks.

Opposite: Tibetan snowcocks (top left) near Dole, pika (top right), musk deer (bottom left) and Himalayan tahr (bottom right) often seen above Namche. See p295.

Retinal haemorrhages

A study conducted in the Khumbu found that 30-35% of trekkers at 5000m suffered retinal haemorrhages. You don't normally notice them, unless they affect a part of the retina called the fovea in which case you will notice a darkening and loss of vision, and upon descent these cure themselves rapidly.

Oxygen saturation meters (O_2 sat)

With the arrival of some relatively cheap battery-powered models some trekking companies now carry them. Oxygen saturation levels vary with altitude (see the table on p281) and vary from individual to individual; values plus or minus approximately 5% are still within the normal range. O_2 sat values also vary enormously between resting and exercising and eating. Normally only resting rates are meaningful. A low O_2 sat is an indication that HAPE may be developing (or that you have a low HVR), or has developed. However, it gives no indication of HACE: somebody can be dying of HACE and still have an O_2 sat that is perfectly normal for that altitude.

OTHER HEALTH PROBLEMS

The Khumbu Cough

Few trekkers manage to escape this one. The extra amounts of cold dry air that you need to breathe in at altitude irritate your bronchi (windpipes). Your body reacts to this as it would to an infection like flu, producing large quantities of phlegm, a mild cough, mild sore throat and a runny nose. Since there is, in fact, no infection it's pointless taking antibiotics but throat lozenges might help so take plenty along. Before you appear to get it use non-medicated ones; once you get the cough try using anti-bacterial ones occasionally because you are more susceptible to a bacterial infection. Other solutions are to wear a thin scarf over your mouth to keep your breath moister, inhaling steam and keeping well hydrated. An inhaled nasal decongestant can help you breathe through your nose so that the air reaching your throat and lungs is more moist and therefore less irritating

Bronchial infection

Bronchitis is an inflammation of the bronchi: sometimes it is caused by dryness (as in the Khumbu cough), asthma or allergy, but sometimes it can be caused by a virus or bacteria. An infection may be accompanied by a fever, shortness of breath, chest pain and a cough producing more and greener phlegm. It can be a viral infection, in which case antibiotics will do nothing, or at altitude it would much more likely be a bacterial infection. It's best to see if the above measures for the Khumbu cough work; otherwise get some rest or return to a lower altitude, eg Namche, and see a doctor.

Dehydration

Trekkers lose large quantities of water, not just through sweating but by breathing harder at altitude. Water vapour is exhaled with each breath and the thinner air means more breaths are required. If the fluids lost are not replaced, dehydration will result making you feel lethargic and sometimes resulting in a headache. The symptoms are similar to AMS so the easiest way to avoid confusion is to always keep hydrated.

A happy mountaineer always pees clear! If your urine is a deep yellow or orange colour you are not drinking enough. Even if you are not feeling thirsty you should still try to drink more. This can include any liquids (soups and tea but not alcohol) and as much water as possible. Many people find that with supper they often drink more than a litre of water, catching up on what they should have drunk during the day.

Hypoglycaemia

Especially after prolonged bouts of exercise, the body can quickly run out of energy (hitting the wall). The solution is to snack frequently and stop often.

Snow blindness

This is sunburn of the cornea, a painful affliction that feels like hot sand in your eyes. It is entirely preventable by wearing sunglasses that block UV light. This precaution is most important not just in snowy areas but also at altitude since the concentration of UV light increases with altitude. Porters often get snowblindness because they don't realize the importance of wearing sunglasses in snow.

If you lose your sunglasses, make yourself two cardboard eye-shields shaped like glasses with two narrow slits for vision. These are surprisingly effective at cutting down UV.

Exposure

Also known as hypothermia, this is caused by a combination of not wearing enough warm clothes against the cold, exhaustion, high altitude, dehydration and lack of food. Note that it does not need to be very cold for exposure to occur. Make sure everyone (porters included) is properly equipped. Symptoms of exposure include a low body temperature (below 34.5°C or 94°F), poor co-ordination, exhaustion and shivering. As the condition deteriorates the shivering ceases, co-ordination gets worse making walking difficult and the patient may start hallucinating. The pulse then slows and unconsciousness and death follow shortly. Treatment involves thoroughly warming the patient quickly. Find shelter as soon as possible. Put the patient into a sleeping-bag with hot water bottles (use your drinking water bottles). Another person should get into the sleeping-bag with the patient to warm him or her up.

Frostbite

When flesh freezes the results are very serious. Amputation may be necessary. Frostbite occurs usually in fingers or toes and takes time to develop unless bare flesh is exposed to winds at low temperatures or is holding cold metal.

Treatment When cold, fingers or toes feel numb, clumsy and lose power. If it's still possible to move them they aren't likely to be freezing although at this point the skin surface can partially freeze unnoticed. If you are worried, stop and rewarm. For fingers swing your arms around to promote circulation and stick them in your armpits. Pain on rewarming means either you frost-nipped them or came close.

With partial thickness frostbite, the flesh turns cold, blue and numb, but the underlying tissue remains normal – soft and pliable. With deeper injury, fingers or toes become wooden, incapable of movement. If you suspect deep frostbite, make plans for evacuation immediately. Don't begin rewarming until in a situation where refreezing cannot occur since this is infinitely more damaging than the affected part staying frozen a bit longer. If evacuation is guaranteed, if only the hands are affected or if damage to the toes is minimal and pain will not impede walking, then rewarming should be done as soon as is practical. Warm slowly and evenly: blood temperature or a bit warmer (up to 42°C) is optimum. If possible, a bath which allows the affected part to be warmed without it hitting the sides of the container is ideal. Rewarming can be excruciatingly painful so consider giving narcotics if available. Ibuprofen 400mg should be administered before rewarming and continued every 6 hours afterwards to prevent formation of natural chemicals which can actually harm the tissues further. Blisters will probably form – clear ones are indicative of partial thickness injury whereas bloody ones mean more extensive damage. Gently dry the affected limb and place clean gauze between the fingers or toes to protect them. The most important part of treatment of frostbite is preventing further injury and infection. A bulky dressing and not allowing the affected part to be used **at all** is the best way to achieve this. See a doctor as soon as possible for assessment of damage and continued care. Nifedepine (Adulat) can also be used to help prevent frostbite (5-10mg of the fast-acting type of tablets only) if your core temperature is good but the side effects are an increased heart rate that can occasionally have unpredictable results at altitude.

Boils

More common during the monsoon, these are usually the result of a staphylococcal skin infection. Early on these can be treated with lots of hot compresses, but if they get tense and fluid-filled, they need to be lanced. This should only be done by a doctor or nurse. Don't squeeze them as this spreads the infection.

Unwelcome bed companions

If you're using your own sleeping bag then it's very unlikely you'll have problems. Renting sleeping bags always carries a very small risk of scabies but not fleas or bedbugs, and this can be further reduced by airing the bag for a day or two in the sun. If you ever use local blankets the risks increase considerably.

● **Bedbugs Bites** are normally small, itchy and in neat lines. Bedbugs do not normally live in sleeping bags because when they are aired there is nowhere to hide.

● **Fleas** All local dogs are carriers and fleas also hide in quilts, blankets and old carpets. Occasionally trekkers pick them up. The small, red, itchy bites are usually congregated around areas such as the tops of your socks, waist, armpits or sleeves. You should try not to scratch, but do wash yourself and your clothes thoroughly. If you can find some flea powder, use this as well.

● **Scabies** Caused by a microscopic parasite this is luckily rare amongst trekkers. It can be caught from sheets or rented sleeping bags (but only if they have not been aired properly) or contact with an infected person, sometimes another trekker. To avoid scabies you should use a sheet sleeping bag within your sleeping bag. The itchy red spots look like pimples without the pus and may, at first, be confused with flea bites. As the parasites multiply, the marks spread widely but not usually on the face or head. Go to Khunde Hospital or the Pheriche Clinic, if possible, or visit a health post. Treatment is a head-to-toe dousing with Scabex. All clothing should be washed and thoroughly aired and your sleeping bag should be left in the sun for a several days. It takes a few days to a week or more for the symptoms, including itching to disappear, even if the treatment has been successful. Occasionally a second treatment may be necessary.

Leeches

These monsoon terrorisers are able to put a sizeable hole in you completely painlessly. Found in profusion in damp forest and damp, deep grass, leeches are adept at penetrating socks and even boot eyelets. Do not try to pull a leech off but apply salt, iodine or a lighted match and it'll quickly drop off. Leeches don't transmit disease but the wound can get infected: clean with antiseptic.

Blisters

Since you spend most of the time on your feet, looking after them properly to avoid blisters is of paramount importance.

Prevention Start with boots that have been worn in. This means not just for a short walk on level ground but with a pack in hilly country. If a blister starts to develop while you're trekking you can usually feel it. There'll be some rubbing, localized pain or a hot spot. Stop and investigate, even if it occurs during the first five minutes of walking or just in sight of the top of the hill. The trick is to stop and tape before the blister develops. Carefully apply moleskin or Second Skin, or a strong adhesive tape. Check that the hot spot is not being caused by the seam of a sock or a seam in your boot. Once you've applied a dressing, recheck it periodically to ensure that the problem is not getting worse.

Treatment If you develop a blister there are several approaches. If it's not painful then surround it (don't cover it) with some light padding, eg moleskin, and see how it feels. If it is painful you may want to drain it. Clean the skin carefully, sterilize a needle by holding it slightly above a flame for few seconds and pierce the blister. Do not cut away the blister skin until it has dried out and is no longer useful for protecting the delicate skin underneath. Put protective tape over it with some cotton wool as padding. Some people, however, put strong, carefully applied tape straight over the blister, with no dressing.

Cuts and scrapes

Most important is getting and keeping them clean and dry so they can heal on their own. Wash with lots of (clean) water to get out bacteria and dirt. A bit of dilute betadine or other antiseptic is fine, but does not substitute for washing with lots of water. Do not clean wounds daily with antiseptics – this will slow the healing. Covering wounds with a dressing, perhaps with some antibiotic ointment underneath, promotes healing. If wound edges are gaping, using steri-strips to pull them together is a good idea, then find a doctor to fix it properly.

Vaginal infections

If you have experienced these before it is worth bringing a course of the medication you were last prescribed in case the infection recurs.

Dogs and other animal bites

These are fortunately rare, but potentially very anxiety inducing. If you get bitten, or even receive a scratch that draws blood, the first thing that needs to be done is thorough washing of the wound (unless serious bleeding is occurring in which case stopping it is the priority!). First use copious quantities of soap and water and then clean again with an antiseptic such as betadine. Animal injuries that break the skin carry the potential for rabies in Nepal. The treatment depends on whether you had the pre-exposure rabies vaccine series (most trekkers don't get it – the chance of needing it is so small). Whether you had the pre-exposure series or not, a break in the skin from an animal needs to be assessed by a physician (preferably not a local one – rabies treatment in Nepal is inadequate). If a potential exposure has occurred, the vaccines, which are 100% effective if given in a proper and timely manner, should be started within about 4-5 days. Wounds should not be stitched/sutured until rabies treatment has been given.

FIRST-AID KIT

This is a basic list to cover the more common ailments that afflict trekkers. Climbing groups, expeditions and trekkers going to isolated areas will need a more comprehensive kit. Quantities stated are for one person.

Drugs easily purchased in Kathmandu:
● **Acetezolamide Diamox for altitude sickness** This comes in two forms, 250mg tablets (in Nepal) and 500mg time-release capsules. One strip of 10 tablets is enough.
● **Norfloxacin or Ciprofloxacin** for bacterial diarrhoea. Norfloxacin is cheaper. They are both broad spectrum antibiotics and can be used to treat many other infections. One strip of tablets.
● **Tinidazole (Tiniba) for Giardia**. One strip of ten tablets.
● **Oral dehydration salts** Some people can drink this stuff, others hate the taste. It is worth remembering that they all are good for you, replacing essential salts. In Kathmandu the nicest-tasting one is "Electrobion" but there are more brands, the most famous is Jeevan Jal. Take 1-3 packets for the replacement of salts and fluids lost by vomiting and diarrhoea.
● **Throat lozenges** Basic Strepsils, Halls and Vicks brands are usually available.

Better purchased in the West:
● **Tape for blisters** Moleskin/Second Skin/zinc oxide based tape (Leukoplast) – for blisters. Cheap low quality tape is available in Nepal.
● **Painkillers** Useful as mild painkillers for headaches, for reducing fever and reducing tenderness or swelling. For longer treks take plenty. Some brands are available in Nepal.
● **Cold medicines/Decongestants** and/or nasal spray are handy for short term use.

● **Plasters/Band-Aids** Assorted plasters and perhaps a stretch bandage would be useful. If you have had knee or ankle trouble previously a good support bandage is well worth bringing.
● **Betadine/Savlon/Dettol Antiseptic** for cuts.
● **Anti-bacterial throat lozenges** Bring several packets for the Khumbu Cough.
● **Gel hand cleaner** A small bottle is particularly handy for trekking and means that you are not washing your hands with possibly contaminated water.

RESCUE PROCEDURES

Assessing the situation

You don't need helicopter rescue for moderate AMS. For severe AMS, oxygen, PAC bag treatment or immediate descent is vital, so get them down rather than waiting for a helicopter that may take hours or even days to arrive.

For other emergency situations think carefully: are you better off going to the Pheriche HRA post or Khunde hospital, or calling their doctors to you – or calling a helicopter? In addition, there are always a surprising number of doctors on treks themselves. For non-life-threatening situations it may be that after seeing a doctor you can descend yourself or be carried down saving the expense of a helicopter rescue, not to mention being able to continue the trek when things have improved, rather than being stuck in Kathmandu.

If somebody has had a serious accident, don't panic. If there is bleeding, apply pressure over the wound, keep them warm and take stock of the situation. Look at all your options logically and carefully.

Summoning a helicopter

The process of summoning a helicopter can take 24 hours or longer once the message reaches Kathmandu because there must be a guarantee of payment (by a trekking company, insurance company or your embassy). How quickly the helicopter comes also depends on the weather. While a helicopter can magically appear in several hours it isn't unusual for it to take several days to reach an injured patient – there are no golden hour rescues.

There are telephones everywhere and a radio at the HRA post. When sending a message include as much clear detail as possible: your names and nationalities, the exact location, the reason for the rescue request and an assessment of the seriousness. Helicopters require a flat area to land on, below approximately 4500m/14,764ft.

APPENDIX C: FLORA AND FAUNA

The best all-round guide to the flora and fauna in this region is *The Story of Mt Everest National Park* by Margaret Jefferies but it can now only be found in libraries.

FLORA

From October to the spring the Khumbu is dry and brown, almost desert-like. In contrast, during the monsoon the greenery is surprisingly intense and flowers dapple hillsides. The wide range of flora includes the rhododendron, gentian, primrose, edelweiss and the beautiful mountain poppy. The forests of the deep Khumbu valleys comprise blue pine, fir, and juniper with birch and rhododendron forests at lower altitudes. Above the tree line is dwarf rhododendron and juniper scrub. The latter is prized by the Sherpas for its fragrant and instantly recognizable smell when burnt, a scent that soon becomes familiar. The highest plant of all is the tiny snow rhododendron.

WILDLIFE

In the Khumbu few wild mammals live above the tree line and even fewer are regularly seen.

- **Himalayan tahr** A large and handsome goat adept at rock climbing. The males are around a metre high and sport a luxuriant coppery brown coat, with a paler mane. They are often seen during the first day or so of the walk above Namche, eyeing trekkers with disdain.
- **Snow leopard** Hauntingly beautiful solo cats, virtually never seen by trekkers.
- **Wolf** Rarely seen, wolves live at the top of the tree line. Their coat is thick and sandy or grey and they use their bushy tail to keep their nose warm while sleeping.
- **Weasel** Quick eyes may see a blur of tan fur around grass and rocks near villages above Namche, even to as high as 5500m/18,044ft.
- **Himalayan mouse hare** A small tail-less mammal that is surprisingly tame.
- **Musk deer** Well under a metre high, this delicate deer is occasionally seen near Dole or around Tengboche in the dark forest. It is illegally hunted for its musk, produced by a gland in the male and used for making perfume. The male has large distinctive fang-like teeth (see photo opposite p289).
- **Common mouse** At night in the lodges there's the telltale pitter-patter across the roof and the occasional scream (not of mouse origin!).

DOMESTIC ANIMALS

In the warmer lower hills a variety of animals are kept. Chickens are kept mainly as egg-producers. There are dogs; and goats are numerous, being sacrificed and eaten during important Hindu festivals and ceremonies. They are very destructive, stripping the ground and shrubs bare of leaves and are responsible for much of the deforestation close to villages. Buffaloes provide milk and meat, and pull ploughs. At high altitudes they are replaced by yaks, naks and various crossbreeds.

BIRDS

Nepal is on some major migration routes and is famed for its varied bird life. Since the local people don't hunt birds, and they are all protected in the park, with keen eyes you should seen the majority of the birds mentioned below. Serious birdwatchers should consult: *Birds of Nepal* by RL Fleming or *Birds of the Central Himalayas* by Dorothy Mierow, both usually available in the Kathmandu bookshops.

- **Lammergeier/bearded vulture** This large and beautiful soaring bird is a scavenger, often seen gliding along the mountain sides above Namche.
- **Griffon** Similar to the lammergeier, but slightly heavier with a shorter, wider tail.
- **Golden eagle** This raptor hunts pheasants, snow cocks and smaller mammals rather than being a scavenger. It is smaller and more agile than the other soaring birds.
- **Danphe/Impeyan pheasant/Monal** The national bird of Nepal, often seen in pairs. The male sports nine iridescent colours and is plump, almost heavy. The female is a plainer brown and white. Good places to spot them are along the trail to Thame and Tengboche, and around Phortse.
- **Blood pheasant** The male has a red throat, red and white tail and bright red legs. They are seen around Tengboche and Dole.
- **Tibetan snow cock** Both male and female are striped: black, white, grey and brown with orange legs. Easy to approach, they congregate in noisy groups at altitudes above Namche right up to the snow line, especially on freshly dug fields.
- **Snow pigeon** They fly in compact flocks and as they wheel around in the sky their colour alternates between light and dark.
- **Yellow-billed and red-billed chough** Black with red legs, choughs are curious and play-

ful but have the annoying habit of attacking tents, ripping the material with their beaks. Together with crows, they are known as 'gorak' by the Sherpas.

● **Jungle crow** Black and slightly scrawny, crows are great camp scavengers.

● **Tibetan raven** ('caw caw') Completely black, these ravens attain nightmarish proportions in the Khumbu.

APPENDIX D: NEPALI WORDS AND PHRASES

Many Nepalis, especially those used to dealing with foreigners, can speak some English. It is, however, really worth making the effort to learn even a few Nepali phrases since this will positively affect the attitude of the local people towards you and you'll be made all the more welcome.

Derived from Sanskrit, Nepali shares many words with Hindi and is also written in the Devanagari script. For many of the people you speak to (Sherpa, Rai etc) Nepali will, in fact, be their second language. Whilst Nepali is not a particularly difficult language to learn up to a basic level, Sherpa is much harder.

Nepali includes several sounds not used in English. The transliterations given below are therefore only approximate. However since pronunciation varies across the country your less-than-perfect attempts will probably be understood as just another regional variation.

Namasté

Probably the first word learnt by the newly-arrived foreigner in Nepal is this greeting, which is spoken with the hands together as if praying. Its meaning encompasses 'hello' and 'goodbye' as well as 'good morning', 'good afternoon' or 'good evening'. *Namaskar* is the more polite form.

General words

How are you?	*Bhaat khanu-boyo?* (Have you eaten your dal bhaat?)
Fine thanks	*Khai-é* (I have eaten)
Please give me	*..... di-nus*
Do you speak English?	*Angrayzi bolnoo-hoon-cha?*
Yes/no	(see below)
Thank you	*Dhan-yabad* (not often used)
Excuse me (sorry)	*Maf-garnus*
good/bad	*ramro/naramro*
cheap/expensive	*susto/mahongo*
Just a minute!	*Ek-chin!*
brother/sister	*eai/didi* (used to address anyone of your own age)
Good night	*Sooba-ratry*
Sweet dreams	*Meeto supona*

Questions and answers

To ask a question, end the phrase with a rising tone. An affirmative answer is given by restating the question without the rising tone. 'No' is translated as *chaina* (there isn't/aren't any) or *hoi-na* (it isn't/they aren't).

What's your name?	*Topaiko* (to adult)/*timro* (child) *nam ke ho?*
My name is	*Mero nam ..... ho.*
Where are you from?	*Topaiko/timro dess kay ho?*

Britain/USA	*Belaiyot/Amerika*
Australia/New Zealand	*Australia/New Zealand*
Where are you going?	*Kaha janné?* I'm going to ... ... *janné*
Are you married?	*Bebah bo sokyo?*
Have you any children?	*Chora chori chon?* boy/girl *chora/chori*
How old are you?	*Koti borsa ko boyo?*
What is this?	*Yo kay ho?*

Directions

Ask directions frequently and avoid questions that require only 'yes' or 'no' as a reply.

Which path goes to ....?	........*janay bahto kun ho?*
Where is ...?	.....*kaha cho*
lodge/hotel	*bhatti*
shop	*possol*
latrine	*charpi*
What is this village called?	*Yo gaon ko nam kay ho?*
left/right	*baiya/daiya*
straight ahead	*seeda jannus*
steep uphill/downhill	*bhiralo matti/talla*
far away	*tadah*
near	*nadjik*

Numerals/time

1 *ek*; 2 *du-i*; 3 *tin*; 4 *charr*; 5 *panch*; 6 *chho*; 7 *saat*; 8 *aatt*; 9 *nau*; 10 *dos*; 11 *eghaara*; 12 *baahra*; 13 *tehra*; 14 *chaudha*; 15 *pondhra*; 16 *sora*; 17 *sotra*; 18 *ottahra*; 19 *unnice*; 20 *beece*; 25 *pochis;* 30 *teece*; 40 *chaalis*; 50 *pachaas*; 60 *saati;* 70 *sottorri*; 80 *ossi*; 90 *nobbi*; 100 *say*; 200 *du-i say*; 300 *tin-say*; 400 *charr say*; 500 *panch say*; 600 *chho say*; 700 *saat say*; 800 *aatt say*; 900 *nau say*; 1000 *hozhar*

How much/many?	*Kati?*	today	*ajaa*
What time is it?	*Kati byjhay?*	yesterday	*hidjo*
It's three o'clock	*Tin byjhay*	tomorrow	*bholi*
hours/minutes	*ghanta/minoot*	day after tomorrow	*parsi*

Food and drink

restaurant/inn	*bhatti*	bread	*roti*
Please give me...	......*di-nus*	cheese	*cheese*
mineral water	*khanni-paani*	boiled egg	*phul*
tea	*chiya*	omelette	*unda*
coffee	*coffee*	salt	*noon*
milk	*dood no*	spicy hot	*piro*
chillis	*korsani china*	sugar	*chinni*
boiled milk	*oomaleko-dood*	beer	*beer*
honey	*maha*	rice spirit	*ruxi*
Cheers!	*Khannus!*	rice	*bhaat*
chicken	*kookhura-ko massu*	lentils	*dal*
buffalo	*rango-ko massu*	potatoes	*aloo*
pork	*sungur-ko massu*	vegetables (cooked)	*takaari*
It tastes good	*Ekdum meeto*		

APPENDIX E: GLOSSARY

ama	mother
bergschrund	gap where a glacier parts from a rock wall
bhanjyang	pass
bhatti	simple hotel
bivvy (bivouac)	small shelter for camping
Brahmin/Bahun	Hindu high priest caste
cairn	pile of stones marking a route ('stone men')
chang	home-brew made from barley or rice; also 'north' direction
chhu	river
chhusa	crop-growing area above main village
chimneying	climbing a vertical crack just greater than body width
chomo/jomo	mountain goddess
chorten	Tibetan stupa (see below)
chotar	prayer flag pole beside house
crampons	spikes that strap on boots to aid walking on ice
crevasse	dangerous cracks in a glacier
cwm	valley shaped like an amphitheatre (Welsh)
dal bhaat	staple meal of lentils and boiled rice
deorali	pass
dhai	curds
dingma	clearing
doko	woven, load-carrying basket
drangka	stream
ghat	river bank or bridge
goan/gau	village
gompa	Buddhist temple (literally: 'meditation')
goth 'goat-h'	shelter or temporary house
gunsa	'winter place', where early crops are grown
himal	snowy mountains
jumars	device used for climbing up a fixed rope
kang	mountain
kani	entrance arch
kharka	grazing ground
khola	stream
kosi	river
kund	lake
la	pass
lha	fenced herding area, also spirits
lho	south
mani wall	wall of stones carved with Buddhist mantras
mantra	prayer formula
neve	smooth high snow-field, accumulation area of a glacier
nup	west
phu	high altitude grazing area at the end of a valley
piton	spike hammered into a rock crack for climbing security
pokhri	lake
prussiks	loops of cord used to climb a vertical rope
rakshi	local distilled spirit
ri	ridge or soft peak
satu	flour

serac	large block of ice typically found in an icefall
shar	east
Sherpa	of the Sherpa people
sherpa	trekking group assistant
solja/suchia	salt-butter tea
stupa	hemispherical Buddhist religious monument
suntala	mandarin orange
tal	lake
tarn	small lake without entry or exit stream
trisul	trident carried by worshippers of Shiva
tsampa	roasted barley flour
tse	peak
tsho/cho	lake
yersa	crop-growing area above main village

APPENDIX F: BIBLIOGRAPHY

TRAVEL GUIDES

Armington, Stan *Trekking in the Nepal Himalaya*, Lonely Planet Publications, Australia,
Bezruchka, Stephen *Trekking in Nepal – A Traveler's Guide*, Cordee, UK/The Mountaineers
Nakano, Toru *Trekking in Nepal*, Yama-Kei Publishers, Japan /Allied Publishers, India
O'Connor, Bill *The Trekking Peaks of Nepal*, Crowood Press, UK
Swift, Hugh *Trekking in Nepal, West Tibet, and Bhutan,* Hodder & Stoughton, UK
Nepal, Insight Guides, APA

MAPS

Khumbu Himal, Freytag-Berndt und Artaria, Vienna, 1978 and 1985
Lapchi Kang, Freytag-Berndt und Artaria, Vienna, 1974 and 1985
Mt Everest, National Geographic Magazine, 1988
Planimetric Map of Satellite Images for National Remote Sensing Centre (Nepal)
    Institute for Applied Geosciences, Germany 1986
Rolwaling Himal (Gaurisankar), Freytag-Berndt und Artaria, Vienna, 1981
Shorong/Hinku, Freytag-Berndt und Artaria, Vienna, 1974, 1979 and 1987

TRAVELOGUES/HISTORY

Bernstein, Jeremy *Wildest Dreams of Kew*, George Allen & Unwin UK 1970
Boardman, Peter *Sacred Summits*, Hodder & Stoughton, London 1982
Bonington, Chris and Clarke, Charles *Everest the Unclimbed Ridge*, Hodder & Stoughton,
    London 1983
Bonington, Chris *Everest South West Face*, Hodder & Stoughton, London 1973
Bonington, Chris *The Everest Years*, Hodder & Stoughton, London 1986
Eggler, Albert *The Everest Lhotse Adventure*, Geo Allen & Unwin, UK 1957
Franco, Jean *Makalu*, Jonathan Cape, London 1957
Gillman, Peter *Everest -- The best writing and pictures from 70 years of human endeavour*
    Little, Brown & Co, London 1993
Hillary, Edmund *Nothing Venture, Nothing Win*, Hodder & Stoughton, London 1975
Hillary, Louise *High Time*, Hodder & Stoughton, London 1973

Holzel, Tom and Salkeld, Audrey *The Mystery of Mallory and Irvine*, Jonathan Cape, 1986
Hornbein, Thomas *Everest the West Ridge*, Vikas, New Delhi 1982
Howard-Bury CK *Mount Everest: The Reconnaissance 1921*
Hunt, John *The Ascent of Everest*, Hodder & Stoughton 1953
Kolhi, Capt MS *The Himalayas – Playground of the Gods*, Viking India 1983
Kolhi, Commander M S *Nine Atop Everest*, Orient Longman, New Delhi 1969
Mulgrew, Peter *No Place for Men*, AH & AW Reed, Wellington, 1964
Norton EF *The Fight for Everest: 1924*, Edward Arnold, 1925
Salkeld, Audrey *People in High Places*, Jonathan Cape, London 1991
Shipton, Eric *That Untravelled World*, Charles Scribner's Sons, NY 1969
Shipton, Eric *The Six Mountain-Travel Books*, The Mountaineers, Seattle 1985
Taylor-Ide, Daniel *Something Hidden Behind the Ranges – a Himalayan Quest*
     Mercury House, San Francisco 1995
Tichy, Herbert *Cho Oyu By Favour of the Gods*, Methuen & Co, London 1957
Tichy, Herbert *Himalaya*, Anton Schroll, Vienna 1970
Tilman, HW *The Seven Mountain-Travel Books*, The Mountaineers, Seattle 1983
Unsworth, Walt *Everest*, Oxford Illustrated Press, UK 1989
Verghese *Himalayan Endeavour*, Times of India 1962
Von Furer-Haimendorf, Christoph *Exploratory Travels in Highland Nepal*, Sterling
     Publishers, New Delhi 1989
Weir, Tom *East of Kathmandu*, The Travel Book Club
Wignall, Sydney *Spy on the Roof of the World*, Canongate, Edinburgh, UK 1996

RESEARCH

Bista, Dor Bahadur *Fatalism and Development Nepal's struggle for Modernisation*,
     Orient Longman, Calcutta 1991
Jefferies, Margaret *The Story of Mt Everest National Park*, Cobb/Horwood, Auckland, 1985
Bhatt, Dibya *Natural History and Economic Botany of Nepal*, Orient Longman, New Delhi
Fisher, James F. *Sherpas – Reflections on Change in Himalayan Nepal*, University of
     California Press, Berkeley, 1990
Lachapelle, Paul A, *Report on human waste management in Sagarmatha National Park* for
     University of Vermont, Burlington VT and School for International Training, Kathmandu 1995
Mierow, Dorothy *Birds of the Central Himalayas*, 1988
Ortner, Sherry *Sherpas through their Rituals*, Cambridge UP 1978
Schaffner Urs Road *Construction in the Nepal Himalaya: the Experience from the
     Lamosangu-Jiri Road Project*, ICIMOD 1987
Sharma, Pitamber *Assessment of Critical Issues and Options in Mountain Tourism in Nepal*,
Stevens, Stanley *Sherpa Settlement and Subsistence – Cultural Ecology and History in
     Highland Nepal* for University of California
Subba, Chaitanya*The Culture and Religion of Limbus*, Subba KB, Kathmandu, 1995
The Himalayan Journal 45 1987-88, Oxford University Press Bombay, 1988
Wilheim, Emily *Chialsa – Disappearance or Revival?*, School for International Training

MEDICINE

The High Altitude Medicine Handbook, Micro-edition, Andrew J Pollard& David R
     Murdoch, Radcliff Medical Press, Oxon 1997
Medicine for Mountaineering ed. Wilkerson, 3rd edition, The Mountaineers, Seattle, 1985
Management of Wilderness and Environmental Emergencies ed. Auerbach and Geehr,
     second edition, C.V. Mosby, Toronto 1989
Mountain Sickness, Peter Hackett, American Alpine Club

INDEX

❏ OTHER GUIDES FROM TRAILBLAZER

Adventure Cycling Handbook	1st edn late 2003
Adventure Motorcycling Handbook	4th edn out now
Australia by Rail	4th edn out now
Azerbaijan	2nd edn out now
The Blues Highway – New Orleans to Chicago	1st edn out now
China by Rail	2nd edn late 2003
Coast to Coast (British Walking Guide)	1st edn late 2003
Cornwall Coast Path (British Walking Guide)	1st edn Mar 2003
Good Honeymoon Guide	2nd edn out now
Inca Trail, Cusco & Machu Picchu	2nd edn out now
Japan by Rail	1st edn out now
Kilimanjaro – treks and excursions	1st edn Jan 2003
The Med Guide	1st edn mid 2003
Nepal Mountaineering Guide	1st edn mid 2003
Norway's Arctic Highway	1st edn mid 2003
Offa's Dyke Path (British Walking Guide)	1st edn May 2003
Pembrokeshire Coast Path (British Walking Guide)	1st edn Mar 2003
Pennine Way (British Walking Guide)	1st edn late 2003
Siberian BAM Guide – rail, rivers & road	2nd edn out now
Silk Route by Rail	2nd edn out now
The Silk Roads – a route and planning guide	1st end Apr 2003
Sahara Overland – a route & planning guide	1st edn out now
Sahara Abenteuerhandbuch (German edition)	1st edn late 2002
Ski Canada – where to ski and snowboard	1st edn out now
South Downs Way (British Walking Guide)	1st edn late 2003
South-East Asia – a route and map guide	1st edn Jan 2003
Tibet Overland – mountain biking & jeep touring	1st edn out now
Trans-Canada Rail Guide	2nd edn out now
Trans-Siberian Handbook	5th edn out now
Trekking in the Annapurna Region	4th edn mid 2003
Trekking in Corsica	1st edn out now
Trekking in the Dolomites	1st edn out now
Trekking in Ladakh	2nd edn out now
Trekking in Langtang, Gosainkund & Helambu	1st edn out now
Trekking in the Moroccan Atlas	1st edn out now
Trekking in the Pyrenees	2nd edn out now
Tuva and Southern Siberia	1st edn late 2003
Vietnam by Rail	1st edn out now
West Highland Way (British Walking Guide)	1st edn Jan 2003

For more information about Trailblazer and our expanding range of guides,
for where to find your nearest stockist, for guidebook updates
or for credit card mail order sales (post-free worldwide)
visit our Web site:

www.trailblazer-guides.com

ROUTE GUIDES FOR THE ADVENTUROUS TRAVELLER

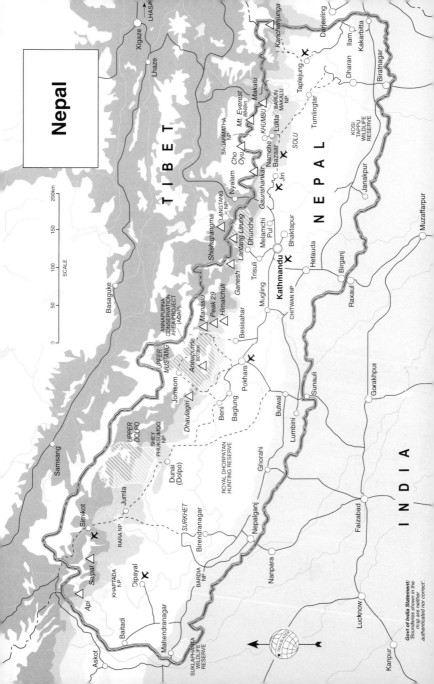

Nepal

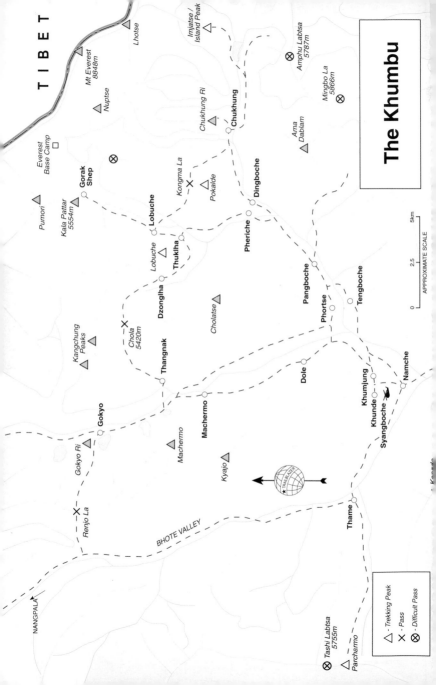

The Khumbu